Bottomless Bag

Again?

Second Edition

again,

By Karl Rohnke

BAG OF TRICKS

KENDALL/HUNT PUBLISHING COMPANY
4050 Westmark Drive   Dubuque, Iowa 52002

Cover Design by Plynn Williams.
Interior Design by Woodshed
   Productions.
Photos by Karl E. Rohnke
   except where noted.

Introduction - Preface - Forward

Let's get these three over with all at once . . .

I started writing **Bag of Tricks** in December 1979 because: (1) I like to write, (2) I had beaucoup ideas and no systematic way to pass them along, except in training workshops for Project Adventure, (3) I had recently completed the book, **Cows' Tails and Cobras**, and needed another writing project, (4) It was wintertime (not my favorite season), and I needed something to do besides pull-ups, (5) There was more than one person who didn't think I could make a go of it.

So now, I'm coming up on fourteen years of writing and producing this unlikely quarterly. Ten years was the goal I gave myself at one time, when people asked how much longer I was going to continue **BOT's**, but now . . . I don't know. I've gotten so used to the routine of "getting out the copy" each three months that I'd probably miss the hassle and certainly the writing.

Things have changed a bit since that first December issue (other than the price). For the first two issues, I did the typing on an old Olympia portable and the copying on an even older ultra-messy spirit duplicator. Then Bonnie Hannable agreed to do the typing, Wilkscraft Creative Printing did the camera-ready photocopying, and my young sons folded, stapled, and licked stamps for an in-house fee.

Since then I have been introduced to the seductive ease of using a word processor. For a dedicated Royal portable typewriter fan, the change over was initially painful, but as time has passed I have unemotionally forgotten how to change a ribbon and mechanically set margins. Now the clack of the keys-on-platen has been replaced by the muted and somewhat comforting sounds of the computer keyboard. Karl . . . Karl . . . Karl — how quickly we change.

I don't think the number of subscribers during the last fourteen years has ever gone over 500, but then it's never gone below

200. Obviously not a big money maker, but it serves the intrinsic purposes mentioned above. I haven't checked, but I'd be surprised if anyone has subscribed for the entire fourteen years, however, some have been faithful readers, and I appreciated that support, particularly those of you who included a regular "howdy" with your yearly renewals; kind of like a quarterly Christmas card.

The original edition of **The Bottomless Bag** represented what I thought was the best writing and most useable copy from the first 38 issues of *Bag of Tricks*. For this revision, I've electronically cut and pasted, re-written, deleted, re-illustrated, added over 200 photographs, made some additions, and ended up with what you have here; over 2 pounds and fourteen years of tricks.

Table of Contents

For easy referencing, I've divided the book into the following chapters. Every activity is also listed alphabetically in the index. (I hated doing it, so you better appreciate it!)

Contents in the following chapters are not necessarily sequenced, except for a couple of items that resulted from an uncommonly organized evening in front of the tube. Refer to the index for specific named events.

DISCLAIMER

It is **important** to remember that:

- Adventure curricula or activities should not be undertaken without the supervision of leaders who have successfully

completed qualified professional instruction in the use of the skills necessary to implement adventure curricula or activities.

- Instruction and suggestions in this book for the construction and implementation of ropes course elements are subject to varying interpretations and the construction process is an inexact science.

- Before any attempt is made to use any ropes course elements whose construction has incorporated any of the materials contained in this book, a qualified professional should determine that safe techniques have been employed in their construction thereafter. Inspections by a qualified professional no less frequently than annually should be made to protect users against accident or injury that can result from the deterioration of materials caused by the use, abuse of the elements.

- The reader assumes all risk and liability for any loss or damage which may result from the use of the materials contained in this book. Liability for any claim, whether based upon errors or omissions in this book or defects in any ropes course the construction of which has incorporated any of the materials contained in this book shall be limited in amount to the purchase price of this book.

An Operational Paradigm

The following four simple concepts are emphasized throughout the activities offered in this book, and as stated, the emphasis is on *simple*. Most "formulas for success" are either so complicated that extensive training is required to implement the model, or the definitions are so couched in educational jargon that the concepts are overwhelmed by the vehicle. Take a look below; hard to go wrong, eh? And this fab-four combo *works*!

1. **Communication** - freely talking and listening to one another
2. **Cooperation** - working voluntarily together
3. **Trust** - emotional and physical
4. **Funn** - spontaneous and encompassing

Trying to achieve the first three goals and have fun at the same time is key, recognizing that if the participants do not enjoy what they are doing or learning, they will not return willingly for more of what you have to offer. Of the four, FUNN* is initially the most important.

* *FUNN = Functional Understanding's Not Necessary*

Here's my guarantee. If you find that using the activities in *The Bottomless Bag Again,* (offered in conjunction with the *Challenge By Choice** credo) does not result in greater fulfillment of your teaching and/or facilitating goals, I'll personally refund the purchase price of the book. I certainly don't gain anything financial by offering a refund, only the satisfaction of letting you know that I am convinced that the combination above works.

If you do want your $$$ back, please don't return the book (I've got lots of them); just pass it along to another educator, and let them have a try.

You can reach me at the National Project Adventure Office; P.O. Box 100; Hamilton, MA 01936.

Challenge By Choice — This easy-off-the-tongue shibboleth refers to a disarmingly laid-back facilitating approach that puts the choice of participation into the hands of the participant. Seems obvious, I agree, but if you think about it, most programs require a consistent level of participation within the curriculum; cognitive or psychomotor. In other words, there is little choice left to the player; it's either perform to a predetermined level, flop in front of your friends, or drop out.

Challenge By Choice encourages the student to consistently try (performance level is *not* key), but also allows occasional time outs if that individual, for whatever reasons, does not feel comfortable with the activity. Consistent malingering is another matter, but knowing that "your turn" does not always mean "your try" is comforting knowledge to a shy, inept, unprepared, or hesitating student.

Reader's Digestive

Ω

Here's something that you might find helpful as you peruse the pages of this book looking for something "meaningful" to present at the next teacher in-service day or for channeling the energy of those hyperactive kids in D Block.

About five years ago I began recording the names of those activities that I found myself using repeatedly during various adventure workshops. As reflected by that compilation of neat-o things to do, I have highlighted in these chapters those included games, initiatives, stunts, and trust activities that are my *very* favorites. (When someone uses *very* as an adjective, that means it's *really* boffo!).

If an Omega symbol (Ω) appears immediately to the right of an activity title, that indicates favorite status. The lack of an Omega icon does *not* mean, however, that the remainder of the topics in this book are page filling losers. Highlighting favorite activities was just something that amused me one evening, so if you find that my preferred anthology is anathema to your own collection of fun-filled crescendos, strike them out *boldly* with a felt tipped pen.

As a brief aside: I chose the Omega symbol not so much that Ω seemed particularly appropriate, but because I couldn't find a heart symbol under *Key Caps*, and Ω seemed the least offensive of what was available. How do you feel about £, or §, or even æ — see what I mean?

The Bottomless Bag Again?!

Second edition

Chapter 1

Warm-Ups/Exercises

Getting a student warmed up at the beginning of a session seems necessary (hours of academia on your backside is enough to make anyone's circulatory system sluggish), and generally proves troublesome: not many students want to be warmed up. So, your initial cardiovascular sequence should be active and unique. Being active is no problem. The take-a-lap-and-come-back-here-for-roll approach has been used and misused for years. But, providing initial and satisfying variety of movement requires thought, inventiveness, commitment (you get to demonstrate), and compassion.

Here are a few warm-up ideas that I have used randomly (not repetitively), which have been well received by most students.

Tag Games

You played some kind of tag games when you were a kid, right? You had to! It was a prerequisite to growing up; a physical and social necessity. Take those "ancient" good fun games, change the rules and lingo a bit to fit the group and occasion, and see how useable they become as unique warm-ups.

Everybody's IT
(The world's shortest tag game) Ω

Simplicity itself: when the game starts everyone is IT, and tries to tag everybody else. If you're tagged, you're OUT. That's it, that's all . . . what did you expect, an essay?

Dizzy Izzy Tag

A vertiginous tag game that lasts lots longer than *Everybody's It.*

Start with 2-3 IT'S. When tagged, rather than being OUT, a new IT must spin around three times before chasing another person. This vertigo pause prevents "tag backs," a heavy rule refinement in serious tag games.

Restrict the running area to prevent fast

runners from never getting caught. The game continues until everyone is obviously warmed up; doesn't take long with most people.

Sore Spot Tag/Hospital Tag

Same rules as *Everybody's It*, except the tagged person must hold the spot where s/he was tagged (with one hand); but that person is still in the game.

The handicap and good humored embarrassment of a tag varies considerably as to where the tag is affixed. It's hard to keep from laughing if the tag was on your posterior, and trying to run with a tag on your foot is a frustrating task.

Hold the first spot tagged with either hand. Hold the next spot tagged with your only free hand. (Tag inventively.) Having no hands left, you may tag now only with your hip — an obvious disadvantage, unless it's you against another hip tagger. After the third tag, you are mercifully OUT OF THE GAME.

Pairs Tag   Ω

Find someone you want to choose and/or be chosen by; i.e. pair up. Don't worry, there's no holding hands in this game. Considering that there are only two of you, decide who is initially IT. That person tries

to tag *only* their chosen partner, who, of course, is you. Now *that's* simple! You have to like this game.

If a tag is made, the IT designation switches over and the chasee becomes the chaser. Taken as is, this could be a very boring game, but the interest stems from the fact that a lot of other pairs are playing exactly the same game in the same small restricted area; the smaller the group, the smaller the game area. Only *fast walking* is allowed and three seconds must elapse between tags, (about the time it takes to spin a 360°).

Pairs Tag is one of those comparatively rare games that works well with large (50+) groups of people. Make sure, even with a large group, that you severely restrict the playing area and emphasize that only walking is allowed.

As facilitator, place yourself as a permanent *pick* in the center of the action. Two pick people would be even better.

Try this. Same game, same rules, except this time you start off with pairs holding hands. Pairs chase pairs . . . get it? *Pairs, Pairs Tag* — I should get a medal!

Elbow Tag

Another aerobic warm-up tag game (Is there any other kind?) that provides enough variety to keep interest high.

If too much running becomes a problem; i.e., a good runner controlling the game, or a poor runner about to expire, include the 7 step rule. The person being chased can take no more than 7 steps before linking elbows. If 8 steps are taken, that person is automatically caught. Why 7 steps? Why not? It's your game, you choose.

Make sure to play the game long enough so that players develop a feel for strategy and are not just running about willy-nilly. Then again, willy-nilly's okay if a group's in that mood.

Ask the group to pair-up and link elbows with their partner. The outside arm should also be held akimbo by placing a hand on the hip.

One or two people are designated as IT. Appoint only one IT at the beginning, until some strategies are developed. The IT must try to catch the only unpaired player within the boundaries (keep the boundary lines close for more action). The fleeing player must link elbows with one of the members of a pair to be safe. The other member of that pair (odd person out!) must immediately take off, to prevent being caught, then look for an available elbow to link with. If the playing area is kept small, a good player can move swiftly from one elbow to another without much running.

Flip Me the Bird

Tie knots in towels to equal about a third of the number of people in the group. These knotted towels are called *birds*. If your budget and sense of humor allows, buy rubber chickens and use them as *birds*.

Assign 2-3 people to be IT. To be immune from a tag, a player must be grasping a bird. Since there are only 6 birds per 18 pursuees, there is much "flipping of the bird." There can only be one bird in the hand at a time. In keeping with the name of the game, the bird must be thrown, not passed, and the throw cannot be made back and forth between paired players.

Needle & Thread Tag — A Strategy Tag Game

Ask your group to form a circle so that each person can, with arms extended to their side, grab the hand of the person next to him/her. The IT person begins within the circle, while the person to catch locates her/himself outside the circle.

Every time the person being chased runs between a pair in the circle, that pair grasps hands, effectively "sewing up" the previously open space.

The object of this one-on-one tag game is for the chaser to catch (tag) the chasee before that person *sews up* the entire circle with extended arms and clasped hands. There is more to this tag game than being simply fleet of foot.

Team Tag, Tag

This tag game is more team-oriented than *Everybody's IT*, and tamer (though no less exciting). Divide any group larger than six into two equal teams and distinguish them somehow (shirtsleeves rolled up or down, armbands, bodies painted red & blue, etc.). Identify boundaries for the playing area that will allow some moderate running. (You'll probably find that this tag game can produce wheezing levels of oxygen debt, even in a small area. If the running area is too extended, you may find that the game's aerobic value will out-distance its play value.)

Players can locate themselves anywhere within the designated area before the signal to start is given. Hearing GO, the object for all players is to tag someone on another team before they are tagged.

Players who are tagged are "frozen," and if two players dispute who tagged whom first, both are frozen. (This is called playing to PAR — **P**recludes **A**rgument **R**ule.) Players can be unfrozen when a still viable member of their own team squirms, squiggles, or crawls through the cryogenetically suspended player's legs. The game ends for a particular team when all their members become iced-up. The last team remaining at ±98.6° are champions — until you say GO again.

Having everyone yell, "Tag!" or "Tagged!" upon tagging or being tagged will add a nice verbal dimension to *"Team Tag, Tag."*

Triangle Tag

A hand-held triangular game for four people. Use this as a quickie warm-up activity.

Ask your group to quad-up in groups of four (I know that's redundant, but . . .), and ask three of the participants to hold hands, forming a manual triangle. One member of

foot designates having lost balance) by pushing on each others' palms in *slooow motion* only. No fast moves are allowed, even to gain an advantage or win.

This low-key contest obviously requires a determined effort to cooperate, coupled with the desire to prevail. Most contests end with both folks simultaneously losing their balance, and that designates a well deserved tie, particularly if both stumbling contestants try to support one another.

Honestly performed, this event is a vigorous and cooperative blend that combines the aesthetic flow of dance and the starkness of one-on-one confrontation.

You better have some breath mints ready for this one, coach!

the triangle is the person designated to be caught, and the other two hand-holders of that triad act as blockers or protectors. The fourth person is IT, and must try to tag the designated odd person in the triangle.

As a safety consideration, do not allow an IT to purposefully try and break through the group's grip. A large person could easily do this, resulting in bruised wrists and fractured trust.

The triangular personnel dance and jump about in semi-coordinated moves to keep the IT at bay. Change roles clockwise every 60 seconds (to alleviate that old tag malady, IT-anoxia), or whenever a catch is made.

Cooperative Competition

Try this slo-mo sequence as a cooperative strength/stretching exercise for two participants. Considering sequence of activities, this is *not* a warm up to use during the first few get togethers.

With a partner (same size or sex isn't necessary), stand toe-to-toe and palm-to-palm. Each participant tries to maneuver his/her partner off balance (moving either

Photo by Gloree Rohnke

Bottoms Up

A one-on-one warm-up stunt that combines strength, balance, and a very odd juxtaposition of bodies.

Sit facing one another and place the bottom of your feet against the bottom of your partner's feet. Legs should be well bent with posteriors skooched fairly close together. Attempt to push against your partner's feet (while putting all your weight on your arms) until both your derrieres come off the ground. You will notice a poignant tightening of the tricep muscles, and an overwhelming urge to smile (grimace?): hold for 5 seconds.

If you find that some pairs are having an easy time with this exercise, suggest that they include another person and try to "bottoms up" with three participants.

Stork Stretch

Seriously folks, do a few ham string warm-up exercises before trying this triad stretch.

Split up into groups of three. Stand facing each other in a triangular configuration. One person raises his right leg and places the right foot on the right thigh of the person to his right, as that person continues the identical action to his right. Right! So, it's everyone's right leg as parallel to the ground as possible, as their right leg is supported on their right-hand partner's thigh. The left legs (3 of them in most

groups) support the trio. (HELP! Take a look at the photo.)

After achieving this unique balanced position, each member tries to lean over and place their head on their right knee, or, depending upon the triangular rapport, on their partner's knee. As you attempt this movement, a certain tightening of the hamstrings will occur, accompanied by various deep-throated guttural sounds.

This "stretcher" is not designed for everyone's body, but the cooperative results are worth an attempt by young limber folks.

Heads and Tails Tag

Ken Demas, National PA Trainer, offers this variation of *Heads and Tails Tag* that he calls *I Declare.* The group, recently well versed in the rules and refinements of *I Declare*, stand ready to play. One person flips a coin into the air (doesn't matter who, just someone who has a coin), and everyone declares their heads or tails affiliation by either placing a hand on their head or on their behind. If the coin comes up heads, heads are IT. All the heads then charge about trying to tag all the tails. If a tail is tagged, he/she indicates their tagged condition by putting both hands on their posteriors, spreading their legs, and screaming, **"I'M CAUGHT!"**

Uncaught tails can free frozen tails by crawling through the tagged player's legs and yelling, **"TAILS FREE."**

The game continues until all the tails are caught, or until 2 minutes and 15 seconds have gone by, at which juncture the coin is flipped again and everyone gets to redeclare what they want to be when they grow up; i.e., heads or tails.

If the players demand a score (hey . . . some people care) count the number of uncaught players after the time limit is announced.)

If the reflipped coin comes up heads for the next round, you've got the routine . . . right?

I changed things a bit, Ken (. . . can't help it, I'm a compulsive changer), but I think this is basically what you had in mind. Ken, did you ever think of the nomenclature ramifications if your wife played this game? *Claire Declare.* Too much, eh?

Sun Salute

In past *PA* workshops, we have asked teachers to show us (workshop leaders) some of their favorite warm-up and/or stretching exercises. The Sun Salute has been mentioned more than once. Here is a sketch outline of the Sun Salute, (below) a contiguous series of twelve body stretch positions. One leads fluidly to two, and flows to three, etc. The positions depicted are ideal examples, but often difficult to achieve (ex. #3). Do the best you can at your own rate, and remember that speed is not a criteria for successful completion.

Invisible Jump Rope

There *is* a reason why boxers jump rope: it's an effective (though somewhat tedious) cardiovascular exercise. Jumping rope is not, as I was led to believe as an adolescent, just an innocuous sidewalk pastime for *girls*. If you continue to think that a twirling rope is a bit on the distaff side, try hopping into a staccato, hot pepper, double dutch set-up for a bit of humble pie. Most students (male and female) respond well to rope jumping in its many forms, if pre-

1   2   3   4   5   6

7   8   9   10   11   12

sented as a means of achieving fitness and coordination.

As you watch an adept jumper windmill his/her way through a complex routine of cross-overs, jig-like steps and double jumps, the uncomfortable knowledge that tripping over your own feet is easy enough, suggests that you don't need a rope to complicate things. In other words, you need a warm-up routine that will allow you to emulate the good guys without having to look bad. (The only time it's okay to look bad is when everyone is looking bad, and even then it's a strain on chronically pumped-up egos.)

So, just pretend. Measure the length of your pretend rope by standing on the rope and bringing the ends up under your armpits. Come on, you can't expect to do all the following tricks if your pretend rope is too short!

Begin slowly, jumping and casually turning the rope in sequence with your hops. See how easy it is to coordinate the hand and foot movements.

Try a trick! Cross your hands (and your arms up to your elbows) vigorously in front of you each time you jump. This crossover move isn't that difficult and will definitely impress your friends. Try a double cross-

over. Nicely done, and not a miss yet.

You, of course, recognize by now that almost anything is possible jumping within this format, so use your imagination — here are a few starters for this anything-goes workout.

1. Try a double jump, a triple . . . then six turns with one jump. If you make it, you have just broken the world's record. (Five turns in one jump is the Guiness record — no kidding.)
2. Try some fancy footwork, any ole dance step that you can think of will do; a jig, a fling, an ëntre chät, etc.
3. Entice someone near you to jump at your pace and initiate a "follow the leader" sequence. At the end of a few wildly impossible moves, hop away from your partner and at a wink, both throw your ropes high in the air toward one another, grasp the falling, flailing rope, and continue jumping without missing a beat. Fantastic!
4. Hop toward someone and jump as a pair, intertwining each other's rope so that your feat is as impossible as it is delightful.
5. End with some kind of Brogdingagian group jump — and not one person has missed a turn. Hot pepper!

Toss-a-Name Game   Ω

If you have trouble remembering a bunch of new names in a just-met group situation and you dislike name tags (Hello, my name is BLANK . . .), this game provides an action-packed sequence that makes forgetting harder than remembering.

Break up into groups of about 8-10 people, and stand in an informal circle. A leader says his *first* name and tosses a fleece ball to his/her right or left. (Make sure that the type of ball or toy you decide to throw from person to person is soft and innocuous enough that even if a person gets blindsided with a throw that no injury or

pain will result. This is important toward establishing trust.)

Continuing in either direction, each person says their first name and continues tossing the ball in sequence until the leader again has the ball. The leader calls out someone's name in the circle (you *do* have to remember at least one person's name!) and *lofts* the ball to her/him, and that person calls another individual's name, etc., etc. Notice that I used the word LOFT, not ZING.

After the ball has been flying about for a few minutes, or more usefully, after you begin to get a feel for all the names in the group, start up another ball, increasing the frequency of names being called and the action. Add a third and fourth ball toward the end of the game just for fun, because at this point, the law of diminishing returns creeps in; names and balls are flying about so rapidly that it's hard to pinpoint who's who, as balls careen off your head and body.

If there are other groups playing the same game, stop occasionally and ask a third of a group (3 groups) to transfer to another group and begin the action again. After a while, announce to the three groups that anyone can change groups whenever

they want to, insuring that everyone gets to hear each person's name.

As a finale, have all the individuals mingle about, with the number of balls in play equal to 1/3 the number of people. Chaotic certainly, but it provides a humorous ending to a functional game.

Don't limit yourself to throwing just balls, introduce a rubber chicken, or stuffed creature of some kind. The players will appreciate this gesture toward reducing the stress of remembering names.

Retro-Eknhor

Standing or sitting in a circle, announce yourself by saying your first and last names backwards, then ask each person, when ready, to introduce themselves to the group. The trick to having this activity received well by the disbelieving students, is to introduce yourself with conviction, pronouncing the reversed mish-mash of letters as if that *were* your name. *Hello, I'm Lrak Eknhor.*

Accept whatever pronunciation is offered by a player; this is not time for syntactic correctness. Offer encouragement to try (nobody's paying attention to proper pronunciation) and congratulations for every attempt. As students struggle with the unknown amidst laughter and potential ridicule, recognize this *silly stuff* as a useful activity for working on trust and compassion.

Bob and Eve like this game.

Bumpity Bump Bump

Saying *Bumpity Bump Bump* rapidly takes between .6 and .65 seconds, (the average is about .623). You need to know this.

Ask your group to "line up in a circle," then put yourself at circle center. The arced

players should be about four to five steps away from you. Point decisively to one of the circled folks and say that person's first name with conviction, following their name immediately with the exclamation *Bumpity Bump Bump*. The person that you pointed to and named must respond by saying the first name of the person to their left, before you finish exclaiming *Bumpity Bump Bump*. If they flub the name or completely forget, that person takes your place in the center, and subsequently attempts to trap someone else. It obviously pays to know who is on your left, unless the person in the center exclaims RIGHT!, before pointing and saying BBB, then you must name the person to your right. *However*, if the center person is male and exclaims right, you must transpose that command and name the person to the left, and if the center person is female and yells left, that's obviously right, right?

Sorry, I just couldn't help it. You were doing such a good job of reading and concentrating, I should be ashamed . . . Everything before the italisized word *however* above is for real, and constitutes a useful name game. Everything after *however* is me fooling around— just playing. Are you smiling? Hope so . . .

Peek-a-Who   Ω

Whatever name-game you have been using (*Toss-A-Name-Game, Whampum*), this bit of whimsical latter-day Peek-A-Boo will further cement faces with names. *Peek-A-Who* is a name reinforcer and a grand excuse for copious laughter.

Obtain a blanket or bedspread for the game; a sheet will do, but it doesn't have the heft or opacity of a good ole battleship gray, keep-the-grass-stains-off-your-knees, USN surplus blanket.

Ask two players (substitute freely) to hold the blanket between them so that the blanket provides a vertical sight barrier that can be lowered and lifted easily. Two chosen volunteers from either team sit on either side of the blanket. When the blanket

is dropped, the two players, suddenly facing each another, must verbally identify one another by name. Second place moves over to the winner's side, and this win me/ lose me action continues until one team has taken over the other team or competitive ennui sets in.

As a variation, ask two players to sit back-to-back (blanket between) and attempt to identify the other player by listening to how their teammates describe the other person. Spelling out names is not allowed.

Whaumpum

This appropriately designated name-game involves a sure-fire attention-getter, the potential of being smacked with an ethafoam sword.

Place yourself in the center of a people circle (8-15) so that the peripheral folks (everyone's peripheral in a circle) are within foam sword length of your reach. Everyone is seated (except you), with legs extended forward. Extended legs are mandatory to prevent getting whacked on the head. Foot hits are de rigueur, head hits aren't.

To start, someone in the circle says the name of someone else in the circle. You (the person in the center) try to whack the named person on the foot before he/she names someone else in the circle, and so on. When you finally end up whaumping someone before they can verbalize another name, that person replaces you in the center of the circle. After you hand the sword to the next IT person, you have 5 seconds to say someone's name, or a sword strike ensues, and you're STILL in the center.

If someone flinches, (photo) that's as good as saying, "Let me take your place in the middle of the circle," and the flinching person does just that.

This game almost demands that an individual learn names quickly. Day dreaming results in a foot whaump. You won't have to worry about lack of attention as the whaumping action develops.

Whaumpum was passed on to me by an old friend and outdoor adventure associate, Dr. Lee Gillis, currently teaching at Georgia College in Milledgeville, GA.

If you don't have access to an ethafoam sword, either (1) write to *Project Adventure* for the price of an ethafoam plank (the makings for ten foam swords), or (2) loosely roll up a newspaper and tape the roll to produce a temporary but useable sword. A rolled up newspaper can hurt (ask your dog), so temper your Daily News attacks.

Photo by Nicki Hall

Chapter 2

Trust Activities

trust can happen in a heart beat. Developed trust is something to protect and cherish; unfortunately there's not much of it around.

The following activities are not presented in any particular sequence or lesson-plan hierarchy. Use the ones you feel comfortable with in context with where your group's *at*, and where you feel they best fit.

Establishing trust is built into almost all the activities in this book. Physically and emotionally trusting one another is one of the necessary foundations toward establishing team work. Without an operating level of trust within a group, very little will be accomplished toward achieving announced learning goals.

Learning to trust one another in this competitive world is not easy, requiring more work and sensitivity than most would imagine. In contrast, loss or diminishing of

A Variation on Stress

Blindfold students before participating on belayed ropes course or high gymnasium elements. Removal of sight and asssociated visual reference points makes balance events very difficult to navigate and commitment elements poignantly felt.

Two cautions:

1. Allow the student to feel comfortable with an event before introducing the blindfolds.
2. Request *volunteers only* for this high commitment activity.

Isn't everything on a volunteer basis? Certainly, but there is a fine line between a conscientious attempt (the expectation) and a volunteer effort that seems beyond expectation.

Having students talk one another up a climbing wall (leader sighted, belayed climber blindfolded) is another fine exercise in trust and communication.

Human Ladder

Purpose: To develop trust, to be responsible for each other's safety, to engage in physical contact with members of your group.

Materials: Several smooth dowel rods, about 3 feet long, and 1-1/2 inches diameter.

Directions: Students are paired and one member of the dyad is asked to hold one end of the ladder rung. The other member of the pair stands opposite and firmly grasps the free end of the rung. The remaining rung supporting pairs, standing close together, form the ladder. (See photo)

A volunteer (not your heaviest student) climbs aboard at one end of the human ladder and proceeds to

move from rung to rung. As the climber passes by, the students holding that just-used ladder rung quickly leave their position and proceed to the beginning of a new ladder line, adding their rung to what becomes an infinitely long ladder.

Note: The direction of the ladder may change at any time, and the height of the rungs being held may also vary.

Considerations:
- Rung supporting pairs should be made up of participants who have about the same body size.
- Do not allow the students to hold the rung in such a position (above the shoulders) which makes maintaining the rung orientation dangerously difficult.
- Encourage the "rung walker" to use people's heads for balance.

Discussion: How did you feel when you were climbing? When you were holding the rung? Did your feelings change after the first climber took their turn? Did trusting some people make your climb easier?

I Trust You, But . . .   Ω

Here's a neat action-oriented way to develop trust within a group. Blindfolds will be necessary for most folks.

Ask 3-4 participant volunteers to stand at one end of a basketball court, right next to the wall or bleachers. Have them assume the hands-up/palms-out (bumpers up), protect-yourself position. At this point they are either blindfolded or have committed to keep their eyes closed. Ask the three participants to *jog* toward the far wall at a steady, controlled pace.

The remainder of the group will be spread out with their backs to the far wall that the blindfolded jogger is approaching, but standing at least six feet away from that wall. Their job is to stop the jogger before s/he encounters, vis-à-vis, the wall. Hand-to-hand braking (bumper to bumper) is compassionate and functional. A couple other members of the spotting group should stand along the side walls to redirect errant runners.

The results are impressive and the student choice is generally to try the blindfolded run again, perhaps next time with a longer run available outdoors. This activity is a useful preliminary activity to the trust fall.

Don't allow *any* fooling around by the spotters. Also, ask the spotters to be quiet during the run in order to increase the jogger's commitment.

Dog Shake

After a group has been working with you for at least a couple weeks, and they obviously need, or are in the mood for, a bit of shared nonsense, tell them (at the beginning of your session) that you have just the right exercise designed to physically loosen up a group.

Don't present this exercise until the group has had a chance to figure you out, and has begun to develop a functional level of trust in your zaniness. You may want to

practice the following routine a couple times before demonstrating it. Pick your practice site wisely.

The *Dog Shake* takes its name directly from the way a dripping wet dog shakes himself (right next to you), kinetically demonstrating a biologically ideal way to initiate the drying process. You will never be able to duplicate the unhinged, explosive wiggling movements that a dog achieves, but in relative slow motion, the human miming attempts are fun and uninhibiting.

To convince an understandably dubious group to join you in a *Dog Shake* is largely dependent upon the instructor's charisma and/or acting ability, for s/he must initially demonstrate the moves (and countermoves) including a running and sometimes garbled commentary which goes something like this: "A dog's shake always begins at the tip of the nose." (Begin wiggling nose.) "It's hard to wiggle the nose without including the cheeks and mouth." (Exaggerate mouth and cheek movements.) "Let's include the ears now (if you can) and the hair" (if you can, I'd like to see it, but it's good for a laugh). "If you are worried about what other people are thinking of you, relax, because here go the eyes." (Roll your eyes randomly in their sockets.) Now, move smoothly (?) and consistently down from one body part to another.) "The whole head begins to bounce around, which starts the shoulders to moving and then the arms can't help bobbing about." "Don't forget the head and eyes." "The chest is part of the shoulder movement, which goes right on down to the waist and hips." (If you have never done the hula, here's your chance: much exaggerated hip gyrations.)

"Are you into it?" "Can you feel the water flying off your body?" "The thighs are next, which start the knees." (Move those knees, while keeping everything else going, of course. By this time, you are nearly 100%

convulsive.) "And then finish it off to the toes." "We made it — now, don't stop." "Do it! — Do it!! — Do it!!!" Continue a full body spasm for about five seconds or so.

People are usually laughing and obviously enjoying your antics at this point. Don't give them time to lose the laughter; ask them to join you in a Dog Shake sequence and begin as above. Talk them through and join them in the Shake. The whole sequence should take no more than 60 seconds.

After you have finished (everyone usually applauds themselves — a nice gesture, really, there should be more of it; i.e., more opportunities which allow that type of relaxed freedom and spontaneous self-approval), demonstrate a **complete** *Dog Shake*. Start your nose twitching and let the movement transfer immediately and directly to your hips — kind of an impulse, manifested in a torso twitch and subtle hip shake. It's hard to verbalize, but try, and if it feels good, it's probably right.

Ask the group to do it with you a couple times and applaud their actions (no matter what spasmodic efforts are forthcoming). Move on to the next exercise amidst a nice feeling of shared spontaneity.

Sherpa Walk

This follow-the-leader, action-oriented walk is probably the longest duration trust activity (other than marriage) that I've taken

part in. It is also a fine activity for developing communication, no matter how outlandish the message means become.

You will need a blindfold for each participant.

1. Cut the blindfolds long enough so that tying them around the head doesn't become an initiative problem.
2. Offer clean blindfolds for hygienic and humanitarian reasons.
3. Use cloth that does not admit light or that can be doubled.
4. Have more on hand than you anticipate needing.

Ask the entire group (8 - no more than 15) to tie on a blindfold. If you have not previously mentioned the trust aspects of participating in a blindfolded activity, those comments would be appropriate at this juncture. To wit, the instructor will not make fun of or make anyone appear foolish because of being blindfolded. Such shenanigans are usually not funny and even so, the loss of confidence is hardly worth the bit of low humor.

You need a story line to relate that gives this upcoming sightless bash some reason for being. Use the following slice of fantasy as an outline to develop your own patter.

"Your travellers' group has adventurously elected to tour an exotic and politically forbidden area of the Asian continent. The charter flight, aboard Xanth Airlines, was difficult to obtain (visa problems) and prohibitively expensive. However, because of personal wealth and governmental leniency, the plane and your group has arrived in the country of Ultimo Sotto Voce to the strains of their national anthem; a 12-note dirge in 4/4 time repeated in endless succession. The reason for this metronome-like anthem is that all the people in USV are deaf (very small and insular country — inbreeding and all that), and wouldn't appreciate a longer or more varied melody: they like the beat. Considering their removed location on the continent (with resultant limited exposure to other people), it would come as no surprise that their meager language (almost a complete lack of syntax: 2 vowels, 5 consonants) is incomprehensible to your group.

Sadly, about a decade ago, the populace became endemically afflicted with leprosy as the result of the unlikely situation of a Polynesian immigrant's having brought the disease via an aborted airline hi-jack and resultant emergency parachute attempt (refer to page 1 story in Leahali Gazette, November 14, 1969 — 'Leaping Leper Leaves Legacy')" etc., etc.

The Problem

After having lightheartedly presented the background information, tell your blindfolded travellers that two Sotto Voce citizens will lead them blindfolded through a sacred area to where the tour bus will pick them up.

Tap two members of the group on the head (SV tour guides) and tell them to come with you so that you can point out the route through the sacred ground. Explain to the remainder of the group that you will return within five minutes and that they should take this time to arrange themselves in some way for sightless travelling.

Take your two chosen leaders (blind-folds now off) and point out a preselected route that you want them to lead the group through. Spend some time, prior to the group's initial meeting, to establish a challenging and enjoyable route. Include: bashing through some bushes, having to crawl under and over something, walking next to water (which you can splash threateningly), passing over and down a 6-8 ft. drop-off, etc.

Explain to the leaders (and eventually the group) that they are not allowed to say anything (language, inflections) that the group will understand, but can make whatever non-specific sounds they like; whistles, clucking, clapping, etc. Guides are not allowed to touch any members of the group (leprosy — remember?). So, obviously, a means of communication must be established in a minimum amount of time. Give the leaders a couple minutes to discuss communication strategies while you walk back and explain the situation to the now highly organized (?) travellers.

Assure the group that you and one other proctor will be silently attending their walk to provide spotting in case of any potentially risky moves. As you see the leaders eventually approach, say, "The next semi-human sounds you hear will come from your Sotto Voce leaders," and then be quiet.

As you walk along with what becomes a very verbal group of travelers, watch for potential danger and, if necessary, put yourself in a good spotting position. Point out the route to the leaders if they seem lost. Watch and listen for situations that will be valuable to relate during the post-trip discussion.

Try to end up the walk in an area that allows the group to be physically close together. After you announce that they have arrived at the "bus terminal" (blind-folds can be removed), and the initial

exclamations of "Where are we?", etc., have been made, ask the leaders to walk the group back through the route to satisfy their curiosities and allow spontaneous sharing of reactions and sensations. Finish up with a sit-down debrief session.

Human Camera

Here's a useful trick for outdoor education teachers or interested educators that I saw used at an O.E.A. conference at Bradford Woods in Indiana.

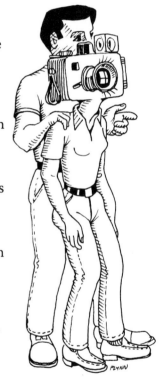

The teaching theme is to demonstrate how you can use a partner as a camera. After having made appropriate comments about how a camera is like a human eye, ask your partner to close his/her eyes, then lead that person to a spot where there is an interesting object you would like to record on their retinal film. Using the human camera's body as an infinitely mobile tripod, set up your partner's head (the camera) in such a way that their closed eyes are directly in front of the chosen subject. Gently pull their ear lobe (or push on the acromion process) to activate the shutter. At this encouragement, the "camera" opens and closes their eye lids (shutter) *very quickly* in order to record the scene. Lead your partner to a few more photographic possibilities and then talk about what you two have jointly recorded.

Vary the scenes from close-ups to distant landscapes. Switch roles after you have talked about the experience with your partner or as a group. I think you can easily recognize that this is not only a shared experience of high quality, but also a trust sequence (unselfconscious touch, no-sight manuvering) that leads to good feelings and a useful pairs rapport.

Trust Fall and Trust Dive   Ω

Refer to the book *Silver Bullets*, pages 80-83 for detailed directions as to the presentation of these classic trust activities.

People Pass Steeplechase

People Passing is a unique hands-on activity for building trust that requires no props, however some preparation time is necessary. The perceived object of this activity is to physically pass a member of the group the distance required to complete a quickly established steeple-chase course.

Rules and Procedures

The steeplechase course must be planned before the group arrives. In setting up the obstacles, be creative, spontaneous, and compassionate. Don't expect more from a group than they can deliver — respect the fine line between challenge and unreason-able risk.

1. Some useable and acceptable obstacles include: moving through shrub growth (not somebody's garden), over shallow water (lots of splashing), down or up stairs, over and down a low wall (maximum of 6'), through the front seat of a car or van.
2. The passers may not move their feet when they have physical contact with the person being passed. As soon as a passer is no longer touching a rider, s/he can run to the front of the passing line and continue the rider's progress.
3. Riders may not touch the ground (any solid obstacle included). Make up your own penalties for an infraction . . . maybe increasing the weight of the rider, or more creatively, switching after each infraction to the next heavier member of the group.
4. Let the group choose the initial rider. Unless the group is from outer space or extremely motivated, the lightest group member is the best bet for this role.
5. The distance covered obviously varies as per the challenge level and the types of obstacles. Try to make the steeplechase course long enough so that the group has to work together for at least 10 minutes.

6. Everyone must be involved in the passing procedures, but it becomes obvious, because of physical limitations and individual prowess, that some people will do more lifting and others more planning. That might be worth talking about.
7. This event can be timed in order to establish a touchstone for future efforts, but if this approach is chosen, the obstacles must be minified for safety reasons.

Boundary Breaking

This excellent exercise was sent to me by Paul Bernard of South Portland, Maine. I have changed the directions slightly and added parenthetical choices to a few of the questions, in order to make the exercise more applicable to all ages.

Procedure

A. Seat the group in a close circle on a padded floor (or provide pillows, etc.).
B. Each person must answer every question, with the proviso that he/she may pass in order to think. If a person passes twice, do not pressure him/her for an answer.
C. Group members should not repeat the answer of someone else, if at all possible.
D. Explanation of answers is not necessary and is, in fact, counter-productive to the flow and mood that you are trying to establish.
E. Limit the size of the group or the number of questions so that the exercise does not become tedious.

Directions to Participants — Read the following to your group.

I'd like you to respond to a series of questions. Every answer you give is the correct one; no one will question your response or react to your answer in any way.

Please do not "cop out" by stealing someone else's answer. We will proceed around the circle, starting with a different person for each new question. If you can't think of an answer, you may PASS, and I'll come back to you.

Speak loudly so that everyone can hear. Be as honest as you can. Remember that we are interested in discovering good things about each other.

We are here as a group only to listen to each person's response. This is *not* a debate. We are not here to disagree, only to seek the person that is in each of us.

As each person answers, begin developing an idea of each person in the group and perhaps a few of the invisible boundaries, held up by ignorance of one another, will begin to tumble.

Boundary-Breaking Questions.

1. What is the best movie you have ever seen?
2. What is the most beautiful thing about people?
3. What is the ugliest thing you know?
4. What do you like to do most with a free afternoon?
5. On what basis do you select your acquaintances?
6. What is the greatest problem in the United States?
7. If you could smash one thing . . . what would you smash?
8. If you had one talent to choose, what would that one talent be?
9. What is the greatest value that guides your life?
10. What quality do you look for in a really good (friend) teacher?
11. Other than a relative, what one person has greatly influenced your life?
12. What gives you the most security?
13. What is the biggest waste you know of?
14. What is your greatest fear?
15. Select a word that you feel describes kids (people) of your age?
16. If you could give your principal (employer) one piece of advice . . . what would you tell her/him?

17. Name the most unreasonable thing that you know.
18. If you could choose to be a book . . . what book would you choose to be?
19. If you were to paint a picture . . . what would you paint a picture of?
20. What do people like best about you?
21. What do you consider to be your biggest fault?
22. When do you feel most lonely?
23. What TV commercial bothers you the most?
24. What one thing would you change in your (life) school?
25. Describe your feelings about (fast food) hamburgers.
26. Choose one word to describe old (young) people.
27. What future discovery are you looking forward to the most?
28. What subject is the most frequent topic of discussion among your peers?
29. If you could be a song, what song would you choose to be?
30. What is the very last thing that you will be willing to give up?
31. What is the best advice you have ever gotten?
32. When you are depressed, what cheers you up the most?
33. If you were tape recording the sound of violence . . . what sound would you use?
34. Who is your favorite rock or new wave or country music star?
35. What is your least favorite food?
36. Describe the ideal family.
37. What is your favorite holiday?
38. If you could have any car in the world . . . what kind of car would you choose?
39. What cartoon character do you identify with?
40. What scares you the most about next year?

Coming & Going of the Rain

This "hands-on" group activity is a classic outdoor education standby that can be used effectively in an adventure program. It can be presented in two ways, depending on how "together" your group is.

Ostensibly, the object is for the group to audibly experience the sounds of a summer rain approaching and leaving a geographic area. If the group cooperates and performs their individual roles well, there is the distinctly rewarding experience of hearing the increasing wind, the pitter-patter and eventual drumming of a brief rainstorm. But I feel the greatest benefit comes from achieving the cooperation and trust level that is necessary for the elements to be realistically heard and felt.

Ask your group (any number up to 50 — more people than that requires "rain helpers") to make a circle and then turn to their right (or left, it doesn't matter). Have them close up the circle by side-stepping toward the center of the circle until they can easily touch the person's back in front of them. Explain that the group will be trying to experience the sounds and feel of a summer rain shower, and that their close cooperation is needed for this to happen.

With the person in front of you (you are standing as part of the circle), demonstrate the movements necessary to achieve the sounds desired, as follows:

1. With your palms flat on the person's back (shoulders) in front of you, rotate your hands to achieve a swishing sound (the increase of wind preceding a shower).
2. Change to a drumming motion with your finger tips on your partner's back (beginning rain drops).
3. Change to a heavier, finger-tip slapping action (harder raindrops).
4. Return to the motions of #2.
5. Return to the motions of #1.
6. STOP, and wait for all sounds to cease.

When you begin #1, at the beginning of this exercise, your partner passes along the motion to the person in front of them and so on, until the motion is returned to you; i.e., feeling the hand rotation on your back, at which point you begin #2, and so on until the sequence ends.

This exercise is much more effective if the group decides to keep their eyes closed for the duration of the "coming and going of the rain."

Pick your geographical location wisely for this group exercise. Do not ask a group of students to "demonstrate" this hands-on exercise with strangers wandering by, and try to pick a spot that is as quiet as possible — no lawnmowers or chainsaws to interrupt the emotionally fragile sound sequence that you are trying to build.

If your group can't handle the touch that is required in this method, place yourself in the center of the circle and have everyone face toward you. Ask the group to follow your lead and you change the sounds when it seems appropriate. Unfortunately in this case, the sounds do not meld as well into one another, but it's still an effective experience.

The "rain" sounds are made by:

1. Rubbing your palms together.
2. Snapping your fingers alternately loud and soft.
3. Snapping multi fingers.
4. Slapping your thighs.
5. Pounding your chest and reverse the order.

Don't Get Cocky With Trust

Orange Jump Center - Orange, MA c.1977

Introductory class of eight pre-jumpers led by a young, but obviously knowledgeable instructor; ruggedly handsome, sporting a full lip moustache that's just a tad rakish and dressed to showcase his high fitness level. His speaking voice is well modulated, but has a barely definable tone of supercilious intent, perhaps latent elitism.

The class progresses well, and it becomes obvious that he has made this presentation many times; pausing for laughs at just the right time, using practiced facial expressions and body movements with predictable glances at his grotesquely

huge Rolex knock-off sky diver wrist watch.

All the above is OK and fits into the commercial high adventure aspect of the experience. The small things mentioned above as criticisms were probably not even noticed by the clientele who seemed enthralled by the instructor's charismatic persona, the drop zone scene and themselves for having chosen to be there. What I did take umbrage with was his penchant for black humor jokes, which seemed to serve no purpose other then elevate his position as being in the know."You have 17 seconds after exiting the plane at 1,800 feet to do something before impacting the ground. You can either utilize that time to deploy your reserve as instructed or kiss your ass goodbye; there's ample time for either choice."

But I think it was more than that, perhaps something he felt about the overt manifestation of danger in parachuting which he couldn't allude to directly. The poor taste jokes may have been an honest attempt to put us at ease.

Making someone comfortable with a newly experienced and potentially dangerous activity (rock climbing, hang gliding, downhill skiing, etc.) in a casually competent way will earn more respect and trust from your students than any number of cute (sometimes tasteless) verbal ploys. But, to be casually competent you must first become definitively competent. Instructors who make difficult tasks appear easy, do so because of inherent capability, experience in the field, and much practice; it just doesn't happen. When you reach that stage of competency, the road toward trust becomes smoother. If you are scheduled to lead a knot tying session, and the knots have to do with personal safety, you must reach a level of personal proficiency that allows you to confidently talk about and manipulate the cordage and knot systems. And, to reemphasize the point I was making about the overzealous jump instructor, jokes about knots slipping and people falling are inappropriate and rarely useful. Beginners do not want to be vividly reminded, particularly in a grossly overt way, of the consequences resulting from mistakes or equipment failure.

I ran into this macabre use of humor recently at a hang gliding instructional area. The instructors were capable, but some were young and instructionally immature. Their fall-go-splat comments were not well received except by the youngest of the students. The following day our group travelled to another instructional venue and had the pleasant experience of receiving lessons from a mature, obviously skilled practitioner, who used a combination of straight talk and humor to charm, teach, and relax a nervous audience. Big difference in approach; big difference in results.

Photo by Peter Steele

Chapter 3

Stunts

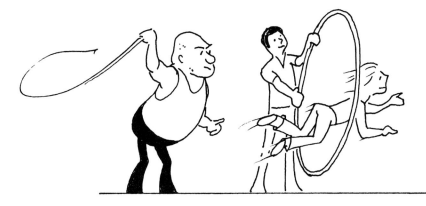

Optical Tricks to Play on Yourself

Roll up a piece of paper (the paper you're reading right now is a good size) so that the core (I.D.) measures about one inch. Hold up the formed tube so that you are looking through it like a telescope (right eye) and hold the tube next to (touching) the knife edge of your left hand — palm facing you. See illustration.

Keep *both* eyes open and let the hole in your palm appear. No hole?

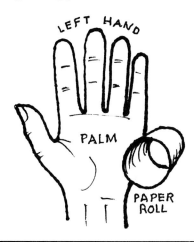

How about trying to see a finger-link sausage instead? OK, get rid of the tube and hold both of your hands about 10-12" in front of your eyes with the index finger of each hand just touching the tip of the other index finger (see photo pg. 152). Do you see the sausage? The sausage has fingernails!

No link sausage? I give up — you're hopeless.

Texas Big Foot

Need a simplistic task that can't be done (almost can't be done)? *Texas Big Foot* takes little time to explain or attempt and provides a humorous low-key task that is bound to fail. If personal expectations aren't paramount and image isn't on self-destruct, it's fun to fail sometimes — particularly as a group.

Ask the group to form a circle (with you included) so that everyone is holding onto their juxtaposed partners; arms around shoulders.

Then announce, with great portent, that this activity is extremely hard to accomplish and that morphological cooperation is essential to success and injury avoidance. Indicate that all the group has to do (in their present arm-over-shoulder configuration) is take three giant steps toward the center of the circle. To be successful, the final step must end with the group still intact, and standing.

Count off the first step, then stop. Offer encouragement and praise. Count the second step — no comments are necessary or useful at this point because of the laughter and convolution of the one-time circle. The final giant step invariably results in falling down by some participants or complete disfiguration of the circle; i.e., failure to achieve the announced goal.

Admittedly a "lightweight" activity, but a nice tone-setter toward shared laughter and unselfconscious touching; also indicates that failing can be fun: no worries, mate.

Stunt-Pole (Sapling) Vaulting

Simple field vaulting is a spontaneous, just-fooling-around child-like activity that involves a good upper body workout and a sense of risk-taking and satisfying movement that encourages continued efforts. Additionally, vaulting is fun and doing it is much more exciting than watching. I didn't

write that last sentence as a "don't be vicarious" platitude; there really is a sense of weightlessness and swift movement that can be achieved with a simple (sturdy, please — no mop handles or skinny bamboo poles) vaulting pole.

Provide a number of hardwood 8' sapling sections that will support *your* weight (i.e., try them out), to big or little folks and ask them to vault from place to place; done simply by jogging forward, placing the pole in the turf (a la TV's Wide World of Sports) and vaulting. I'm not going to burden you with a detailed or anytailed explanation of the kinesiology of vaulting, and you shouldn't have to explain, either. If the pole is held and planted solidly, and a person thrusts forward from that pivot, forward progress (hopefully, free of the ground) will occur. If not, there's plenty of time, soft grass, iced tea, and tries left.

If the vaulting pole ends up akwardly angled twixt a person's legs, you might want to try some coaching with basic technique suggestions, like: "Don't let the pole end up between your legs."

If rapidly gained expertise indicates a desire for self-testing, set up a vault for distance over grass, sand, or even a small gully. If the situation presents itself, don't ignore a wet or muddy area as consequence for a grand challenge.

Sacky Hack

Undoubtedly one of the most frustrating and infectiously popular and portable pastimes to come from California in a long time is the frenetic, small circle, down-time beater called *Hacky Sack*.

Essentially, the Hacky Sack is a small (about scrotum size) stitched leather bag filled with cherry pits. I'm not kidding about the pits. I've never cut one open to check (and considering the price, I doubt if

I ever will), but I have been assured by native Californians that there are indeed cherry pits inside . . . there must be something exotic in there to justify the price tag; maybe it's the stitching.

The game idea is to kick this small sac, or strike it with some part of your body (as in soccer, contact with hands, arms, and shoulders is verboten), so that someone else can also experience the personal embarrassment of completely missing or misdirecting this miniscule ersatz soccer sac.

I will admit that trying to keep the sac aloft for an established number of hits, kicks, etc., is a just-one-more-try affliction that is not only individually insidious but wildly contagious.

You might assume from my irreverent tongue-in-cheek comments about various players' abilities, that use of a Hacky Sack is an elitist activity. Not so! Everyone has the same opportunity to look inept and descended from Son of Maladroit. Skill level obviously increases with practice, but not everyone has 10 hours a day to kick around a pit sack, so here's a suggestion or two for those of you who are employed or married.

I have invented the Sacky Hack, for us hackers who want almost instant gratification from our physical endeavors. Simply do this. Blow up a balloon that has a couple ounces of water in it and kick away. The sloshing water provides erratic flight characteristics (the challenge), but the size of the balloon allows a better-than-average chance of making contact (the satisfaction).

If even this slowed-down version gives you trouble, fill the balloon with helium, and after the first kick it will disappear, providing the opportunity to seek other diversions that require less practice time . . . like windsurfing.

Body Sac

There's something about the game Hackey Sac that makes me uncomfortable. I suspect part of the reason is that I don't kick the sac very well, and being quickly identified as a quick twitch/no contact kicker, a high functioning footy group that is trying to establish a "world record" gives off palpable "you can play, but . . ." vibes that rattle the maladroit ego and elicit the quintessential cop-out comment: "This game sucks!" Well . . . it doesn't, as evidenced by the laid back, "Don't say you're sorry, man" kicking circles that seem to appear whenever there isn't a basketball available. How come so popular? To wit, Hackey Sacs are easily transportable, necessary play space is minimal, the rules are super simple, competition against self is de rigueur, and the eye/foot coordination necessary is transferrable to other games.

Kicking the small seed bag around is fun, if not somewhat elitist, and therein, I think, lies the rub; the amount of time necessary to gain the requisite kicking skills to gain satisfaction often results in a round ball retreat. How about trying a game that allows the use of already practiced skills while the new ones are being brought up to satisfying snuff; i.e. satisfying to the player. Enter Body Sac, a recent full-body contact variation pursued by a playful handful of folks from the annual OTRA (Oklahoma Therapeutic Ropes Association) Conference at Camp Redlands.

During a break, on the first day of the conference, I watched Jose maneuvering a regulation Hackey Sac around with an impressive level of below-the-waist skill, as he waited for the inevitable two or three other kickers that seem to appear whenever a scrunchy seed sac takes foot flight. I watched the foot, knee, ankle sequence for a couple minutes, then remembered a whimsical purchase I had made the week

before at Child's World — I'm a toy store junkie. Searching and groping around inside my highly organized game bag, I eventually found the new purchase; a macro seed bag that looks just like a Hackey Sac, but about 3-4 times as large. Manually flipping my BIG sac casually up and down, I ask Jose if he has ever played Hackey Hand? Intuitively (ego preservation) I had eliminated the crux of my intimidation; i.e., not being able to control the flight of a small object with my feet. Now we were going to play at (not play at a game, just play) keeping this comfortably sized object aloft by using hand contact only. Open hand whacks made more sense (to me) considering the size of the new seed sac, and the admonition on the packaging that stated unequivocally, "This play sac was not designed for kicking." There it was in black and white, a justification for developing a new game, and particularly since the sac came without any instructions, (except what not to do).

Jose and I manually smacked the sac around a bit, suggesting to one another after a few hits that maybe we could keep score, which we did. But before we could set a standard, others were attracted to our gymnastic hits and saves and were, of course, immediately included within our non-elitist cadre of, prehensile, upright/primate, manually dexterous, sac-whackers.

Recognizing that this was a "new" sport being established, the suggestions for satisfying play came fast and furious from the hands-on participants. Here's what resulted from that intensely creative play period, on the friendly fields of Camp Redlands, Oklahoma — ". . . where the winds come whistling down the plains . . ."

- No points are scored if the sac is whacked manually. Hand hits are strictly utilitarian, used only to keep the sac aloft— off the ground and in play.

- Points are scored as follows: one point for foot contact, three points for contact with any part of the body between the waist and the neck, (not to include the serve) and two points for cranial contact.

- After any scoring contact, the sac must be passed to another player before an additional score can be recorded. This pass can be made manually or otherwise.

- Unlimited manual hits are allowed by each player before the sac must be passed on.

- "Carrying" the sac to control its flight is not allowed.

I think the game was well received because: (1) The group made up their own rules. (2) The use of hands was allowed, to keep the game moving (as contrasts Hackey Sac, where misses and starting over are frequent and eventually tedious). (3) The entire body can be used innovatively to score points.

Ed Note: I have tried this game with a regulation Hackey Sac, and it plays *almost* as well.

Funny Face

After having experienced the *Mirror* and *Anti-Mirror* activities (See *Silver Bullets*, pg. 170), *Funny Face* is a natural and predictably hilarious follow-up sequence that produces some of the most distorted facial expressions seen since the third grade.

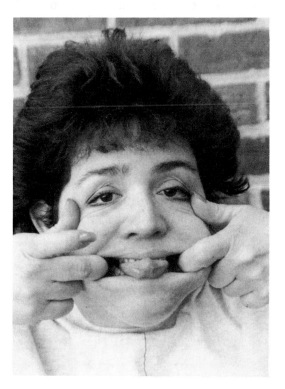

Announce to the entire group that the purpose of this encounter is to try and make everyone else smile. And, although smiles are ordinarily well received, in this case, even the slightest upward tilt of your mouth is cause for elimination from the circle *and* the game. If you generally have trouble not smiling and can't suppress a giggle, you're meat for this zany activity.

Split your large group into smaller encounter circles, say 5-7 per silly set. The rules, recently established and constantly being amended, state that after the GO signal, everyone in the circle tries to make the other members smile. If you slip and show the slightest smile, you are eliminated, and can then step back and watch the experts do their thing. A participant is not allowed to touch another player and all eyes must stay open — otherwise, anything goes. The facial and anatomical gymnastics that result are indescribable.

When the group is reduced to the last two or three, stop the action and announce that these stone-faced competitors are the regional champs and will go against the other regional champions (whoever is left from one of the other smaller encounter circles) in a face-off. This final *face-off* can result in some classic moves and reactions.

Don't approach this activity seriously. (Can it be done?) The value of *Funny Face* lies in the spontaneous reactions of the players and the unselfconscious participation that generally results. People, particularly adults, like to have an excuse to be silly occasionally. Everyone not in the final face-off is part of the cheering squad.

Prone Mortars

I'll present the essence, you provide the rules.

Get some (a dozen) used bicycle inner tubes from a bike shop (it's good PR for them, 'cause they just throw the tubes away). Also, get some (or make) large (5" x 5") bean bags. Don't use ball bearings as bag fillers.

In a large room (gym, field house) or outside, lie on your back with half a dozen bean bags within reach. Put your feet (the legs follow, if you noticed) inside an inner tube and spread your legs to tighten the tube. The double section of tube in front of you is the propulsive element of a leg-supported slingshot. Put a bean bag onto the double rubber and fold it around the rubber so that when you pull it back (to-ward your head), the bag can be released and propelled forward. With your feet held at about a 45° angle to the floor, the flight of your bean bag (considering the "quick twitch" characteristic of the rubber) will arc satisfyingly toward whatever target you have in mind. These projectiles are fairly innocuous (if the arc is high enough), so even some person-to-person catapulting shouldn't be dismissed.

Try:

1. Accuracy contexts (use hula hoops as targets).
2. Knocking over objects (plastic pins).
3. Distance contests (everyone else uses the same bean bag and rubber?).
4. Sliding shots on a slippery gym floor (lower the angle of incidence) to score points; a la shuffleboard.
5. Shooting at people who are walking perpendicular to your flight path — like an arcade game. Provide whatever protective gear seems necessary as to the speed and weight of the bean bag.
6. Just shoot for the fun of it — try vertical shots straight up; that's a lot of fun. Run away . . . Run away . . .

Fast Draw

Since you already have a number of small pocket mirrors around for use in the game

Mirrors & Mortars (*Silver Bullets*, pg. 26), try this fast-action, one-on-one confrontation.

Hold the mirror on your hip, as if you were reaching for a six-gun. In a paired-off situation, with the potential Wyatt Earp's standing about 10 yds. apart, you are ready for a showdown. The first fast-draw artist to hit an opponent's retinal area with a flash is the winner. Play again, or challenge the champion. Note the opportunity for inventive role-playing.

When two people face off, the sun must be situated so that each player has approximately the same light angle to use, otherwise one player has a distinct advantage. Skewing the angle might not be a bad idea to develop parity amongst combatants.

Have the pairs stand farther apart to offer a more difficult target. There will be no doubt in a players' mind (light overload via the optic nerve) when they have been flashed.

If the thought of "gunfighting" does not appeal, have the two flashers face up-sun toward a shaded wall. Using an agreed-upon target on the wall, the fast-draw contests can be considerably less sanguinary.

Think of team contests, although team affiliation isn't the appropriate word in this case — think . . . family (the Earps, Dalton Brothers); or show down (Jessie James, Hole-in-the-Wall Gang, etc.). Picture groups of mirror wielders trying to "wipe out" the opposing flashers. Such a contest could begin in an open field and spill over to a wooded or building area. Have you ever been flashed from behind a Shag Bark Hickory?

Solar Shoot Out

During a recent workshop, some of us were fooling around with mirrors, flashing reflected sunlight onto a shaded wall and watching the dancing spots of light form a random "atomic movement" display. None

of us were in a hurry to do anything meaningful or competitive with the mirrors (it
was a F.U.N.N. moment — Functional
Understanding's Not Necessary), being
content with watching the crazy scooting of
light circles on the bricks. Inevitably,
someone shined a blast of reflected solar
light into another participant's eyes — the
retinal response was predictable and
immediate — YEOW — combined with a
reflexive head jerk. Shades of *Fast Draw*,
leading to talk about other fast-draw games
with mirrors and resulting in this new
histrionic variation of earlier flasher games.

In the past, fast-draw aficionados would
either face one another in a reflected ray
shootout (the first person receiving a retinal
hit was the loser) or more sanguinely, all
arriving at a specific mark on the wall with
the winner designated as the first light spot
arriving at that mark.

Shouts of "I'm first!" followed by
unbelieving and good-humored expletives
indicate the difficulty of maneuvering and
identifying your own light spot. To alleviate
this confusion and give more people a
chance to join the fun, ask a group of
people (determinators) that equal the
number of mirror-wielders to line up
against the wall facing the ersatz Jedi
warriors. Each light shooter should be
paired with a determinator, whose back is
against the wall. When the signal is given to
"draw" (after each shooter has properly
"holstered their weapon"), the shooter tries
to hit his/her partner's retina with a solar
blast. When this happens (believe me,
there's no doubt when the retina receives
such a massive light overload), the receiver
yells "HIT" and throws one arm overhead.
Such a display indicates without question
or argument who is the fastest mirror in the
west — or east, or wherever you happen to
be standing.

A Rope Trick

This trick is a solo take-off of the *Almost
Infinite Circle* stunt, as defined in *Cows'
Tails & Cobras*, pg. 69. The object is to
form an overhand knot in a rope that is tied
to an individual's wrists; i.e., both wrists,
without taking off the rope, untying the
wrist knots or cutting the rope.

Solution:
1. Take a bight in the center of the rope.
2. Pass this bight under either one of your
   wrist loops.
3. Pull the bight through with your other hand
   and open it to a size that will accommo-
   date your hand.
4. Pass the bight over your hand and pull the
   bight down and through the wrist loop.
5. An overhand knot should form before your
   wondering eyes.

If you include a metal ring as part of the
bight, it will become part of the formed
knot — complemental legerdemain at no
extra cost.

The Dollar or Buck Jump

This idea provides a fun filler at the end of a
class period when you have a few minutes
before the bell, or as a surefire series of $$$
contributions at a cocktail party.

If you have all your debts paid and have
a spare dollar bill pocketed, place your
buck on the ground and tell the students
that anyone who can jump over the bill
lengthwise earns the dollar.

The catch is . . . they must grab their
toes (or tips of both shoes) and *not let go*
while they jump, continuing to hold on for
one second after landing.

Additional physical/financial stipula-
tions —

1. You must jump forward over the bill.
2. You may not fall backward (long jump
   rules are in effect).

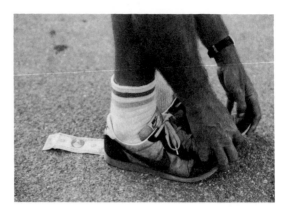

3. Start with your toes as close to the bill as possible.
4. The jumper's heels must clear the vertical plane of the end of the bill after the jump.

If you are strapped for funds, you can use a piece of paper the same size as a dollar with an **IOU** written on it.

Be sure to try this tricky and difficult event yourself before you start handing out cash — you may even want to put two bills end-to-end because of the shrinking dollar . . .

Occasionally an adept someone will make the jump successfully. Further challenge that person (double or nothing?), by asking if they can make the jump in reverse — much harder.

Beerhunter

This game (stunt) is not for everyone, but the name and resulting nonsense appeals to a baser sense.

The name is based on the movie "Deerhunter," in which there is apparently (I haven't seen the flick) a Russian Roulette sequence that is quite dramatic. To approach the drama without the negative ramifications of firearms, substitute a six pack of beer for the revolver.

If your imagination has not already grasped the crux of this foamy gambit, allow me to elucidate . . .

Take one (1) of the cans in a six pack

and shake it with gusto. Place the shaken can next to the other five cans and (with everyone's eyes closed) mix up the cans. Place all the cans back into the cardboard six-pack holster . . . I mean holder.

The six players then choose a can and hold it in front of their faces. With everyone's thumb inserted in their respective pull-tabs (triggers), the stage is set for drama, suspense and a face full of foam.

Hey . . . I said the game wasn't for everyone, but you have to admit there is a certain primitive panache to the foamy format. I like the name of the game... sounds better than Dr. Pepperhunter.

Flubber Ball

Take the ball and run with it — if you can catch it. Take your favorite inflatable sport ball and inject it with a heady dose of helium. Your ball won't float away, but the results are noticeable, particularly with *Moonball*. If the ball is made of light-weight material or is thin-walled, the ball will react more dramatically to the helium — the ultimate thin wall/lightweight ball being, of course, a balloon.

I suspect helium help is against somebody's U.I.A.A. formal rules, so beware using your flubber ball in sanctioned games.

I wonder how a cage ball would handle if filled with helium?

While were on helium — Did you ever breathe in some helium from a store-bought balloon and then try to talk? If you need an ice breaker to start a session, get a couple helium balloons, take a couple snorts, then recite "Mary Had a Little Lamb . . ."

Take a small bite from the rubber in the neck of the inflated balloon. This will give you a place to suck helium, and it won't pop the balloon — most of the time.

Rodeo Throw

It appears that not many folks use "hula hoops" for hip spinning now-a-days, although keeping that infernal circle above my hips is still a task that befuddles my ability to hula-spin. Curious storekeepers ask, "What are you going to use all them hoops for?", as scientists, educators, mathematicians, and recreation specialists find an increasing number of uses for these simple but intriguing plastic hoops. There's even segmented hoops available now so you can create whatever size you need for an activity, also allowing after-class break down of your hoops for storage or travel.

Try the following activity on a wooden gym floor (a rubberized gym floor provides too much friction). Throw a hoop away from you with an underhand toss and in the same motion, impart a backward spin to the hoop. The hoop will travel, spinning and gently bouncing, away from the thrower until the backward spinning motion overcomes forward momentum, causing the hoop to spin in place for a second then eventually return in the general direction of the thrower.

Practicing this type of throw is preliminary training for the next event; the *Rodeo Throw.* Try to have lots of different sized hoops on hand to include as many people as possible.

Two participants stand next to one another at one end of a gym; one as the runner and the other as thrower. (This presupposes that some practice throws have already been made.)The thrower spins the hoop on the floor (as above) and the runner attempts to sprint out and dive through the vertically spinning hoop without knocking it over. Timing is important, as the best chance to scamper through the hoop is when it briefly spins in place. Two trips through the hoop is possible, but requires a good throw, quick feet, and/or a small bod.

Variations quickly present themselves from this simple beginning, as people align themselves differently (opposite ends of the gym for simultaneous throws and dives), or try increasingly difficult tricks (feet first through the spinning hoop).

Squirm

Place a *slightly* deflated beachball (Moonball) between the foreheads of two participants. The object is to maneuver the ball from forehead to knees and back up again, without touching the ball with your hands (elbows, arms, etc.). Mucho balls; mucho action.

Balance Practice

Remember how, at the circus, the clowns would balance plates or a chair at the end of a long pole that was planted on the chin or forehead of the performer? That type of balance skill takes a lot of practice, and more time (or patience) than you have available in a 50 minute class.

Try some small-scale balancing "tricks" using a 1" x 3' wooden dowel. Almost everyone can gain some immediate success and satisfaction from balancing such a rod vertically on the palm of their hand. It will, predictably, require some hand, arm, and body movement and, in some cases, jogging this way and that to keep the rod from falling, but that's fun and given to repetition.

As skill or luck increases, try balancing the rod on your chin, forehead or even your nose. Contests for maximum vertical time aloft or distance covered while balancing are natural incentives. Also try tossing the dowel from person to person; i.e., from balanced position to balanced position. Try a 180° toss (half spin) from hand to hand. Try a 360° toss! Try not whacking yourself, or your partner, in the head.

I've noticed people balancing peacock feathers in much the same way as using the dowels above, but the challenge is considerably reduced because of the feather's slow movement due to lightness and air resistance. Safer too, and getting whacked by a feather seems oxymoronic enough to just let it happen.

Rug Remnants

I'm sure you have seen or perhaps used small, four-wheeled scooters designed for free-wheeling movement on gym floors.

They seem like a lot of fun, but cost prevents their widespread use.

Some frugal and inventive teachers have substituted sections of rug remnants for scooters for use on smooth-surfaced floors (wood, not Tartan). You put a small section of rug on the deck (fiber twist to the floor), sit on it, and get pushed around by your DP (designated pusher).

Here's the next step: cut some sections of rug (this is where that old saying, "cut-a-rug" came from — no, really!) somewhat larger than 12" long and glue (sew) velcro strips onto the back side so that two pieces can be used as "rug skates" for whatever slip-and-slide game you have in mind. The velcro strips aren't really necessary, but they look snazzy.

Olympic speed-skating records (around the gym) are a natural and are sure to be broken repeatedly. I timed one "skater" for the length of a gym at just over 7 seconds!

Seat Spin

If your group is fairly dizzy anyway, ask each person to try this simple maneuver.

Sit on the gym floor (the slipperier, the better), and throw or thrust your extended legs to the right or left in order to initiate a spin on your buttocks. As soon as the spin has started, tuck your knees and arms up to your chest to feel the immediate acceleration and rapid spin rate; a la figure skaters. If you can hold two revolutions before tipping over, you are doing well.

This simplistic spin-a-roo stunt does not work well on asphalt (hot top), grass and recently plowed surfaces.

The world's record for glute spinning is held by Tillie Haversac, who in 1987 at the Paramus mall, spun around 14 times before losing her all-American lunch (hot dog, large Coke, and a Twinkie). Awesome!

There's a physics lesson in here somewhere.

Another Nonsense Knot

Here's a nifty sequence to establish a quick solution to an impossible problem. Ask if anyone can tie an overhand knot in a short piece of rope (3'-4') if both ends are being held by the person attempting to tie the knot.

The following illustration provides the simple solution. "Now, why didn't I think of that?"

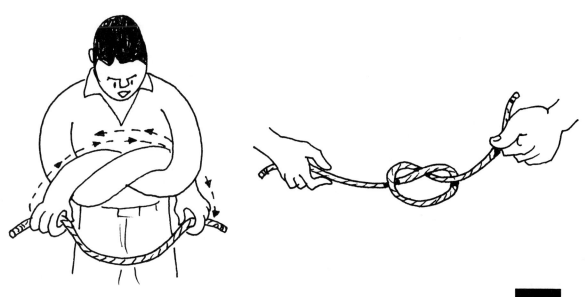

Scooter Swing

This swing-on-wheels idea came from Dave Villandry of the UMPA (Urban Modification of Project Adventure) program in Cambridge, Massachusetts.

I have observed other people trying this swinging idea in past workshops, but I recently tried it myself and can now attest to what I was observing; people having fun and being challenged.

For this activity, you will need a floor scooter (essentially a 12" x 12" section of 3/4" plywood that has four ball-bearing casters attached on the bottom of the plywood in each corner), and a dangling rope somewhere near the center of the gym. Use of the 20' gymnastic climbing ropes that many schools still have, will work fine. You will also need a person with a helmet on, and lots of other folks to stand in a circle around that person.

Brief reference to the helmet situation, because I'm sure it caught your attention. In some instances of adventure programming, you are safer with a helmet on, and this is one of those times. The Scooter Swing activity is not dangerous, but an unplanned fall to the floor is possible. Make me feel better, wear the helmet.

Ask the group to make a large people-circle around the rope to be used. The chosen participant stands on top of the scooter and grips the rope. Someone moves in from their position in the circle and gives the center person a shove to get started, which scoots the rider toward the far circumference of the circle, where they are pushed back toward the other side of the circle. This compassionate reciprocal pushing and scooting continues in a random fashion until the person tires of the ride or detaches from the scooter. As long as the rider holds onto the rope, a fall is simply slipping off the scooter and sliding to a stop on the floor. Do not allow riders to use black-soled shoes, or the gym floor will suffer as will your rapport with the custodians.

As the rider becomes more adept, the

circumference of the circle can be expanded considerably.

This is fun, folks — give it a try. It's a natural for making up games. Two games to try:

1. After each successful push across the circle, expand the circle's circumference by half a step until the rider eventually slips off the scooter.

2. Place a ten pin (or empty tennis ball can) in the center of the circle. The rider starts on the scooter at the edge of the circle somewhere. The group attempts to knock over the ten pin using the rider as the "bowling ball." The rider tries to miss the ten pin by foot movements and body English. Count the number of shoves necessary to knock over the pin. The circle's circumference remains the same throughout each attempt. The larger the circle, the more chance the rider has of missing the pin.

Alert the folks in the circle to the danger of getting whacked in the ankle by the scooter, particularly if the person riding it flips it with their foot.

Scooter Spin

The set-up for Scooter Spin is simple, and it goes like this . . . Place two, four-wheel gym scooters in the center of a basketball court or other large smooth floor area. Ask a helmeted volunteer pilot to lie on top of the two scooters (chest and pelvic area on the scooters). Offer the rider a knotted end of a 20' rope; any substantial rope that's easy to grip.

Begin to slowly rotate the rider on a foreshortened section of rope — this allows you (the spinner) to establish yourself as the central power source for the accelerating rider. As the centrifugal force builds, slowly let out

the remainder of the rope, while maintaining the rider's speed (which to a first-time, wide-eyed pilot will seem in excess of Mach I.) I'd estimate the rider's actual maximum speed at 15 m.p.h.

A Caveat

According to the immutable laws of physics, if either you or the rider lets go during the spin sequence, both will travel apart from one another with equal velocity. Practically speaking, you will end up meeting the floor with surprising abruptness and the solo pilot will continue (at speed) toward the first solid object encountered beyond the boundary of the smooth surface. The resulting impact is impressive; don't let it happen!

Tie a slip knot in the rider's end of the rope and place it over his/her hand. Tie an overhand knot about 12 inches above the slip knot so that the rider can hold onto the rope without experiencing constricting pressure from the slip knot. Also put a figure eight loop in the spinner's end of the rope to allow maintaining solid contact.

If the set-up allows (field house, parking lot, Logan Airport), release the rider at top speed and see what kind of maximum distance can be achieved. There must be a formula that can be experimented with that relates centrifugal rotation to distance.

As a *Challenge By Choice* quick-stop mechanism, the rider can drag his/her feet if speed seems excessive.

Helmets should be worn by all riders, and you might even want to put one on too. Goggles and silk scarf are optional.

Scooter Slalom

Use the same type of scooter explained previously in the Scooter Swing. You will need a minimum of two scooters, but having a few more keeps things moving; i.e., less standing around and waiting.

This aerobic activity requires that the students work in pairs. They will be "scooting" through a slalom course set up on the gym floor in an attempt to establish a time. Each additional attempt offers a chance to better their record. Emphasize pair self-satisfaction, because time comparisons with other pairs are inevitable.

The rider sits on a scooter and puts his/her feet on top of a second scooter. The second member of the pair stands behind the rider and provides the GO, by pushing. The slalom course, a sample of which is outlined in the illustration, should include a few right angle turns, a couple "hairpins" and a straightaway — be inventive (tough, but realistic).

A couple people in the group with digital watches can be timers until their turn comes up. As the pair attempts to make their fastest trip through the slalom markers (cones), it become obvious that the pair which works together (the rider uses his/her hands as outriggers to aid balance and turning), shows the most improvement. There is an infectious quality to this activity, because each pair is sure they can "do it faster next time."

Rules

1. One pair on the course at a time.
2. For each pylon or cone touched, a second is added to the total time. If a marker is knocked over, add two seconds.
3. If the rider's feet come off the front scooter and touch the floor, the ride may continue. If the rider's posterior hits the floor, the ride is over.
4. Slingshotting the rider is not allowed.
5. Rider and pusher must maintain physical contact throughout the run . . . particularly over the finish line.
6. Riders should wear a helmet.

Try to set up the slalom cones (using the entire gym floor) so that the start and finish is at the same end of the gym.

As this activity uses up a lot of energy, a pair should be encouraged to switch roles as rider and pusher. This suggestion is usually well received by the pusher.

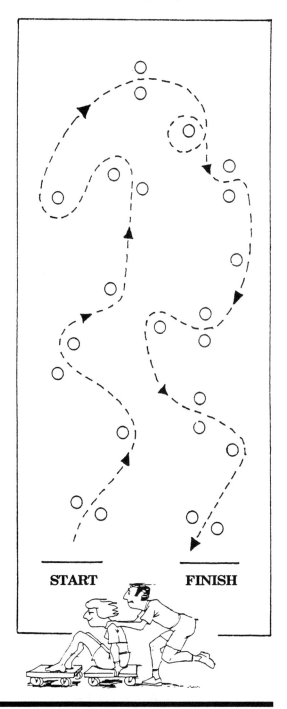

START   **FINISH**

Snowflake

"The simplest are the funnest."

Obtain a mess of loose styrofoam packing material; say a small box full. These ultra lightweight objects are your "snowflakes." Did you know that no two pieces of styrofoam are ever exactly alike? No, really . . . that's true; I read it somewhere.

Climb to the top of something (staging, tree, ladder, astrodome) and launch a snowflake or two. Watch their slow and erratic descent. I'll bet it would be tough for a person down below to catch one on his/her tongue.

Note from the U.S.D.A. — Dispose of all tongued styrofoam pieces because of inevitable hygienic concerns. If your floor area is "clean enough to eat off of," recycle the missed "snowflakes." If the floor's cleanliness is suspect, you can play "Squash the Grub," a quaint foot-stomping survival activity indigenous to the African pygmy.

Do not let these descending pieces of styrofoam enter your mouth; they don't taste good (they don't taste at all), and sucking one in can be detrimental to continued breathing.

Snowflakes — of Descending Velocity and Permutations

Yesterday, I was absently rifling my hand through a box of "snowflakes," when I noticed that there were three different basic shapes represented; the cup, the peanut, and the figure 8 types. Since no one was watching (you have to be somewhat reserved, as President of the Corporation), I tossed a representative sampling into the air and noticed that their flight (descent) characteristics varied considerably — thus, the crux of this in-depth inquiry. (I had approached *Scientific American* magazine with the results, but snowflakes in June were of "topical interest only," so . . .)

The cup shape was definitely the most predictable and the slowest descender. I'd suggest its use with special needs groups or those needing a higher success ratio: not much challenge, but definitely a floater worth watching.

The peanut configuration varies considerably because of an apparent inconsistency in the manufacturing process. A "good" peanut shape falls fairly predictably, providing a catch ratio consistently higher than 50%. The mutant peanuts, however, are devils to predict and establish — in my mind, the most difficult and frustrating objects to tongue successfully. Be prepared to grade your "snowflakes" for descent consistency, if success is the criterion. Some groups could care less, so you know what do do in that case.

Finally, the figure 8, a beautiful piece of aerodynamic foam that is both predictable and frustratingly difficult to catch — a sportsperson's paradox that is akin to the skill of nabbing catfish by hand. The whirling *and* spiral descent of this snow-flake will test the mettle and oral dexterity of your most adept student: quick twitch muscles are key for these video game-like descents.

So, there you have it; as definitive a treatise on styrofoam bit descent as you will probably ever read — and, once again, *Bag of Tricks* was there first.

The Rope Push

Halve your group and ask each half to stand on either side of a marker line (chalk line or rope). Hand them a 60-80' length of rope (any diameter or material) so that each side has an equal amount on their side of the marker line. Mark the center of the rope with a piece of tape. At this juncture, they are probably ready for a good old Tug-O-War, BUT the object this time is, at the end of a one minute time limit, to have more of your rope on their side than they have of their rope on your side! WHAT? Right, fox, this is a rope push, not pull. Here are a couple rules to ease the transition from tradition to chaos.

No one on either team is allowed to cross over and touch the other team's turf or person (no intentional contact). Tug-ging on the rope is tabu — only push. Throwing the rope *is* allowed.

Judging this event is well-nigh impos-sible, but who cares? And, a tie is usually well received by all, except the most die-hard competitors. This confused bash may be worth trying again, so suggest taking a minute or two to develop team strategies and subterfuges, or sneaky initiative ideas.

Double Dutch

Using the same section of rope that you used for *The Turnstile* (**Silver Bullets**, pg. 156), double it so that each section is about 20' long, and with one piece in each turner's hands, have them turn a "Double Dutch" tattoo on the floor or street. If you don't know what Double Dutch is, ask any street-wise student, because verbalizing the sequence is harder than doing it . . . well, maybe not.

This is the stuff of pure nostalgia for some, an aesthetic and physical awaken-ing to others, and flagellating frustration for most. I have seen young women perform feats of endurance and skill among, on top of, and underneath those spinning double ropes that would make a *Sports Illustrated* photographer's index finger itch. Try

stepping into those whirling ropes for a little "hot pepper"; it's a humbler!

Orange Teeth   Ω

Try this simple stunt and listen to the "Hey-how-do-you-do-that?" comments. It's a programmatically useful and funny lunch time diversion.

Cut an orange (thin-skinned oranges work best) into quarters and eat the edible part down to the whitish rind. Take a knife and cut the peel as indicated in the crude drawing below (all my drawings are crude), to form teeth.

Adjust the rind in your mouth so that the exterior of the peel faces in (white out) and fit the edges of the rind between your lips and gums. Tasty, eh?

Your reversed ascorbic false teeth are now in place. Stick your tongue through the "teeth" slots for a touch of bizarre realism.

CUT LINES

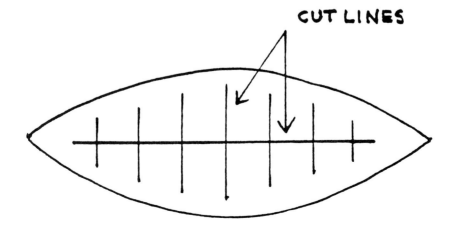

Chapter 4

Just Plain Games

The Travesty Concept

Somebody in a group always seems to be looking for the easiest (sneakiest) way to accomplish something. It's just human nature I suppose that, as you set the operating parameters for an initiative game or problem, someone in the group will try to outguess you or come up with some outlandish manipulation of the rules to achieve a goal.

For example, getting a group of people over a twelve high foot wall is a well known classic initiative problem, and unless you specifically say that "the Wall extends indefinitely in both directions," someone

will ask if they can just walk around the Wall to get to the other side.

I realize that you can't knock initiative (afterall, that's the name of the game) but the ridiculous back door ploys have always bugged me. Ex. "How come I can't just walk through the poison peanut butter to get the rope if I have to come back here anyway?"

So now when someone asks if they can stretch the rules, I just invoke the *travesty concept,* which states that a group can do anything they want to achieve a goal, **IF** what they choose to do is satisfying and enjoyable for the group.

"So sure, if you folks want to solve this problem by just walking around the Wall, that's cool, but let's talk about that decision . . ." or "Walking through the poisoned peanut butter isn't as much fun as swinging across, but go ahead and walk across if that's satisfying to the group."

Try it out. Explain what the travesty concept involves, then let the group make their own rules about following the rules. You may be surprised, that when a group has the choice of challenging themselves they often end up choosing the most difficult potential solution.

The Point of the Game

I think this is what you might call a "party" game, but it has the ingredients — with slight modifications — of a useful group game that emphasizes cooperation, being comfortable as the center of attention, thinking on your feet, good-natured humor and incisive thinking.

The object is to have one or two people (volunteers) leave the room and upon returning, to try and determine what "the point of the game" is that the group has decided to play. (If two people leave the room, upon returning, they operate as one person; i.e., a team of two.)

The out-of-room volunteers begin the action by asking questions of the large group. Any number of questions can be asked, but a time limit for questioning is set. Before a deadline is reached, the person asking the questions must correctly determine . . . *the point of the game.*

For example, the group decides that all answers to the questions must be responded to sequentially in a pre-determined order by members of the group; i.e., 1-15, or however many people are in the group. If the person asking the questions determines that the group is indeed answering the questions in that manner and makes the discovery within the time limit, then he/she "wins," and receives a standing ovation or whatever.

Sequential answering is a fairly easy game to discover, but if you add an alphabetical twist to the answering, the "point" is not so sharp. For example, each person answering in sequence must also use sequential alphabet lettering in order to begin the first word of their answer.

Example:

Question #1 - Is what you're thinking of in this room? Answer #1 - Always keep your questions to the point. (Emphasize A in *always* as the first letter of the alphabet.) Question #2 - Was my last question too nebulous? Answer #2 - Bob is a better judge of that. Question #3 - Which Bob do you mean? Answer #3 - Can't you be more specific? This ploy obviously makes discovering the point of the game more difficult and immensely humorous to the "in" crowd.

Also try: (1) Alternating male and female players as those answering each question. Obviously, the answers need have no relevance to the questions, as only the alternating of sex is significant. (2) Each answer must include the name of a prominent article in the room.

Use shoe size, height, or age for other sequential ploys.

Point of the Game is a rainy day gem that may well last the entire period.

Help Me Rhonda

This is a minimum prop, small group word game that is usually well received by older students (folks who can spell). Divide a larger group into triads or troikas. Each group of three must have a piece of paper and pencil (pen).

The leader (not necessarily you) calls out the name of a person (three to six letters in the name) with no repeating letters — try RHONDA. The designated recording secretary of each group spells the name at the top of a sheet of paper, like so:

R   H   O   N   D   A

The leader then calls out the name of a category, say "animals." The troika must then list as many animals as possible underneath the letters of the name RHONDA, so that each animal's name must start with R-H-O-N-D or A. E.g., <u>O</u>wl under <u>O</u>, <u>D</u>og under <u>D</u>, <u>A</u>ardvark under <u>A</u>, etc.

The teams score one point for each acceptable answer, and two points for each animal name that no other team thought of. Choose other categories for additional contests, and let the players choose the categories. Try - "flowers," "cities," "trees," "brand names of foods," "sports," etc. If the students in the group are math, English, science or whatever majors, specialize the categories: "protozoans," "circulatory system," "bones of the body," etc.

What's-the-Key? Games   Ω

As I've mentioned in previous game write-ups of this genre, the play rationale (other than fun, which is a taken-for-granted ingredient, or I wouldn't be writing about it) is twofold: (1) The puzzle encourages players to "see" solution possibilities other than just the obvious answer; i.e., emphasizing lateral rather than vertical thinking — "taking the blinders off," so to speak. (2) Allowing participants to experience the frustration, discomfort and anger of what it's like being on the outside of a group.

Players sit in a circle and the leader says, "I'm going on a trip to Boston (or wherever) and I'll take anyone along who wears the *proper* clothing — we are going to Boston, after all!" The leader then describes his own sartorial set-up and asks if anyone would like to join the trip —that person who's dressed appropriately, of course.

The correct attire (top half) is whatever the person immediately to your right is wearing and the de rigueur bottom half attire is what the person to your left is sporting.

Skip a person to the right or left if you think the answer is too obvious.

Bang, You're Dead
(Around-the-Ole Campfire Game)

This game is another example of the I-know-there's-a-clue-but-I-can't-figure-it-out collection.

The object is for a group to figure out why whatever you're saying is true or why their reply is wrong.

In this particular game, for example, you say, "Bang. You're Dead!", point to anyone, and then wait for a response from someone in the group indicating whom they think you shot. The guesses begin slowly and the frustration level grows apace as you indicate, apparently without reason, who has been shot. Then you begin again with another, "Bang. You're Dead!" exclamation.

The key-clue in this particular game is, whoever makes the first verbal response to your statement "Bang . . ." is the victim. Too easy? Try the game and see how long it takes for the group to figure it out. Remember, "Truth is obvious, after its discovery."

Other clues could be body or limb positions. If the group becomes adept at spotting clues, try using "eraser clues"; i.e., body movements or positions that indicate just the opposite for a clue. Example: If your legs are crossed, then an uncrossed leg position is the key.

Be aware there has been some negative feedback received as to the "*Bang, You're Dead*" title of the game — too violent. Try changing the game and name (*Troika* - a team of three) with the following presentation: "A connection has been formed between the following three people (name any three people). Who caused this bonding? The answer is the same as in the *Bang, You're Dead* approach.

Hands Down

People generally see what they want to see or perceive only what is being shown to them. Magicians count on this tunnel vision to make their sleight of hand appear to be "real magic."

This simple problem (demonstration, actually) is designed to point out that the obvious facts are not necessarily the combination needed for a solution. Also that lateral thinking (looking beyond the obvious) is necessary in an initiative situation to come up with a functional answer. Contrast this to vertical thinking, where the individual(s) fixate on one only one approach.

Obtain five lengths (about 6") of any type of matching material; e.g., pencils, dowels, sticks. Kneel down on the floor, pavement, ground, etc., and place the five pencils on the flat area in front of you so that a pattern is formed — any pattern will do.

For example:

Indicates the Number 3

Indicates the Number 1

— or whatever your imagination produces.

Ask the group surrounding you to indicate the number from one to ten that this arrangement of sticks demonstrates. Set up two or three different patterns so that the group gets to see and guess additional numbers that you are depicting.

The Gimmick — As soon as you set down whatever fanciful combination of sticks your imagination conjures up, place your hands on the floor next to the sticks with the number of fingers exposed indicating the number you have in mind. (See photos above.) The sticks do not indicate anything. Change the pattern of sticks and change the number of figures you leave out (two fists on the ground is zero; two hands palms down, fingers extended, indicates the number ten).

Someone will eventually figure out what you are doing. Use that person to maintain group interest by asking them to name the number indicated by each new pattern. If no one catches on, place your hands closer to the sticks or try throwing the sticks over your shoulder and ostentatiously slapping your palms on the area in front of you.

Be sure to finish up this exercise with a brief statement of what you were trying to accomplish, and what the gimmick was, because there will inevitably be a couple folks still baffled by your overt/covert display of digits.

Passing Crossed or Uncrossed

This around-the-campfire game is historically played with a pair of scissors, but can be as effectively played with two pencils, two sticks, etc.

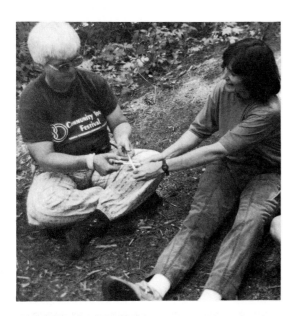

A leader initiates the activity by passing two pencils to the person sitting to their left or right in the circle. The leader says one of two things, "I am passing these pencils to you crossed," or "I am passing these pencils to you uncrossed." The leader indicates to the group that each person is to individually receive the pencils and then pass them on crossed or uncrossed, also verbally stating both how they were received and how they are being passed; i.e., crossed or uncrossed.

Confusion begins when a player receives the pencils parallel to one another and the passer says, "I am passing these pencils to you crossed." The group looks to you for confirmation that this person is bewildered. Your confirmation of the passer's correct assessment and action increases the confusion. Why are obviously uncrossed pencils being passed "crossed"? As in all these where-is-the-key problems, the in-hand pencils have nothing to do with the crossed or uncrossed situation.

The "key" is the legs position of the person doing the passing and the legs position of that person to whom the pencils are being passed. For example, the person receiving the pencils says, "I am receiving these pencils crossed." (Are the passer's legs *crossed* or uncrossed?) And, "I am passing them uncrossed." (Are the receiver's legs crossed or uncrossed?)

"I see, said the blind man, as he picked up his hammer and saw."

I've Got the Beat

Utilizing any object or even your own finger, establish a simple beat by striking that object on a table, floor, etc. There should be no more than 8-12 movements to the beat. Perform the movements of the beat a couple times in front of your group, so that they have a chance to understand and attempt to remember what you are doing. After you have performed the sequence 2-3 times, tell them that, "I have the beat." Then offer them the object to tap with and ask if anyone else thinks they have the beat. If your beat sequence is simple enough, you will have a couple volunteers who think they can duplicate your actions.

As in all these do-as-I-do problems, the key is not the obvious movement or sound, but is revealed as a pre- or post-movement, position, or sound. In this case, a *deep breath* or *clearing your throat* before starting the beat is the indicator or key to a "successful" beat. The key can be any number of things, but the group must begin to realize that the answer to these types of problems (and many initiative type problems) is often not the visually obvious one.

Predictably, the people who think they know how to duplicate your beat are concentrating on exactly what your physical motions are with the beat object. If, after a few tries, no one has "The Beat," make the *throat clearing* before starting more obvious. It is amazing how zeroed-in some people can become to extraneous actions that they think are essential movements. As obvious as you think your actions are in trying to expose the "key," there will still be some myopic individuals who say, "Do it one more time." I can commiserate, having been that short-sighted person more often than I'd like to admit.

Your Add   Ω

This simple, no-prop game has so many good things going for it that you should try it right now. Grab a partner — husband, roommate, wife, sibling, anyone with a few fingers (10 digits are not necessary; in fact, amputees have an advantage).

Tell them to put their hands behind their backs (command is SET!), and on the

word SHOW! both players, standing vis-á-vis, thrust their hands forward with from 0-10 fingers extended. The first player to come up with a calculated total for all fingers is champion.   Example — 1st player shows 8 fingers, 2nd player shows 2 fists; total is 8. Also try subtracting and multiplying, using a third player's one hand finger total as the subtractor or multiplier.

If your group is involved in an extended workshop or retreat (more than one day), this game can emphasize spontaneous interaction between people. Whenever two people approach one another, one can say SET!, which is all that's needed to initiate a quick *Your Add* contest, leading to further conversation, maybe friendship, further involvement — perhaps even marriage, financial commitments, pets, two cars, wall-to-wall carpeting, kids — what more can you ask of a simple game?

Which Way? Softball

Trying to referee this game can be as confusing as trying to follow the rules. Where a player runs after hitting the ball, in ordinary softball, is predictable, but by radically changing the base-running rules, a traditional game becomes a physical *and* intellectual challenge.

1st inning	Run the bases in reverse.
2nd inning	2nd base becomes 1st base. 3rd becomes 2nd. 1st becomes 3rd.
3rd inning	When the ball is hit to the right side of the field (or infield), the player runs to 3rd base first and proceeds around the bases in reverse. If the next batter hits the ball to the left side of the field, then the player runs to 1st base.

If the players are on base, they must determine which is the correct direction to run, based on where the ball is hit.

Another Name Game

After a group has played some other game to learn everyone's name (Ex. Toss-A-Name Game), this quickie serves nicely as a review. It's a quick-thinking, speedy-action, couple-laugh, name tune-up.

Everyone stands in a circle with you initially in the center. Point to someone and say, "Right" — then say the complete name of your school. For example, "Right, Lakeview Elementary School." The person that you pointed to must say the name of the person to their *right* before you finish saying, "Lakeview Elementary School." If they flub the name or don't say anything, then that person takes your place in the

center of the circle. If you say, "Left". . . etc., etc.

To make the game more difficult, say, "Three Right," or "Two Left," indicating the person 3 or 2 spaces to the right or left.

If the group is large (20 or more), put more than one person in the center. This game is somewhat like *Speed Rabbit*, but more goal-oriented.

Paper Golf

Chasing a golf ball around the links is a comparatively unphysical means of spending exercise time, from a cardio-vascular standpoint. I'd like to further reduce your oxygen uptake by introducing you to *Paper Golf*, a fiendishly clever, intriguing, and fascinating paper and pencil game of golf.

You will need 18 sheets of unlined paper to duplicate an 18 hole course. The size of the paper is up to you, but generally the larger the paper, the more demanding (not physically) the game becomes.

The following illustration depicts a typical Paper Golf hole set-up. Your imagination and golf experience will allow you to make up the other 17 holes on separate sheets.

The game is best played by a foursome (that's golf talk for 4 players playing a round — 9 or 18 holes — together), but can be played by any number; i.e., until the pen or pencil lines become confusingly intertwined.

To Play

Player number one places the point of his/her pencil or pen directly on the paper anywhere between the two markers designating the tee. (It quickly becomes obvious that this paper game of golf uses the same vocabulary and rules of regulation golf, and as such, provides an enjoyable method of teaching the basics of the game without

suffering the frustrations of "keeping your head down," "maintaining a straight left arm," "controlling the back swing," etc.)

The player eyeballs the distance from tee to green, recognizing the obstacles that will increase the score and planning a first move (drive) that will place the ball (tip of the pen) in a safe area for the next stroke.

After the player has planned her drive, she must *close her eyes* and keep them closed for 5 seconds before moving the pen. Only one continuous move (straight or curving) may be executed. If the pen tip *ends up* in a bunker or hazard, strokes are added to the score.

The player must then plan the next stroke (with eyes open) and execute the stroke (eyes closed) toward the pin (hole). To finish the hole, the pen tip must end up directly in the open area of the hole.

As you develop each hole on the separate pieces of paper, use your imagination to vary the obstacles and distance and thus the par value for each hole.

How're Ya Doin'? Just Fine, Thanks

Ask a group of 10-15 students to put on blindfolds, and then arrange themselves facing you (continue talking so they know where you are); shoulder-to-shoulder. Then, starting from the right or left of the line, have them count off, and remind them to remember *their* number.

Depending upon whether this is your first blindfolded initiative problem, you should mention the trust aspect of no-see situations. Assure the group that you will not do anything to jeopardize their safety or embarrass them. Considering that trust is such a fragile and sometimes hard-won group feeling, value and nurture the group's trust as your most valuable teaching tool in adventure education.

Lined up, numbered and waiting, ask each participant to ask the person to their immediate right or left this question, "How're ya doin'?" Each person asked will answer, "Just fine, thanks!" Continue this verbal flood of questions and answers so that all the participants hear the repetitive Q&A's at least 3 or 4 times.

Now, have the participants mill around (still blindfolded) in the hands-up-palms-forward-protect yourself position until their sequential number positions have been entirely scrambled.

Ask them to stop and return, shoulder-to-shoulder, to their initial numbered position. They are allowed to talk, but the only thing they are allowed to say is, "How're ya doing'?" "Just fine, thanks!"

In order to further involve the first and last person in line, ask the group to *line up in a circle.* Line up in a circle? Are you kidding? No, really . . . can you do that ?

Pick and Choose Ω

Ask the entire group to line up behind a designated throw line on the gym floor (there's lots of lines around, just pick one of them) and give the group at least 50 old tennis balls (or fleece balls). Place a plastic milk carton or waste basket approximately 20 feet perpendicular from that throw line marker, then place another one to the left of that perpendicular line about 25 feet from the marker, and finally a third container to the right of perpendicular and 30 feet away — so that it looks like this: (There are two sets of containers in the illustration.)

Using a two minute time limit, ask the group to see how high a score they can achieve by throwing or bouncing the balls into the containers. The closest container scores 1 point; the second, 3 points; and the third, 7 points.

The group must separate themselves to become either a thrower or retriever. The throwers must remain behind the throwing line. The retrievers may stand any place

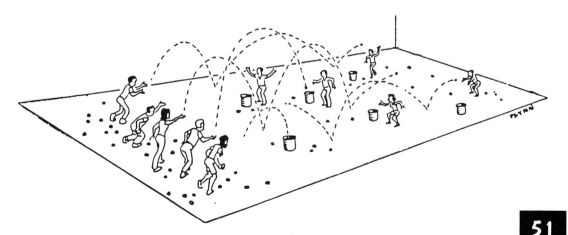

they wish, but may not "help" the balls into the cores; their job is simply to retrieve missed shots and get the balls back to the throwers as fast as possible. Once the clock starts, the throwers and retrievers may not exchange positions, but may switch before the next attempt.

This is a group decision-making game. Resist the temptation to make "facilitating" suggestions and let the action flow. The game is obviously designed to play more than once.

Think about adding another container 5' further out that scores 10 points, to stimulate interest and increase the difficulty of the decision-making process. Add a rubber frog to the throwables and indicate that it scores double. This is not a serious game . . . but having fun is serious business.

A Game Called Blockhead

Steve Butler, a playmate of note, brings by games and toys from time to time and this particular store-bought item has potential. The commercial name of this bought-in-a-box game is *Blockhead.* The game para-phernalia (those things that come tumbling out of the box) are brightly colored wooden blocks of varied shapes. The blocks are about one to three inches in length or width, and are not easy to describe because of their polygonal makeup — lots of square corners, not many round.

With a playing partner(s), the game object is to construct a balanced stack with the blocks. Each player(s) chooses a block, as their rotating turn comes up, and adds it to the precarious spire. If the stack falls as the result of their misplaced block, they are designated "acting blockhead" until the next tower topples.

It's easy to recognize how this type of game fits well into an adventure curriculum.

1. A sense of risk-taking and uncertain outcome is constant.
2. Conversation and decision-making are ongoing.
3. The blocks can be home-made by the students. Make macro blocks for maximum action.
4. Instructions and proctoring are minimized, while action, anticipation and creativity are undeniable.
5. Occasional and expected failure is an accepted part of the game.

Caveat: Don't use cinder blocks.

Mine Field   Ω

Empty your bag-o-tricks on the floor and ask the students to rearrange all the play goodies so that they are randomly and equally spaced within an approximate 15" X 40" rectangle on the floor. Outline the rectangle with rope, tape, webbing, string, etc.

The object of creating this fabricated

mine field is to provide a maze-of-mines venue through which a blindfolded person can be verbally guided to "safety". Verbal directions must come from the sidelines; i.e., the verbal leader is not allowed to stand next to or touch his/her partner.

This picky-foot jaunt from boundary to boundary is timed. For each "mine" touched, there is a 30 second time penalty added to the final time. Have each pair trade their blind/leader positions after an initial attempt.

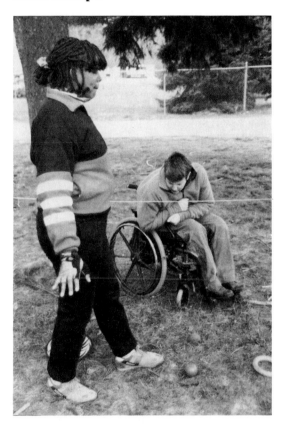

If you have the time, and using a stop watch seems counterproductive toward what you are trying to accomplish, just let the various pairs work their way slowly through the maze, counting the number of "mine" contacts for comparison with a later attempt.

For a touch of surrealism, try adding 20-30 set mouse traps to the mine field. These small traps might be deadly to a mouse, but a shod participant will hardly notice the trap release. The SNAP, however, is a definite indicator that a mine has been touched. **DON'T USE RAT TRAPS** — they hurt!

An alternative mine field can be set up in a large outlined (rope) circle. The activity is pursued in exactly the same way, except each pair is headed for the center of the circle where a squeeky toy has been placed. First foot/sound contact with the toy WINS. Winning involves getting to watch, and waiting for the next pair to WIN.

For intense militant action, try the pursuit variable of releasing a heat-seeking missile (HSM). Pairs and rules are as above.

In this game action, the blindfolded player is called the Sidewinder Missle, a highly accurate and devastatingly destructive missile. This Missle (SWM) is aimed at a target on the far side of the room (chair, table, etc.) and is set in motion by the person giving step-by-step instructions. If the SWM touches a mine, he/she must remain motionless for 30 seconds.

Sixty seconds after the SWM is launched, an anti-missile missile is also launched. This second blindfolded player represents a heat-seeking missile and is trying to destroy (tag) the SWM before the target is reached. If the HSM touches a nugget, he/she must freeze for 25 seconds.

Filling the floor with SW and HS missiles provides a mutated military mélee of more than modest proportions. Great fun for all, warhead affiliation notwithstanding.

Warp Speed   Ω

This neatly-wrapped initiative problem involves getting to the solution by operating at warp speed. The problem itself is a variation and extension of *Group Juggling,* (**Silver Bullets**, pg. 112).

Choose one soft, grabbable throwing object (fleece balls are good — lacrosse balls are bad) for the fast-paced action. Ask the group to form a circle (about arm's width between people). Include yourself in the circle and make sure either you or someone has a digital stopwatch. (Remember, the group will be attempting to reach *warp speed*, so the timing mechanism *has* to be accurate to the nearest 100th of a second.)

Ask everyone to raise one hand and to keep it raised until they have received the thrown object from someone, at which point they can put their hand down. (This simple game-facilitating-request has caused more confusion than a judo teacher in a karate studio. Tell a group to raise both hands and catch the ball with their teeth — no problem, but ask them to raise only one hand and the questions flow non-stop.) Also ask everyone to *remember who they throw to and who they receive from*:

You (instructor) start the action by throwing the ball to someone on the far side of the circle. Don't worry about starting the stop watch; the group is simply establishing a pattern. That receiver throws to anyone else across the circle who has their hand raised, and the throwing continues until you receive the ball last. Go through the pattern one more time to cement the sequence and to build confidence.

Now ask the watch holder (not you or the person you throw to) to time a sequenced throw/catch attempt by starting the clock when you say GO and stopping when you say STOP. Whatever time you achieve is your current WORLD RECORD.

Ask the group how many seconds faster they think the sequence can be done, realistically. If the first time established for 20 people is 16 seconds, maybe 12 seconds as a final time would be a prudent guess —

certainly not in the *warp speed* category, but an acceptable beginning.

More attempts and misses are made until the next level of time is achieved amidst considerable conversation, and some trial and error. Ask for an even lower time commitment, which will probably be met with hoots of disbelief from the more conservative throwers, and cries of *"Let's go for it!"* from the slingshot-armed zealots.

As each level is achieved, persist in asking for a lower time. Allow changing of positions in the circle and whatever time saving ploys their imaginations come up with. Don't be strict with the rules, because remember, there really aren't any. Also, as the group's time decreases become more of a cheer leader. Indicate that reaching *warp speed* describes an entirely different dimension of accomplishment, and is characterized by intense group vibrations

and a subtle changing of the way things appear; clearer, simpler perhaps.

When someone finally suggests dropping or rolling the ball over everyone's sequentially outstretched hands, your time should come in below one second — a substantial accomplishment for a team that first guessed 12 seconds as their ultimate goal.

Strange things happen at *warp speed.* "Beam me up, Scotty, there's no intelligent life down here."

What's Up? Dock! — A Mine Field Variation

Purpose:

- To develop cooperation, trust and imagination through physical and verbal group activity.
- To develop group support and awareness of the problems of the physically disabled.
- To develop the capacity for taking responsibility in guiding others and in following directions.

Explain to the class that this is a group activity designed to test their concentration and ability to give and take directions. Tell them you will need two volunteers — one a rower and the other a dock worker. The rower will be trying to maneuver his boat through a rock-strewn channel and land at the dock. Explain that the rower is the lone survivor from a ship that exploded. He was blinded in the explosion but escaped in a small rowboat.

The dock worker who saw the explosion is now trying to guide the blind rower to safety. The other students are to be the rocks and channel sides. Some of them should stand in two lines along the channel (boundaries), while the others (rocks) may stand, kneel or sit at random in the channel area. When the rower docks successfully, or bumps into a rock or channel boundary,

both he and the dock worker lose their turn and must choose replacements. While the new rower is putting on his blindfold, the "rocks" should change positions in the channel.

The game continues until everyone has had a turn at being rower or dock worker.

Procedure:

Set up the boundaries for the channel — sides and length. Have the rower stand at one end wearing a blindfold and standing with his back to the dock worker who will be at the other end of the channel. The other students should place themselves at random in the channel area to be the rocks and channel sides.

Dock Variations

- Try offering a touch of acoustic realism to this trust/communication problem by adding some "authentic" ocean noises. Begin to create the sound of wind and rain (vocally and with whatever props are immediately available). As you might expect, the dock worker soon has to yell to the rower above the crashing waves and howling wind. The rower, in turn, has to struggle to understand the wind-tossed directions.

  While these actions somewhat alter the tone of the exercise, the bond between the dock worker and the rower is enhanced as both jointly struggle to work together under adverse conditions.

- Allow more than one rower to attempt simultaneous passage through and among the "rocks, buoys and reefs." The dock workers shout their directions from the sidelines in a cacaphonous chorus reminiscent of the game *Hog Call.* Blindfolded rowers must return to the start if they are unfortunate enough to make contact with an obstacle.

Moonball Ω

Moonball is an excellent one-prop-game that develops coordination and fast reactions. Play becomes intensely competitive, as a group competes against its last best effort.

Scatter your group (any size, but use two or more balls as the group size demands) on a basketball court or a field. Use a well-inflated beach ball as the object of play. The group's objective is to hit the ball aloft as many times as possible before the ball strikes the ground. Depending upon the group, set a goal of 50, 75, 100 hits to add incentive.

Rules:

1. A player cannot hit the ball twice in succession.
2. Count one point for each hit.
3. Two points are allowed for a kick.

Not too complicated, eh?

The tension and expectation builds as each "world record" is approached. Moonball is popular with all ages, because it's simple to understand, requires little skill, and involves (like it or not) everyone. This is a particularly useful activity to initiate when a new group is just getting together, especially if you want early arrivals to become involved and not just self-consciously stand around, wondering why they came.

Moonball Variation

I'll tell you something honestly. *Moonball* has programmatically saved my bacon on a couple occasions when I needed a quickly explained, moderately active game for people standing around at the beginning of a session wondering why they were there. (That last sentence seems a bit run-on, but I'm talking now, not writing, and you know what I'm saying.)

After you have messed around with Moonball, here's a variation, and Lord knows this isn't the only one. Beachballs (aka Moonballs) give vent to flights of curricular creativity, because what else are you going to do with a gaily colored, balloon-like ball that doesn't pass or bounce worth beans, or kick with any predictability?

Ask the group, after playing basic hit-the-ball-37 times, to see how many times the group (6-60+) can hit the ball in sequence through all the players without, (1)

letting the ball hit the ground, or (2) missing a sequenced player. Alternately, see how fast the ball can travel from player to player in sequence; i.e., through the whole group. If the ball touches the ground, assign a time penalty — say 5 seconds. The ball must be hit, not simply passed.

Set up a regular Moonball game and record the most number of ball strikes (hands only) during a one minute time limit. Only count those hits that are not preceded by a ground bounce. The ball must touch each player sequentially. Allow the group to arrange themselves in whatever position they decide is best to achieve the greatest number of hits.

When the ball begins to leak air (it's bound to happen eventually — these things only cost $1.27), try a quick round of *Five-a-Side Flatball*.

Moon Ball Debrief Considerations:

- When the group eventually reached their numerical goal, did they stop or did they continue hitting the ball, trying to establish a higher score? Why did they stop when the goal was reached? Did you tell them to? Why did they keep going? Did you encourage them?

    If a group continues to hit the ball after their numerical goal is reached it's a fair indication that the majority are having a good time, and provides an excellent example of what positive competition is all about.
- When the ball was being batted around, where where the players looking most of the time? At each other? At you? At the ball? What difference does it make where people are looking?
- There is little emphasis on who's hitting or not hitting the ball, and only fleeting regard as to how well or poorly the ball is being struck by the players. The person making a great saving hit might

regard their own prowess with some significance, but by the time they anticipate the exclamations of "Nice Hit!" or "Way to Go!", the ball has already been hit by two or three other people. The same situation holds true for the hapless swing-and-miss player who cringes, waiting for the hoots of dirision that don't come, because everyone is too intent on getting the ball in the air again in order to start another sequence.

- The implement of play for Moon Ball is significant. Have you ever played a heavy duty competitive game with a beach ball? A beach ball was chosen for the game Moon Ball because it's recognized as a play object for the beach. It's lightweight, easily hit, non-threatening, gaily colored, hard to control even with practice, and inexpensive. If we had chosen a volley ball for the game Moon Ball, the emphasis and feel for the game would have been considerably different and definitely more competitive.

Moonball - Big Leak Variation

When your beach ball finally splits (literally), extend that split to a size that allows you to put a pair of shoes inside the ball. As you travel, the ex-Moonball provides a colorful way to transport your muddy field shoes without getting your clothes dirty. I'm not kidding — this works. Colorful conservation at its finest.

Unholy Alliance

This is an advertisement of sorts, but also an introduction to a surprisingly complex decision-making tug-o-war.

Project Adventure, Inc., sells this 4-way tug rope, and I'll quote directly from the description (no permission or quote marks needed, I wrote it) in the Ropes Course Source catalog.

Use of these 1" diameter multiline ropes gets away from the pull-your-arms-off contests so characteristic of single rope tug-o-war. With 4 teams of up to 15 participants each, players are able to develop strategies and temporary affiliations that bring people back for "just one more try."

These soft-to-the-touch ropes have an impressive tensile strength of 17,000 lbs. That multi-ton strength, in conjunction with the 4 - 30' spliced lengths, precludes any danger of rope breakage under strain.

The 4 lengths of rope are eye-spliced in the center (4 galvanized thimbles around a 5/8" diameter galvanized drop forged steel ring. Each rope end is back-spliced.

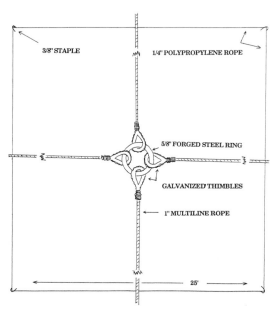

UNHOLY ALLIANCE

How to Use the Alliance Tug Rope

Procure or purloin a 100' length of old 1/4" polypropylene (or some such cord) and tie the ends together (splicing looks better) to form a rope circle as it lies on the ground. Marking every 25' of this rope length with tape, change the circle to a square. This rope square designates the boundary marker for the game. Stake out the square using 3/8" staples. If you are on asphalt STOP, and find some turf. People really get into this activity and occasionally fall down. Grass stains are OK, scabs aren't.

Since each of the 4 pulling ropes is only 30' long, it doesn't make much sense to put more than 15 pullers on a length — there just isn't room for more to pull efficiently. Nonetheless, split your group into 4 equal smaller groups and ask them to assume the pull position (whatever that means). Do not allow the last person to tie into the rope. As a matter of further safety, don't allow any knots to be tied in any of the ropes.

As the Pull Master (PM), take the 4 pulling ropes and set the center ring into the center of the boundary square so that the 4 ropes are perpendicular to the 4 sides of the boundary rope; a north, east, south, west kind of thing.

The PM advises, "Take up the strain," at which time all pullers slowly begin to put pressure on the ropes. After a couple seconds of holding the ring on center, and as the pressure increases, the PM shouts PULL and steps quickly and nimbly back.

The action has obviously begun, but the deception and strategy during the first pull-off usually gives way to pure physicalness. It takes a couple pull-offs for the teams to discover how brief alliances with the pulling teams to their right and left can sometimes produce victory for their team. This very physical game is an announced *antitrust* activity.

A win is achieved when a team pulls the center ring over the section of boundary rope that marks their part of the square. If the ring goes directly over any of the 4 right angles, it is a *NO PULL*, and the teams begin again from a starting position.

Make sure you let the teams try this activity often enough so that team strategies

can develop.

If you are the *Pull Master*, watch out when you yell "PULL" at the start, as rapid movement of the ring can result in a horizontal PM.

If you plan to put together your own 4-way pull ropes, please be sure to choose rope that is advertised as stronger than the estimated combined pulling power of the participants. I'd also suggest using metal thimbles for the splices and at least a 1/2" diameter *drop-forged* ring in the center. Do not allow anyone to grab the ring or spliced thimbles during a contest, broken fingers could result.

This activity can be exhausting — don't count on a full period's participation. Establish smaller groups; share the pain.

Shark

Objective: To gain the most points while travelling as a group from island to island through shark infested water.

Materials:

Large field
1/2" X 4' diameter plywood circles for each group to use as a "ship". Use sandpaper to smooth the circumference edges.

Procedure:

1. Divide students into two groups with 8 to 10 members per group.
2. Give each group a "ship" and instruct all members to hold onto its sides.
3. Groups are to run with their "ship" until a staff member yells "Shark!" Then all members jump on board the "ship." The first group on board with *all feet* off the ground gains a point.

    Repeat this procedure several times, yelling "Shark" when the teams least expect it. The first group to reach the finish line gains 5 points.
4. Add up points to determine a winner.
5. Debrief allowing the group to come up with ways to improve on their time.
6. Repeat the activity.

If this one on one competition is not well received, indicate that each group's individual final time will be added together to produce one grand time. In this way, everyone can try to determine how to best improve each group's performance as it relates to the added scores.

To Tell the Truth

A party game? I suppose, but also a useful and entertaining get-to-know-you-better tool for a group that has already spent some time together.

Arrange chairs in a circle so that there is one chair per participant, including yourself.

Procedure:

Participants in the seated circle ask a question aloud that can be answered either yes or no. Each person silently answers the question by remaining seated (a *no* response), or moving one seat to the right (answers *yes*). No conversation is necessary, but repartee is expected, contagious and encouraged.

If someone answers a question "no" (example — Did you brush your teeth this morning?) and the person seated to their left thinks "yes," then a lap sitting situation develops. With ensuing positive and negative responses, multi-lap people piles invariably develop.

Make sure your chairs are substantially constructed. Ostensibly, the idea is to develop lap stacks by question responses and then try to move everyone back to a single seat status by asking "moving" questions.

Rules:

1. Questions must be oriented to yes/no responses only.
2. Answers to questions must not be self-

apparent. Examples — Do you have on long pants? Are your eyes blue?
3. Questions begin in sequence around the circle until everyone has asked a question (or passed, if that is their choice), and then the questioning continues spontaneously.

Concerns:

Limit the type of questioning, if necessary, or as you perceive your group. Sexually-oriented queries or those that pertain to bodily functions are best avoided. The end of the game occurs when:

1. Everyone returns to and occupies a single chair (improbable).
2. No one can think of another can-you-top-this question.
3. You like the lap that you are sitting on and decide to continue the questioning, interfacing as a diad.

Variation

Whenever a chair is left empty, remove it from the circle and see what develops: a quadriceps delight.

Shoot Out

This game can have either a lot of rules or very few, depending upon how it's presented and "where the players are at."

If the group is into fantasy and fun, the extra rules and ritual are usually well received. If the group is young and active, they will want action and less explanation.

Give the groups what they want — it's a good work-out either way.

General Rules (add or subtract appropriately)

The playing area can be inside a gym (field house) or on a marked field (football, etc.). There is a certain intimacy gained inside a gym that seems to add to this running, throwing mélee.

You need two teams of about 5-15 people. Separate the two teams (however you decide to split the groups) and give each member a softee (flexible flying saucer) or a soft-flyte (a nylon foldable saucer with a surgical tubing rim), making sure that each member of a team has the same color saucer.

At this juncture, explain to the teams that they must develop a verbal insult to hurl at the other group. The insult should not include any obscene words or ethnic slurs, and may be delivered as a group in unison or by the chosen DI (designated insulter).

After some in-depth insult discussion, the groups line up facing each other about 30 yards apart. All *Shoot Out* participants must, at this point, holster their saucers. This is done by sticking the saucer into the waist belt of their shorts, pants, etc., in such a way that a quick draw can be accomplished. (Gentlemen should be aware that shoving the disc too far down into their "holster" might result in a pre-game injury that could remove them from the competition. Substitutions are not allowed, so be careful).

As both groups ritualistically glare at one another, the signal to begin is given. All members, of opposite groups, stalk slowly toward one another (VERY purposefully — you know, like in *High Noon, Gunfight at the OK Corral*, etc.), until they reach a line that separates the groups by about 10 yards. When both groups are aligned, the DI says, "When you were a baby, you were so ugly that your mother fed you with a slingshot!" or some such invective. The responding group, shocked and infuriated by such an incisive remark, says in unison, "Oh Yeah?!" This traditional response is the signal for everyone to go for their saucers, which weapon *must* be thrown within 2 seconds after the first throwable is released.

If a thrown saucer hits a player *below*

the waist, they must die a dramatic, histrionic and noisy death (like in *Rio Lobo*, or *The Magnificent Seven*), and lie on the floor or field until that segment of the game is concluded.

After a softee is released, that color only may be picked up by a team member as the participants dash about trying to find and pick up a spent saucer and, at the same time, trying to protect themselves. Players may knock a thrown softee aside, but may not catch a saucer that has been thrown at them.

Play continues until all members of one group have been properly "drilled," "plugged," eliminated. The groups then realign themselves at opposite ends of the field to discuss strategy and prepare to give or receive the next insult.

There is obviously a lot of tradition and ritual that must be enjoyed (relived) to make the above "work." If the group is young and more into activity than tradition — line them up as before (10 yards), and let them blast away at a given signal.

Jugball

An innovative, active game that encourages recycling, from Dan Hussong in New Jersey.

"About the game itself, *Jugball* is played on a field hockey field (can also be played indoors), using a 'beat up' tennis ball. The 'Jug' is made by cutting off the bottom of a one gallon plastic milk jug. (Run a piece of electrician's tape around the cut edge, as it reduces the chance of being scraped and also preserves the jugs.) Players hold their jugs by the handle. Have all the students who plan to sign up for this activity bring their own jugs. One student who lives on a dairy farm volunteered an unlimited supply, so we were all set to go. I cut the jugs as uniformly as I could, but found that many students wanted to "customize" their

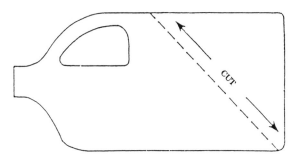

own jug and I encouraged this. 'Jaws,' 'Super Scooper,' etc., were born.

The object of the game is to advance the ball up field by throwing and catching the ball with your jug, and eventually hurling the ball into the opponent's goal.

Some worthwhile restrictions to place on energetic high school students are:

1. No physical contact.
2. No running forward with the ball, only lateral or backward movement allowed.
3. No close-range shooting (the arc on a field hockey field serves as a good boundary line).
4. To alleviate 'scrums' with an entire class trying to pick up a ground ball with their jugs, allow players to pick up a 'dead' ball with a bare hand and throw it high overhead.

Pre-class warm-up exercises are sometimes more fun than the game itself. I like to bring out a bag of tennis balls and have the class start out playing catch and then do a little group initiative. An example would be forming two lines facing each other and establishing the goal of moving a ball through every jug as quickly as possible. This gets them in the mood, and they work hard together to beat the clock instead of each other.

Jugball has been well received by most groups and we haven't introduced it to the Freshman class yet; Freshman love to do anything new, exciting, and physical!

We are adapting it to an indoor setting

in the second term as an elective choice. Our auxiliary gymnasium is perfect for it, as we let the ball play off the walls just like in Raquetball or Jai-Lai. After two weeks of witnessing this mania, we are convinced that Jugball is here to stay . . ."

Drop Dead Ball

The idea for this highly aerobic game comes from an activity book called *Keywords*, given to me by a participant (Ian Hoey) in a games workshop at the University of Ulster in Coleraine, Northern Ireland.

Divide your group in half and ask the players to visually distinguish themselves somehow — rolled up pant leg, hats/no hats, shorts/no shorts (better interpret that last one correctly, coach).

Throw a fleece ball or rubber ring into the dispersed group. Whoever catches it may run until tagged or has thrown the ball to another member of his/her team. *The object is to pass the ball 15 times amongst the members of the group before the ball touches the ground or is intercepted by the other team.*

Rules:

- Throws may be made to any team member, but not to the same person twice in a row.
- If a person is tagged while holding the ball (two hands below the clavicle) that person MUST throw the ball as hard as they can WITH THEIR NON-DOMI-NANT ARM toward the farthest goal, and within 2 seconds of having been tagged. The ball cannot be caught by either team.
- After the ball rolls dead it can be picked up, but only by a member of the oppo-site team. If the ball is thrown over the goal, the ball can be picked up and brought back to the goal line before being thrown back into play.

- When a team reaches 15, they score a point. The ball then goes immediately to the other team so that the restart isn't a time-wasting hassle.
- Another way to keep things moving. When a team reaches 15 consecutive throws, they start again immediately from zero to try and score another point. The onus continues to be on the other team to tag a runner and inter-cept the ball.
- If the use of numbers by both teams is confusing, assign letters to one of the teams. When the letter team completes sequential throws from A to O, a point is scored.
- If you want the game to last a bit longer (like six hours), ask the teams to num-ber themselves sequentially and pass the ball in sequence from player to player in order to score a point: a game to last the semester for sure.

I have taken great liberties in present-ing and changing the rules of this game (as always) — I expect you to do the same.

Follow Me!

An indoor (not necessarily), fast-moving, perceptual game that allows total participa-tion without intimidation.

A player volunteers to briefly leave the room, and a leader is appointed among the remaining people in the group: 30 people per group is better than 10.

When the IT person returns, the leader initiates a movement (clapping, finger-snapping, head-rubbing, anything visual). Whenever the leader changes a movement, the group must immediately follow his/her lead. The IT tries, amidst all this confusing movement, to identify who the leader is; i.e., the person initiating the changes.

Indicate that the group should not all look at the secret leader — it's a give-a-way. When the leader is finally caught, he/she

senting people as rapidly as possible using the above suction technique and without having the card fall to the ground.

You will find that as you transfer the card from person to person (or attempt to), it is important for the sucking person to choose that proper moment to blow (small puff, actually) when the potential sucking person has built up sufficient vacuum potential to allow the transfer to take place. Actually it's, I blow, you suck — you blow, he/she sucks. Does that help?

I hope you recognized my compassionate choice of card size; I could have suggested a 3" x 5."

Definitely a game for all seasons and no reason.

can be the next IT or anyone else who wants to volunteer.

The game action is fast-paced and fun. Try adding music from a BOOM BOX to establish the game pace.

Suck and Blow

This is a very intense game. Actually, the game name should be *More Suck Than Blow,* but why split hairs about something so meaningful?

Before I offer the very minimum game rules, you need to practice a bit to be ready for the aerobic challenge in store for you. Go get a 4" x 6" card. Hold the card up to your pursed lips and suck hard (not suck actually, just draw in air forcefully enough to keep the card positioned on your lips). A good suck will keep it there for maybe 3-4 seconds. Try it a couple times. Have contests with your friends to see who can keep a card juxtaposed to lips the longest. Tilting your head back invokes the *travesty* ruling, so don't do it.

OK, here's the game. The object is to try and pass the card around a circle of con-

Catch 10

Here's a fast-paced, blatantly competitive game for 3-6 people, that I remember developing with a group of friends on the beaches of southern California many years ago. At that time, we used a regulation football, and that's still cool, but you may have more luck with a diverse group using a frisbee (the 97 gm. model, of course).

The playing area can be any field area that doesn't have obstacles to run into or trip over. There are no boundaries. Grass, as in most active outdoor games, is the best playing surface, unless a beach is handy, and that is absolutely the ultimate barefoot surface for jump-around, feel-good, land-on-your-head games.

The object is to try and make the person you are throwing to, miss the frisbee, for which slip of the fingers a point is disawarded. When a player accrues 10 points, she/he is out of the game and the remainder of the players continue until only one remains; that player with the least number of points.

The throws are made in keeping with a

pre-game determined sequence (Pete, to Jill, to Rod, to Liz), and continues this way unless a player, who has just missed a frisbee, thinks he/she has been taken advantage of for one reason or another and shouts, "STOP" (or whatever invective comes to mind). The offended player gets to make a standing throw with the frisbee at the person who made them miss, from a measured distance of 10 yards. In the event of either a miss or catch, the frisbee continues in the new throw/catch sequence direction — opposite to the way it was going.

Gentlemen's rules are in effect throughout; i.e., when a throw is made, the catcher **must** exert a 100% effort to snatch the frisbee, but if the disc drifts beyond catchability, the point is added to the thrower's total; if the catcher obviously dogs it or short-arms an attempt, the point is his.

Catch 10 strategy — Running toward the person you are throwing to is OK and is actually a good offensive move, but a player must throw the frisbee from a distance of at least 10 yards away from the catcher. Trying to keep the sun at your back is another bit of Top Gun gamesmanship that works.

Try to make *Catch 10* as much a running/catching game as possible by lofting high throws well beyond where the catcher waits or by running to place yourself as a potential catcher near to the person you will be throwing to. Think up strategies, add rules, change rules; make the game yours.

Frantic   Ω

A good game has an easily identifiable aura of tradition; e.g., *Kick the Can, Stick Ball, Tip Cat*, etc. For a good game that just hasn't had enough time to be established, the most expeditious route to traditionalist acceptance is to develop and establish a

vocabulary surrounding the game and its play. Remember: "knucks down," "ring-ring-a-levio," "àlle-àlle-in-free," "one patata-two patata . . ." etc., all important spoken parts of the games, essential to proper play, fun to mouth, and incrementally traditional. *No one* escaped from JAIL without having two feet inside the jail and shouting ÀLLE-ÀLLE-IN-FREE.

Here is a unique game that requires little skill, includes any amount of people and is 100% active. The name of the game is *Frantic* and the object of play is for a group of any size to keep an equal number of assigned tennis balls moving about a gymnasium floor until six penalties have been indicated by the referee.

The vocabulary, which remember is the key to contemporary tradition, goes like this:

Rabid Nugget — A moving tennis ball.

Hectic — A stationary tennis ball.

Berserk — A referee's scream, designating a penalty.

Frenzy — An elapsed time period measuring six Berserks.

Logic — A tennis ball that becomes lodged unintentionally on or behind something.

Illogic — A tennis ball that is craftily stuck on or behind something.

Paranoia — A player's feeling that the refs are picking on him/her.

Rules and Use of Terminology:

If thirty players are on the gym floor, thirty *Rabid Nuggets* are thrown, rolled or bounced simultaneously onto the floor by one of the refs. There are three refs; one at each end of the court and one off to the side at midcourt. It is the duty of the two refs on the floor to try and spot *Hectics* and to generate a hysterical scream (a *Berserk*) so that all will recognize a penalty. The group has five seconds to start a *Hectic* moving again or another full throated *Berserk* is issued. The *Berserking* ref must point condemningly at the *Hectic* until it is again provided impetus.

Every fifteen seconds after a start, the sideline ref puts an additional *Rabid Nugget* into play until the final *Berserk* has been recorded. The team is allowed six *Berserks*, at which juncture the ref on the sideline, who is responsible for timing this melee, jumps up and down waving his arms and yelling, "*STOP-STOP-STOP.*"

The team intent is to keep the *Rabid Nuggets* moving as long as possible before six *Berserks* have been recorded. This time span is called a *Frenzy*. After a *Frenzy*, ask the group to talk about and develop a strategy in order to keep the *Rabid Nuggets* moving for a longer span of time; i.e., increasing the duration of the *Frenzy*.

Rule Refinements for Frantic Freaks:

A rabid nugget must be kicked (only kicked) randomly or to another player. It may not be held underfoot and simply moved back and forth. This rule was recently included to counter the basically sneaky player who's always looking for a way around the rules in the guise of initiative.

If a rabid nugget becomes a logic or illogic, the ref must get the nugget back into motion. An illogic receives an immediate *Berserk*.

There are no official time-outs except for double loss of contact lenses or sun stroke. Frostbite was considered, but it's still possible to kick a nugget with numb toes, so continue play.

Balloon Frantic Ω

The rules to this slow-motion photogenic game nearly duplicate those of tennis ball *Frantic*. *Frantic* with balloons is best played indoors in a high ceiling gym or outdoors on a windless day.

Ask each participant to roundly inflate a 12" balloon, and tie off the neck (Don't use so-called "penny balloons." They are too small and don't provide enough action.) Inflate at least 6-8 extras to serve as throw-ins for the 15 second rule, or as replacements for the inevitable broken balloons (Boomers). Remember, these are 12" balloons. Get your moneys worth, blow them up **BIG**.

The rules for both games are identical, except for the start. Ask each player to throw their balloon into the air, rather than having the ref start things with a kick.

Be sure to have a camera or video camcorder on hand, because the

technicolor action of BF is color poster material.

Braaaaack-Whffff

Everyone gets one balloon (I'll be writing the word balloon a lot, so let's have capital **B** stand for balloon). The **B**'s should be purchased in as many different colors as possible; ecru, vermillion, puce, etc. Also, buy decent sized **B**'s; the small penny **B**'s don't remain aloft long enough or provide enough action for these games.

Ask everyone to stand inside the "key" at the end of a basketball court (or fabricate your own round boundary area), and blow up their **B**'s just short of popping. (Have some spare **B**'s available.) Don't tie off the **B**'s neck, just hold on and get together with other folks who have the same color **B** as yours.

The Contest

One person representing each color lets go of their **B**, allowing it to jet willy-nilly about. Wherever it comes to rest, another team member of the same color advances to that point with their **B** filled and cocked and releases their rubber missile in an attempt to further their team's distance from the circle's perimeter.

This pattern continues until all the **B**'s have been released. The team color champion is, of course, that final **B** which is the furthest from the circle. (Have a 50' tape measure on hand for disputed distances.)

There is practically no skill or technique involved in this game, so no one seems to care who wins. The fun is in the doing.

(off the floor) by batting the **B** with announced parts of their body, including hands, which must remain clasped. If the **B** touches the floor, the group receives a penalty point. Players keep track of their own penalties.

Start the groups off slowly by announcing that they may hit the **B** with hands only. After about 30 seconds switch to "alternating hands and heads." Then every 30 seconds or so call another switch. "Alternate heads and noses. Try heads only. Knees only. Alternate knees and noses. Try heel to chest." "Chests only"; which usually causes most of the groups to dissolve in frustrated laughter.

Ask if any one kept score. Yeah teams!

Booop Ω

Blow up *one* of the balloons and tie off the neck. Ask your group of 3-4 people to join hands in a circle and try to keep the **B** aloft

Fire in the Hole Ω

It's time to put the **B**'s away — permanently. You're going to like this! Divide into groups of 3-5 with your **B**'s.

Place 3-5 B's between your 3-5 person group. Position the B's carefully at about mid-torso level. As in dealing with dynamite charges, it's the placement that counts. Then, put your arms about your partners' bodies and prepare to squeeze, BUT... before initiating any psycho-motor synapses, the group shouts together, **"Fire in the hole!"** — that's to warn bystanders of the impending explosion(s). You don't need any further instructions after the squeeze starts.

Try standing in a circle so that each person is facing the person's back in front of them. Have each person place an inflated **B** between her/him and that person — initiate a group squeeze.

Try a one-on-one squeeze to share a poignant moment.

If a particular **B** is giving your small group a problem, ask for help and other squeezers, I'm sure, will hurry over to add their contractions and emotion toward a final solution.

Comet Balls   Ω

Old socks, weighted with sand or rocks, have been thrown around by kids for years and years; I can remember making them and breaking windows (inadvertantly, of course) in the 40's. I also remember putting flour in socks at Halloween time, and then whacking people with the powdered sock leaving a huge while mark where contact was made, but that has nothing to do with now; just reminiscing.

The New Games Foundation popularized this spontaneous fun by replacing the sand and rocks (which doubled as a weapon) with a Nerf ball and calling the centrifugal device a something-or-other, it's a whimsical name that I can't recall.

Did the old spinning sock have a name when you were a kid? I can't seem to remember ever calling it anything but a "rock sock"; a sobriquet that mothers and homeowners near my turf learned to hate.

As part of a game Steve Butler and I invented called *Foes & Questors*, we "re-invented" the rock-sock as a sand-sock and called it the Mage's Mortar, a sand-filled sock thrown with a mortar's flight, producing a devastating penalty if you were unfortunate enough to be within 10 feet of the point of impact. (But not half as devestating if you received a direct hit.) Admittedly, I'm getting off the original subject (I think), but the point is that these weighted socks are multi-use items that are great fun to experiment with, particularly in open areas.

Here's how to make a modern "rock sock" that we now call a *Comet Ball*. Buy the least expensive ladies' knee high socks that you can find. I like the brightly colored socks rather than flesh colored ones, because the resulting Comet Balls look more like a toy and less like a drawn and quartered panty hose.

Squeeze a tennis ball into the end of the sock. Done. Wow, was that easy! Oh, I forgot to mention; try to buy queen size knee highs—you get better centrifugal leverage with your throw. Make sure your arms are short enough to handle the ex-tended sock (longer legs help too); it's kind of embarrassing to whack the ground everytime you try to spin the sock.

Let's play some catch with a weighted sock. Keep moving farther apart as you become more adept at throwing and catching. See which pair of throwers on a football field can move the farthest apart and still make a catch.

After throwing one of these panty-hose sock rockets you will appreciate why they say a Comet Ball compares to an old rock sock, as a Porsche is to a VW.

Try and snatch the flapping tail of a descending Comet Ball. A proper catch is always by the tail; receiving the ball in-hand displays an appalling measure of gaucherie.

The first few tries at throwing for distance are usually wildly inaccurate, and dangerous if you are standing too near the thrower. A discus-like spin produces the farthest and most errant throws; some tosses heading straight up! Watch out for these wildly enthusiastic throwers.

There are a couple games you can play using Comet Balls, but I'm not going to tell you what they are. I think just throwing them for fun is where its at. (*Silver Bullets* pg. 25; if you *must* know.)

Off the Wall (Indoor Frisbee Game)

This atypical frisbee game (Is there a typical frisbee game?) is an elitist variation of the old *GUTS* model. This is not a game for everyone, because considerable skill in throwing and catching a frisbee is required. But wait, let me offer the rules before you skip this game and miss out on some off-the-wall elitest fun.

Arrange and disperse 6-8 people to each end of a vacant gym. As in the game

Photo by Nicki Hall

GUTS, a frisbee is thrown back and forth with the attempt to make the other team miss (drop the frisbee). The major rule change here is that the frisbee may hit the back or side walls (or any other obstacle that can be aimed at; a backboard, for example).

Further Rules:

1. Ceiling shots result in a "no throw" — neither team adds or subtracts a point.
2. Short throws also result in a "no throw" situation.
3. The frisbee must approach the defenders between a 45 degree and horizontal level, or a "no throw" results.
4. Impossible-to-reach shots are judged individually and result in some memorable arguments.
5. Skip shots are allowed if the frisbee reaches the defenders at a minimum of knee height to the catchers.
6. Only one hand catches are allowed unless the decision of both teams is to make the game easier, and then two-hand catches are OK.
7. Tip or rebound catches (from player to player) are OK, and in a heated contest can be spectacular.
8. No "flying missile," knock-your-fingernails-off shots are allowed. Direct shots are acceptable, however; i.e., not off-the-wall.
9. A two-three or possibly four-point throw can be made, by hitting 2,3,4 (or more?) objects before the frisbee is dropped to the floor.

Off The Wall is a fine game for the talented frisbee thrower, but its drawbacks include:

1. At least a moderate skill level is required to enjoy the game.
2. Only a comparatively small number can play.
3. An entire gym is needed to play.

Frisbee Shuffleboard

Since you have taken over the gym for a game of *Off The Wall,* try this subtle variation of shuffleboard.

As in shuffleboard or horseshoes, two players compete against two other players. The object is to throw/slide your team's frisbees (3-5) into the key (circular) area at one end of the gym from the far end of the gym. Throwers stand just beyond the out-of-bounds line under the basketball backboard.

The basketball key area is divided into three smaller areas. The closest (and smaller) area is worth 3 points. The next area scores 2 points and the far area 1 point. If the frisbee is touching any line, no points are scored.

Smooth, low, gliding (on the floor) throws work best. With additional practice, it's possible to knock an opponent's frisbee out of a scoring area, or into one. Each team must use a different color frisbee to avoid confusion and wrestling matches. Also, try using "softies" (foldable frisbees) for this game.

Basic Killer

Object — For an unknown killer to "kill" all the people involved in the game, before they discover who s/he is.

Set-Up — There are many ways to pick a killer, but the easiest and fastest is for the leader to ask everyone to close their eyes, and then walk briskly and obviously around and among the players, touching one of them on top of the head to indicate their sanguine role.

Rules:

To "kill," the killer must wink at a player. If the wink (not a blink) is recognized as the gift of eternal sleep, that player is dead and must histrionically die, ending up flailing about or shuddering on the floor/ground while emitting outrageous sounds of agony, outrage and defeat: This is not meant to be a subtle role. DO NOT die immediately after being killed. Give the killer a chance to move away by waiting 15-30 seconds until your terminal sequence begins.

The group mills about the playing area, eyeing each other carefully (you must keep your eyes open). When someone thinks they know who the killer is, they shout "J' accuse!", or more domestically, "I accuse!" The accuser must be seconded by another player within ten seconds or the initial accuser is eliminated (bumped off) by the referee's (you) pearl-handled revolver.

However, if there is a *second*, you (the referee) say, "On the count of three, I want you both to point accusingly at the killer." If both players point at the same person and it is, indeed, the mass murderer — the game is over. If the accusers point at different people, you quickly reach for your symbolic revolver and polish off the two maladroits who have so crassly offended the group's sensibilities. The game continues until the killer is caught or until all the players have been killed; a feat worthy of applause and a couple rousing "good shows!"

Variations

1. Allow the killer to pass on the death knell by shaking hands and pressing the victim's wrist with an extended index finger. It is obviously not necessary to kill every time a hand is shaken. So then, here we go about the room enthusiastically shaking hands with everyone and looking frantically for the deadly digit. All the above rules for basic killer apply here also.
2. If the vibrations of all this noise and cascading bodies is distressing, try the following "nice" variation. Everyone in the group must go around the room whispering something nice to each player they encounter, except, of course, the killer, who will whisper something having to do with your demise. For example, "I sure like your knees," or "That blouse is outstanding," or "Your crew cut is _____." The killer might say, "Here comes the kiss of death," or "Tomorrow you die," etc.

Some parents don't want their kids playing a game called *Killer*. Some adults also don't want to play a game called *Killer*. Refer to the game *Alienation* (next page) for a killer-like alternative activity.
3. If the games are dragging a bit and you want to speed things up, introduce the plague variation.

Whenever a player is killed, s/he can (after waiting a few seconds to let the killer move on), take others players down with them by touching (the plague) someone as they fall to the floor. That infected player can then pass it on to another poor soul if they are slow enough to be caught. The dying person cannot run around the room tagging a series of people, nor can the initial person with the plague fall on the killer. If the killer carelessly gets caught in a plague sequence, then it's either fast-talking time or just keeping a low profile.

It always seems that everyone gets in on the fun of these games except you — so here's a way to pick the killer and join in the game yourself.

Everyone joins together in a cluster and puts one fist into the group center with a thumb sticking up. You announce (with everyone's eyes closed, including yours) that you are going to squeeze a person's thumb once. That person will then reach

around all the extended thumbs (all eyes still closed) and squeeze someone else's thumb twice. The person with the double squeezed digit is the killer. Neat, huh?

Play *Killer* more than once to discover some of the subtleties and stratagems that make this game so popular.

Alienation

Killer's not a bad game, and with the right group can be loads of fun. But, with the evening news invariably reporting another murder, the name and context of the game has fallen into disfavor, particularly with the parents of young student players.

So, here's a variation that involves a different name and subtley different rules, but for you aficianados and true Killer fans, fear not, the action and anticipation still approach neurotic proportions.

Game Objective - At the end of an established time period (24 hours), for you to be on a team that has either the most humans or aliens; the greater population obviously takes over the earth, and even more significantly WINS.

Set Up and Rules -

- One player is designated as the Ultimate Alien [UA] at the beginning of the game.

If you want to be included in the play action, here's how to pick an Ultimate Alien so even you don't know who that nefarious person is. All players stand in a tight circle with their eyes closed and extend one hand forward with their thumb sticking up—like a hitch-hiker. You reach into that mass of thumbs and squeeze one (1) thumb definitively. Then with dispatch, the person with squozen thumb, finds another available thumb amongst the many and squeezes it twice (2). The person with the twice pressured thumb is IT. Get it? Good!

If someone wants to play, but doesn't necessarily want to be the UA, all they have to do is not extend their thumb; no thumb, no squeeze. Perfect.

- The UA is given eight 1/2" slug washers (these are about the size of a quarter, 1-3/8" in diameter). One person, not playing the game, is responsible for delivery of the washers to the UA. This person's identity is revealed to all at the beginning of the squeezing sequence so that the UA can make appropriate and unobtrusive contact. If the number of players exceeds 20, add more alienation washers to maintain the action.

- In order to alienate someone (turn that player into an alien) the UA must try to deliver a washer to that person without being seen. The criteria for a successful transfer is that the washer must be found by the player after the transfer is made; i.e., without knowing where it came from. A proper alienation scenario involves physical contact with the washer by the person finding it, although this rule is often ignored by slipshod players.

- If a player recognizes that an alien is trying to alienate him/her, to protect themselves, all they have to do is point at the alien and quietly say, "You're human." At that juncture the alien returns to human form and operates as a human until either the time is up or they once again get alienated.

- If a human catches the UA passing a washer, and says "You're human" the UA will acquiece and calmly pretend to resume a human demeanor, BUT that condemned alien can *never* become human and will lie or do whatever is necessary to make the other players believe that he or she has joined their human condition. The UA then, when appropriate, continues to pass on alienating washers.

This is basically an anti-trust game and should be announced as such. If everyone is aware of the game's objective (having agreed-upon fun) then the potentially pejorative aspect of the game simply becomes part of the excitement. If every game you play resembles *Save The Whales*, a certain level of off-the-wall, counter-culture play will be excluded from your Bag of Games. I'm emphasizing variety of fun here, not confrontational scenarios of philosophical concern. Remember F.U.N.N.?

Trash Ball

Divide your group into half and situate them on opposite sides of a volleyball net (fortunately, the playing dimensions of a volleyball court exactly duplicate the NCAA Trash Ball specs.). Offer each group an equal amount of *dry* trash. (There is a wet trash variation of this game called *Garbage Ball (Gaabidge Ball in New England)*, but permission slips from parents and custodians are required.) An example of dry trash is — wastepaper, small cardboard boxes, light plastic, etc.

Make sure there is an ample amount of trash: trash equals action.

On the GO signal, each team tries to put their trash over the net. Do not set a time limit for the game, rather indicate that you will signal when the game is over. This unexpected signal prevents a team from collecting all the trash and throwing it all over seconds before the time limit.

The winner is, justly, that team with the least amount of trash within bounds on their side of the net. So that the teams won't suspect favoritism by the referee, the ref must write down on a sheet of paper the proposed time limit for each game.

This melée of random physical movements and laughter is a philosophical breakthrough in experiential education, ranking right up there with Mud Wrestling.

Boffer Bonkers

This simplistic, blatantly competitive game is one of the most aerobic and least serious one-on-one confrontations I know of.

Bonkers can be played as teams, but the pure form is one balloon, two players. Action on a gym floor is most convenient because of the permanent boundary lines.

Use the center line of a basketball court to place your well-inflated balloon. Both players, armed with a boffer, back off to the next parallel line — I'm sure this line has a name, but you'll recognize it because it looks very much like the one that you put the balloon on. The playing area is designated by the distance from one back line to another.

Play begins with each player, kneeling on their back line, facing each other and ritualistically slamming their boffer against the floor three times in rhythm with the other player's similar efforts. On the third hit, both players rush forward and try to hit the balloon past their opponent's back line *so that the balloon hits the floor* beyond the line. An offensive player is not allowed to physically cross over their opponent's back line.

A point is scored when the balloon touches the floor.

Best two out of three is guaranteed to bring your heart rate up to 150 BPM, unless you have chosen a real maladroit as an opponent (or vice versa), in which case you must go best 7 out of 10.

Aggression Bonkers allows a player to cross over his/her opponent's back line. A point is then scored by either hitting the balloon to the floor (as before) or bouncing the balloon off the back wall. If you are playing on an outdoor basketball court, the back wall rule is waived — a winning shot in this case puts the balloon off the court; i.e., out of bounds.

If you wish to play Team Bonkers, simply supply more people with Boffers. Do not substitute 2' x 4's for regulation ethafoam swords or bats because splinters

may cause the balloons to burst. Am I kidding? Right!

Boffers can be purchased from most athletic supply catalogs. Save some $$$ and make your own from pieces of old gymnastic mat material called ETHAFOAM. Use 2" thick sections and cut the swords to any size that appeals. Don't substitute styrofoam for ethafoam — the former breaks easily and being hit by styrofoam hurts. *Project Adventure* sells ethafoam.

Samurai & a Kamikaze Variation

The game, *Samurai*, is explained and pictured in the *More New Games* book, from the New Games Foundation, of California. The book may be purchased from *Project Adventure*.

The reason I mention the above is because Samurai has become a workshop favorite. In addition, a recent *Project Adventure* workshop group developed an embellishment to the game that is worth passing along.

There are a number of game success ingredients included in Samurai that almost guarantee acceptance and active participation by almost any group.

1. Rules can be quickly explained and easily understood.
2. Participants can unobtrusively remove themselves from the game, if they so desire.
3. Role-playing is encouraged and applauded.
4. Simple physical skills are used.
5. Satisfaction results from both participation and observing.

A bare-bones description of the basic game follows: (refer to the *More New Games* book for additional details)

Ask your group to form a circle around you — about 4' - 6' between people. Armed with a boffer (ideally) or any easily manipulated and innocuous sword-like weapon, the person in the center attempts to symbolically eliminate everyone in the circle with high or low slashes of their ersatz sword. These slashes are token strokes only; actual contact must be avoided or the players in the circle will either lose trust and disperse, or lose trust and retaliate.

If the Samurai (person with the sword) slashes high, each participant included within the arc of the stroke must duck or lose his/her head and be eliminated (falling to the ground). If the sweep of the sword is low, a hop must be made, or their legs are removed, as is the player. Mid-torso, belly button shots are not acceptable, as any certified Samurai knows. All of this martial manipulation is accompanied by inscrutable yells of the Samurai and groans of dismay and simulated agony of the players — a cacophony of oral action and reaction.

The last person to remain standing is the next Samurai.

After the basic game has been played a couple times, try the following variation.

As the game begins, place a second

similar sword in the center of the circle. As the Samurai begins his/her circular sanguinary forays, anyone in the circle can try to grab the second sword (boffer) without being hit (actually hit) by the Samurai. Then, mouthing whatever challenge or oriental invective comes to mind, the two adversaries have at one another in a duel to the finish.

Rules for the Duel:

1. No slashing strokes allowed -- only thrusts to the torso. This is a safety rule to protect a player's eyes.
2. A Win is achieved by touching your opponent, with the tip of the boffer, on the torso only – head and appendages do not count as a touché.
3. Do not use a rigid pretend sword (modified 2' x 4') for this duel.

If the Samurai wins, the challenger joins the other downed player and places his/her sword back in the center.

If the sword-snatcher wins, all the previously vanquished players stand up and return to the game and the new Samurai takes over against a full circle of players.

Mirrors & Mortars

I think this game is unique. I have only tried pieces of it as parts of another game, but its potential is worth developing — the action and reactions are fast and well received. Here are the objects of play and an outline of game possibilities.

Mirrors

These surrogate laser reflectors can vary in size from the small purse type, to as large as you can afford or attempt to carry. The mirror serves as a weapon. If reflected sunlight is seen by an opposing player, that player is frozen temporarily (movement from the immediate area is restricted for 2 minutes). A small mirror is easy to carry, but is hard to aim accurately. A larger mirror, say 10" x 12", reflects considerably more light and is easier to aim because of the more visible light beam. There is no doubt whether you have been zapped by a mirror; the reflected glint of the sun sets off a retinal alarm that's hard to ignore.

A pre-game joint decision that adds to the game's enjoyment is the agreement that all players hit by a light flash must punctuate their retinal trauma by falling down and simultaneously yelling, thus indicating to the light wielder that s/he has scored. Picking off a player from 200-300 yards is great fun and strategically useful. Getting hit is kind of fun too.

Various ploys can be used to counteract the flash. (1) Don't look at a person who is trying to flash you. (2) Wear a set of goggles (we call this prop, the *Goggles of RA*), that are somehow woven into the game's storyline to provide immunity from the mirror's devastation. (3) Try reflecting the sun back at the person initiating the flash: called the Quid Pro Quo Flash or QPQF (pronounced simply, Cue Pee), to knowledgeable players. (4) Try to maintain as much of a "downsun" position as possible. Be careful though, a large mirror is capable of reflecting *360 degrees*, depending upon the sun's position in the sky.

Mortars (Second Weapon)

A mortar is represented by a knee-high woman's sock with a tennis ball insert. (See **Comet Balls**, this chapter.)

The sock mortar is used as a weapon by lofting it (like a mortar is projected) in a long parabolic ar. The rules concerning such a throw are: (a) The mortar, to be effective, must land within 10 feet of the opposing player. (b) The mortar must achieve at least a 10 ft. apogee (height) to be armed. (c) All players (including the thrower) within the 10 ft. diameter devastation zone are "frozen" for two minutes.

If the mortar's *tail* is caught during its descent by the proposed victim, the thrower and anyone within 10 ft. of him/her are frozen for three minutes.

Long-arcing throws (50 yds. or more) are possible by twirling (discus fashion) the sock before letting go.

Ultimately, there should be some definable reason for all this flashing and twirling; perhaps a team competition of sorts? Pattern it after the game, *Capture the Flag*, where each team seeks a particular object and must take the retrieved talisman to a winning area. To extend the length of the game, use two retrievable objects.

The obvious limitation to this game is the need for sunshine. A perfectly clear day is not necessary, however, because intermittent clouds add a different twist to the game; reducing the power of the light wielders. If it's an absolutely gray day, refer elsewhere in the 2 1/2 pound book of adventure activities that you are currently reading for help in choosing a substitute something.

Admittedly, the above rules are not in logical order and the context is a bit shaky, but here's your chance to make up your own rules. We have used the socks and mirrors successfully as part of the game, *Foes & Questors*, so I know they work as "weapons": fun to use and fun to avoid.

Tree Soccer

During an adventure curriculum workshop, a group of us got together before dinner to play a bit of pick-up soccer. Teams were quickly arranged, but no one could agree on how large the goals should be, or where they should be located. A suggestion was made to use two large trees as the goals.

The trees were about 40 yds. apart on an otherwise open field. The object (scoring a goal) was simply to hit the tree trunk with the soccer ball; all other rules remained the same, with the following two exceptions. (1) There are no out-of-bounds. (2) After a score, the opposite team is allowed to make first contact with the ball from wherever it carroms after hitting the tree. Considering the above, it's apparent that there are no timeouts or stoppage of play — a very aerobic game.

Asteroids

The game, *Asteroids*, is an active offering of benign mayhem and a useful lead-up to the game *Ankle-Biters*.

Provide each player with a throwable object that they wouldn't mind being hit with: nerf balls, fleece balls, or objects of that genre. I would not want to be hit with a tennis ball, red playground ball, lacrosse ball, or shot put.

Ask the group (from 10 to 100) to spread themselves out within a definable playing area; this game works best in a gymnasium, because of the built-in boundaries. At a signal, all players loft their "throwable" object in the air. Each person must then, with great dispatch, grab a thrown object (after it hits the floor and being sure that it is not their own), and using this as a weapon, try to hit someone, recognizing that speed is essential, because everyone is trying to do the same thing.

If you are hit, sit down — you're out (don't fret, the game doesn't last long). Continue playing until only one player is left, and then start another round before the champion has a chance to gain a breath — usually ensuring that a champion does not repeat or get a chance to repeat.

Considerations:
- A player may gather as many throwable

objects as he/she wishes, but must drop them immediately when hit.

- Large balls may be hand-held by a player to serve as a deflector of other thrown objects.
- Balls may not be caught.
- This is a self-elimination game; i.e., if a player feels threatened by the game or just doesn't want to play, he/she can simply sit down and remove themselves unself-consciously from the action.

If you would like the action to continue longer, refer to *Ankle-Biters*, or require multiple hits for elimination.

Ankle-Biters Ω

Each player (warrior) is issued a foam sword and three lives. The object of the game action is to become the last player remaining as a warrior.

Each player tries to eliminate the other players by hitting them (no head shots) with a foam sword: each hit subtracts a life. After being hit three times (being whacked three times in succession by the same adversary is unchivalrous and illegal), the afflicted warrior immediately loses his/her sword and metamorphoses into an Ankle-Biter. In this new role, the downed player loses use of his/her legs and must assume a kneeling-on-the-turf position. An Ankle-Biter may pivot from this position off either foot, but such restricted mobility is the limit of lateral movement allowed.

From this demoted status and position, the angry, alienated Ankle-Biters may fight back against the warriors by attempting to grab their ankles if a sword-wielder is unwise enough to step within the pivotal area of one or more Ankle-Biters. Having an Ankle-Biter or two tightly gripping a leg causes a noticeable restriction of mobility with resultant decrease in sword-fighting efficiency.

Play continues until all the warriors, save one, have metamorphosed into Ankle-Biters. Restrict the play area for more action. A wrestling room presents an ideal "field du combat." A grassy field is also well received, except by the person responsible for getting out Ankle-Biter grass stains.

If your budget cannot handle supplying that many swords (hey, everybody can't play polo . . .), give each player a softie

(flexible frisbee) or a nerf ball to use as a "soft-war" weapon: 2' x 4's are not suitable surrogate swords. These items must be thrown to effect a hit (head shots are still illegal), therefore, each item is commonly owned ordnance and can be used by any still active warrior. Ankle-Biters, as self-professed pacifists, shun weapons of any kind and would not tolerate their use within the ranks. Although Ankle-Biters share a common physiological affliction, they are extremely territorial and ethnically chauvinistic; truly a formidable character. The ankle grip of a mature male Ankle-Biter has been compared to the leverage torque developed by the Jaws-of-Life (an auto extrication tool) — awesome!

The game plan above was written over eight years ago and since that time, Ankle-Biters has changed a bit. It has become the most well received active game used in a workshop setting. The rules are basically the same, but the nerf (fleece) ball has replaced the sword. Some new rules:

- When hit by a fleece ball, you must drop to one knee and randomly throw however many balls you have in your possession. The thrown balls must travel beyond your pivotal reach.
- At this juncture, you can either (1) become an ankle-biter, or (2) wait for a ball to roll within reach and get back into the action.

There is literally no end to this game and I sense that this fact, plus the rapidly changing player roles is what makes *Ankle-Biters* such a popular activity.

Aerobic Tag Revisited — Results in Hooper

Aerobic Tag (*Cowtails & Cobras*; original edition, pg. 100) provides a non-pareil, cold morning warm-up activity. In order to explain a new variation of Aerobic Tag

called *Hooper*, I'm including a brief re-counting of the rules.

Aerobic Tag

1. Teams of equal number (also try for skill, size, sex split . . . good luck) are needed and players must be easily distinguished by the timekeeper — use pinneys; light shirts/dark shirts; pants rolled up or down, etc.
2. The object is to maintain team possession of a play object (frisbee, softie, nerf ball) for 30 seconds (depending upon the interest and physical level of the players).
3. Players may run with the object, but if tagged by a player on the opposite team, they must release the object within one second or risk losing a point to the other team.
4. A point is scored if a team keeps possession of the play object for 30-60 seconds. If the play object is on the ground, it is still in possession of the last team that touched it.
5. Play begins again, after the score, when the timekeeper throws the play object straight up.

As a result of having played this game over the years and having recently discovered that using rubber deck tennis hoops as the play object on windy days is best (frisbees always end up blowing out of bounds), the game *Hooper* evolved, and it's a winner.

Hooper

You need a rubber deck tennis ring and four hula hoops as props for this game. Rules of play for Hooper are identical to Aerobic Tag with these exceptions and additions:

1. The four hula hoops are placed on the field of play to form the corners of an imaginary square. They should be at least 20 yards away from one another.

2. A team has to keep possession of a rubber ring for 15 seconds, at which juncture the timekeeper yells, "HOOP."
3. To score a point, a player whose team has maintained possession for 15 seconds and hears HOOP, must place him/herself inside one of the hula hoops and catch the rubber ring by having it actually "ring" his/her hand. This catch is most easily accomplished by bringing all the fingers of the hand together and overlapped (not the thumb) to form a "spear." (see photo on pg. 93)
4. Both feet must be inside the hoop for the point to count.
5. If two players both grab the rubber ring during play, the timekeeper yells, "RE-LEASE," and one of the players immediately throw the ring as high as possible overhead.
6. Some boundaries are necessary to prevent cross-country runners from dominating play, but keep the lines far enough apart to allow unrestricted running.

Hooper combines the aerobic value of a tag game with the skill and strategy necessary to play position and make a difficult catch. This is a three-star game — take the time to wade through the words and give it a try. Refer to the game Drop Dead Ball, for another aerobic tag variation.

All Catch Ω

Have at least one *soft* ball available per player. One person throws a ball up to a height of at least ten feet. Someone else must catch that ball. If the ball is caught, that ball and another one are thrown up together, and those two must be caught by someone other than the person who threw the ball. This adding-a-ball sequence continues until a ball is dropped.

This initiative game is a real fooler. It's an adept group that can achieve six balls in play without a drop.

Up Chuck Ω

Played almost identically to *All Catch*, except. . . . Each player has a soft throwable ball. On a signal everyone must throw their ball at least 10 feet high. The object is to catch a ball you didn't throw. Leave all missed balls on the ground so that they may be counted. This negative score provides a

goal to best for the next throw. The ideal scenario is for everyone who throws a ball to catch a ball; i.e., no drops.

If the group is working well together, and quickly accomplishes the task, add more balls (two per person) to up the ante.

Add-on-Tag (also called Tusker when played with ethafoam swords) Ω

The object of this duo running game is for one IT-pair to catch another pair and become a catching quartet (hands joined to form a line) and catch another pair to become a sextet, etc. Only the two people at the end of the line are allowed to tag a fleeing pair (one hand anywhere . . . well, almost anywhere). If the line breaks at any point, a catch is disallowed. This catching sequence continues until only one fleeing pair is left and, as undisputed champions of speed and chicanery, become exempt from further chase and harassment.

To prevent injury, do not allow pairs to run through or under the catching line. Restrict the playing area so that the game is active, but not so small that the catching line becomes an unbeatable seine. In the past, I have set up three fixed boundary lines and left the fourth boundary to be an imaginary line marked by my extended arm presence. This allows a comparatively small play area to begin with (when it's hard for a single pair to catch another pair), and an incrementally growing area, as I occasionally and unobtrusively shuffle a few feet back. The students are so much into the game that no one notices my gradual extension of the boundaries: I haven't been caught yet!

Night Exercises

If students are spending the night away from home at an outdoor education center or retreat and the evening hours are warm enough to support some nocturnal activity at your site, try these four feel-comfortable-with-the-dark games. Don't limit these activities to just elementary-aged folks — I've experienced excellent results (positive feedback: "Hey, that was fun . . ." comments) from adults in adventure curriculum workshops.

Commandant

The object of the first game is for one person (The Commandant) to keep all the rest of the players from making it back to home base in the dark. You will need one powerful flashlight and a portable home base. The portable home base isn't necessary, but it allows some flexibility in choosing game sites. An automobile makes a good home base. The field area that you choose for play should be free of rocks and stakes and whatever else could put holes and dents in people.

The Commandant stands at home base and counts to 50 slowly, while the rest of the players scatter to begin their nocturnal scamper back to home base, hopefully unseen. Each player must physically touch two large announced objects (trees, cabin) out in the field of play before they are allowed to try and get back to home base. These two objects must be in the Commandant's field of vision and at opposite ends of the field (at least 90 degrees apart).

The Commandant may either stay near the base or roam far afield in order to try to catch someone. A catch is made if the Commandant spots someone and can call their name. At the initial stages of the game, a name must be used. Toward the end of the game, as people are dashing toward home base, simply hitting a player with the light is enough for a "catch." A successful player, upon touching the home base, yells, "FREE." A caught player walks back to home base, and shares humorous insights about nocturnal bushwhacking with the previously-caught players already there.

The first person to make it back FREE is the next Commandant, if the game is to be played again.

Considerations:

Certain chances are being taken by playing this fast-moving game in the dark. Players move quickly, with severely reduced vision, and although a certain amount of retinal adaptation takes place (night vision: a good teaching topic for an outdoor education center), there is still the chance that someone can trip and fall over or onto things that shouldn't be there, or run into unseen branches, etc. If you know the area (to be played in) well, the chances for injury are probably minimal, otherwise I'd have to recommend against this game.

The chance-taking on your part, as sponsor, group leader, etc., is the responsibility that you have as the decision-maker. Can this game be played safely within the parameters of the players' maturity level, the physical geography of the area, and whatever Murphy-like laws control each 24 hours?

Whooo?

Another nighttime acclimatization game which allows a player to travel and/or hide alone in the dark without having to be very far from other players or home base . . .

Ask for six volunteers to be hiders (ersatz owls, if you will). The number of hiders will vary as to the size of your group.

Six hiders is sufficient for about 15 seekers. These folks hide in whatever wooded area avails itself in your camp area, recreation center, etc. The hiders try to pick a spot that allows their clothing to blend into the dark and shades of gray, afforded by the luxuriant patches of poison ivy.

Each hider takes about a dozen identically numbered pieces of small paper with them, and heads for their chosen hiding spot. Giving the hiders a few minutes to situate themselves, the seekers begin their individual search.

Each hider has the option to make a characteristic sound occasionally in order to help the searchers, particularly if no one is even getting warm (cold, warm, warmer, etc. — you know!). This compassionate rule is included to not only help the seekers, but gives the hider a role other than just hiding.

When a seeker actually makes contact with a hider, the found body soundlessly hands a numbered piece of paper to the discoverer. When a seeker has collected a predetermined number of slips or a particular numbered sequence, he/she can retire from the game and either watch the proceedings or try to confuse things with animal calls of their own.

The game helps younger players get used to the dark, and affords an engrossing evening activity that appeals to all ages.

No flashlights allowed. Make sure the hiders are well dressed if the temperature is cool. Sitting motionless in one place for a period of time is a good reminder (or lesson) of how physical activity helps to maintain body warmth.

Izzat You?

A nocturnal hunt that sometimes shows things and people as they aren't.

In an outdoor setting, split your group

in half. Ask which group would like to be the outdoor hiders first. Take that chosen or volunteer half outside to a well-known or established trail, not far from the main cabin or building. The area along the trail should be partly cleared; i.e., not dense undergrowth. Visibility should be such that no street lamps or building lights can be seen.

Talk to the hiding group about how motionless objects (people) in the dark can take on other forms that appear to be rocks, stumps, logs. Indicate that as hiders they will want to cover all parts of their body that stand out (white skin or clothing), and camouflage body parts so that they blend into the surroundings. Then begin hiding members of the group along the trail, following these rules and guidelines.

Hide people individually unless there is reluctance to stay alone, and then, allow a pair to hide together.

A hider must be in a partially exposed position. Completely concealing a person behind something is not allowed. Try to blend the hider with the natural surroundings; a rock, tree stump, etc. A hider must be no more than 20 feet away from the trail.

The seekers wait patiently in the building until the leader of the hiding group comes back and announces that all is ready. Guidelines for seekers are as follows:

1. The object of the game is to find as many of the hiders as possible.
2. Point scores are kept for each team.
3. The seekers are taken to the trail head and told that from here on, they can expect to find hidden people on each side of the trail.
4. The seekers may not leave the trail.
5. When someone thinks they have spotted a hider, they call others over to have a look. If the consensus (vote?) is that there is actually someone there, the attending instructor shines his/her flashlight directly at the spot indicated by the seekers. If a hider is revealed, the seekers get a point. If there is no one there, the hiders get a point.
6. If all the seekers pass a hider on the trail, the instructor will call the group back and point out the hider with a flashlight. The hiders then get a point, and that particular hider can join the group and silently cheer on his/her group.

This procedure continues down the trail until the last hider has been found or is revealed. Points are added up to establish a nocturnal champion. The teams then reverse roles and the game is played again.

The reason that the seekers remain indoors until the hiders are set, is to show what a difference retinal adaptation (night vision) makes toward safe walking in the dark. In an outdoor education setting, this exercise is a natural lead into a discussion about the adaptations that nocturnal animals make toward existence in a re-duced light environment: mention bats, owls, cats.

I have personally led this game many times and can attest to its popularity. There is something exciting about being hidden only a few feet away from many probing eyes and remaining uncaught. Many of the hiders report that they heard strange noises as they waited silently for the seekers to reach their hopefully hidden area.

Do not allow any flashlights to be carried, except those held by instructors.

Mission Impossible

Finding a nighttime game that is fun, non-threatening, and safe is not an easy task. This active game (capture-the-flag genre) was suggested recently as a fun-for-all-ages, after-hours contest.

Object - For a team to find hidden papers

(secret documents that outline plans which are of global significance) and return them to a home base without being caught.

Game Set-Up

Divide the playing area into three or four distinct sections. These sections should be well defined by a fence, hedge, road, etc. An instructor hides the documents (make up a manila folder that looks official) in some outdoor portion of one sector, making sure that some part of the folder can be easily seen.

Each player is told to bring a flashlight or is supplied with one. Without fail, everyone at summer camp has at least one flashlight. (Have you noticed the recent American fascination with expensive flashlights that's evidenced by exotic catalog ads that claim wondrous and amazing things for devices that supply portable light? Miniaturization; lithium batteries, high-tech bulbs, waterproof to 600', case and compass included. I even read about one recently that fires tear gas toward the area it illuminates — what every camper needs, at only $37.95.)

The two teams must establish their own home base from which to operate, and as a goal area. A home base can be located in any of the sectors. The situation that makes this game different from other similar games is that no one knows in which sector the papers are hidden, so that offense and defense from both teams must infiltrate all areas to look for the papers and prevent them (once found) from being brought back to a safe haven; i.e., home base — game's over!

The flashlight is each player's weapon. If a player is hit by a light flash, she/he must return to home base before starting their quest again. Considering this "flash" ability and the necessary wide dispersal of players, the chance for an exciting finale is evident.

As a safety consideration, don't include any playing area that has picket-like stakes protruding from the ground or neck-level rope or cable hazards.

Thanks to Donna Bayliff, a teacher at the Fox Lane Middle School in Bedford, New York, for this nocturnal game idea.

Frog Wars

For this game(s), you need:

1. Spot markers - 9" diameter rubber or plastic gym markers. Enough for 1/2 of the players.
2. Fleece balls (tennis size) for at least 1/2 of the players, plus a few extra.

These items (and many other game goodies) can be obtained from *Project Adventure, Inc.*, P.O. Box 100, Hamilton, MA 01936 (508) 468-7204. A full-color equipment catalog is available; ask for one — tell 'em Karl said it was OK. (It's free anyway, but it makes me look good.)

Want to know how to play the game(s) before reducing your equipment budget? Good idea.

Hand out spot markers (henceforth referred to as lily pads, which is obviously what they were meant to be), to half the group. This lily pad group designates a team, and the players are called "Rana Pipiens" (RP's) — a rather common greenish amphibian with great jumping ability.

The other team is assigned as many fleece balls as you have to hand out. DO NOT substitute tennis balls for fleece balls: when hit, they hurt. The members of this fleece ball armed team represent Rana Pipien's greatest predator, the pre-pubescent male (PPM).

Object - For the frogs (RP's) to move their entire herd the length of a basketball court (timed effort) while the pre-pubescent males (PPM's) attempt to prevent this movement, for reasons that make sense to this age group. Teams change roles after an attempt and then compare times.

Procedures & Rules

1. RP's move by flipping their lily pad forward onto the gym floor and double foot hopping onto the pad. The lily pad throw must be at least 3' minimum. Any length throw beyond the minimum is accepted, but obviously increases the frog's vulnerability to being hit.

2. A player is safe from being hit while standing on a lily pad, or with a pad in hand.

3. A player can be hit by a thrown fleece ball while hopping, in which case they must return 1/2 the distance to the starting point, and begin hopping along again.

4. When a player reaches his/her goal (far end of the gym), they achieve super frog status and may return to the lily pond (double-footed hops still required) to aid their frantically hopping cousins. Super frogs are immune to fleece ball strikes, so they may try to shield their more vulnerable green friends in transit until all RP's have completed their journey — stop the clock.

5. PPM's must throw from behind the black out-of-bound lines that parallel the basketball court, in fact, which delineate the court itself.

6. Fleece balls may be retrieved by any PPM from any place on the court, then refer to #5. If a PPM throws from inside the line, their shot does not count and they must refrain from throwing for 30 seconds.

7. Optional - If a super RP catches a fleece ball, that ball is removed from the game.

Game #2

Same basic rules as above, except whenever an RP is hit, the PPM thrower takes the frog's place on the lily pad and reverses hopping direction; i.e., moves to the opposite end of the gym.

The starting position for this game is mid-court.

If you need an active game that rarely ends, this variation of *Frog Wars* is just the thing. Lots of throwing, nebulous and transitory team affiliation, a modicum of confusion, and loads of random action.

Lily Pad Soccer

Remember the lily pads (rubber gym spots) that you used in *Frog Wars*? Get 'em out again for a fast pinball-like game of indoor soccer. If you want a fast game with NO body contact, here it is:

Two teams — two balls. If possible, use the new fuzzy indoor soccer balls or even an appropriate sized NERF soccer ball. Or, use a red play ball or beach ball or Earth Ball, or whatever you want.

Each person gets a lily pad and can pick whatever location on the gym floor that suits them, but once situated, they cannot move except to pivot on the foot that is planted on the lily pad.

Two balls (no team/ball affiliation) are constantly in play, so even if a goal is scored, action continues. The goal ball is simply thrown back onto the gym floor. If a ball comes to a stop between players, give it a lateral (not toward a goal) kick.

Soccer rules are somewhat followed to keep the game from dissolving in chaos, which isn't all bad either.

Count Down

This simple activity combines action, anxiety, team effort and humor with a minimum of explanation and props.

Ask a group of 10-30 to form a circle so that everyone is eventually facing front-to-back, as if you were going to do a *Lap Sit*, (*New Games* book). Give a fully inflated balloon to a designated captain and explain that the balloon is to pass through everyone's legs (front to back or back to front, their choice) until the circle is completed. Each person is allowed one-half second for the passage between their legs. If there are 20 people in the group, to be successful the group must complete the circle in 10 seconds (in this case). Blow an airhorn or sound some other raucous noise-maker to indicate that the group has been engulfed in asbestos-impregnated Fluff or whatever inventive disaster comes to mind. If a balloon breaks, the full disaster is immediately experienced.

If you have just finished playing *Balloon Frantic* so that there are enough balloons for each person, try the same through-the-legs game with this variation. Each person starts with a balloon marked with their initials (felt-tipped marker). The game ends (same timing system) when each player gets their own balloon back. Try a double rotation or clockwise one way and counter the other.

Since everyone now has a personalized balloon, ask them to take care of that balloon over the next few hours (or days) to see whose air container has the most staying power. Use 4" diameter of remaining balloon to establish a terminal criteria.

Such a long-term inoffensive imposition can result in helping to maintain contact between group members beyond their initial get-to-know-you activities. Especially effective in a camp or retreat setting when a group will be together for an extended period.

Make a big deal about daily balloon checks, making humorous inferences about sizes, hot air, wrinkles, staying power, etc.

Predator & Prey

A field game for the younger student (grades 4-7) that requires no props, and which is particularly useful in an outdoor education setting.

Object

For a chosen student (predator) to visually "kill" all the rest of the players (prey) by calling out their names and where they are hidden. The killed prey then joins the predator and attempts to capture still hidden prey. Captured prey may not call out names until the word FLUSH has been called. (See FLUSH rule.)

Rules & Procedures:

The initial predator is a volunteer or is chosen in whatever way you think is appropriate.

The predator stands on an elevated area – small hill, back of a pick-up truck, etc.
The predator is not allowed to leave the assigned area.
The prey is given one minute to hide in a place that allows them to see the predator; i.e., not 100% concealed.
The predator may, at any time, say FLUSH, at which time all the remaining prey must leaving their hiding places, advance a brief distance toward the predator, and rehide. After saying "FLUSH," the prey has 20 seconds to rehide. All predators must close their eyes or put on blindfolds during this 20 seconds.

The game continues until all the players have become predators except one, who is designated an endangered species and becomes the initial predator for the next game.

Be sure to play the game in an area that allows many and varied hiding places.

Italian Golf

I've had a lot of fun with this throw and catch game, punctuated as it is with upward cultural thrusts of manual emotion. If that verbal mish-mash doesn't make any sense, refer to the expressive catching position (see photo below), and its reference to an emotional Italian hand and arm gesture.

The hidden agenda of Italian Golf is to offer a game that teaches by example the rules, vocabulary and etiquette of actual golf combined with a format that is low key and enjoyable enough to encourage 100% participation.

You will need about a dozen rubber deck tennis rings. These soft rings are obtainable from various physical education equipment catalog suppliers and from Project Adventure, Inc. As far as I know, deck tennis rings are used on the deck of a ship to play a game that resembles tennis, when hitting tennis balls off the court (into the ocean) doesn't make economical sense. The rings are soft, but substantial enough to allow a good long throw. People seem to like holding and throwing the rings, just for the sake of doing it — I suspect dogs would like them, too.

The Game

Break up into small groups of 2, 3, or 4. Four players together designates the classic golf FOURSOME. As you stand where you are, look around and try to envision a

playable GOLF HOLE — something in the 100-300 yd. category with perhaps a DOG LEG and a couple obstacles (tree, pond, car). Declare "This HOLE looks like a PAR 8," or however many throws you think it will take your team to HOLE OUT. The first person in your group to DRIVE (throw a ring) gets set on the established TEE and throws to another person in the foursome that has assumed a catching position some distance toward the HOLE (final destination).

To legally catch the rubber ring, the catcher must extend a hand (palm toward face) upward with fingers and thumb held together so that the incoming ring will encircle the hand and pass over the wrist to the forearm. Anything less is a miss, and the STROKE (throw) must be taken again. Once the catcher establishes a position, that person must return to his initial position, at which point the next thrower in the foursome sequence takes over at the point of the last miss, and play continues. Each throw is counted as a STROKE.

The foursome continues throwing and catching in sequence until the "HOLE" is reached. The SCORE is recorded on the SCORE CARD, then the next hole is conceptualized and attempted.

Spend some time letting the players throw and catch before the game is explained. The throw/catch is an enjoyable preliminary to the game and gives the players a better idea of how far they can throw accurately and also how well they can't catch.

Be inventive in establishing holes, taking advantage of natural WATER HAZARDS, and other OUT OF BOUNDS obstacles. Particularly intense HOLES include brief sojourns into and out of buildings.

Keep score over a series of HOLES so that FOURSOMES can compete against one another. If two foursomes are playing a hole one after another, golf vocabulary that fits the occasion includes: PLAY THROUGH: LET OUT SOME SHAFT: NEVER UP, NEVER IN: BIRDIE-EAGLE (or more likely DOUBLE BOGEY): NICE HIT: HOW MANY DO YOU LIE?

Have you figured out the Italian connection? Hold up your hand, palm facing you, in the approved finger together catching position. Shake your hand and arm up and down vertically in this position 3 or 4 times to alert your thrower that you are ready. Get it? Maybe you have to be there. The gentleman in the photo on pg. 87 is my father who, at age 85, *still* beats me at real golf.

The Wave   Ω

Everybody needs a chair. Flimsy chairs do not work well for this highly active game that involves moving your posterior rapidly from one chair to another. Come to think of it, I don't know of any chair that will hold up to a charging 250 pounder, bereft of compassion and consumed with the desire to park his/her well covered posterior in the only remaining empty seat. Sounds like fun, eh?

Sit in a circle with the chairs fairly close together. Designate (ask for a volunteer — maybe you) a person to leave his/her chair empty and stand within the circle of seated bodies. As soon as the IT person moves toward an empty chair, it must be filled by the person sitting next to the chair that will result in a clockwise or counterclockwise movement of people. As one person moves, the next person must be in motion, etc., etc., in order to fill the rapidly vacating seat sequence. When this game gets moving, the rapid seat changing results in a wave-like flow of people that looks impossibly choreographed.

When the IT person finally gets his/her posterior into the appearing/disappearing empty chair, the inevitable displaced person must immediately look for and pursue the elusive empty chair: there are no timeouts.

Change directions (from clockwise to counterclockwise or vice versa) occasionally in order to confuse and confound a floundering IT — you'll know when. Play until quivering quadriceps plead for relief (or you run out of replacement chairs). This is one of those games that has to be played to appreciate the potential for (1) fast, physical action (2) unselfconscious touch (3) copious laughter, and a sense of posterior abandon that borders on chaos. Get into it.

As with all these person-in-the-center games, if someone gets stuck in circle center, they have the option of walking up to any other player and saying, HELP ME! The approached player is encouraged to take the beleagured IT person's place as a compassionate pragmatic gesture — because they might need help in another situation later in the program.

After the action has really established itself, suggest that someone leave their chair and try to dash across the circle to a chair that has been vacated by another chance-taking player. Once this chaotic concept is understood and appreciated, the helter-skelter dashing and dodging has to be seen to be appreciated.

Striker   Ω

Remember when you were first learning to play soccer? "No hands, use your feet . . . phweeet . . . penalty — hand ball. Come on, kid, use your feet."

Are you kidding? I spent every adolescent waking physical hour (except in glandular timeouts) learning how to throw, catch and smack balls of various types, and now my hands are appendages-non-grata.

Here's a game that offers relief from the foot fetish aficionados, called *Striker*, and you are *not allowed* to kick the ball. Score one for the prehensile let's-play-catch fans.

Obtain a 16" beach ball ($1.27 at Zayre's) and inflate it roundly. Halve your group on a playing field and ask the two teams to separate by about 10 yards. The team with the oldest player can elect to either receive or smack the ball. The team that initially delivers the ball (smack-off) begins by having one player loft the ball and having another player hand-strike the ball so that it sails toward the other team. Or, as an alternate START, have the two shortest players pair off for a jump ball. Play has begun, so here are a couple rules.

1. The ball cannot be hit with any part of the body except the hands and arms. Why? Because it's my game and my rules, so I'm getting even for all those years of hearing "... keep your hands down!" Besides, I'm an only child.
2. No purposeful body contact is allowed.
3. There are no timeouts, penalties (self-enforced rules; usually by the biggest, strongest player), or whistles. Play is continuous. After a goal is scored, a member of the defending team is allowed to pick up the ball and gets a free hit toward the far wall.
4. Strike only with an open hand.

A score is achieved by hitting the ball over the end line or hitting the wall at the end of the gym. If more than 20 people are on the court, put another beach ball into play.

Five-a-Side Flatball

This is one of those "spontaneous genera-tion" games that occurs full-blown as the result of some serendipity and more than a dollop of PGE (playful group energy). *Five-a-side* also plays better than it reads, so give it try when group energy is high, after a heady game of *Striker*, perhaps.

Deflate a Moonball (aka beach ball) to about 66-2/3 maximum to provide the object of play.

Ten players make up the official roster for this fast-moving game with five players arranging themselves on each side as opposing teams. Use the basketball lines near the end of five court that are parallel to one another and about 6' apart to act as boundary designators. The two teams line up facing one another. Team players should be a little more than arm's length away from one another and facing the members of the opposite team. The sug-gested lateral boundary line is just beyond the last player in line.

Object — To smack the flattish ball over and past the opponent's line using only the front or back of an *open* hand.

Rules:

1. Players must stand with their toes on the line while waiting for a playable hit.
2. When the ball approaches, a player may make one pivot step forward to smack the ball, but may not make purposeful physical contact with an opposing player.
3. A point is scored if the ball crosses the opposing player's line. If the ball sails *over* that player's waist height, no point is scored.
4. Play begins with a back-handed hit of the ball (called a backy).
5. The ball may not be picked up, held or carried.
6. Five consecutive hits of the ball per side are maximum before the ball must be touched by someone on the other team.
7. Kneeling is not allowed.
8. Penalties are judged and assessed by the players.

Only play Five-A-Side in a warm ambi-ent temperature situation, otherwise the ball easily splits its seams.

If the ball splits a seam as the result of all this whacking about, insert a balloon into the hole and inflate it until the beach ball assumes its 2/3 flat appearance. And . . . ah . . . don't forget to tie off the balloon before resuming play.

Onion Jousting

Here's *OJ* in a nutshell.

Outline a circular area bout 5-6' in diameter using an old section of webbing or sling rope. Two people stand in this circled area, each armed with two teaspoons (tablespoons, for the less adept), and one small onion. Considering that each contestant (this activity is wildly competitive) has a spoon in each hand, place the onion in the spoon of the non-dominant hand. The contest is to try and dislodge the onion from the spoon of your opponent.

Rules: (without which, play becomes warfare; "moral equivalent of ". . . notwithstanding)

- A player must not step out of the circle.
- You are allowed to hit your opponent's onion or spoon with your free spoon. Any other contact can result in forfeit. If an onion is dropped, the player having dropped the onion loses. If both onions are dropped simultaneously, the first onion to hit the ground loses.
- Combat begins by both players eyeballing each other, and ritualistically clicking the bowls of their free spoons against one another twice before any offensive action is allowed.
- You may substitute a mango for the onion, if both players agree to the change.
- Raw eggs, of course, replace onions for the ultimate macho contest: *mano-a-mano* until *huevos ranchero* is achieved.

Clothespin Tag

A pinchy good addition to your tag game collection.

Give each player four clothespins (the spring type that hold tightly, and which used to be made of wood and are now usually fabricated of plastic, and don't look and feel as good as they used to). If you want a faster game, offer less pins per player. Also, remember that restricted boundaries mean more action and enjoyment. Widely spread boundary markers favor good runners, and you are quickly back into the I-want-to-play/don't want-to-play schism that downgrades an otherwise good game.

Game

Each player tries to get rid of their pins by attaching them to other players' clothing (everybody wears shirts). A player's 4 pins

must end up on 4 separate runners. The first player to successfully attach all four pins is the champion. A pin must remain attached for 5 seconds to be valid. A player cannot rub up against another player or the wall in order to dislodge a pin(s). Redistribute the pins and begin again if interest remains high.

If the thought or possibility of pinched breasts and genitals (sounds funny, but it isn't) is a concern, allow only dorsal attachment of the pins. Dorsal pinning adds considerably to the skill level of the game. Players look like swirling matadors as they attempt to set their spring-loaded *banderillas*.

Speed Rabbit   Ω

You may recognize this stand-in-a-circle activity as an old beer-drinking game, because that's exactly what it is, but I've changed the rules slightly so that rule infractions result in people switching, rather than mandatory beer-quaffing. The fast and ludicrous action, however, remains the same, so chug away for nostalgia's sake (better use soft drinks for a student group — I have a feeling that parents may complain otherwise).

Ask the game initiator to stand in the center of the circle. Her/his job is to point to a person in the circle and say either (1) elephant (2) rabbit or (3) cow. The signified individual and the two people to her immediate right and left must perform a ritualized and symbolic pantomime sequence before the center person can count to 10. If the sequence is not done correctly or in time, then the offending person must take the place of the initiator. If the sequence is performed correctly, then the initiator points to another person until someone eventually makes a mistake or

doesn't complete the sequence within the allotted time.

The animal sequences are as follows and, of course, can be (should be) amended or added to as play continues. Noah was pretty good at this game.

Elephant

The person pointed to: (1) Extends their right arm forward, palm down, hand lightly cupped. (2) Brings the left hand under the arm and up to pinch the nose. (3) Flaps the right arm up and down, as in flapping their trunk. The two players to the right and left of the flapping trunk must establish "ears." (See photo)

All this happens simultaneously before 1, 2, 3 . . . 10 is reached.

Rabbit

1. Center person hops up and down.
2. Person to the right stomps his/her right foot. Person to the left stomps his/her left foot.

Cow

1. Center person interlaces fingers of both hands and presses both palms out away from her/his body, resulting in both thumbs pointing to the ground.
2. Side people must grab a thumb and mime a milking motion.

Make up your own series of sounds and motions for a chicken, horse, porpoise, skunk, dog, etc. To increase the action (chaos), and eventually end the game, begin to put more and more caught people into the center.

Hand Grenade Relay

If you have trouble with the Ramboesque title, try *Lob It*, or *Hook Shot Relay*.

This game is designed to move a group from one activity to another without having to say, "Let's all walk (or jog) over to the next event." Or, it can be used simply as a low-key competitive activity that is different enough to spark some interest and let's-do-it action.

Divide your group quickly into smaller groups of three or four players. Give each group a 4" diameter playground ball that is not fully inflated; this less-than-round adaptation cuts down on the rolling action.

Indicate that each member of each group will, in on-going sequence, lob (straight arm, overhead style, like lobbing a hand grenade), the ball toward a goal. The "goal" is moving the ball through, over and around a series of natural obstacles in order to deposit the ball at a distinct final destination. Obstacles can include: through a swing set, dog leg around a tree, over a backstop, through a swinging tire, through the front seat of my car (doors open), up and down stairs, and many etc.'s. Design the course with imagination, eschewing predictability for unsuspected challenge.

Continually emphasize that the throwing motion must be "hand grenade" or basketball hook shot style. This limited orbital lob will handicap the best throwers in the group (a leveling ploy) and keep the teams closer together.

Rules:

1. Each person and team keeps track of their own score as they alternate throws toward achieving the final goal (perhaps a lob into a 55 gallon drum from a minimum peripheral distance of 30 ft.).
2. Each throw must come to a stop before the next team member can pick up the ball.
3. The next lobber must have one of their feet on the spot where they picked up the ball.
4. Any ball thrown rather than lobbed is a no-throw, and must be repeated with the other arm.
5. The initial person-to-person sequence must be maintained.
6. Teams do not have to wait for one another, and so, can sequence their lobs as rapidly as they like, although there is no reward for finishing first.
7. Teams may not interfere with one another or touch each others' balls.

Hooper Relay

Using the same format as played in *Hand Grenade Relay*, throw a rubber hoop (deck tennis ring) as the object of play.

Rule changes include:

1. The hoop can be thrown using any hands-only propulsion; i.e., no Jai-Alai type implements allowed.
2. The thrown hoop must be caught to be counted. A missed hoop results in another recorded throw from the same starting point. The catcher may change position, however.

3. To make the catch more difficult, require that the hoop be "ringed" over an extended hand in order to count (as in the game *Hooper*).

Because of the high incidence of missing the hoop in long throws, some interesting decision-making situations develop as to throwing distance and catching ability.

See *Italian Golf.*

Initiative Problems — No Props

The Reversing Pyramid

Divide your class into groups of 10 and ask those 10 people to arrange themselves into a 4-3-2-1 standing pyramid, like this —

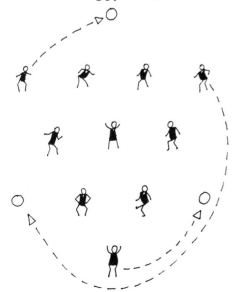

Once pyramidally arranged, ask that symmetrical group of 10 to reverse the apex and base of the pyramid (triangle) by moving only three people. Simple? How come you looked at the answer?

Count Off Ω

This initiative activity appears so simple that you may initially ignore its possibilities. Try it with a group during some down time, or if there are a few minutes before the change of class bell.

Ask a group of 15-20 people (the numbers may vary, but try to have about one person per number) to count to twenty without pre-planning who is going to say which number, and try to do this without having two (or more) people saying the same number simultaneously. It seems easy — it isn't.

No verbal or visual signals are allowed. Also, begin this activity when the group is not in a circle. A circular arrangement lends itself to a speedy solution.

Anyone can begin by saying, "one," then someone else tries to sneak in a "two," and then a quick "three," "four," and then "fi.." "five," and back to zero to begin again. How come? Two people tried to say five at the same time. Get it? Got it! Good.

Everybody Up

Using this cooperative exercise is a useful way to introduce the concept of initiative problems.

Ask two people of approximately the same size to sit on the ground (gym floor) facing one another so that the bottoms (soles) of their shoes are opposed, knees bent, and grasping each other's hands. From this stylized sitting position, ask the duo to try and pull themselves into an upright standing position. If the pair is successful (most are), ask them to seek another partner and try three people, then four, etc., until the entire group makes an attempt. Criteria for a successful attempt are: (1) Hands grasped so that an electrical current could pass through the group. (2)

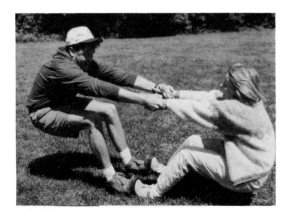

Foot contact with the same electrical set-up. (3) All derrieres off the ground at about the same time.

Something that began as a simple cooperative stunt soon becomes an initiative problem that includes the entire group.

An expanding group will functionally find that the seemingly logical circular configuration of bodies cannot be continued beyond 8 people or so. A change of thinking (initiative) must be employed to come up with a solution that allows large numbers (50 people) to complete the problem.

If an adrenaline-pumped group of 8 or 10 jogs over to you, after having stumbled and jerked to a tenuous standing position, and breathlessly asks, "Did we do it right?" — need I say what your answer should be? Are they high? Yes. Do they feel good about their effort and themselves? Yes. Did they do it right?

An alternate or additional way to present this problem is to ask the participants to sit back-to-back and try to stand as a pair, a trio, etc. Do not allow interlocked arms for safety reasons (shoulder dislocation possibilities).

Popsicle Push-Up   Ω

This cooperative activity can be used as a simple-four person stunt, or you can continue to add people, ending up with a useful large group initiative problem.

To set up the initial four-person attempt, ask for four volunteers that can do at least one push-up. Ask one person to lie face down on the ground, as if preparing to do a push-up. The second person lies face down, perpendicular to the first person, so that the tops of his/her feet are on top of the first person's upper back. The third person repeats the procedure, using the second person as their foot rest. The fourth person fits in this weave so as to connect everyone in a square configuration. Everyone should be face down with their feet (instep) on someone's back.

On a signal, everyone does a push-up and, if done together, there will be four raised bodies, with only eight hands touching the ground: simple, but impressive.

If one of the participants has trouble getting up (foot pressure on their back might cause a problem), tell them that you will count to three before saying GO, and that the "permanently prone" individual should attempt a push-up on the count of two, offering just a bit of a head start.

After your groups of four have had some fun with this quartet push-up (including a 360° rotation attempt while in the up position — doomed for failure, but worth a laugh or two), ask the group to continue to

add people to one of the quads in an attempt to include the whole group (4 to infinity) in a mass popsicle push-up.

There is more than one solution to this initiative problem, and the technique outlined above is not the easiest. Remember, solutions are not important; how the group reacts to the problem and one another is key

This problem is characteristically time-consuming, not from the standpoint of discovering a workable solution, but because of how long it takes a group to decide on a technique and implement it. The attempt needs a leader; don't appoint one, let it happen.

People who cannot do a push-up or have back problems can still include themselves in the group solution by lying face down on a strong person's back and, using their arms, try to assist their partner during the push-up attempt — a sharing of strength.

Popsicle Push-Up Variation

I've seen a couple innovative variations recently of this highly useable initiative problem. The variations were the result of my presenting the problem in a simpler, more direct way. In the past, I have always demonstrated the tic-tac-toe grid solution (above) and so all the attempts to add extra people were variations of that theme. Now, I simply say (with no demo), ". . . try to get your entire group supported off the ground with only the participant's hands touching the ground. The group must support themselves at least a half inch off the floor for five seconds. See photo at left.

Try this approach and I'll bet you will see solutions you never knew existed. After the problem has been solved appropriately, you can show them what a "proper" Popsicle Push-Up looks like, because it's fun too, and worthwhile doing together.

Blindfold Line Up   Ω

Sitting here at 32,000 ft. (so announced by the Eastern Airlines captain), on the way to Puerto Rico for some monkey business, I was trying to think of a topic, game or event not yet detailed in past BOT's, and this old workshop standby (*Line Up*) came to mind. Flashed-to-mind is more like it, because by some memory malfunction, I had left this excellent initiative problem out of the collection in *Silver Bullets*. I don't want to be overly effusive, but this simple exercise in communication and trust is one of the finest. It "works" best with a mature group of participants: K-6 teachers either adapt or move on.

Group size can vary from 8-15. If participants number from 20-30, ask half the group to try the problem while the others observe. Tell the observers that their solution should occur in less time because of what they perceive and communicate to one another — don't count on this actually happening though. Observed experience does not effective participants make.

Ask the group (when assembled in front of you) to close their eyes and keep them shut for the remainder of the problem. Even some adults have trouble with this request, so offer blindfolds in this case and require their use with younger groups. Also emphasize the Challenge By Choice aspect of this, and all, Project Adventure activities. If someone really wants (needs) to take a peek, what the heck, take a peek.

Using the "bumpers up" position (both hands in front of the face, palms facing away) for protection, ask all the folks to mingle about slowly without talking. This is done to change everyone's position so no one knows who is where. After about 10-15 seconds of this giggling, shuffling affair, ask them to stop, keep their eyes closed, put down their hands, and listen to the pre-problem instructions. At this

juncture, tell them this is an exercise in communication and trust; communication that they develop among themselves and trust that they are not going to be made fun of, or purposefully made to appear ridiculous.

Indicate that you are going to assign a number to each participant and that you will do this by walking among them and tapping each person on the shoulder, saying a number at the same time. To facilitate your job (because I always forget), ask everyone to raise a hand and to lower that hand when they receive a number from you. Dig?

Supposing that there were 12 people in the group, you now have 12 sightless, numbered, disoriented folks who have no idea what to anticipate next. This approach is purposeful but not unkind, because you now say, "I want you to line yourselves up, shoulder-to-shoulder (or back-to-front, or hand-in-hand; doesn't matter) by number from 1 to 12 without saying a single word; i.e., no talking."

If blindfolded people can look dumbfounded, they will — you just hit them with a blockbuster request. There will be some utterances or halting questions. Re-state the problem, emphasizing that talking is not allowed.

After some stumbling about (physically and conceptually), ideas begin to actualize and progress is made, albeit slowly. Mentally record specific observations about what's happening, so that you can facilitate a discussion afterwards, or simply in order to relate a humorous vignette that they *can't see.*

Clapping, tapping, stomping, skin-writing, whistling all have their place in this primitive evolution of communication. Having two or three of the above techniques attempted (at or on you) simultaneously can be somewhat confusing and uproariously funny to observe. The value of video-taping this activity goes without saying, which is an odd thing to say, because I already said it. Say what?

Offer encouragement when deemed necessary to assuage growing frustration.

Allow 10-15 minutes for a solution. If the group is still largely disoriented after 10 minutes, ask them to stop, keep their eyes closed, and wait for you to touch their shoulder, at which touch they loudly announce their number. Then let things continue apace for another few minutes.

When it's obvious that the sequenced solution has been achieved, ask them to open their eyes and count off. Allow a couple of minutes for the explosion of conversational sharing that predictably occurs as the result of pent-up, who-did-this and you-did-thats.

As facilitator, mention or ask about: frustration, fears, trust, applicability, leaders, followers, and don't worry about humor, there's plenty at the tip of every rested tongue.

Initiative Problems — Minimum Props

Polar Bears Around the Ice Holes

This odd, story telling game has been around for decades. See if your mom and dad remember it.

You need three or four dice (I'll bet that's wrong — it's probably three or four die, or more appropriately, two sets of dice; you know what I mean), and a couple 1' x 1' squares of white styrofoam. The one inch measurement isn't critical, anything that looks like an ice cube is OK. I recently found some very realistic plastic ice cubes in a novelty store (no imbedded bugs) that make great props for this game.

These squares represent the 6 faces on a di. Any center hole in a di is an "ice hole," so dice 1, 3, and 5 have ice holes; 2, 4, and 6 do not. "Polar bears" are the di holes around the center hole, so di 3 has 2 polar bears around an ice hole.

If the following combination shows up, what should I say?

POLAR BEARS

ICE HOLES

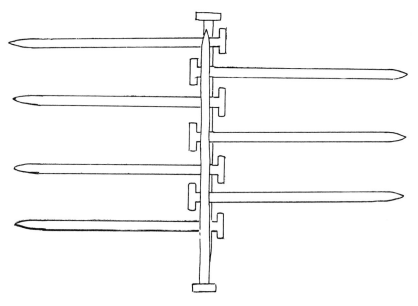

PORCUPINE PROGRESSION

"I see one ice hole and 6 polar bears, but only 2 bears are around one ice hole."

What do the plastic ice cubes have to do with the sequencing? Nothing, they are strictly window dressing.

Is this confusing for students? You bet — I love it.

The Porcupine Progression

During a recent workshop, a participant offered this problem to our group. This is a particularly appealing and useful initiative problem because:

(1) The solution is neat and attractive (a why-didn't-I-think-of-that type).

(2) Small. inexpensive and easily obtainable props are required.

(3) Initially, there appears to be no solution so that when the visually satisfying nail arrangement is acheived or demonstrated, the word "impossible" becomes less of an obstacle next time.

Offer the following props to an individual or a small group. Thirteen 40 penny common nails (that's lumberyard talk for 5-1/2" long nails with a big round head), one of which should be started vertically in a small piece of wood. The problem is to balance the remaining 12 nails on the head of the vertical nail.

It doesn't take long to figure out that a solution beyond a stack-'em-up attempt is necessary. I don't mind admitting that the final answer to this "impossible" problem slipped by my steel-trap cognitive capabilities. An M.I.T. freshman workshop participant conjugated the right stuff in about five minutes. Obviously, I could have come up with the same simple answer, but I wanted the group to feel that it was their solution. The above illustration indicates the bi-lateral nail arrangement, leading to a final solution.

Lay the bottom nail on a firm surface, then alternate the next 10 nails on top of this first nail. Lie the top nail on so that its

head is opposite to the bottom nail's head. Grip (pinch) this symmetrical nail arrangement at both ends and place it on the head of the vertical nail. This may require some fiddling about, but this low center of gravity arrangement balances surprisingly well. Eureka! Voila! Neat-o!

Porcupine Considerations

- The nails do not have to be any particular length, but I have found that the longer and larger common nail type are the easiest to work with and are more visual.
- The current "world's" record is 84 nails on the head of one nail.
- To make this problem more portable, pre-drill the block with a drill-bit the same size as the diameter of the nails being used. In this way, the vertical nail can be easily set and also removed.
- Have two or three Porcupine Progression sets available for use if the group numbers over 10 participants: More props = more action.
- If you need a light weight PP set for travel, buy some aluminum gutter nails or potato baking nails, and use a cut block of ethafoam in place of wood.

Save the City

The object of this compassion-based initiative problem is to transport a radioactive isotope (tennis ball) from beginning to destination without letting the isotope touch the floor (reverses the ionization of the sub-floor re-bars, resulting in a decomposition of structural integrity and collapse of the horizontal supporting mechanism (floor), or touch any body part (I won't go into detail about the anatomical consequences — too brutal).

It's your group's civic and humanitarian responsibility to use the available customized lead shield transporters (plastic milk carton with the bottom cut off - see *Jug Ball*) to transport the isotope up, over and across a few well-chosen obstacles.

Rules:

- Isotope (ball) must touch only the transporters (jugs).
- Isotope must make contact with the interior of each transporter; i.e., the ball must be transported from jug to jug.

Considerations:

- Establish a deadline for completion. This is a timed event.
- As a variation, require that everyone choose a place to stand and then have to stay there — pivot action on one foot allowed.
- Each student must supply their own decorated isotope transporter, (to keep you from having to slice up beaucoup milk cartons).

Mirage

This simple set-up could become a classic in communication confusion. The object of the exercise is to see if a group member can communicate to the remainder of the group (pencil and paper in hand) the geometrical abstraction (see illustrations) that has been given to him/her.

Four separate pictorial attempts are made with four separate abstractions, following these guidelines:

1. The presenter vocalizes the abstract illustration with his/her back to the group.
2. Again, verbalizing a different abstract figure, but this time facing the audience. Gestures are allowed by the communicator, but no questions may be asked or answered.
3. Now, face the audience and use gestures only: no talking or making any sounds (except laughter, which is hard to stifle at this point).
4. And, finally, facing the audience, gesticulating to your heart's content and responding to the group's question.

After each attempt, allow the group to compare their separate drawings with one another and with the master abstraction. Note which attempt produces the most accurate representation and discuss why you think this is so.

These illustrated abstractions are examples that have been used successfully in the past, but they do not represent any holistic, spiritual, religious or secular anything. Make up your own and I suspect you will get the same humorously insightful results.

Tangrams

You have probably tried to solve puzzles like these (illustrations) at one time or another, but on a smaller physical scale. A group solution of the puzzle necessitates some sense of spatial relationship and an appreciation of leader/follower rules to efficiently discover the figure forming positions for the jigsaw-like pieces.

Cut the puzzle pieces from 1/2" fiber board (an inexpensive and fairly tough plywood substitute) or whatever durable material you have available. Cut the sections much larger than the commercially packaged pieces, in order to facilitate group interaction.

Use the measured distances as proportion guides only. If you want the figures bigger or smaller, keep the proportions the same and cut away.

After the group has solved the problems, or occasionally not come up with a solution, ask a question or two about how the group interacted (or ignored one another) to stimulate conversation about something other than rock 'n roll, the local sport's franchise, or blemishes. Here's an effective way to allow a person to express him/herself about something that's not a news item or a self-centered topic.

An interesting exercise in communication skills results from asking two people to sit back-to-back on the floor, supplying one of the individuals with an assembled Tangram puzzle and the other participant with the jumbled pieces of an identical puzzle. The person with the assembled Tangram attempts to verbally explain to her partner how to put the pieces together to achieve congruent solutions.

The procedure can be hilariously turtle-like or impressively swift. A joint working knowledge of geometric vocabulary makes the task much easier.

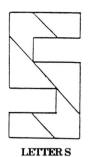

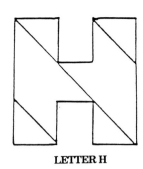

LETTER S   **LETTER H**

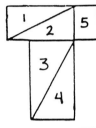

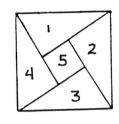

LETTER AND SQUARE

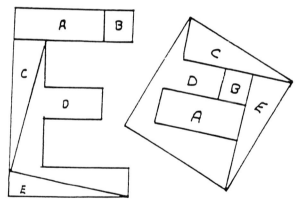

LETTER E AND SQUARE

Stepping Stones

Divide your group into smaller groups of five. Each group is given 4 rubber (plastic) gym markers or 4 rug sections or 4 whatevers and asked to physically cross the width of a basketball court as quickly (timed) as possible. Allow 2-3 minutes of planning time before the start.

Rules:

- Only the markers can be stepped on.
- If someone inadvertently touches the floor, he/she must return to the start, and anyone touching that person must also return.

Considerations:

- Try to emphasize efficiency and group cooperation in your debriefing.
- Try different combinations of gym spots and group sizes.
- Ask the group to combine their "islands" toward facilitating a group solution.

A-Frame

Here's a small group problem that requires a unique solution. The idea for this interesting initiative problem was received from Tom Steele of SUNY Cortland, who originally heard of the details from a group of German exchange students.

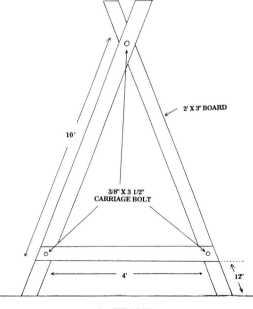

A - FRAME

The object is to move the A-frame apparatus with one person aboard, from point A to point B (30 ft.), using the five available 18' sling ropes. The solution to this problem works best on grass.

Rules:

1. The A-frame must maintain at least one point of contact with the ground at all times and never more than two points of contact. The frame cannot under any circumstances be dragged; the consequences are just too dire to mention.

2. Only one person can make actual body contact with the A-frame apparatus and he/she must avoid contact with the ground. The remainder of the people must stay at least 10 ft. from the A-frame when it is in use. This 10 ft. minimum is obviously necessary because of the radiation hazard involved in A-frames of this sort.

3. The ropes (not acid resistant) may not touch the ground (copiously covered with contact activated sulphuric acid) at any time during the passage over the restricted area.

A Solution (Not to be offered to the students)

Tie the five sling ropes to the apex of the A-frame using a series of bowlines, clove hitches or whatever knot(s) you feel comfortable with. Stand the frame vertically (2 points of contact at the base) and ask one of the six participants to stand on the horizontal cross bar. As this individual rocks from side to side (each left/right rocking motion is coupled with a thrust forward), the other five participants support the A-frame with the previously attached sling ropes. There is scant chance of the frame and rider falling over if the rope holders remain alert.

The A-frame itself can be built from lashed saplings or more uniformly from sections of 2" x 3" lumber bolted together with three 3/8" x 3-1/2 carriage bolts.

The Straw that Broke the Bottle's Back

Problem — To pick up a 12 oz. glass bottle (Samuel Smith's Nut Brown Ale is a good one) with a plastic straw.

Rules:

The bottle must remain off the floor, desk, etc., for five seconds. No other props (glue, rubber bands, etc.) are allowed: one bottle/one straw. No knots are allowed to be tied in the straw.

Solution — Bend the straw about two thirds of the way down — or one third of the way up. Stick the bent straw into the bottle orifice until the bent part flips partially open and seats itself against the interior shoulder of the bottle. Lift the straw and the bottle follows.

Gymnasium Jungle Cruise or a Rolling Raft Adventure

This dynamic initiative problem has all the right ingredients for fun and challenge. The only limiting factor that I can anticipate is the need for Rabid Nuggets (used tennis balls); you're going to need lots of them.

The challenge is to move your entire group from one side of the gym to the other side, using only the following props:

1. A 4' x 8' section of 3/4" plywood.
2. 200 to 300 Rabid Nuggets (depending on the dimensions of the gym floor being used).

3. Four stout broom handles with a rubber cane tip affixed to the end of each.

As always, the gym floor is covered with a horrendously corrosive substance that can't be touched without dire consequences; i.e., starting over. The available props are resistant to all noxious substances.

Has your imagination conjured up a solution yet? Rowing/paddling over, on top of all those nuggets sounds like it could be interesting.

John Hichwa, at the John Read Middle School in West Redding, CT. (1993 Middle School teacher of the year! - Yeah John!!!) sent me the included photo, and a newspaper article covering his *Rolling Raft Adventure*.

Quotes from that article include, "The teacher (John) randomly divided the class in half, gave each group a plywood sheet, 200 tennis balls and four dowels. Instructions were limited — get to the other side by propulsion of only the people on the raft. He also told them not to race. The only thing we want you to do is see if the groups can be successful."

"There are many ways to propel a rolling raft, and not all the plans were good ones. A member of a successful team described their strategy at the debriefing

held after the first crossing."

And the article continues in great detail about how the groups made or didn't make their trips across, but I'm not going to include any answers and spoil the discovery for you and your "teams." Make sure you bevel the corners of the plywood section and sand off all sharp edges. As soon as my source of Rabid Nuggets (used tennis balls) fills the ole nugget bin to overflowing, I'll try out my rubber-tipped J-stroke.

Hawser

This is a no-hands, Action Jackson game that requires a team to work hard and cooperate toward doing something that no one on the team has ever tried before.

You do need a 20'-25' length of hawser for the game. Hawser is defined as large

diameter (circumference) rope, and that means, in the case of this activity, minimum 2" diameter— bigger if you can get it. Rope this size is generally very expensive if you buy a long length, but rope manufacturers often have remnants left over from a special order or from the end of a large spool that they are willing to sell for at least 50% off. Ask for remnant hawser.

Just to give you an idea of size and weight, I received a 26" long section of 9.5" circumference braided nylon hawser recently. It weighs 57 pounds. A section of rope this size is perfect for the game HAW-SER.

Here's how to play:

A team of six must move the hawser 100 feet without using their hands and without manuvering the rope onto their shoulders. The rope must be moved by feet only.

Starting position is standing within a circle made by the hawser. Finishing requires moving the hawser the required 100 feet and then re-establishing the circular configuration with all team members inside. This is obviously a timed event.

Give each end of your hawser to a player and ask them to see who can tie the fastest bowline. No reason—just fun. See photo pg. 118.

Poker Chip Initiative Relay

The program objective of these sequential initiative problems and incentive chip awards is to provide a continuing interest in low ropes course elements beyond the initial group participation that involves the here-it-is-give-it-a-try level.

As you attempt to follow the time setting and point subtraction system, remember that time parity between two systems will depend on the group's ability to function as a team in contrast to individual adeptness. Vary the elements and times as fits your situation and group size.

The immediate objective is, after establishing a total time (three or four initiative problems in sequence), to bring the time back to zero or into the minus category. The group is essentially competing against themselves. The less time it takes to complete the initiative problems, then the less time needs to be subtracted from the total. The total time, for consecutive completion of all three elements, is the time block from which the remainder of events will be subtracted. The emphasis is on both team efficiency (initiative problem participation) and personal ability (individual attempts at challenging events).

Different colored poker chips are awarded for seconds achieved by individual effort. White - 5 seconds Red - 10 seconds Blue - 15 seconds

As these chips are pooled at the end of the relay, a final time is established.

Time Setting Events

- Nitro Crossing or Electric Fence
- Wall
- Beam

These three elements are to be attempted by the group in sequence with no timeout allowed between events.

- Time Chip Events
- *Tension Traverse* - 2 seconds for each 12" that the participant passes beyond the 15 ft. mark (round off to nearest five digit) and a 15 second bonus for making the entire cable.
- *Fidget Ladder* - 15 seconds for each rung made with the feet (both) beyond the starting rung. Hand and foot contact only. There is a 60 second bonus for touching the tree with the forehead.
- *Track Walk* (including end swing) - 60 seconds for completion without falling. 45 seconds - one fall, 30 seconds - 2 falls, 15 seconds - 3 falls.

A typical Initiative Relay attempt by a group of 12 participants might look like this:

- The Nitro Crossing takes the group 8 minutes.
- The wall - 5:30.
- The Beam - 6:30. Total time for the three consecutive events - 20 minutes. This is the time base to subtract subsequent "Poker Chip" events from.

Average group times for the "chip" events are:

Tension Traverse	5:15
Fidget Ladder	5:45
Track Walk	4:30
	15:30

Subtract the "chip" time, 15:30, from the initial 20:00 established time to get a final time, which acts as a goal for future attempts.

Paul's Balls Variation   Ω

Refer to page 21 in *Silver Bullets* for a write-up on the group initiative, *Paul's Balls*. If you are having trouble finding the discarded paper cores needed to make the problem function — try this.

Suspend a plastic milk crate at about the same height as 8-9 of the paper cores can be stacked (16-18'). Use a four-corner suspension system so that the box hangs true and doesn't tip easily. Arrange the cord rigging so that the box can be lowered easily in order to remove balls.

Use the suspended crate as the target for all your super shooters (as in Paul's Balls). Not a bad variation for not much $$$.

So that you don't think my reference to the book *Silver Bullets* above isn't just a thinly veiled author's commercial come on, here's a brief synopsis of the rules.

Give a ball to each member of your group. The timed object is to see how long it takes to "shoot" all those balls into the suspended box. Remember to do it twice so

Object Retrieval or Chuck-A-Hunk

This splendid initiative problem involves all the good stuff — thinking, imagination, action, fantasy, risk and an attractive solution.

The object is for a group to retrieve a fairly heavy (10 lbs.) object that is located near the center of an outlined diameter of approximately 30'.

You will need the following props and geographical set-up:

- 1 - 2' section of 2"-2-1/2" diameter hardwood log
- 1 - length of retired belay rope that is longer than 50' (static rope is better)
- 1 - length of 9mm sling rope or 1" webbing that measures 18' long
- 1 - locking carabiner
- 1 - ammo can or bucket with bail
- 1 - substantial hardwood tree to locate near the center of your 30' diameter outlined area. This tree must stand alone within this circle and display a trunk/limb bifurcation (crotch) at a height of 12'-15'.

that the group can stategize about how to improve upon their first attempt, and revel in their faster second attempt.

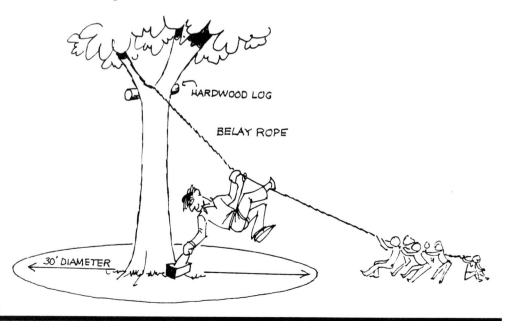

HARDWOOD LOG

BELAY ROPE

30' DIAMETER

Rules:

- Only the props listed above can be used to retrieve the object.
- If *anyone* touches the ground inside the circle, the person *closest to the object* must start again from outside the circle.
- Set a time limit: 20-30 minutes is reasonable.

The Meuse

If you own a copy of the old *Cows' Tails and Cobras* book (early issue, black cover), look under "Board Stretcher" (pg. 75) for a primitive presentation of this event. Paul Radcliffe has revived this old initiative problem by writing up a nifty full-o-fantasy

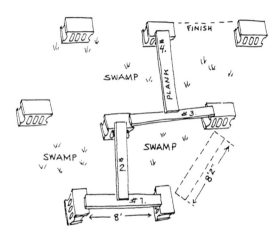

introduction and physically extending the problem by adding more "islands." Here's Paul's write-up — you can blame the illustrations on me.

Goal:

"In search of rare pink porpoise eggs, your expedition team must safely cross the bogs of Lost Swamp. Surprisingly, you have discovered that the boggish water of the swamp is still inhabited by saber-toothed beavers, sneaker-snapping turtles, and the leather-liking Great White Bog-Water Shark. Careful study by your team seems to indicate that their continued existence is directly dependent upon eating whatever "fast-food" is available in the swamp, with amazing regularity. Your precise calculations suggest that you have only ____ minutes to safely cross the swamp before the feeding frenzy will begin again. Time allowed is a function of group size and perceived prowess. Twenty minutes for a group of 10 is about average."

Rules:

1. Your team must start from the same departure point only using 4 boards and rope available.
2. Passage can only be made by staying on high ground and avoiding all contact with the swamp's water; high phosphoric acid content.
3. Should team members or props come in any contact with the water, you must return to the departure point and start over.
4. Subtract one board to make the eventual solution more difficult.

Prop Tips

- Use 4" x 4" x 8" boards for the planks. 2" x 4" x 8" boards nailed together will also serve this function.
- Use cinder blocks for the "islands."
- Allow use of a 12'± section of 9mm rope.

Remember, placement of the cinder blocks is key to making this initiative problem work. Spend some time before the students show up, making sure that the "islands" are in a functional position.

The Great Egg Drop

Your task is to design a delivery system that will protect a raw egg dropped from a height of approximately 8 feet.

Your challenge is to achieve this goal using the *LEAST AMOUNT OF RE-SOURCES*.

Your resources are limited to 20 straws and 30" of 1/2" masking tape. *YOU MAY NOT USE ANY OTHER MATERIALS.* Please keep an accounting of how many straws and how many inches of tape are used in developing your delivery system.

In addition to constructing your product(s), it must *HAVE A NAME*, and you will be expected to deliver a brief creative promotional pitch highlighting benefits and features of your design(s).

All groups have been given the exact same task and will meet together for presentations and product testing in 20 minutes.

Remember, finishing early and using less raw materials helps to make your product look better to the buyers, but the essential criterion is a whole egg after the drop.

Hint: Share your vision, work hard, but more importantly, work smart!"

If your eggs keep breaking, it may have something to do with excess dietary mercury contamination in the chicken's feed resulting in a reduced shell calcium level. Certainly something to complain about.

Eggsactly right!

Bridge It

I'm sure you have been to conferences or clinics where they "teach" communication procedures, team-building, pyramidal management, organizational and developmental skills — need I impress you (bore you) any further? What it comes down to is, are you learning anything about the jargon-loaded skills mentioned above, or are you being burdened with a series of valid but often inappropriate techniques for whatever "people" skills are being touted?

I was recently introduced to a "people" skills teaching game that sparked total enthusiasm, resulted in an engrossing task and was (hallelujah) fun.

Split your group (15-20) in half. The method employed for this halving is worth repeating, also. Rip two full page pictures out of a magazine and cut them up into jigsaw-like pieces to equal the number of people in the group (so that the pieces from both pictures equal the total number of people). Toss all the pieces willy-nilly into a container and ask each participant to draw out one piece. After all the pieces have been drawn, ask the players to pool their pieces to make a picture — two defined pictures, two random groups. Try to choose either appropriate or humorous pictures — cigarette or Kotex ads are probably not appropriate. You get the picture.

You will need the following props x 2; i.e., one set for each group.

    4   styrofoam cups
    8   8"small diameter sticks (to be gath-
        ered previously by the participants
    1   roll of masking tape
    1   small box of LEGO or Tinker Toys or
        the like
    1   paper & pencil (or pen)
    1   set of terminology

You will also need the following items to be used by both groups.

    2   card tables
    1   sheet or blanket
    1   chair for each person
    2   rooms

Set-Up Procedure:

Place the card tables next to one another. Hang the sheet or blanket vertically over the separation point of the tables. (How you suspend the sheet is your pre-initiative problem). Divide the chairs equally on each side of the sheet.

Place all the props for each group on separate tables.

The terminology mix-up could read like this: Side A - The word *top* means *bottom*; *side* means *under*; and a subtle laugh means *high*.

Side B - The word *tape* means *wide*; sticking out your tongue means *how many*; and crossing your right and left index fingers means *parallel*.

Add or subtract words to increase or decrease the confusion.

Procedure

Explain to both groups that the tangible purpose of this exercise is for each separate group to build a bridge toward the other group (sheet) so that the bridges meet and look as much alike as possible. Do not offer any guidelines except to say that only the offered props may be used. Try fabricating a story about two countries that are separated by a body of water, but want to establish a trade and cultural relationship. The river is plagued by bad weather and almost constant fog. The countries have a common language, but the dialects differ considerably.

In order to establish a necessary dialogue between groups, three five minute meetings have been arranged (be very strict on the timing) at a common meeting site (another room). As the members adjourn to the meeting room, remind them that they must not look on the other side of the sheet; offer blindfolds if necessary.

Only one member from each group may talk at each meeting, and the pair must sit facing one another, separate from the other people in the room. No comments from the group are allowed during this time (only laughter!).

The timing of the planning and building sessions should look like this:

Separate groups are shown their building area and props and are allowed seven minutes to talk over the problems of building the bridge (amongst themselves, *not* with the other group), and to begin construction if they choose to.

The three meetings are arranged as follows:

1st 5 minute meeting of the chosen group representatives in a separate room. (A new representative should be chosen each time.)
7 minute discussion and building time back at the site

2nd 5 minute representative meeting
5 minute discussion and building time

3rd 5 minute final representative meeting
10 minute race to get the work accomplished. Be strict as to the deadlines.

Then comes the unveiling (and groans or dismay or shouts of glee), and a period of time set aside for debriefing the process,

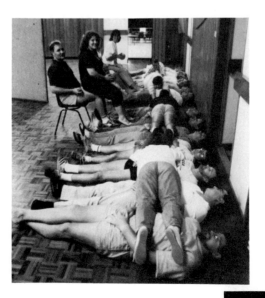

levels of accomplishment, and comparison of approach.

The physical result is apt to surprise you as to the architectural accuracy achieved.

The problem and process is engrossing, revealing, and fun.

If you are short on props, try *Body Bridge It.* (photo pg. 113) Use the same format as above, but substitute bodies for the more typical props to actually construct matching bridges. This is an intiative problem where you really get *into* the solution. Get ready for some unselfconscious touching and uncontrollable smiling.

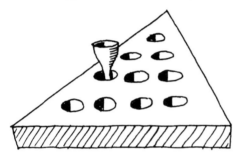

Chinese Checkers Pyramid

The Cracker Barrel restaurant off I-75, just outside Chattanooga, TN, serves a fine meal for a decent price, and you get grits whether you want 'em or not. As part of the down-home hospitality (it comes with the grits), you will find a multi-holed triangular time-spender included on the table among the sugar, salt, and just near the ketchup. I'd mention the fresh carnation flower arrangement (no plastic), but you wouldn't believe that.

A "time-spender" is something offered by the establishment to keep you from getting antsy or bored while waiting for the waitress. This particular gimmick is fairly common, but it's unique in that its solution is applicable to use as an initiative problem by substituting people for golf tees.

The problem is illustrated as follows:

On this particular dining table, the pyramid holes were filled with upside-down golf tees. One hole is left empty (any one). The announced task is to begin jumping tees (any tee with any other adjacent tee), until any further jumping is impossible. If only one tee is left, you are congratulated highly, if two are left, you get a "nice going," and on down the scale until your family's genetic I.Q. is questioned.

For your purposes, simply substitute people for golf tees and use rubber gym spots (like in *Frog Wars*) as substitutes for the holes. Since everyone in the triangular arrangement is involved with the problem, there is usually keen enough interest to maintain attention to the task. Lots of discussion, trial and error, some frustration, and challenging enough to ensure another try. Thank you, Cracker Barrel Restaurant off I-75.

38 Special

Is a person who measures 5'6" tall the world's shortest giant or the world's tallest midget? It's all in your point of view.

Reproduce the illustrated multi-shaped polygons below so that you have enough copies for each student in your class. Ask the participants to count the number of triangles within a hexagon. You will find that

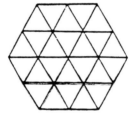
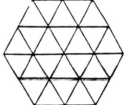

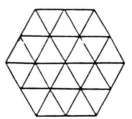

the numbers will vary considerably from the correct count (38 triangles) because it's all in your point of view. Use this simple exercise as a jumping-off point for a discussion of how people "see" solutions. Does the correct answer come from the individuals' working on their own, or from people who shared their results? This visual sit-down problem is a natural preliminary to more physically active initiative problems.

A Lightweight Idea

Haul out your stash of balloons. Ask each member of the group to blow up and tie off a balloon. Use a 12" balloon so that you can achieve an inflated size that is large enough for decent whack-it, smack-it action.

As the balloon-festooned group hangs on your every word, point out a steeple-chase route that you had planned previously. In laying out the course, think OBSTACLES: trees, fences, indoor/outdoor, bleachers, ups and downs.

On a signal, have the players move to the first obstacle from a starting line, and continue through the course without ever gripping their balloon.

- The balloon must remain airborne at all times.
- If the balloon touches the ground, the player either loses 15 seconds, or must

repeat the previous obstacle (their choice).

- No one is allowed to hit the balloon twice in succesion. (This applies only if you are playing as teams)
- If a balloon breaks, the player must reach into their pocket for the single spare held in reserve. Blow-up procedure follows and the steeplechase continues.
- If the second balloon breaks, that player is disqualified for the time being. "Time being," according to the bureau of weights and measurements is 150 seconds (151 seconds during a leap year).

Touch My Can

Object — For a group of about 15 students to make physical contact with an empty beer can without making physical contact with one another. Hair longer than 4" is not "recognized" by the rules committee as a portion of the body.

Circle the Circle

Ask your group to form a hand-in-hand circle. Place two hula hoops together between two people (resting on their grasped hands). See how quickly the people in the circle can cause the hoops to travel around the circle in opposite direc-

tions, through each other (i.e., hoop through hoop), and back to their originating position.

If you have a large group, use lots of hoops.

Hoop Relay

Halve the group and have each half form a queue facing you. The folks in this file should be holding hands front-to-back.

This relay requires two starters, each holding 3-4 hoops. Each starter, on a signal, begins the action by placing a hoop over the head of the first person in line and as soon as that hoop moves to the 3rd person in line, the 2nd hoop is started, etc. If the starters want to become part of the action, they simply start the last hoop and become the first person in line.

When the first hoop reaches the last person in line, that individual runs to the front of the line with the hoop, grabs the hand of the now 2nd person and starts the hoop moving toward the end of the line. Continue until the original front line person returns to that position.

The game can be made somewhat more difficult (physically and emotionally) by requiring that each person reach between his/her legs before grasping the hand of the person in front or in back of them. Come on Karl, be serious! Your choice . . .

Two In a Row

Using a piece of retired kernmantle climbing rope (a fifty foot section will do nicely) as a jump rope, ask a group to see how many people can make two consecutive jumps as a group without anyone missing. Twenty people is challenging, but certainly not impossible. There must be a world's record for this bouncy event: I've seen 30 people make two consecutive jumps, three actually.

Change "turners" occasionally to combat arm fatigue and to keep a consistent turn and arc. To be an effective and constant turner is a valued street skill.

The Turnstile   Ω

Using the same section of rope as above, begin turning at a slow rate and ask

the group to see if they can *all* get through the spinning rope from one side to another by:

- Going through *one at a time*.
- Making one jump as the rope turns.
- Not missing a beat of the rope between people.

If someone hesitates and the rope makes a turn without anyone in there to jump, the entire group must begin again.

Not a hard assignment for one person or two or three, but a cooperative and often frustrating group challenge.

When the group eventually achieves this goal, ask them to try the same chal-lenge, but this time to operate as pairs; i.e., they must make it through the spinning rope with a partner. As triplets?

#10 Tin-Can Foot Pass

Try to pass a #10 can (empty) from foot-to-foot (shoes on) around a seated people circle. That's it. GO! Time this event.

Variations:

- Shoes off
- Let the can touch the ground twixt feet.
- Use two cans and start them in oppo-site directions.

Chapter 6

Sit-Down, No-Sweat Activities

The Bow Knot - Everyone's Common Experience

Ask a few people to untie and retie their shoes (loafers and velcro users are excused), and note the different finger manipulations used to end up with what we accept as the common bow knot.

In these days of both parents' working and not as much classic parenting being done, many traditional learn-it-at-home skills have been shunted aside and either not learned or picked up, as we used to say in the Army, by OJT (on-the-job training, a common service acronym for whatever you learned by experience or military osmosis).

An exception to this pervasive learn-it-at-school attitude is the highly complex (if you make the mistake of trying to think about what your fingers are doing) knot arrangement that holds your shoes onto your feet — the bow. This kindergarten knot used to be taught by family and is as

sure an indication of your lineage as any other invalid ethnic or cultural touchstone.

Are the laces thrown across one another at the start? Definitely Germanic; or are the twin strands folded and placed just so? This purposeful start indicates French background and probably Freudian anal. If the laces are turned concurrently into two equal bights and tied directly together (the so-called Bunny Ears technique that's popular with harassed mommies that compassionately relate unsavory tasks and tastes to kitties, puppies, bunnies and iguanas), you might rightly suspect Italian or Scandinavian. Be aware, however, that there are some controversial theories extant concerning this ethnic grouping by digital dexterity. Academicians take note — here's a thesis topic that I'm sure no one has pursued and just in time for summer study: esoteric, dreary, and practically useless — perfect!

Come on, Karl, do I have to wade

through all this folderol just to find out what the game is? Yes, and since you're this far, don't complain, 'cause here we are at the start.

As I've said in past workshops, using speed contests for teaching knots is counterproductive and potentially dangerous. I can't think of a time, except in rescue situations, when it's necessary to tie a knot rapidly. But, speed contests relating as to who can tie their shoes the fastest provide 10-15 minutes of good-humored, fast-paced competition, the results of which don't depend upon a well-tied safety knot.

Designate a common starting position (1) laces draped toward the floor on each side of the shoe (2) one lace in each hand (3) the first overhand knot already tied, etc. Also indicate if this is a one or two shoe contest — the double shoe situation demanding more skill and conditioning, and not so much dependence on a couple of lucky moves.

A digital watch makes the contest more exacting and intense, as contestants often finish hundredths of a second in front or behind other competitors.

I've had a lot of fun with this simple activity and utilizing a non-serious approach, I'm sure you will, too.

Wordles

In recent workshops, I have been using these word puzzles more and more to avoid going outside during inclement weather, and somewhat more significantly to practice brainstorming techniques.

Make up a series of 3" x 5" cards as outlined in *Silver Bullets* (pg. 102). Rather than offering the small number of cards as suggested, for variety and for larger groups, make up about 30 wordle cards (one set for each group of 5-6), and offer the cards to the groups, announcing that they have 20

minutes to figure out as many as they are able. How they approach the actual problem is up to the group.

When time is up, have all the groups get together and share their solutions. Be prepared to allow more than one answer per card, because some of the responses prove to be as ingenious as the puzzles. Spend some discussion time talking about what technique the group found to be the most efficient in figuring out the various letter and symbol combinations.

Will students really sit still long enough to work together on these word problems? Have them look out the window at the collecting snow, puddling rain, etc., then suggest a few outdoor activities . . .

Here are 90 wordles that I gleaned from various game books. I'd like to say that I made some of these up, but although I enjoy the ingenuity inherent in wordles, I don't have a bent for creating them. I *did* make one up, however — it's #51 in *Silver Bullets* and #91 in this book. I apologize to anyone who made it up before I did — it's yours; no hassle -— don't sue me!

1.   GREENNV

2.   <u>10 J Q K A</u>
      FACTS

3.   __GO___
      JAN 6 FEB 3

4.   LOOK KOOL CROSSING

5.   SIDK DKIS

6.   HIS . TORY

7.   HE
    NOW RE

8.   <u>21 LB. 18 LB.</u>
      HAND FOOT

9. $\dfrac{I}{8}$

10. 1935 ALONG 1975 1983

11. PpOpD

12. ✓✓ ✓
    C O U N T E R

13. EILN PU

14. IT

15. SIGHT LOVE
    SIGHT
    SIGHT

16. HO
    HO
    + HO

17. .THAT'S

18. TILL IME

19. H-O-P-E-S

20. OFTEN
    OFTEN NOT
    OFTEN NOT

21. VAD ERS

22. 1/4 1/4 1/4 1/4 1/4

23. HAND
    HAND
    HAND
    DECK

24. F AR E FAR W

25. CY CY

26. SHRIF

27. T
    T
    + T

28. BUDGET
    ^

29. WIRE
    JUST

30. BALLO-T

31. COME CO

32. PERFORMANCE
    PERFORMANCE

33. COLOWME

34. CLOSE
    CLOSE
    CLOSE
    CLOSE

35. W. I

36. WEEKKKK

37. XQQQME

38. YUO'ER

39. NIRENDEVOUSGHT

40. COPI COPPY COPY

41. LEAN
    REVO

42. H/E/A/D

43. LET/GONES
    BE /GONES

44. LOI'MVE/YOU

45. SEA SON

46. $ $ IT

47. <u>HEAD</u>
    LHEOEVLSE

48. MOTH
    CRY
    CRY
    CRY

49. ME QUIT

50.   O
    M.D.
    Ph. D.
    L.L.D.

51. <u>ii ii</u>
    o o

52. <u>STAND</u>
      I

53. DICE
    DICE

54. O! — 144

55. LOYOUOK

56. CYCLE
    CYCLE
    CYCLE

57. KNEE
    LIGHT

58. GROUND
    FEET
    FEET
    FEET
    FEET
    FEET
    FEET

59. HE'S/HIMSELF

60. DOCTOR
    DOCTOR

61.   R
    ROAD
      A
      D

62. SIDE SIDE

63. YOU/JUST/ME

64. BAN ANA

65. <u>ONCE</u>
    A TIME

66. NOON LAZY

67. F   F
    R   R
    I STANDING I
    E   MISS   E
    N   N
    D   D
    S   S

68. RRRRRRR
    RRRRRRR
    RRRRRRR
    RRRRRRR
    RRRRRRR
    RRRRRRR
    RRRRRRR

69. <u>T I M E</u>
    ABDE

70. ED
    +<u>ED</u>

71. TIMING TIM ING

72. MCE
     MCE
     MCE

73. WHEATHER

74. ME NT

75. ALL world

76.   M
     DISHOES
          M

77. ECNALG

78. 2UM
    +2UM

79. H O

80. HIJKLMNO

81. IECEXCEPT

82. BJAOCKX

83. PAS

84. YOUR PaAnNTsS

85. GESG

86. ONE
     ONE

87. ISSUE ISSUE
     ISSUE ISSUE
     ISSUE ISSUE
     ISSUE ISSUE
     ISSUE ISSUE

88. NA FISH
     NA FISH

89. _____ IT

90. LAL

91. THHAENRGE

Wordle Answers

1. Green with envy
2. Hand over the facts
3. Go on a double date
4. Look both ways before crossing
5. Mixed up kids
6. A period in history
7. He came out of nowhere
8. Wait on hand an foot
9. I over ate
10. Along in years
11. Two peas in a pod
12. Check out counter
13. Line up in alphabetical order
14. It remains to be seen
15. Love at first sight
16. Tally-Ho
17. That's beside the point
18. Till the end of time
19. Dashed hopes
20. More often than not
21. Space invaders
22. Close quarters
23. All hands on deck
24. Few & far between
25. Cyclone
26. Short shrift
27. Teetotal
28. Balanced budget
29. Just under the wire
30. Absentee ballot
31. There's more to come
32. Repeat performance
33. Low income
34. Foreclose
35. I'm upset
36. Long weekend
37. Excuuuse me
38. You're confused
39. Midnight rendezvous

40. Copyright
41. Lean over backwards
42. Headquarters
43. Let bygones be bygones
44. I'm in love with you
45. Open season
46. Money market
47. Head over heels in love
48. Mothball
49. Quit following me
50. Three degrees below zero
51. Circles under the eyes
52. I understand
53. Paradise
54. Oh, gross!
55. Look around you
56. Tricycle
57. Moon light
58. Six feet under ground
59. He's beside himself
60. Paradox
61. Cross road
62. Side by side
63. Just between you and me
64. Banana split
65. Once upon a time
66. Lazy afternoon
67. Misunderstanding between friends
68. Forty-niners
69. Long time, no see
70. Added
71. Split second timing
72. Three blind mice
73. Bad spell of weather
74. Apartment
75. It's a small world after all
76. Mom breaking dishes
77. Backward glance
78. Forum
79. Half an hour
80. Water
81. i before e except after c
82. Jack-in-the-box
83. Incomplete pass
84. Ants in your pants

85. Scrambled eggs
86. One on one
87. Tennis shoe
88. Tuna fish
89. Blanket
90. All mixed up
91. Hang in there

Verbal Enigmas

This is an unusual month — Santa, snow and so on. This is an unusual paragraph too. How quickly can you find out *what is so uncommon about it?* It looks so ordinary that you may think nothing is odd about it until you match it with most paragraphs this long. If you put your mind to it and study it, you will find out, but nobody may assist you, or possibly may not want to. Go to work and try your skill at figuring it out. Par on this paragraph is about half an hour. Good luck — and don't blow your cool.

Answer — The letter E is not used anywhere in the paragraph. E is the most commonly used letter in the English language.

The F Words   Ω

When I recently read about this perception test, I knew what was expected, if not the exact answer; i.e., I knew the gimmick. I still came up with the wrong answer. And now that you're aware something is up, you had better look really closely at the following paragraph, because if you don't get the correct answer, I'll just have to say, "I told you so."

You have 30 seconds to read and study the following 16 word paragraph. During that time you are to determine how many times the letter F appears. GO!

FEATURE FILMS ARE THE RE-
SULT OF YEARS OF SCIENTI-
FIC STUDY COMBINED WITH
THE EXPERIENCE OF YEARS

Even after people are told the correct answer (most guesses are off by at least 2) they still cannot see all the Fs. How come? Gives you something to think about, and if there's more than one of you at the other end of this sentence, something to talk about.

The correct answer? Come on! Look *real* closely. You tell me. There's no trick, just F's.

Gooney Likes

Add this tricky word game to your collection of no-prop, sit-down, where's-the-key? games.

Begin by saying, Gooney likes the MOON, but he doesn't like the STARS. The object of the game is for your audience to guess why Gooney likes some things but doesn't like others. Gooney likes BILL, but he doesn't like JOHN. Gooney likes FEET, but he doesn't like SHOES. Gooney likes the color YELLOW, but he doesn't like BLUE.

Can you guess what the key is? Don't feel badly, it took me 15 minutes and a couple generous hints before I discovered the gimmick; Gooney likes gimmicks, too.

Gooney likes TOOLS, but he doesn't like GEAR. Gooney's favorite word is BOOKKEEPING. He likes BEER, but not BREW.

Gooney likes any word with double adjacent letters . . . LETTER, BOOK, SHEET, SOOT, etc. Ooh! That's SOO easy . . .

Caught Ya Peekin

This teensy game (*Gooney likes teensy*) may warm the cockles of your heart. The cockles are anatomically located just proximal to the mitral valve, and are largely responsible for flutters (ref. . . . "she caused my heart to flutter"). Cockles function better when warm.

Sit or stand in a circle so that everyone can see everyone. The object of the game is to catch someone with their eyes open. I'm not indicating that you should keep your eyes closed, just that if someone in the group sees you with your eyes open, they say, "Caught Ya Peekin." If this is an elimination game, you are then OUT, because you were caught with your eyes open. The game continues until only two or three people are left.

If you want to play the game so that no one is eliminated, just keep playing after you are caught, and continue the game until it's over; i.e., someone decides to change the game.

If, in a flash of intuitive insight, you determine that the best strategy in this game is to never close your eyes, you automatically win the "smarter-than-thou" award, and the silent condemnation of all those timid souls that play by the obvious rules. A Steve Butler game — which he plays very well.

Rainy Day Code Quiz

On a day when you would just as soon not be outside, pass out this list of crazy codes and ask small groups (3-4) to see how fast and accurately they can come up with correct decoded answers. This activity is not a test of any kind and shouldn't be presented as such; it's simply a way to provide an interesting sit-down topic that will encourage discussion, ideas and cooperation.

1. 101D
2. .22 CR
3. 10Y in a D
4. 186.280 MPS is the SOL
5. 7th IS
6. 10 - 4 GB
7. 7 W or the W
8. 52 C in a D
9. 4x4 is 4WD
10. 60 S in a M
11. 12M in a Y
12. 31 F in B's
13. 26 F at HJ
14. 9 out of 10 D recommend C with F
15. RADD 3 men in a T
16. 4 Q in a $
17. 11 M on a FBT
18. 1 BW in a gigawatt
19. The SR of 4 is 2
20. 99 B of B on the W
21. 26 L in the A
22. .44M = MMD
23. R & F of the 3rd R
24. 88 K on a P
25. 4 Q in in a G

Answers to Rainy Day Code Quiz

1. 101 dalmatians
2. .22 caliber rifle
3. 10 years in a decade
4. 186,280 miles per second is the speed of light
5. 7th inning stretch
6. 10-4 good buddy
7. 7 wonders of the world
8. 52 cards in a deck
9. 4x4 is 4 wheel drive
10. 60 seconds in a minute
11. 12 months in a year
12. 31 flavors at Brigham's
13. 26 flavors at Howard Johnson's
14. 9 out of 10 dentists recommend Crest with fluoride
15. Rub a dub dub, 3 men in a tub
16. 4 quarters in a dollar
17. 11 men on a football team
18. 1 billion watts in a gigawatt
19. The square root of 4 is 2
20. 99 bottles of beer on the wall
21. 26 letters in the alphabet
22. .44 magnum = make my day
23. Rise and fall of the Third Reich
24. 88 keys on a piano
25. 4 quarts in a gallon

Patience Puzzles

I had included some of these word puzzles in an earlier BOT's. I listed them because they made you think (not *too* hard) and the solutions were satisfying. Recently, I came across this bunch, but with a difference — no solutions were offered.

Not only was my cerebellum, et al., being titillated, but I was subtly challenged. So, I'm passing the list and the challenge on to you. My first time through I came up with 6-7 answers. Presently, there are still 6 that still have me stumped — but I'll get 'em — just a matter of time.

If you have no idea how these initialism enigmas work, the answer to #3 is: 8 <u>d</u>ays minus 24 <u>h</u>ours equals 1 <u>w</u>eek. *Of course!* "Truth is obvious after it's discovery." Have fun and don't tell me the answers.

1. M. + M. + N.H. + V.+ C. + R.I. = <u>N.E.</u>
2. "1B in the H. = 2 in the <u>B.</u>"
3. 8D. - 24H. = 1 <u>W.</u>
4. H.H. & M.H. at 12 = <u>N.</u> or <u>M.</u>
5. 3 <u>P.</u> = 6
6. 4J. + 4 Q + 4K = all the <u>F.C.</u>
7. S. & M. & T. & W. & T. & F.& S. are <u>D.</u> <u>of W.</u>

8.	A. + N. + A.F. + M.C. + C.G. = <u>A.F.</u>
9.	T. = <u>L.S.</u> State
10.	23 Y. - 3 Y. = <u>2D.</u>
11.	E. - 8 = <u>Z.</u>
12.	8 P. = 1 <u>G.</u>
13.	C. + 6 D. = <u>N.Y.E.</u>
14.	<u>S.R.</u> of N. = 3.
15.	A. & E. were in the <u>G. of E.</u>
16.	My F.L. & South P. are both <u>M.C.</u>
17.	"N.N. = <u>G.N.</u>"
18.	N. + P. + S.M. = <u>S.of C.</u>.
19.	1 + 6 Z. = 1<u>M.</u>
20.	B. or G. - F. -M. = 0
21.	"R. + R. + <u>R.</u>"
22.	A.L. & J.G. & W.M. & J.K. were all <u>A.</u>
23.	N. + V. + P. + A. + A. + C. + P. + I. = <u>P. of S.</u>
24.	S. + H. of R. = <u>U.S.C.</u>
25.	P. & N. & D. & Q. & H.D. were all <u>C.</u>
26.	Y. - S. - S. - A. = <u>W.</u>
27.	Y. + 2 D. = <u>T.</u>

Have You Ever . . . ? Ω

Here's how to use these *Have You Ever . . .* questions as part of an action packed get-to-know-you game.

Ask everyone to chair-up in a circle so that each seated player has a chair except you, and you're at circle center. There should be at least 6" between chairs.

Ask your best *Have You Ever . . .* question, remembering to emphasize that to ask a question, you have to have experienced what you are asking about. I can't ask, "Have you ever parachuted from a plane?", unless I had made a jump myself.

The seated people react to your question by answering either yes or no; a person answering YES answer must get up and find an empty chair, NO remains seated. The person in the center of the circle asking questions is also going to be looking for a chair, so that slow moving YES responders have a better than average chance of ending up in the center and finding themselves responsible for asking the next question.

No one is checking to see who answers YES or NO, so the game format allows each participant to play to their own level of comfort or enjoyment. Challenge By Choice? I'd have never guessed.

Emphasize compassion for one another so that dashing for an empty chair doesn't become a do-or-die flying leap that results in possible injury and spontaneous furniture dismantling.

If you don't have any chairs for the game, simply ask the standing players to grasp hands and continue that hand holding arrangement until a player answers YES. The gaps between vacated hands are quickly filled by fast moving players.

If the questioning begins to assume an obviously embarrasing tack, as facilitator, move slowly during the next seat race so that you end up in the center, and from there are able to redirect the questioning.

Some of the following 500+ questions are meant for adult groups. Choose your questions wisely, remembering there's only about 1/4 inch difference between appropriate and inappropriate.

For a small group (15 or so), a round of competition *Have You Ever . . .* might be just the thing. To begin, make sure that everyone has a seat in the circle; no one starts in the center. Questions can be asked by anyone. A YES response allows a single move (chair) to the right; NO stays where they are. The first person to move all the way around the circle and return to their own chair, **WINS**, and so does everyone else because that means it's time for the next game.

If someone moves into a chair that is already occupied by someone else (A NO responder), have a seat anyway; i.e., in their lap. Triple and quadruple lap sitting is not only commonplace, but feels good too.

Recognize this classic lap-to-lap moment as Kodak photo-op. #14.

Just to tempt you to take the WHOLE *Have You Ever...* test, my score for this list is 352 honest, affirmative responses. Scoring includes responding to questions with multiple answers.

What does a high score on this test indicate?

I don't know, but if you come up with a quasi-rational answer, don't tell anyone; I'd like to keep this test pure— pure fun I mean.

Have You Ever . . .

- been in a parade?
- eaten two raw oysters?
- been bitten by a dog (broken skin)?
- watched 4 VCR video movies in a row?
- participated at a nude beach?
- seen a moon bow?
- broken an established school athletic record?
- helped an animal give birth (not your wife)?
- been to a professional world championship game?
- viewed an autopsy?
- given a shot?

- taken blood with a hypodermic needle?
- performed CPR in an attempted life-saving situation?
- actually used the Heimlich maneuver in a life-threatening situation?
- developed and printed your own B&W film?
- free dived below 30 feet (no scuba gear)?
- swum 50 yards non-stop underwater?
- flown in a glider?
- operated a bulldozer?
- eaten — tripe; cow's tongue, pig's knuckles, brain, mountain oysters?
- seen 43 urinals in a row? (below)
- been within 25 feet of a bear in the wild?
- been to a high school reunion after 20 years?
- caught a wave with a surf ski?
- walked on stilts?
- written a "letter to the editor"?
- climbed a tree to rescue a cat?
- seen the rings of Saturn (not a photo)?
- seen a whale in the ocean?
- been within 25' of a shark in a natural setting (no boat or flotation device)?
- been towed aloft beneath a parasail?
- thrown a curling stone?
- been stopped for speeding?
- done push-ups in an airplane?

- traveled more than 1,000 miles continuously on a train?
- traveled more than 1,500 miles on a bus?
- stayed up all night studying?
- drank more than 10 cups of coffee in a 24 hour period?
- spun a hula hoop around your waist at least 20 times without stopping?
- snapped a leather bull whip?
- had an idea that was eventually used by thousands of people?
- written something that made you cry?
- shaved your legs?
- inadvertently flipped a canoe in 40° (plus or minus) water?
- done over 20 pull-ups (male), 10 pull-ups (female)?
- played catch with a raw egg until it broke? (below)
- as an adult, gone to a costume party in a costume?
- made love in a water bed?
- kept a piece of chewed gum overnight and chewed it again?
- been submerged in a submarine? (not Disneyworld)

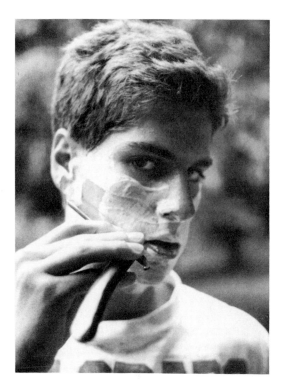

- fired a machine gun on full automatic?
- eaten fiddleheads?
- shaved with a straight razor (entire face or legs)? (photo above)
- eaten dandelion greens?
- used a breath-activated animal call; e.g., crow call?
- purposefully aimed a loaded gun at someone?
- worn a hand-tied bow tie?
- had a manicure?
- had a paid-for massage?
- owned a watch that cost more than $500?
- owned a watch that worked for more than 10 years?
- slept more than 14 hours straight (no chemicals or pills)?
- ridden a "century" on a bicycle?
- owned a bicycle that cost more than $1,000?

- held your breath for more than two consecutive minutes?
- done an inadvertent 360° spin in a braking car situation?
- kept a diary as an adult (over 12 months)?
- stayed in a motel/hotel that cost more than $100/night?
- shared a meal (2 people) for more than $100?
- tried a recreational drug?
- had a wart removed?
- had one of the following as an adult (over 21); whooping cough, diphtheria, chicken pox, measles, mumps?
- worked a night shift?
- had a job on a boat or ship at sea?
- seen a polar bear in the wild?
- seen a koala bear in the wild?
- seen a panda bear in the wild?
- been tied up as a restraining move?
- tried on a straight jacket?
- been to a morgue?
- ridden a multi-speed, muscle-powered tricycle?
- shot a crow?
- listened to a heavy metal album from beginning to end, non-stop?
- laid down in a casket?
- held someone's corporeal ashes?
- had altitude sickness?
- given blood?
- carried a pack weighing more than 60 lbs. for more than 5 continuous miles?
- cried because of a movie scene? a song? an aroma?
- had a parasitic infection?
- seriously pondered what quasars are expanding into?
- read at least two of Carlos Castenada's books on Don Juan?

read the following children's books?
- *The Black Stallion*
- *Black Beauty*
- *The Phantom Toll Booth*
- *Lad, a Dog*
- *Whitefang*
- *Superfudge*
- *The Lion, the Witch and the Wardrobe*

- taken a picture of your anatomy on a copying machine? (photo below)
- belonged to a national fraternity or sorority (Greek)?
- shot flies with a rubber band?
- had an IV administered?
- owned a BB gun?
- worked for less than $1.00 an hour (not babysitting)?
- read a complete book by kerosene or candle light?
- tithed?
- eaten frogs' legs?
- had a Mohawk haircut?
- colored your hair orange, green, purple,

or blue?

- purposefully jumped off something more than 10' high? (not into water)
- killed a songbird?
- returned an entree at a restaurant?
- owned a CB radio?
- volunteered a day's work as a service (no pay)?
- been to a chiropractor for an adjustment?
- been Rolfed?
- been to an EST seminar?
- been a participant (student) on a ropes course (excluding the military)? (photo)
- thrown a live hand grenade (pin pulled)?
- owned more than 10 credit cards at one time?
- participated as part of a real search and rescue scenario?
- won a state championship (not necessarily athletic)?
- drunk 16 ozs. of beer in one quaff (without taking a breath)?
- ordered something "flambe" in a restaurant (not a pupu platter)?
- bought and drank a bottle of Ripple or Thunderbird wine?
- worn lace?

- written a letter of more than 10 pages?
- made a long distance call of more than 10,000 miles?
- suffered from Montezuma's revenge?
- had heat exhaustion?
- had frostbite that caused blisters?
- treated someone with hypothermia?
- urinated outdoors in less than minus 20°F?
- experienced an outdoor shade temperature of more than 110°F?
- experienced an outdoor temperature of under -35°F? (no wind chill)
- been in every state of the U.S. (all 50)?
- built a fire on a frozen lake?
- slept on a frozen lake?
- made butter?
- made ice cream by hand (no electricity)?
- written something with an ink pen (not felt or ball point)?
- sat at a desk at school as a student that had an ink well with ink in it?
- ridden in a Rolls Royce?
- been to a double feature movie?
- owned a pair of white bucks?
- been to an opera?
- seen a stage play in NYC?
- been to a pro game in at least three major sports?

- fallen more than 15 feet onto an unyielding surface?
- sanded an entire hardwood floor?
- been in a yurt? (photo above)
- spun wool?
- been a bartender at a commercial bar?
- had your hair styled?
- refinished a piece of furniture?
- owned more than one cat at a time?
- tried a Nautilus workout?
- hitchhiked over 200 miles?
- jumped a train?
- totaled your car?
- forgotten a good friend's name when introducing her/him?
- wallpapered a room?
- painted a house (exterior)?
- seen a living amoeba?
- thrown any object more than 300' (not downhill)?
- eaten an entire meal using chopsticks?
- swum a mile in ocean water?
- paddled an open canoe at least one mile off shore (ocean)?
- drunk at least 25 different imported beers (not at once)?
- gotten intoxicated on grain alcohol (190 proof)?
- dug up a human skeleton?
- owned a Rolex watch?
- owned a pair of "penny" loafers and put a penny in them?
- carried more than $5,000 in cash?
- reduced your waistline by more than 6"?
- lost more than 50 lbs. of body weight?
- been stuck in an elevator for more than 8 minutes?
- walked to the top of the Washington Monument?
- worn braces on your teeth?
- had your initials entered on a commercial game computer as one of the best ten scores?
- spent more than $10.00 on computer games in one day?
- operated a motorcycle?
- driven a 16 wheeler?
- ridden a unicycle more than 100 yards without falling?
- heard the "buzzing of the bees" during an electrical storm?
- confronted a stranger because of something they were doing (breaking in

line, hitting a child, etc.)?

- ridden a bicycle more than 750 miles on a trip? (photo below)
- missed a plane?
- stayed out all night, as a minor?
- had the "whirley beds"?
- meditated regularly with results?
- spent over 24 hours without seeing or talking to another person?
- gone 24 hours without eating anything?
- bleached your hair (even partially)?
- swallowed a raw egg straight from the shell?
- done a one-arm chin-up?
- flown in a helicopter?
- been in a dance contest?
- ridden a bicycle up a hill longer than 5 miles, non-stop?
- ignored a ringing phone (no recorder screening allowed)?
- climbed a ladder more than 50' high?
- had to have a tetanus shot because you stepped on a rusty nail?
- hit a golf ball more than 300 yards?

- had 5 pieces of bubble gum in your mouth at one time?
- read a book of over 1,000 pages?
- been a Boy or Girl Scout?
- bought a copy of *The Joy of Sex*?
- had a subscription to Playboy or Playgirl magazine?
- typed over 60 w.p.m.?
- spoken a foreign language fluently?
- rented an XXX rated movie?
- wondered where the numerals and letters came from in a digital watch?
- shaved your head?
- had acne?
- ditched a blind date?
- had a tooth pulled?
- bush-whacked 5 miles (no trails)?
- walked in the woods nude (shoes allowed)?
- tried hang-gliding? (photo above)
- flown in an ultra-light?
- received a belt other than white in Karate, or one of the other martial arts?
- run at least two continuous miles in soft sand?
- bench-pressed your own weight?
- tried roller skis?
- had poison ivy on your genitals?
- had a dog lift his leg on you?
- had a dog try to mate with your leg?
- been bitten by a human (broken skin)?

- been knocked out?
- cracked a windshield with your head?
- lost your driver's license?
- owned a car that cost more than $30,000?
- had a ride in a Model A or T Ford?
- spun a doughnut with a motorcycle?
- run a mile in less than 6 minutes?
- lost over $100 in cash?
- played a game that involved taking off your clothes?
- climbed a building façade (bottom to top)?
- owned a knife that cost more than $100?
- been more than 300' below the earth's surface?
- raised bees?
- stayed back a year at school?
- had a marriage proposal turned down?
- turned down a marriage proposal?
- eaten an entire apple — seeds, core, and all?
- owned a Cuisinart?
- purchased wall-to-wall carpeting?
- water skied on one ski?
- gone over a jump on water skis?
- dived using a helium mixture?
- had to make decompression stops on the way up from a deep dive?
- dived under ice with scuba gear?
- caught an octopus by hand?
- spent the entire night in a (a) bus terminal (b) train station (c) airport?
- had part of your body tattooed?
- broken a window purposefully as a vandal?
- played stickball on a city street?
- ridden on the outside of a trolley?
- used skates that needed a key?
- been so nervous that you threw up?
- cut an entire lawn using a push lawn mower (no engine)?
- moved more than a "yard" of dirt by hand (shovel, only)?
- buried a treasure and made a map?

- been to an Outward Bound school as a student?
- been an OB instructor?
- climbed inside a commercial clothes dryer?
- slid down a laundry chute?
- driven a vehicle on a frozen lake?
- seen St. Elmo's Fire?
- seen the Aurora Borealis?
- seen foxfire?
- seen a true mirage?
- ridden on a steam-powered train?
- ridden on a camel?
- seen real quicksand?
- competed for prize money in a sport?
- seen lightning during a snow storm?
- been aboard a Navy warship (while commissioned)?
- watched the sunrise in a foreign country?
- travelled outside the U.S. to work?
- been refused entry to a foreign country?
- been in a crowd of more than 40,000 people?
- performed a magic trick before an audience (not family or friends)?
- owned a cowboy hat as an adult?
- made a piece of functional furniture?
- done a flip off a diving board?
- worn your hair to your shoulders (male)?
- gone six months without shaving (male); your legs (female)?
- been in a crevasse?
- used an ice axe for climbing ice or snow?
- placed a piton?
- counted to 1,000 just for the heck of it?
- written out a googol?
- played Monopoly where somebody won in less than 30 minutes?
- experienced tear gas?
- lived in a dorm?
- lived in a condemned building?
- swung on a rope from one point to

another that covered more than 30 horizontal feet ?

- worn an article of clothing regularly for more than 20 years?
- had a tire blow out at over 55 mph?
- carried the same knife for over 10 years?
- said, "You can do it," to someone, knowing that they probably can't?
- put a bumper sticker on your car that has a heart on it?
- said, "Go for it" when you knew that you probably wouldn't?
- swung on a rope and let go into water?
- struck out in bowling?
- slept between satin sheets?
- gone to sleep during a college (university) class?
- been chased by an animal (not a human or dog)?
- been in a sanctioned bike race?
- competed in a national championship?
- competed in a world championship?
- strung barbed wire?
- been dumped on (fecal contact made) by a seagull or the like?
- observed a bird of prey in a stoop?
- owned a DeSoto, Packard, or Studebaker? An Edsel?
- surfed (board or body) in waves over 10'?
- undergone fraternity hazing; i.e., "hell week"?
- eaten a Twinkie? eaten two Twinkies?
- gone a week without using deodorant?
- been able to spell hors d'oeuvre or hemorrhage?
- been accused of having an accent?
- paid extra money for a vanity plate?
- sold a painting done by yourself (not to family)?
- been on a TV game show?
- seen the movie, Psycho?
- dived into a swimming pool and lost your shorts or top, as the case may be?
- soloed in an airplane?

- won an official eating or drinking contest?
- run a toll booth?
- attended a parochial school?
- seen someone break a world's record (not on TV)?
- performed an athletic task at 30 years old plus, better than when you were 20?
- stayed up for 48 consecutive hours?
- gone to sleep at the wheel and ended up off the road?
- changed the oil and filter in your car?
- owned a comic book that cost 10 cents?
- purchased a mail box?
- hot-wired a vehicle?
- driven while so drunk that you don't know how you arrived at your destination?
- spilled a hot cup of coffee in your lap while driving?
- driven a vehicle over a mile in reverse? (not in a circle)
- owned a pair of sunglasses that cost more than $75 (non-prescription)?
- broken the posted speed limit by more than 40 m.p.h.?
- hit 15 consecutive free throws with a basketball (not necessarily in a game)?
- gone more than 100 miles out of your way because of a map reading or directional error?
- rolled an automobile over, or have been in one that has rolled over?
- been the first person to give aid at an auto accident?
- lighted a flatulation, or have seen it done?
- tried to use a dowsing rod?
- bought a cup of coffee or Coke for a nickel (not a special)?
- bought a condom in a men's room?
- jumped off a bridge into water?
- used a glass-cutter?
- paid more than $8 for a six-pack of beer?
- won or lost more than $50 gambling?

- found more than $50 in cash?
- driven a car with opposite hand drive for more than 5 miles?
- written a poem? (not an assignment)
- had snowblindness to any degree?
- been in mud up to your waist? (photo)
- seen a flying squirrel "fly"?
- gone through a stop sign at over 30 m.p.h.?
- flown first class?
- set off a fire alarm on purpose (the kind that requires breaking glass)?
- eaten a sit-down meal and discovered that you had no money to pay for it?
- chewed on a piece of raw sugar cane?
- taken the husk off a coconut?
- pretended to be Superman (has to include the cape)?

been on top of:

- Sears Tower? (Chicago)
- Statue of Liberty? (New York)
- Empire State Building? (New York)
- Trade Center? (New York)
- Prudential Building? (Boston)
- St. Louis Arch? (Missouri)
- Space Needle? (Seattle)
- CN Tower? (Toronto)

- started a fire without matches or a lighter (not just smoke)?
- speared a fish while snorkeling?
- cut down a 12" minimum diameter tree with a chain saw?
- slept outdoors two weeks in a row?
- paddled a open canoe in Class III water?
- been above the Arctic Circle or below the Antarctic Circle? (not in a plane)
- fired a .44 magnum pistol?
- butchered, cleaned and eaten a fowl?
- had to personally kill a dog or cat for humane reasons?
- done needlepoint?
- climbed a mountain over 12,000 feet?
- cross-country skied with a pack (tent, sleeping bag, etc.)?
- made love outdoors (no tent or tarp)?
- been 50' up in a tree?
- knitted a sweater?
- fallen through ice at least to your waist?
- parachuted from a plane?
- rolled a kayak successfully; i.e., 360°?

- completed a marathon (26 miles)?
- successfully climbed a 5.6 (minimum) pitch?
- soloed in a wind surfer for over 1/2 mile?
- streaked at a gathering? (photo at right)
- competed in an organized triathlon?
- seen an animal underwater bigger than yourself (not at Seaworld)?
- been mugged?
- fired a 12 gauge shotgun?
- seen a child being born (not a movie)?
- been in a coed nude sauna or hot tub?
- been across the International Date Line?
- crossed the equator in a boat?
- slept out overnight in less than 0°F temperatures?
- had morphine administered for pain relief?
- broken a bone?
- won a medal or trophy in competition (25 years or older)?
- held a live poisonous snake in your hands? (photo below)
- milked a cow or a goat?

- ridden a horse bareback?
- been near death?
- made an impulsive purchase for more than $1,000?
- cheated on your income tax return?
- made an obscene gesture at someone while driving your car?

Photo by Dan Madden

- caught a fish that weighed more than 25 lbs.?
- written a fan letter?
- touched a live electric fence? (photo above)
- driven or ridden on a motorcycle at over100 m.p.h.?
- saved someone's life (other than drowning)?
- jumped into the water from over 35'?
- rappelled over 165'?
- driven a one-owner car over 150,000 miles?
- driven over 1,000 miles in one day (24 hours)?
- eaten 1/2 gallon of ice cream at one sitting?
- seen a human die violently (not on film)?
- seen an iceberg (at least automobile size)?
- taken an ocean dip in January-February on the New England coastline (complete immersion, no wet suit, etc.)?
- made up a game that you play regularly?
- gone ten years without seeing a son/daughter? mother/father?
- done silk screening?
- gone to bed before midnight on New Year's Eve (after your 21st birthday)?
- smashed an alarm clock?
- stolen a motel towel?

- told a smoker, face to face, that you *do* object to his/her smoking?
- built a doghouse?
- met a movie celebrity?
- driven at over 100 m.p.h. for over five minutes?
- hopped a freight?
- flattened a penny on a railroad track? flattened a penny and a nickel together?
- written some serious graffiti in a public place?
- had gum stuck in your hair?
- mooned someone? been mooned?
- had an out-of-body experience?
- taken a ride on/in a shopping cart as an adult (in store only)?
- tried a pinch of Skoal twixt your cheek and gum?
- been transported as a patient in an ambulance?
- run over a dog?
- eaten canned dog food? eaten canned cat food?
- removed a bottle cap with your teeth?
- shingled a roof?
- worn a gold chain (male)?
- been hit by a car as a pedestrian?
- written a letter on birch bark?
- cut down a 12" minimum diameter tree with an axe?
- taken a dip through lake or ocean ice?
- played Santa Claus for a group other than family?
- been to an auction and bid on something over $50?
- cut and split a cord of wood?
- hiked 20 miles in one day?
- been on a rollercoaster that turns upside-down?
- played a musical instrument in front of an audience (not family)?
- flown in an airplane for more than 8 hours non-stop?
- appeared on live network television (not tape)?
- had an acupuncture treatment?

- travelled in a communist country?
- had something you've written published?
- had a loaded gun pointed at you?
- had to stay in a hospital for longer than two consecutive weeks?
- ridden on a bicycle-built-for-two?
- been involved in a barroom altercation?
- spoken to a group of more than 200 people?
- driven a car across the United States more than once?
- scuba dived below 50'?
- seen a bat in a cave?
- had a blind date?
- passed out from excessive alcohol consumption?
- punched anyone in anger (adult)?
- had a root canal?
- showshoed?
- been to a black tie function?
- spent a night in jail?
- fired a compound bow?
- rafted Class 5 white water?
- been on a glacier?
- been to 7 different countries?
- seen an active volcano?
- coasted downhill on a bike at over 50 m.p.h.?
- discussed evolution with a fundamentalist?
- experienced a paranormal event?

Additional suggestions for the use of these questions . . .

- As an icebreaker: These simple answers/questions lead to shareable "war stories" that lead to other war stories, etc. Everyone seems to have an adventure vignette that serves as an invitation to further friendly and listenable can-you-top-this? stories.
- Use as a means to stimulate discussion or initiate creative writing attempts in an academic setting. This can be achieved by handing out a list pertinent to your age or experience group (you choose) or by asking students to verbally answer a series of *Have you ever . . . ?* questions.
- Verbally ask the questions, then ask the participants to raise a hand if they answer yes to a question. In this way, all the participants can see who has done what, and it also allows sharing of certain poignant experiences, if the person with their hand raised wishes to share the experience: *Challenge By Choice.*
- In your instructions, don't forget to add that raising hands is voluntary from question to question, so that if a particular query is impositional, embarrassing or objectionable, no one need feel obliged to respond.
- Don't try to figure out a reason why or how these questions have been sequenced, because there is none. The questions are randomly listed with absolutely no psychological or psychiatric intent . . . just fun, mates.
- Make up your own list or series of questions, or adapt these, to best fit your audience or demographic needs. There are approximately 510 questions in this extensive anthology.

No Competition Scenarios

Impulse Ω

This lightning-fast, hand-holding game is suitable for practically any age level, and particularly for a group that likes to compete against itself.

Ask your group to form a hand-in-hand circle around you. A larger group, in this case, will observe more taking place as the impulse travels the circle and will usually have more fun than a smaller group — say 30 versus 10.

Using a stopwatch (can you believe those electronic LCD watches? — flashing rapid-fire numbers from who knows where and accurate to 1/100 of a second. Functional and oozing mystique — what a deal!), time how long it takes to send a hand squeeze impulse around the circle. Ask an individual in the circle to start the impulse and to simultaneously say *"GO"* and, eventually, *"STOP"* when the impulse returns.

Repeat the attempt a number of times to see how much the group can improve their speed (cooperation, physical reaction, anticipation, efficiency). Vary the activity by trying the same thing with everyone's eyes closed and compare times. Additionally, ask the initiator to start the impulse going in both directions at once by squeezing his right and left hands simultaneously. See if the impulses can pass through one another, or if they get lost at the juncture.

Circle-centered impulses can be passed in a variety of other ways. Slaps, bumps, smacks, whistles — this can be a very intense experience. Experiment!

Clap Wave

Circle up, Podners! I mean, line up in a circle, then start a clap wave. You clap, then the person next to you (right or left, doesn't matter), then the person next to the person next to you, etc., etc. This sequenced clapping has to be done quickly, you know . . . like a wave.

Let the wave travel around the circle a few times in order to establish the rhythm. Try reversing the wave in mid flow. Try clap waving with everyone's eyes closed.

Now that you have the idea (the zen of undulation), try initiating the following sounds and movements.

- Two or three claps in sequence
- Stomping and clapping alternated
- Whistling
- Make up sounds and movements
- Send two different sounds in opposite directions

Handicapped Lunch

A gustatorially masochistic idea from Loraine Baxter, at Sarasota Palms Hospital in Florida. You have to experience this one to believe it.

First Task — Pair-up before lunch.

Lunch should require some assembly, such as making sandwiches, ice cream sundaes, etc. One member of each pair is blindfolded. The other member cannot use his/her hands.

Second Task — To eat lunch.

The two handicapped team members must obviously help one another to locate the food, put it together, and eventually get it into their mouths.

Since this is a working lunch, allow enough time for sufficient preparation, civilized eating, and fun. To quote Loraine, ". . . not only is the attainment of the goal its own primary reinforcer, it's also a great spectator sport."

You Tear Me Up

Ask your group to either put on blindfolds, or close their eyes (*challenge by choice*) for this exercise. The blindfold (eyes closed) participants are not allowed to ask questions, but can talk freely among themselves.

Hand each participant a sheet of paper that is equal in size, and ask them to sequentially:

(1) *fold the paper in half and tear off the bottom right hand corner.*
(2) *Fold the paper in half again and tear off the upper right hand corner.*
(3) *Fold the paper in half again and tear off the lower right hand corner.*

OK, eyes open and compare the results. Just a simple exercise to emphasize how people interpret ambiguous instructions, allowing Murphy's law full rein. Ambiguous directions produce disparate results.

If you follow the above directions, is there a right way or wrong way to fold and tear the sheet of paper, Murphy notwithstanding?

Now, line up in a circle, and face each other back to back.

Body English

A group tries to spell out a well known word by using their bodies as letters. (Forming letters with the fingers is not allowed — too easy.) Another group tries to decipher what the first group is trying to say. The groups switch roles from time to time so that everyone gets the chance to be histrionic

and contorted. *Body English* encourages discussion, decision-making, cooperation, and laughter.

Categories   Ω

After you have been in the adventure education business for awhile, someone will eventually ask, "I hear that you do a good job facilitating groups, could you plan something significant for my weekend group?" Being a nice person, and responding to their flattery, you say, "Sure, this weekend would be fine. How many people are in your group?" "Well, quite a few are away this weekend, so we shouldn't have more than 80 or 90."

AArgh! Gulp! HELP!!!

Here's two suggestions: (1) Don't work with groups larger than 25. (2) If you *have to*, start your large group session with *Categories*.

Ask the large group (If there are more than 200 people, you may have to use a loud speaker. Don't look at me . . . you got yourself into this.) to separate quickly into smaller groups that you are about to announce. Alternate 50/50 splits (only two groups) with multi-groups (many choices).

Be upbeat and directive in your presentation; keep the groups moving. As soon as the milling around has slowed and distinctly smaller groups have established themselves, give the participants only time enough to look at one another, say hi, then announce the next categorical split.

The following list is extensive and much larger than you would want to use during one presentation. When I'm "doing" Categories I seldom present more than 10-12 groupings. Look through the list and pick those categories that appeal most to you. Be careful not to use an inappropriate choice considering the age or maturity level of the recipients. Deciding who scrunches or folds toilet paper might not be the best idea for a middle school group. (See photo next page)

Categories List

- Clasp your hands and fold your thumbs. Is your right or left thumb on top?
- Fold your arms. Is your right or left arm on top?
- Have someone look at your eyes and tell you what color they are.
- Which leg do you put in your pants (shorts) first?

- Are you wearing jewelry? Wrist watches and wedding rings don't count.
- When you clap, is your right or left hand on top? Parallel hands?
- When you tap your foot to music, do you use the right or left foot?
- Do you print or use cursive when you write a letter?
- Using your index finger as a pencil, draw an imaginary circle in the air. Does your finger travel clockwise or counter clockwise?
- Again, using your index finger as a pencil, draw a profile of a dog on the desk top. Is the dog facing right or left?
- Which is your dominant eye? (Provide dominant eye test procedure)
- With which eye do you give a spontaneous wink?
- Thinking of clearing a ditch or low fence, off which leg do you jump?
- Standing, facing the foot of the bed, on which side do you get in? Which side do you sleep on, if you sleep with someone else?
- What is your shoe size?
- What month were you born in?
- Can you roll your tongue? Can you turn your tongue upside down?
- What is your astrological sign?
- What is your blood type?
- After a store purchase, do you count your change or not?
- How many blood related siblings are there in your family counting yourself?
- After taking bread out of the bread bag, how do you reseal the bag? Spin? Fold? Which direction do you spin the bag? Or, do you spin just the top?
- When you apply a "twistie" to the top of a plastic bag, do you turn the twistie clockwise or counterclockwise?
- When you lick an ice cream cone, which way do you rotate the cone?
- When standing casually with your hands in your pockets, are they in your front or back pockets?
- Men. Do you carry your wallet in your right or left back pocket?
- Do you pull toilet paper off the top or bottom of a roll? Remember to establish a don't care category.
- Are you a scruncher or a folder—toilet paper? (photo)
- What color underwear do you have on right now? Make sure to signify a no underwear category.
- Do you pronounce tomato with a long or short a? Same question with aunt?
- When you insert your mail into a mail box, do you check to see if the mail has dropped, or do you just pop the envelopes into the slot and leave?
- When you sit on your hands to warm them, are your palms up or down? This one could have some serious implications.
- Do you pick up pennies from the ground or ignore them?
- Do you shower primarily in the morning or at night?
- Is your auto's gas cap on the left or right of the car (driver's seated orientation)?

- When you perform the isometric exercise of trying to pull your joined hands apart, is your right or left hand on top?
- Do you shave primarily with a blade or an electric razor (depilatories don't count)?
- Do you generally wear auto seat belts or not? Do you put the seat belt on before or after you begin driving?
- When you ride a bike, do you wear a helmet?
- If someone asks you to turn around, which way do you turn?
- When you sit down on the ground, which hand touches the ground first? When you get up do you use the same hand?
- Which way do you swirl liquid in a glass (brandy in a snifter)?
- When you open an envelope, do you use a letter opener (knife), or tear it open?

Bombs Away

I hesitate reporting on this oral debacle because, despite the funny results, the activity itself is demeaning and, in fact, has been (probably still is) used as a fraternity hell-week harassment. (The photo below was taken in 1956 as part of my own college hell-week experience.) But after receiving a letter from Bill Hallowell relating how much summer campers enjoyed his modified approach — well, here it is in its 1950's unexpurgated form and Bill's more acceptable fun format.

Hell Week Variation

Inject (hypodermic needle) a raw egg with asfedida (spelling is probably wrong, as this is a phonetic attempt at a word I haven't used in 30 years). Asfedida has the salubrious effect of immediately rotting albumen and yolk, and producing an appropriate foul odor.

The trick (bad joke) is to drop (10-20 ft.) the liquid part of the altered egg into the oral cavity of a coerced kneeling person. (See photo) This is *NOT* an activity to engender trust and compassion, but (and I hesitate to admit it), the results are very funny — if your oral cavity is the one not being used as a target.

The above scenario has been recorded only for its historical significance. The author suggests trying the following set-up in a camp situation for some obvious fun. As presented here, the activity is an end in itself, but could easily be included in a game or as a benign consequence for doing something wrong in the game.

Jello Drop

"We do a Jello Drop at summer camp each year and it is very popular with the 8-13 year-old group. Although they may not readily admit to it, the counselors have a blast with it, too.

Materials:

1. A pan of Jello (any flavor) cut into cubic inch blocks.
2. Elevated platform (baseball backstop, step ladder, low roof).

Once set up, this is an easy, fun activity requiring cooperation, coordination, and a steady mouth. The dropper climbs up any elevated platform with the pan of Jello (pre-cut) in hand. S/he carefully drops one cube at a time into the wide open mouth below. A ten foot drop makes for a good splat when the catcher is off by an inch. A large group of spectators/participants makes it fun, because everyone ends up laughing at each other. Once I had half a cube dribble down the inside of my T-shirt. The other half was dangling between my teeth and lower lip.

Try it . . . you'll love it."

Funnel Your Fun

While I was attending college in the late '50's, it was the rage to fire water balloons from one side of the football stadium to the other amid beery shouts and high-pitched distaff shrieks. Being more often a target than a perpetrator, I missed out on how a water balloon could be fired such a long distance. Rumors of rubber bands and angles of incidence were appealing, but so were the initiators of high-pitched shrieks, so my ballistic education remained unfulfilled.

My next exposure to ballistic ballooning was in Boston, as members of rival skulling crews fired balloons at one another on the Charles River — a formidable distance. I was once again at the receiving end (a spectator, actually).

During the first years with *Project Adventure* (early '70's), there was much physical and academic curriculum experimenting going on. One of the more interesting ideas was to make Physics 101 less text-oriented and more hands-on. Pupils would venture out to the ropes course and determine qualitative and quantitative values of such erudite items as height of elements, mass of logs, mechanical advantages of pulley systems and levers, etc. As part of this in-depth academia, a potential Pulitzer Prize winner suggested firing water balloons for distance on the football field to determine how mass, parabolic arcs and inertia affected accuracy. (I'll admit the cognitive aspect was a bit shaky, but we're pursuing the fun/function formula here.) The results were entirely nonacademic and inconclusive, as students joyfully committed themselves as non-moving targets to prove their nebulous findings. Also, the use of football goalposts and bicycle tires as a slingshot combination did not provide the impressive distance results I had previously observed.

Finally, as the result of a recent *Foes & Questors* game, I have the formula for sure-fire, hyperthrust, long distance, slingshot water ballooning. Two game participants (Joan and Phil) brought a new weapon that they wanted to introduce and as the result of an impromptu, long-distance demo, the other players enthusiastically accepted what was soon called a "Funnelator." This slingshot device was capable of firing small water balloons over 100 yards. Impressed? Here's how.

You need two 10 ft. slections of 5/16" diameter surgical tubing (sells for about $.43/ft.), a large plastic auto oil funnel with a long neck, and many penny balloons.

Drill the upper lip of the funnel (5"-6" diameter top) with a 1/2" drill bit on both sides of the circumference so that the 5/16" tubing can be inserted and tied off with an overhand knot. Slip a 3/8" slug washer over the tubing end before inserting and tying this knot.

Have two people hold the separate surgical tube sections (the slingshot) over their heads and stand 6'-8' ft. apart. A third person (making up the Funnelator team) places a small, water-filled balloon into the funnel and gripping the long neck, pulls it back and down (down to gain a higher arc), and releases smoothly.

If the two rubber band holders are able to stand on benches, step ladders or someones back (piggy back style), the balloon can be launched at a higher arc to achieve greater distance.

It's a good idea to fill the funnel hole with putty (or whatever) to prevent an occasional flashback of water as the balloon breaks because of too rapid acceleration.

If some of you extremists are not pleased with the 100 yard distance, purchase another set of tubing, drill another set of adjacent holes in the same funnel, and prepare for FAA regulations of your missile.

Contests from opposite ends of a football field, with more than two sets of Funnelator teams functioning, provide cooling competition on a hot day.

Considerations:

- Do not fire a Funnelator directly at another person; i.e., no arc. A ballistic water balloon packs a big punch.
- Tie a knot in the end of each section of tubing to provide a firm grip for the holder.
- Check the tubing for tears, particularly near the knot/funnel contact area.

Funnelating is an end in itself — don't worry about reasons for doing it.

Jack & Jill

My mother taught me this silly scenario years and years ago, and considering its entertainment potential for young children, I think it's worth learning. If you have children or work with children, they will like this — it plays better than it reads.

Take a small, ripped-off piece of tissue paper (toilet tissue or Kleenex-type, about the size of your fingernail), moisten it with some saliva, and stick it to the nail of your index finger. Do the same thing with your other index finger. Don't get bogged down by neatness — any ole torn piece will do.

Sit down and rest your hands (index fingers extended) on your knees. There is a little dialogue that accompanies the imminent action, and it goes like this:

"Two little blackbirds sitting on a fence; one named Jack (wiggle the right index finger) and one named Jill (wiggle the other index finger)." "Fly away, Jack!" (lift your right hand rapidly to a position behind your head and simultaneously exchange and extend your middle finger for the index finger. Then, as rapidly, bring your hand back down to your knee. All this is done in one smooth action. The middle finger is now extended with no tissue attached, and the index finger with tissue affixed is held tucked under the hand.

"Fly away, Jill!" (Perform the same procedure with the left hand.)

"Come back, Jack!" (Switch fingers of the right hand again by raising the hand as before and making the switch behind your head. Now the tissue is again apparent.)

"Come back, Jill!" (Same return sequence with the left hand.)

This covert digital display will amaze and mystify young boys and girls, and they'll want you to do it again and again before they figure out what the trick is. Older children (our age) may also be initially baffled, but usually won't admit it.

I just timed the whole Jack Magic sequence and it takes me about 15 seconds from start to end.

A nifty trick that I'm pleased to pass along. Thanks, Mom.

Existential Volleyball

This funny title indicates nothing more than good ole *Moonball* with a goal orientation.

The group (any size) divides in half and faces one another over a line (rope on the ground, painted gym line, etc.). The announced object is to score points for your team by hitting the beach ball over the line and onto the opponent's turf, but the hidden scenario involves more magic motion than competition, as evidenced by the following lack of rules. (Paradoxically, it often takes more words to define less rules.)

1. Any hit over the line must pass the line on the level or while ascending; i.e., no downward hits (spiking).
2. The ball can be hit as many times on a side as deemed necessary by a team.
3. There are no side or end boundaries.
4. Anyone can serve from any position.
5. Rotating players is either allowed, not allowed, or partially allowed.
6. There is no such thing as "carrying the ball," except when you actually carry the ball.
7. Rules can be modified to include a one-bounce-on-the-floor variation.
8. Any part of the body can strike the ball. Foot serves are particularly impressive and non-effective.
9. If point-keeping seems more significant than pure excellence of play, bombastically announce a change of serve after every point. Lower your voice an octave and exclaim, "Side out!" while pointing toward one of the teams with one hand and holding the other hand overhead with three fingers extended. If anyone asks what you are doing, say, "Your ad, serving two" . . . gets 'em every time.

Final Point Clarification — To win, a team must be ahead by two points when 53 points is reached. Keep things moving by alternating answers (yes or maybe) to all players' questions.

Tattoo

It's hard to appreciate the use or enjoyment of this multi-ball activity unless you become involved, but the activity satisfies a need for movement, accomplishment, and personal satisfaction, in addition to being more totally kinetic and visual than any other group activity I can think of, besides rock 'n roll.

Give each participant (10-50 people) 3-4 rabid nuggets (tennis balls) and ask them to arrange themselves behind the mid-line of an indoor basketball court; facing toward

one of the backboards. (For this throwing sequence to work, there must be a wall behind the backboard; i.e., no bleachers.)

Indicate that on GO, they are to aim and throw their hardest in order to hit the basketball backboard, and continue throwing, attempting to produce a drum-like "tattoo" sound on the backboard. After firing their initial nuggets, they must nab a rebounding ball or 2 or 3 and continue this fire-at-will mêlée.

All the nuggets will not rebound back to the throwers, so a couple volunteers must position themselves somewhere under the backboard to retrieve stray projectiles. Being a retriever is not as crazy as it sounds, since all the throwers are aiming well above the downcourt volunteers' heads. A ricochet might bounce off your head or body, but the potential and minor consequences make the "under fire" position more attractive.

Let the action continue for a couple minutes. The sound and movement are rewards in themselves. In addition: (1) Those people who like to throw and throw well can "chuck" as many balls as hard as they want to and cheer their own efforts and accuracy (because no one else is paying attention or can tell who's throwing what where). (2) Those folks who can't throw well can either throw a few nuggets or none at all without fear of censure, because (as above) nobody's watching *their* efforts.

After things slow down a bit (2-3 minutes), ask each person to retrieve and hold a couple nuggets. Indicate that you want to start the same activity, but this time by throwing with the other arm (opposite their adept one). The results are humbling and laughable. Almost everyone does poorly, except the ambidextrous few, so reluctance to try is quickly put aside. After 30 seconds of high arced and poorly aimed throws (and much good-natured ribbing), let them finish up with a few *good ones* by letting them return to their natural throwing arm.

Nugget Alternatives

1. Ask a nuggeted group, standing at one end of the basketball court (backs against the wall) if they can hit the far wall with a ball thrown by their "opposite" arm. After a few attempts (some success, some not), let them finish up with a couple throws with their "good" arm.

2. Request that everyone pair up for the next activity, the "Howitzer Throw." The object of this command/response bit of cooperation is to have one participant tell his/her blindfolded (eyes closed) partner where to throw a ball in order to hit a target (backboard, championship pennant, buzzer, etc.). The partners may not touch one another; only words of direction are allowed. Six shots at one target are delivered and then another target is chosen. People should not become target material. Switch roles after a few attempts.

Where the Balls Are

It becomes soon obvious that to properly offer the preceding tennis ball activities, you need "beaucoup" balls. From past experience, the following sources for used balls are worthwhile pursuing.

Best — Make a deal with a tennis club or tennis pro to barter or buy their used balls. Tennis facilities use an inordinate amount (hundreds) of balls, retiring them after only a few sets. Tell the owner (usually wealthy) that the balls are to be used in an educational program and are not to be recycled for proletarian court play.

Not Bad, But Seasonal — Check the

rooftops of a school's gymnasium. Gym roofs are invariably flat (that's why they leak), and they eat tennis balls (and shoes, locks, golf balls, etc.).

Poor, But Good for a Few — Stand around a municipal tennis court and sneak off with out-of-bounds balls. Be fair, though — let the ball come to a stop.

Balloon Blow-Up

If you are looking for a no-holds-barred histrionic way to demonstrate the teacher/actor role so often used in adventure presentations, try on one of these vivid mime roles.

Lie on the floor in a semi-fetal position with the tip of your thumb pressed against your lips. Begin blowing on your thumb, producing noticeable hissing sounds. (This is the sound of air entering the balloon – you.) Visualize your cramped body as a deflated balloon and try to think of air entering your arms and legs, and why type of movement your limbs would make as they begin expanding. Make the movements sequential and convulsively realistic. Also, be patient with the movements, remembering how long it takes to fill a large balloon.

Keep blowing and filling until your limbs begin to swell and force you into an eventual scarecrow-like standing position. Keep blowing until you are absolutely filled to your limit (cheeks puffed out, on your tiptoes, arms and legs rigid with air), and then BURST with a loud verbal POW or BANG or whatever you do best. You rapidly decrease in size, deflating toward the floor, all the while emitting loud, air-release, hissing sounds, until you end up in a heap on the floor.

A variation — Instead of bursting, simply let your air out, and like a balloon thus treated, jet yourself willy-nilly around the

room until all the propulsive air is gone.

Fried Egg Simulator

Watch for bruises on this one; i.e., don't get carried away during the hot frying pan time slot.

Begin again in the fetal position, but on your knees, face down on the floor. You are, in this position, an unbroken, fresh egg. To begin, ask someone to tap you (breaking your shell) and then flow onto the floor (face down, spread-eagle).

Imagine an egg being broken onto a hot frying pan and try to duplicate, with body movements, the rapidly increasing formation of bubbles under the albumen; i.e., their constant formation and bursting. Can't picture it? Go fry an egg, and then, be one! Use your imagination (well-honed by this time) and finish off the sequence.

To make these silly mime sequences more meaningful to your audience, tell them what you are (to properly align their imaginations), but not what you are going to do — your actions should take care of that.

Inch Worm

Sit on the turf facing your partner. Inch toward one another until you, and he or she, are close enough to sit on each other's feet. Grasp your partner's upper arm with each hand.

Now, decide which direction you two would like to travel. Lateral movement is out, so it's either north or south. After deciding, the partner (in whose direction you're headed) lifts her/his derriere off the ground and moves a foot or so toward whatever goal you have in mind: be reasonable. The second partner now lifts off the ground and in a cooperative, bug-like movement duplicates the step above and moves toward her/his partner.

Attempt to keep your bottom on your partner's feet and help the action by both pulling with the arms and slightly lifting the feet. Coordinate your movements and eventually speed up the process so that your pair is indistinguishable from a Loctanis herodipus, inching comfortably along a branch.

PDQ   Ω

During workshops and in various classes, I've discovered that a sit-down session facetiously dubbed, the "Play Determinant Quotient" (PDQ), acts as a fine deinhibitor, is good for more than a few group laughs, and clearly illustrates the instructor's role as actor and co-participant.

In your own presentation of this semi-skilled and mostly useless potpourri of shenanigans, the value extends from the participants' attempts, rather than the dialogue that comes so easily and vicariously.

Indicate to your seated listeners that you are going to introduce, by demonstra-tion, a progression of "things to do," and that you would like each member of the group to approximately duplicate your manipulations, sounds, movements, etc. Explain that all these nostalgic doings are self-tests and are to be scored individually on a pass-fail basis. Further indicate that the "tests" are initially easy and become progressively harder.

All of this preliminary patter is to develop interest and psych the group for trying something new, mysterious, and with a bit of pizzaz. If your earlier presen-tations during the workshop (class) have been effectively spontaneous, your audi-ence (you are an impromptu actor, after all) will eagerly anticipate the next bit of zaniness.

The PDQ "Test"

1. Take your right index finger and insert it into your mouth and attempt to make an oral popping sound by levering the finger of choice against the inside of your cheek and

151

rapidly out of your mouth (keeping the lips pursed in an approved manner).

Author's Note — Attempting to write about these facts of profitless dexterity is probably as tedious as reading about them. It's predictably more fun to digitally abuse your cheek than to read about it; so back to your finger and lever away. Have you ever seen someone try to "pop" their cheek and achieve only a fleshy "sploop"? It's funny, and entertainingly useful in a group setting as the expert poppers attempt to aid the hapless sploopers.

1. (a) Try the opposite finger in the other cheek: historically more difficult.
2. Snap your right finger and then the left finger, achieving a distinct snapping sound. Remember — all these performances are on a pass/fail basis. Goodnaturedly emphasize the failures and jokingly remark on outstanding efforts.
3. Snap all the fingers of one hand against the thumb in rapid succession, achieving three or four distinct sounds.
3 (a) And with the other hand and fingers.
4. Mention that the next test is entirely conceptual and that only YOU will know if you passed the test.

Point your index fingers at one another so that the finger tips actually touch one another. Do this about 10-12 inches in front of your face. (Photo below) To "pass" the test, you must *see* a small link sausage visually form between your fingertips. This is definitely a pass/fail test; you either see it or you don't. Don't laugh — I'm being serious . . . kind of.

If people (you) are having trouble making this visual connection, tell them to look beyond the fingers or to cross their eyes. If *you* still can't see the sausage, I don't know what to say: I'm sorry. Better drop this one from your test list.

If you slightly separate your fingers, the link sausage (which has fingernails on each end — gross!) will float in mid-air. Keep trying.

If you juxtapose all four fingers at once, you get multiple linked sausages.

5. I'm not going to try to depict this next one, at least not "by the numbers." It's an age-old, two-handed trick used to

delight young children (and young minds) by opposing palms, juxtaposing and intertwining the middle fingers, twisting the palms against one another in opposite directions, as the fingers find their way, and finally causing the middle fingers to flip-flop in opposite directions. It is amusing to watch and fun to help someone try to accomplish this fairly intricate, but well-known movement.

Another remember — You are trying to present a series of maneuvers that *will* result in occasional and obvious failure, in order to share the consequences of trying a new and possibly intimidating task.

6. Cup your hands and blow *across* (like across the top of a bottle or bullet shell) the small aperture formed between the second and third joint of the thumbs. This produces a hollow hooting sound that is the newfound delight of practicing youngsters and anathema to their parents and teachers.

You can extend or supplement this "test" outdoors by placing a blade of grass (wide blades for deep sounds, narrow blades for higher notes), between the thumbs (as above) and blowing directly *on* the tightly held blade. The grass acts as a vibrating reed, producing a variety of animal and unearthly sounds.

7. You can finish this formal (?) part of the testing sequence by demonstrating something difficult that you can do. Try whistling loudly through your teeth. Or, touching your tongue to your nose. Or, playing a recognizable tune (I've always had good luck with "You Are My Sunshine") by cupping your hand in your armpit under your shirt and...you know!

The folks in your group (more group than audience by this time) are beginning to demonstrate with alacrity those ridiculous pranks that not so long ago amused their friends and aggravated their teachers and parents.

A couple of tested maneuvers that have proven humorous and acceptably bizarre are: (a) Put your finger in either ear and seemingly extend it into your oral cavity, resulting in an obvious and moveable bump in your cheek (use your tongue, please!) (b) Produce a nose-breaking sound by cupping your hands over your nose/mouth area and convincingly "pop" your nose by subtly snapping a thumbnail against your teeth.

I don't think there is any need to list more of these PDQ's, because each group knows more than enough tricks to further your purposes of relaxing overly serious seminar participants and demonstrating an engaging level of play. Even the participants who don't actively take part are taken by the spontaneous nature of the responses and the level of group enjoyment. The test, after all, is no test at all, but simply an invitation to play.

Mrs. O'Grady — A genuine no-prop deinhibitizer that's more fun than embarrassing.

With about 6-8 people (including yourself) standing in a circle, ask the person to your left or right the following sequence of questions and also indicate to them what their reply should be. This is a very traditional game:

You:	"Did you hear what happened to Mrs. O'Grady?"
Them:	"No, what happened?"
You:	"She died!"
Them:	"How did she die?"
You :	"With one cocked eye."

At this juncture, you close one eye tightly and hold it closed until the game is over. The person who was answering your questions then asks the identical series of questions to the person next to her, and this continues around the circle until all the participants have, "one cocked eye."

When the questioning role is yours again, continue to add embellishments to the way Mrs. O'Grady died. E.g., "With her mouth awry" (and twist your mouth grotesquely to one side); ". . . breathing a sigh," ". . . with her leg held high" (lifting one leg off the floor); and ". . . waving goodbye." By the time all of these movements, sounds and postures have been continued by all members of the circle (as the questioning creeps humorously and interminably around from person to person), physical fatigue and a certain hysterical monotony allows an unselfconscious abandonment to the game. Why else would a semi-sophisticated adolescent stand on one leg, waving a hand absently with one eye closed, his mouth twisted to one side, while emitting a series of metronome-like sighs?

If you have student leaders or another teacher that can initiate the questions, you can begin other O'Grady circles. Don't include more than 8 people in a circle for obvious reasons of physical fatigue and tedious repetition. If things are going too slowly the next time the questioning comes around to you, include two "things to do" in your obituary.

You do not debrief this "theater in the round," simply enjoy it.

Leather Bubbles

I like this! And I really like the long bubble life. These four paragraphs are taken directly from the Adventure Counseling Curriculum Guide of the Hamilton-Wenham Regional School District, Hamilton, Massachusetts.

"From time immemorial, the blowing of soap bubbles has been a form of amusement for children, young and old. A formula is here given for a solution which will produce bubbles of surprising size and durability.

Half an ounce of soap — preferably castile — is cut into shavings, put into a pint of water and gently heated until the soap is dissolved. The solution should be allowed to cool and should then be filtered. Into three parts of this solution should be mixed two parts of glycerine, and the mixture thoroughly shaken in a bottle. It will at first be clear, but will soon become turbid. After a day or two, the solution will be found to be whitish or turbid at the top and clear underneath. Pour off the turbid portion and use the clearer part for the blowing of soap bubbles; or, better, siphon out the clear portion and keep it for use.

A bubble made from this glycerine liquid will *last for hours*, if not disturbed by draughts of air, and if allowed to rest on some soft woolen fabric. New clay pipes should be used in the blowing of the bubbles, and contests may be held in the blowing of the largest bubble or the most lasting one.

A pleasing game for all ages is played by arranging a cord, or some sort of screen, across the room, the bubble-blowers taking opposite sides. The object of the game is to blow the bubbles and force them over the dividing line into the enemies' territory, by using small, oriental-type hand fans. A piece of cardboard from a box or the back of a yellow pad works okay, too. The opposing side tries to fan them back again. Every bubble that bursts over the territory of either side counts as a point against that side.

BIG Leather Bubbles

A fellow named David Stein manufactures a whimsical device called the "Bubble Thing," which makes bubbles in the 3'-12' category and sometimes "as long as a bus!" Dave's instant bubble mix is, "Mix one cup of Joy or Dawn dish detergent with 10 cups of water. For longer lasting bubbles, add 1/4 cup of glycerine or Wesson oil to the soapy mixture."

The bubble-making device looks like . . . it really doesn't look like anything I can think of. It's a plastic rod with a loose triangular arrangement of filigree cloth (like rick-rack, but different) draped below the rod . . . you better get one.

For use summer or winter. "Winter bubbles crystallize into rainbow-colored spheres, then shatter."

Autograph Seekers

Here's a means of achieving some emotional adventure and sizeable amount of vis-á-vis stress.

The following list represents your autograph worksheet. The task is to select any ten of the following 25 items below by placing an X in front of each of your choices. A player will then seek the autograph of an interviewed person to fit each of the ten categories or conditions that you have X'd. The autograph signifies that you have actually talked with a person and have asked the necessary question(s) to determine if that person fulfills what the item indicates. You must have a different autograph for each of the ten items. No winners or losers in this game, just a good time and some personal growth.

1. Thinks the President is doing a good job —
2. Born under my astrological sign —
3. Prefers to work alone —
4. Likes liver —
5. Reads poetry —
6. Looks attractive to me —
7. Has a part-time job —
8. Likes break dancing —
9. Might be intimidating to me —
10. Believes in magic —
11. Owns an Alligator shirt —
12. Has a tattoo —
13. Appears to be friendly —
14. Likes mint chocolate chip ice cream —
15. Plays a musical instrument —
16. Advocates openness —
17. Drinks beer —
18. Enjoys competition —
19. Sleeps in a waterbed —
20. Drives a sports car —
21. Uses Nautilus —
22. Wears Jockeys —
23. Has had a root canal —
24. Likes the President —
25. Thinks UFO's are real

This activity requires some moxie with a dash of chutzpah, and is subversively arranged by teacher-types to initiate conversations. The actual autograph-seeking can be accomplished within a school setting, but stalking real world folk is much more adventurous and satisfying. Be careful, though, you might initiate more conversation than anticipated and end up with a friend — and you know how friends are, they can be so demanding and personal . . . and tie up the phone, too.

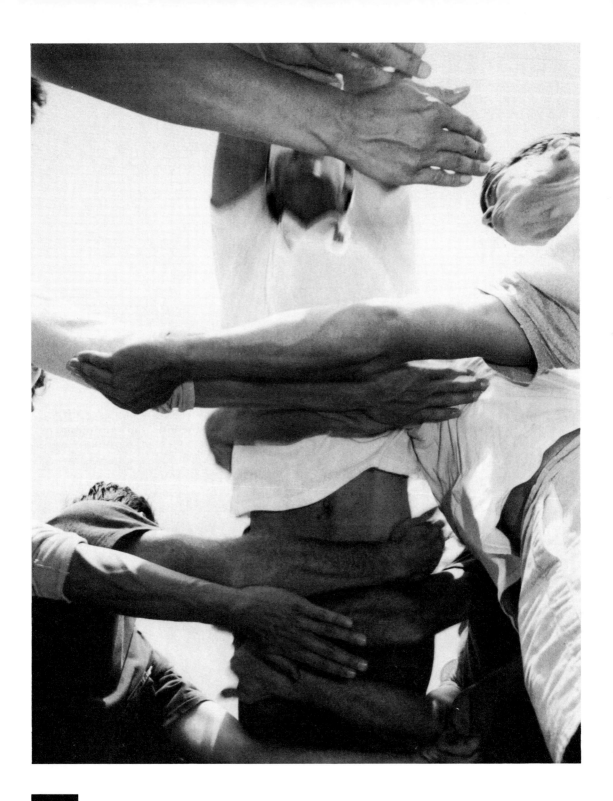

Chapter 8

Curriculum Tidbits

located and say START. Measure thirty seconds (60 seconds is interminable) of beats and times 2 for a minute's total.

If people want to know if or why their pulse rate is high or low for their age level, be noncommittal; this low-key line-up is not meant to serve as a diagnostic clinic.

Another 50/50 Group Split Ploy

Always looking for another unobtrusive way to divide a group in half? This sit-down/stand-up ploy recently showed up at a workshop, and does exactly what it's supposed to.

Ask your group to pair-up. Indicate that one person of the pair must decide to stand the other sit. All standing players make up one group (team) and the sitting players represent the other.

If there is an odd participant, quickly put them on the team that *you* think might

Pulse Line-Up

Having people form a line because of height, age, etc., is useful as an ice-breaker and as a means of revealing something about yourself without bragging. Add this simple line-up to your collection.

Ask people to line up as to their standing pulse rate. Let them determine what their pulse rate is right there, right now. Show them where the carotid pulse is need another person, or ask him/her to choose a standing or seated position. Odd people also tend to liven up a homogenous grouping.

I haven't used this technique often enough to know if the standing/sitting choice produces a different dynamic or skills discrepancy between groups. I'm sure if you make up a valid-sounding theory and couch it in pedagogic terms (cognitive, affective, psychomotor) that whatever you say will be well received. Sound familiar?

Dial-a-Quote

"The difference between my quotations and those of the next man is that I leave out the inverted commas." — George Moore

Need a quote, a word, or a phrase to fill a blank in your proposal? I think most of us at one time or another have searched about for the right words or phrase to express what we felt, but couldn't synaptically release. Sometimes a proposal will be accepted if the right text buttons are rhetorically pushed. Here are some "buttons" to read through and use to the best of your needs.

All of these words and phrases have been used and stated in a variety of ways before, so don't feel guilty about borrowing them, because they are part of what should be a shareable pool. I collected them from a series of books (including some stuff from *Cows' Tails & Cobras*, *High Profile*, and *Silver Bullets*, that I forgot I had written), introductions, letters, articles, and whatever I deemed was generic and useable enough for the dial-a-quote process. If you see something here that looks like your work, be flattered — I like what you said, and I'm sure someone else will, too. You have contributed to idea-sharing at its best. Note that I have left out the quotation marks, hopefully making it easier for you to borrow a phrase or two.

Dial-a-Quotes

Trust, within the framework of an adventure curriculum, is gained with patience,

thoughtfulness, and care, over a period of time, and can be damaged or lost in a few seconds.

Unfortunately, many children grow up in such a protected environment that the chance to learn day-to-day survival skills never materializes.

Each task is designed so that a group must employ cooperation and some physical effort to gain a solution.

The problem-oriented approach to learning can be useful in developing each individual's awareness of decision-making, leadership, and the obligations and strengths of each member within a group.

They also serve to break down some of the stereotypes which exist so comfortably in our social network.

Initiative problems are a non-pareil for building morale and a sense of camaraderie — when a group need a morale boost or a means of gaining behavioral insights, a well-chosen game or initiative problem was a surefire and enjoyable way to accomplish that goal.

If what you are presenting is geared only to successful completion, and failure is non-existent, then boredom replaces challenge.

Reasonable risk-taking is part of living.

Games can provide the morale growth and sense of camaraderie that facilitates group cohesion and enthusiasm for the program.

It's hard to turn your back on obvious fun.

Trust is a powerful and essential education tool; it is the key to personal involvement.

An individual will seldom take a physical or emotional chance, if they perceive callousness and unreasonable risk as part of that risk-taking.

A group surrounded with positive experiences and successes will experience trust, growing apace with personal confidence.

. . . a chance to try potentially difficult and/ or frightening activities in an atmosphere of support and caring.

. . . being able to "back off" when performance pressures or self-doubt become too strong, knowing that an opportunity for a future attempt will always be available.

. . . respect for individual ideas and choices.

. . . their eager wish to participate illustrates clearly that people will respond to challenging, enjoyable, and meaningful activity curricula.

Risk is normal in the daily lives of all human beings and is essential to their education.

Safety is an essential ingredient, but to deny or reduce the risk factor in educational units is to run counter to the educational process itself.

Adventure activities have been used effectively by a variety of teachers, counselors, therapists, camp directors, and church leaders.

. . . an effective, engaging way to bring people together to build trust and to break down the artificial barriers between individuals and groups of individuals.

These **PA** activities have been evaluated as having improved self-concept, improved the ability of members to take risks, and improved the ability of group members to cooperate and work well together.

. . . Thus the ropes course is not simply a series of cheap thrills and military oriented obstacles...

. . . there is a good feeling in knowing that there is something to be worked toward before success can be expected.

. . . lessens their normal sensitivity to failure because the activity is engrossing and fun.

. . . the group was laughingly supportive of any effort, no matter how inept.

. . . increased confidence in his/her physical and psychological ability to overcome problem situations.

. . . unafraid of failure, because of the supportive nature of the group and the knowledge that if I continue to try, I'll probably improve.

. . . keep the curriculum fresh, exciting, and non-repetitive.

. . . increased level of agility and physical coordination.

. . . the use of teams, points and competition has consciously been minimized.

. . . as a person matures, s/he needs to handle the anxiety that precedes any new venture.

Students are regularly out in weather which ranges from sunny and warm to cloudy and close to zero.

. . . sufficient for conditioning and remains within the realm of fear, fun and functionality.

. . . a willingness to appear inept in front of others.

PA is unprecedented in its success in providing students with activities which are focused on enhancing self-esteem and mutual support.

. . . solving problems that are designed so that group members must take advantage of their combined physical and mental capabilities in arriving at a solution.

. . . develop abilities that contribute to group decision-making and leadership.

. . . foster appreciation and respect for differences existing within the group.

. . . appreciation of the interdisciplinary nature of real problem solving.

PA would self-destruct in a few years if teachers used only a few successful activities over and over again.

Games emphasize fun, give and take, a non-competitive nature, and play for the joy involved.

Adding outdoor adventure to our curriculum allows us to address the needs of more students.

By emphasizing team sports, we offer those students who are not team-oriented another chance not to participate, to become a discipline problem, or to become disillusioned with physical education.

Adventure activities require complete concentration of all of one's faculties and energies.

These activities offer opportunities to learn and develop lifelong leisure and physical activity skills.

. . . a physically exciting and accepted philosophy toward education of the total person.

Teachers using adventure curriculum activities have reported that their adventure adaptations are successful beyond all expectations.

Positive educational change regularly occurs as the result of accepting and reshaping adventure activities.

Adventure training works because people need the stimulus, respond to the vehicle and like the results.

Adventure training allows most students to achieve beyond their initial expectations with a resultant growth of self-confidence.

Adventure training defines compassion, trust, and commitment through jointly experiencing a series of demanding and exciting activities.

Adventure-based activities are designed to supplement, add to and embellish traditional programs — not replace them.

The emphasis is not on how well you perform, but how well you try.

The obvious results, measured in personal satisfaction and growth of self-esteem, more than compensate for a winning score.

. . . activities which offer fine physical and mental challenges and a satisfying spectrum of accomplishment levels.

Because of the various stresses involved (fear of failure, physical harm, human fallibility), there are unparalleled opportunities for the establishment of trust

Adventure education activities provide physical and mental challenges with pizzaz.

A consistently high (but accomplishable)

level of expectation, demanded and created by both the intrinsic and external forces.

Students need to be convinced that not just anyone could have done this, and that the teacher *cares* that the goal is reached.

A success orientation in which growth is supported and encouraged and in which the positive is emphasized.

Encouragement is one crucial ingredient in resolving the conflict between high expectations and the need for a successful experience.

An atmosphere of mutual support in which cooperation, encouragement and interpersonal concerns are consistently present.

A sense of enjoyment, fun and the opportunity to laugh at a situation, each other, and one's self.

An approach to learning which makes use of group problem-solving, which allows for a variety of personal contributions and which presents problems that can't ordinarily be solved individually.

The rewards are set up for group effort, rather than individual success or competition.

The use of a learning environment that is more complex, more engaging, less predictable and less familiar than a school classroom.

The merging of intellectual, social, physical, and emotional learning and development.

A significant amount of cognitive work, related directly to abstractions and questions previously developed in the classroom, or subsequently to be developed.

The combining of moments of active involvement with moments of personal and group reflection and evaluation.

An awareness that teachable and learnable moments are unpredictable but necessary ingredients in a curriculum.

A definite organization and structure which define the limits of the experience and states expectations but within which the participants have freedom to make decisions, choices, and mistakes

An economic and structural reasonableness which allows the curriculum to effectively compete for dollars and other resources within an educational economy which is limited in its resources.

An individual will seldom take a physical or emotional risk if they perceive unreasonable risk as part of that risk-taking.

A group surrounded with positive experience and success will experience trust growing apace with personal confidence.

Trust is gained with patience and care over a comfortably long period of time and can be damaged or lost in a second by carelessness or inconsiderate behavior.

Program activities must regularly display an element of fun.

If what you are doing is so geared to successful completion that failure is non-existent, then boredom replaces challenge.

Be ready to personally attempt whatever you are asking your students to try — right there, right now. Involve yourself regularly in curriculum activities — let the students see you succeed, fail; laugh and live with them.

Operating with *calculated abandon* and being *reasonably unreasonable* sounds good, but be aware that programmed adventure differs from pure adventure in that the path and outcome of the programmed approach are known. Operate to your known level of safety.

Setting a Tone

Charlie Harrington (former Pittsburgh Steeler rookie and all-time Adventure rookie), uses an amusing and attention-getting way of indicating an infraction of the rules while a group is attempting an initiative problem (touching the "electric fence," landing in the "poison peanut butter," etc.). His flagging tool is a brightly colored bandana, stuffed casually but noticeably in a back pocket. Upon spying a blatant (or subtle; sometimes called sneaky) infraction, Charlie throws his

marker to the ground (a la the NFL) and shouts "HEAVY LUMPS"; which exclamation has no significance, except to draw attention to the infraction and its perpetrator.

This delightfully superfluous action and announcement is a fine example of what an adventure instructor can do to add to the enjoyment of, and instill fantasy into, an obviously fabricated situation.

Training Truisms

- . . . people are usually capable of achieving well beyond their self imposed limits.
- . . . most people are stimulated by reasonable risk and challenge, and that the accepted risk or challenge does not have to be physical.
- . . . people will try harder when given the choice to try, rather than being directed or coerced into "trying" — *Challenge By Choice.*
- . . . most people have forgotten how to "play" without the crutch of win/lose competition.
- . . . there's more value to failing forward than failing to try.
- . . . the best performers are not necessarily the best leaders.
- . . . students will consistently attempt difficult tasks, if convinced that their teacher/mentor is also willing to occasionally share the same risk.
- . . . effective communication involves the pleasant paradox of more listening than talking.

Splicing Made Hard

Learning to splice three-strand rope with an experienced teacher at your side is no great task. Learning to splice from an illustration is self-flagellation of the third kind (the

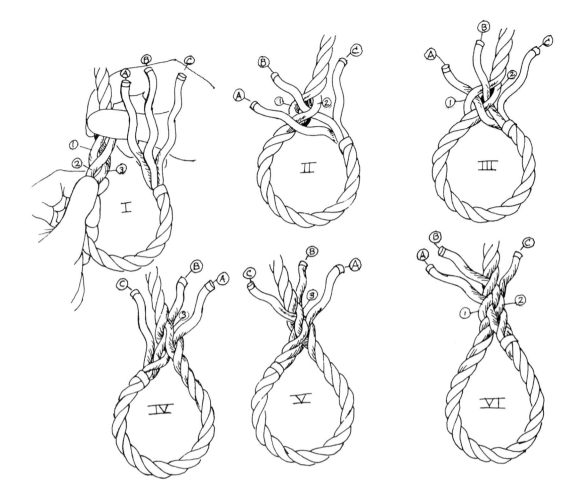

fourth kind involves trying to follow instructions over the phone).

Here are a few illustrations that are clearer than most, depicting steps toward producing an eye splice: start flagellating.

Of the three most common splices (eye, short, and end), the eye splice is the most commonly used.

Note that illustration 4 is the obverse of 3, and also that illustration 6 has been turned back over.

If you get stuck and can't figure out what you are doing wrong, don't call. My number isn't (508) 469-7685.

Good Cents

How many pennies do you have hoarded? I should ask, how many are reluctantly stored, because who really wants those omnipresent coppers that seem to reproduce themselves and appear everywhere they shouldn't — under dressers (where they get caught by the vacuum and make a clinkety-clank sound all the way up the tube), washing machines, bureau tops, etc.

It bothers me to buy things that cost $1.41, because of the $.04 change. Then what do you do with the pennies? Toss them into the family loose change receptacle of choice, (glass carboy, fruit jar, giant clay piggie, etc.), then roll 'em for deposit at the bank.

If you have functional age children, you can make the inevitable counting, stacking, and stuffing seem exciting for about 15 minutes — then it's split for the video, leaving oceans of sifted pennies on the rug for you to rake together and put away — 'till the next time.

Spend them. For what, penny candy? . . . no such thing anymore. Stores frequently ask (via cute cash register signs) for your pennies — until you try to pay for something. Sure, at $1.41, they love your penny, but 141 of them?

It would make an interesting movie theme to offer someone a million dollars if they could spend (actually in-the-store spend), ten thousand dollars of pennies within a reasonable time span. (Save your trip to the Casio — that's 1,000,000 pennies and considering that one hundred pennies weigh 10 ounces, a quick Nautilus membership might be in order as a prerequisite to the competition.)

Birthday Penny Largesse

Before a birthday bash for one of your children, grab handfuls of cents and liberally sow your back yard with these copper discs. There's usually a bit of guilt associated with the first couple of sweeping tosses, but the surreal sensation of sowing money indiscriminately to the winds is actually quite satisfying.

The objective benefit — When the vibrating kiddos, surfeit and wired from a parentally planned sugar overdose, swarm onto your metallically seeded yard, they will soon discover the unburied treasure and digitally rake them up with gusto, to be ferried home in the cute little birthday bags that you cunningly provided—and horded in someone else's fruit jars.

Take Them to the Mall

This plan, although effective and satisfying, hints of subversive or revolutionary action; have a good rap ready for the 17 year-old mall security guard.

Let your kids throw pennies by the fistful into those hokey mall fountains that have signs telling you to keep out. A worthy charity will probably (I wish I were sure, but . . .) benefit, children love the excess, and your copper coffers begin from zero again.

Posterity Plan

Put the pennies in a bottle or jar and bury them, all of them, and make a treasure map — great fun — with the idea that some future generation of _____ (insert appropriate surname) can dig them up and cash in on their numismatic value as a downpayment on a Porsche (or whatever monumental extravagance you and I will never be able to afford).

A Penny Stunt

Ever tried to see if you could pick up a penny from a table (bar) top by just placing your flat palm against the coin, lifting and closing your hand to a fist and somehow miraculously finding a penny nestled there?

Performing such feats of worthless dexterity is entertaining for awhile, but after the third or fourth time, it's a bit ho-hum. The challenge can be extended by using more pennies and seeing how many can be lifted and grasped in one swipe — personal world records are a natural.

So, how do you do it? . . . Sweaty palms help. Place the fleshy part of your palm (just below the root of the index finger) on top of the first coin. Press down hard, but as unobtrusively as possible (be cool, remember, this is part skill, speed and *trick*), for about 3 seconds and in one swift motion, lift and close your hand. Considering a

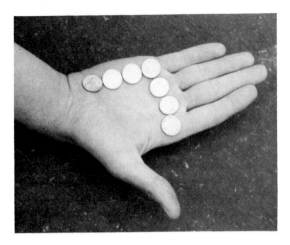

expenditures, we purchased and mixed a concoction gustatorially referred to as generic or macro-GORP. The ingredients were:

1. Foil-wrapped chocolate Hershey kisses
2. Shelled (shells on) roasted peanuts
3. Grapes (with seeds)

All of the above items were admittedly tasty and attractive to the palate, but required a pre-oral digital commitment that slowed consumption and increased attention to what was going over the lips (and onto the hips?). It was reported — after a brief period of initial dismay — that the generic GORP allowed more time for the tactile enjoyment of spontaneous mouth-stuffing.

There was some movement to substitute prunes (with pits, of course) for the grapes. The prune group liked the idea because a prune kind of looks like a big raisin. The idea was ultimately rejected because of the large colon movement that was inevitable, considering how much GORP was being munched.

After buying a quantity of the above items, mix them all in an opaque plastic bag — so that no one can see what they are grabbing.

This reporting is a bit whimsical, but generic GORP was actually a hit. Try it for a change of pace.

Thanks to the Nantahala Outdoor Center staff for participating in this oral experiment and to Gary Nussbaum (Radford University, Virginia) for buying the stuff.

couple optimistic if's, you should find a penny in your palm when you look — unless you used a dime on the table and if a penny shows up, let me know *that* trick.

A couple of practice grabs and you'll have it, I think. Beefy palms help. If the coin keeps falling from your hesitating grasp, moisten the side of the coin that contacts your hand (your choice — saliva, beer, Perrier).

After mastering the single coin move, attempt two coins, then three, etc. Continue to place the coins on the table so that they make contact with the fleshy part of your palm.

Refer to the photo above for Alberto Gunizau's (1982 World's Penny-Lifting Champ; runner-up '83-84 largely because he lost the tip of his middle finger in a bowling accident), patented start, which is aptly referred to as "Gunizau's Gamble." Beyond the initial 8 coin arrangement, it's up to you. See you at the nationals.

Oral Adventure

I was involved in a workshop recently where truly prodigious amounts of *GORP* were consumed by the participants (the instructors helped). As a means of reducing the predictable oral intake and associated

True Grit

I'm not going to spend a lot of words on this, because it sounds weak — you know, like I'm just filling up space, but I know this simple activity works and for certain audiences, it's ideal therapy.

In the 60's, I worked as a "trail teacher" for an outdoor education center in California, taking sixth grade students on ecology hikes, leading campfires, teaching basic biology, etc. During this week of residential "camping," we regularly provided craft time so that students could use forest products (acorns, pine cones, bark, etc.) and their ingenuity to create a handmade object d'art. Usually, the slap-dash final product was a pencil or napkin holder or some such semi-useless, "Isn't-that-nice, dear" circle-file type geegaw.

But, the significance of this hands-on activity was that students gained a tactile sense of what they could achieve with some elbow grease, personal commitment, and time. Kind of like the occasional occupational rewards that we don't get enough of.

Many 4" x 4" pieces of 120 grit sandpaper were provided as an incentive to "improve on nature." What really happened is that some students who had *never* done anything manually worthwhile (to them or anyone else, I suppose) got turned on to making things smooth, or "soft," as they used to say, with sandpaper.

You say, come on, Karl, what's the big deal with the sandpaper and what's the next game, anyway? I say, it *is* a big deal to provide a student with a low-cost activity that provides immediate and deserved satisfaction.

Try this yourself. Come on, if you're going to smile and shake your head, you can at least try this little experiment. Find a *small* piece of hardwood (oak, maple, teak) and, using a knife or some such tool, give it round contours. Then, starting with 80 grit sandpaper, further smooth the edges and take out all the grooves and scratches. Then progress from 80 grit to 100 grit to 120 to 150 to 220 to 320 to 400 and finally, to the magic 600 grit sandpaper. When you start using the bigger numbers (finer grit paper), the tactile enjoyment of making your object

"soft" is a sensory adventure not to be denied.

I have seen troublemakers, bored kids and non-achievers gain an inordinate amount of satisfaction from this coarse to super-fine grit progression toward achieving the luster and practically unbelievable smoothness that 600 grit paper allows.

Practical tip — buy garnet or aluminum oxide sandpaper: Don't waste your time with glued-on grit.

Touch the finished product to your cheek — your lip: Nice, huh?

The Constrictor Knot

Having used, written about, and taught knots for years, it's a treat to discover a "new" knot that is easy to tie and uniquely useable; i.e., serves its own purpose.

The constrictor knot literally acts as a clamp for whatever objects you want held together, and in conjunction with a half hitch, it's ideal for hauling boards up into a tree. Learn the knot, and uses fairly annouce themselves.

Geoffrey Budworth, author of *The Knot Book*, offers this tip for tying the constrictor knot: "If the object you want to tie the knot around is soft, use hard cord for the tieing. If the object is hard, use soft material to tie the knot. The effect will be the same. In each case it will grip like a boa constrictor."

Adventure Games Teaching Suggestions

1. Establish rapport with the individual players right away. Do this in a casually competent way; don't come on strong.
2. The key to including the student who arrives late is to continually extend an open and welcoming invitation to all new players.
3. Establish yourself as a player as well as the teacher right from the git-go.
4. Begin with games that provide easy access and have few, easily explained rules.
5. Let the players stretch their bodies and their feelings slowly at first.
6. Explain the game's structure and rules as clearly and simply as possible, and do it in a style that encourages participation, playfulness, fantasy and fun.
7. Combine description with demonstration.
8. After a brief period of play, ask for questions. If a particular question suggests an interesting variation, you might use it as an opportunity to empower the players, allowing the group to take charge of, or even name the game.
9. Extend an invitation to play. Don't demand participation; always offer choices.
10. If, as the leader, you are able to demonstrate the game with appropriately outrageous or foolish words and actions, you can serve as a model, encouraging all the players to cast aside their inhibitions and join you.
11. Before a physically active game, point out any qualities of the group's physical make-up that requires special safety procedures.
12. When presenting games, always look for opportunities to make the game fantasy or imagery come alive.

A CHECK LIST

I wrote down these topics many years ago as a means of reminding myself and the workshop participants what we were trying to accomplish during a debrief, and also as a self-check list of my responsibilities as a group leader. It still reads well, so pick and choose what makes sense to you and use what you don't agree with as discussion topics.

Initiative Problem Debriefing Topics

Leadership & Followership - gotta have both; who's who and when to be which

Group Support - toward achieving a decided-upon goal; group vs. individual

Peer Pressure - does it exist? what are it's positive and negative aspects?

Negativism/Hostility - how do you handle it positively?

Efficiency - toward achieving a group goal or nebulous world record

Competition - differentiate between positive and negative aspects of competition

Spotting - importance; attention to; how to emphasize, trust

Sexism - which activity? where? don't emphasize who; key in on why; be a moderator, not an instigator

Carry Over - how fabricated initiatives effect real-life decisions and patterns

Fear (physical & psychological) - use as a tool, not as a prod

Joy/Pleasure/Fun - and the last shall be first (or should be . . .) Without these three, forget the list above.

The Role of the Instructor

Problem Presenter - To instill interest, humor, and willingness to TRY.

Rule Reinforcer/Tone Setter - Be strict, but compassionate; make the problem real.

Safety Factor - Do not allow unsafe acts or attempts. Be realistic, not stultifying.

Arbitrator - When the going gets rough, arbitrate to prevent "hands on" decisions.

Encouragement - If a group is working hard with negligible results, encourage and cajole, but don't provide answers. You are facilitating, not teaching.

Sounding Board - Don't take sides; ask open ended questions, and give noncommital answers.

Don't Teach - Present the problem and encourage as above, but let the group come up with a solution. The answers are not up to you.

Facilitate - To facilitate means to make something easier. This applies to the debriefing procedure, not coming up with the solution itself.

A Polygonic Quickie

Peter Richards, Atlanta, Georgia, suggests a twist of an old initiative problem (Blind Polygon) that makes it even more useable; no props necessary.

"Remember the one with a length of rope and blindfolds, where you try to make a perfect square with the rope? Here's a new twist: Have your group *join hands* and, blindfolded, try to make a perfect square or triangle, etc."

· It works.

How Old Do I Think I Am? A Circuitous 50/50 Group-Split Ploy

If the game you intend to play doesn't have to start *right now*, try this revealing share-something-about-yourself method of halving a group.

Ask the oldest players to begin forming a line to your left and facing you, youngest to the right. Most importantly, indicate that no one is to reveal their age; i.e., let the line form by where each person *thinks* they should fit in: no declaring or digital displays allowed. Allow a couple minutes for this to happen, as the banter and repartee is an important part of the communication and cooperation you are trying to facilitate. (This ploy works best with a group displaying a wide chronological age span, but can also be used with a school class by requiring that their age position be to the nearest day. It seems that someone's age is always of interest, no matter how wide or narrow the span.

After the line stabilizes (no one jostling for a new generational position), ask the people to declare (volunteer only) their ages, starting with the youngest. Offer much applause for the oldest, no matter what the actual age, and call that person the most venerable (or experienced) — not the oldest. There is occasionally someone who has grossly over or underestimated where they should be in line. If their chosen position casts them in a good light, make note of it. If a 40+ individual ends up in the 20's section, move right along to . . . asking the youngest end of the line to walk around toward the most venerable end until each person in the group represents half of a vis-á-vis pair. Starting with the oldest/youngest couple, ask each *pair* to count off, 1-2, 1-2, etc.

All the 1's over here, and 2's over there, equals a well-divided group — by age, anyway.

Rather than declaring their numerical age, ask the self-designated line to establish their chronological position by stating something of world significance that happened during their birth year. If some one whimsically says, "I was born that year"; that's a fine answer.

Pickup Prelims

Need two equally numbered teams? Are you about to choose the two best athletes (best friends) and ask them to pick sides? Don't! The results are predictably devastating to the last chosen few (overweight, inept, unpopular, ethnic, blemishes, too tall, too short, too something).

Try a few of these low-key pickup techniques, and you might find that the students will look forward to the next set of zany comparisons.

The following is a list of comparisons that hopefully will give you close to a 50/50 split, and if parity isn't achieved, at least the students will experience the fun of personally comparing a non-threatening object, fear, action, etc., and also of becoming part of a group, albeit only briefly. (See *Categories*)

Also us we:

(1) color of eyes
(2) When you sit down on the ground, which hand touches the ground first?
(3) When your hands are folded, is your right thumb or left thumb naturally on top? Also, when you fold your arms, is your right or left arm comfortably on top? (Both the following have to do with heredity.)

(4) Born in the months January through June, move to the left; July through December to the right.
(5) When you lick an ice cream cone, do you lick to the left or right? Which way do you rotate the cone?
(6) When putting on pants, left leg in first, or right leg in first?
(7) Both socks on before putting on shoes, or one sock, then a shoe?
(8) If you turn around for some reason, do you turn clockwise or counterclockwise?
(9) Do you jump off your left or right foot to clear a ditch?
(10) Split up into Horoscope sign groups and then choose two equal groups of six signs. What?

So, there's a start, and be assured that there are lots of other things to compare. Try not to choose comparison themes that will prove to be embarrassing. Chubbies to the left, beanpoles to the right . . .

Accessible Ropes Courses

Four sites I know of, currently involved with using ropes course elements with the physically disabled:

Camp Courageous of Iowa
P.O. Box 455
Monticello, Iowa 52310-0455

Bradford Woods Outdoor
    Education Center
Indiana University
5040 State Road 67N
Martinsville, IN 46151

University of New Hampshire
New Hampshire Hall
Durham, NH 03824

Accessible Adventures
250 NE Tomahawk Island Dr. #309
Portland, OR 97217

I have been following **Camp Courageous** (above) via their newsletter for over ten years. They do an unbelievably good job with mentally and physically disadvantaged campers. The Camp operates *entirely* through donations, so if you have time, money or equipment to offer, they will use it well.

Government Surplus Wants You!

This article on Federal Surplus Property may prove to be the most valuable (monetarily) bit of information that I have made available over the past years in BOT's, and I don't know why I haven't mentioned this goldmine of gear previously. Preoccupied with other games and goodies, I suppose.

There was an article written in 1979 about the stupendous amount of good, useable surplus gear available to certain qualified groups. The article was written by Jack Shakeley and was distributed by the Grantsmanship Center, a non-profit educational institution. I will be quoting from this article. If what I quote and edit seems interesting and you think your center, school, etc., may qualify, I'd suggest writing for the entire article from: The Grantsmanship Center, 1031 South Grand Avenue, Los Angeles, California 90015. Cost is $1.10 per copy. The name of the article is "Federal Surplus Property: Need A Submarine Cheap?"

I have been going to the surplus property center in Taunton, Massachusetts, for years, picking up various gems for our program at ridiculously low prices. Some of the items included: Cross Country skis (10th Mountain Division, c. 1950); navy wool bib pants; poplin wind pants; desks; chairs; chalk boards; parachutes (sized from about 20' diameter to 50' — and that last number is not a typo). I won't mention the prices, because you wouldn't believe me.

There are also items there in the warehouse that have questionable value, but are so attractive that you just have to have one. I'm thinking particularly of a silver-coated fireman's suit that included the coat, pants, and a large-visored hood. What a buy, and just the thing for riding the zip wire or playing *Foes & Questors*. I also remember buying one hundred mailbag hooks for a *dollar*. How can you pass up anything that costs a penny? . . . and if you are going to buy one, you might as well have a hundred. Anyway, I would have been embarrassed to buy only one.

As an interesting aside — My father (Radm. O.C. Rohnke, U.S.C.G. Ret.) in 1955 was captain of the Coast Guard icebreaker Eastwind (WAGB 279), operating as part of Operation Deepfreeze, then commanded by Admiral Byrd.

When I was nosing around the cold weather surplus material at the G.S.A. in Taunton, Massachusetts, I spied some particularly heavy looking bib-type pants. On closer inspection, I saw the stenciled words EASTWIND and the date - 1955. *These same pants had been aboard my father's ship over 30 years ago.*

My dad has been retired now for over 20 years, and lives in Bradenton, Florida. I asked him if he would like to have the pants. He smilingly turned them down, observing sagely that they didn't fit into his tropical lifestyle. Too true — good thinking, Ace! So, I'm keeping them tucked away for that trip to the Arctic or Antarctic that I need to take in order to tick it off my "Have you ever?". . . list.

So, who's eligible for all this federal largess? I quote directly from the above-mentioned article. "Basically, there are three eligible organizations. First and largest, is the public agency. This group includes all state, county, municipal, and local government units.

The second group is non-profit health and education agencies, with a few other non-profits thrown in. These include hospitals, medical clinics, health centers, schools, colleges, universities, child care centers, museums, etc. Every non-profit organization must show evidence of non-profit status by the IRS, which means a 501 (c) (3) letter of determination.

The third group of eligible organizations is a little unusual. These are the organizations that conduct activities called service educational activities of interest to the Department of Defense. Falling within these groups are the Red Cross, civil air patrols, Boy and Girl Scouts, Boys' Ranch, etc.

Every year the federal government declares more than 4 billion dollars' worth of goods as excess. Of this amount, about 3 billion worth is declared surplus. Perhaps as much as 400 million of this surplus finds its way to eligible non-profit organizations and local governments."

I'll include a few addresses to write to for specific state information. I'd include more, but these are the only ones I have left from the original article which lists addresses for all the states. Get yourself some mailbag hooks; they make great fetishes.

New York

NY Bureau of Federal
Property Assistance
Bldg. 18, Campus Site
Albany, ny 12226
(518) 457-3264

Pennsylvannia

Dept. of General Services
Bureau of Surplus Properties
2221 Forster St., Box 3361
Harrisburg, PA 17125
(717) 787-6996

Rhode Island

RI Dept. of Administration
Div. of Purchases
State Warehouse, Box 8268
Cranston, RI 02920
(401) 464-2081

Massachusetts

Mass. State Agency for
  Surplus Property
Park Sq. Bldg., Rm. 502
31 St. James Avenue
Boston, MA 02116
(617) 727-5774

Maine

Allocations Officer
Maine State Agency/Surplus Property
State Office Bldg.
Augusta, ME 04333
(207) 289-2933

Missouri

Missouri State Agency for
  Surplus Property
117 N. Riverside Drive
P.O. Drawer 1310
Jefferson City, MO 65101
(314) 751-3415

MAILBAG HOOK
$ 0.01

Chapter 9

Ropes Course Construction

There is a disclaimer at the beginning of this book pertaining to, among other things, "the construction and implementation of ropes course elements." (Second paragraph) I want to make sure you read that page again. The actual building of a ropes course element doesn't require a degree in engineering, but there are a number of things that can go wrong, like not following directions.

If you are a hands-on type of person, and the idea of building your own series of ropes course elements appeals; go for it. However, I cannot take responsibility for on-site variations of the following elements, for misuse of their implementation, or for failure to not use suggested building materials.

Throughout this chapter, whenever I indicate the placement of a 1/2" staple, I will follow the word *staple* with a parenthetical (V) or (H). (V) = vertical, and (H) = horizontal, concerning the orientation of the staple to the axis of the trunk. (V) generally indicates a belay or support staple. (H) indicates a climbing staple.

Jus-Rite Descender

Situation — Anxious 135 pound belayer looking up at an equally anxious 200 pound climber who's looking down from a precarious perch that s/he is about to detach themselves from (FALLING!). The anxiety quotient can be uppped significantly by adjusting those people-poundage figures.

The rope holder *knows* when that chunk of beef falls, the weight differential twixt belayer and climber *will* result in an impromptu meeting (vis-á-vis) an undetermined but disconcerting number of feet off the ground. There is a small matter of hot hands and derrière, but at the moment of leaving the ground, that is of secondary concern.

You have probably seen this sequence enacted more than once and have experienced firsthand the anxiety referred to earlier. My feeling is that the more dynamic the belay, the less pressure the system (rope, cable, bolts, belayer, swages, climber) has to statically absorb. Programmatically, I have advocated over the years not having the belayer tie into an anchor point (ONLY on a ropes course, bottom belay situation - belayers on a rock face MUST tie into an anchor) and not belaying someone more than 30-35 pounds heavier than the belayer, with some poundage leeway recognized for the skill and experience of the belayer.

Enter . . . *The Jus-Rite Descender* . . .

Cut an 8"± x 10' hardwood log and skin it. Spring-time beech wood strips as easily as skinning a snake, and autumn oak has comparative suction bark, but, notwithstanding your bark peeling efforts, whatever hardwood you choose will do the job. Use a two-handled drawknife for the debarking procedure, keeping the bevel of the blade up if you are skilled in hand-tool woodcraft, or bevel down if you are like me. Wear gloves to protect your knuckles in any case.

After the stripping process, take your PHD (posthole digger) and dig a 3-1/2' deep hole approximately where you would stand to belay a specific ropes course element. Now, you and a building buddy take that bare-bone log and "Iwo Jima" (Iwo Jima is a verb in this case) it upright

into the hole.

In New England, a log should last about five years, unless you are lucky enough to have used a locust log, in which case the wood will probably outlast your next three dogs. To increase the log's use in-ground, liberally soak the wood/soil interface with a liquid wood preservative. And, if you copiously slosh some of this same miasmic stuff onto the log's surface each year, your descender will last longer than tenure.

Now you have an impressive 6'-7' of stripped trunk sticking out of the ground, and well tamped, I hope.

Using a stepladder, climb to a level where you can drill down on the trunk, and, starting dead center, drill an 11/16" diameter, 45° angled hole to the length of a 16" auger drill bit. A power drill and alternator will make short work of this task, otherwise,

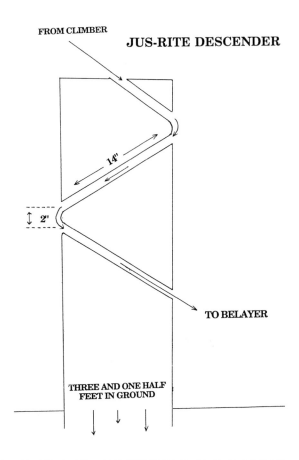

FROM CLIMBER

JUS-RITE DESCENDER

14"

2'

TO BELAYER

THREE AND ONE HALF FEET IN GROUND

plan on a grand arm workout with a bit brace.

The drill bit should exit about 12-14" down from the top of the log. Measure down vertically about 2" from this hole and drill back into the log so that the angle of the drill is approximately the same as the top shaft. Repeat this procedure on the other side of the log so that you have a total of three 11/16" x 14" shafts descending from the top center in a zig-zag pattern down and through the log.

Reeve the belay rope through the top hole and on down, using as many shafts as necessary (until its *jus-rite*), depending upon the weight of the potential faller. The rope comes out the bottom hole at about three feet from the ground and travels directly to the belayer. A classic belay stance can be used, or simply hold onto the rope with two gloved hands. There is certainly more image in the Gore-Tex; Capilene; Vibram; 60/40; leather-gloved stance . . . but two hands works just fine.

The 45° angle of the shaft precludes a shearing effect on the rope, and the two or three inches between holes on the side of the log provide friction over a longer path than a mechanical device permits. The system is adjustable for different weights of climbers by adding or subtracting shafts, or by having the belayer shift one way or another around the log. As an anonymous ropes course practitioner from the U.K. commented . . . "this drilled log is FBI" (fabulously brilliant idea). Thank you.

CAUTION: If you let the rope "sing" through the holes by dropping someone too fast, the rope may become surface-scorched. Heat that will scorch the mantle of a rope, can also damage the kern.

Use of the log allows a minimally trained lightweight individual to belay *any* sized student. Knowing that you are not going to be pulled off your feet and/or get your butt blistered by a fall provides a contagious confidence that further nudges the hesitating student to try.

A teacher's comfortable confidence level is a predictable series of adventure teaching plateaus. The higher plateaus, reached by experience and confidence, result in a casually competent style that allows you to say with believable conviction, "You *will* be safe!", "The rope *will* hold!", "The knots *do* work!", etc. If your presentation is halting, unsure and faulted with an occasional nervous "Oops," well — would you confidently tie in?

The one obvious drawback to this massive belay helper, aside from a certain lack of portability, is that use of the log is limited to only those ropes course elements that do not require the belayer to laterally follow the climber, but then, how many students have you seen someone accidentally fall from a *Burma Bridge*? You can count them on one or two fingers, right?

Heebie-Jeebie

Performance Objective

To walk across a taut cable using crossed ropes for support, which ropes decrease in usefulness as the participant approaches midway on the traverse.

Material Needed:

115'	3/8" cable
3	3/8" strand vice
8	3/8" cable clamps
3	7/16" serving sleeves
50'	5/8" multiline rope
15	1/2" staples
4	1/2" rapid links

Construction Details:

The *Heebie Jeebie* serves as a useful connector between two other high ropes course events. As such, the choice of support trees is dictated by whatever juxtaposed high elements you plan to connect.

Install a belay cable at what seems to be an appropriate height as per the other contiguous high ropes course elements. If this particular *Heebie Jeebie* is being built separately, go for as much height as the trees and your vertigo quotient allow. Remember when measuring and cutting the belay cable, to add at least 18' for the safety back up loop; that's 9' for each support tree, probably a generous ammount, but better generous than one inch short.

About 12' below and parallel to the belay cable, install another length of 3/8" cable between support trees. Remember, since this is not a belay cable, back up loops aren't necessary.

Measure up from this cable about 5' on each support tree directly above and vertically in line with the anchor bolts, and at that 5' mark, drive in a 1/2" staple;

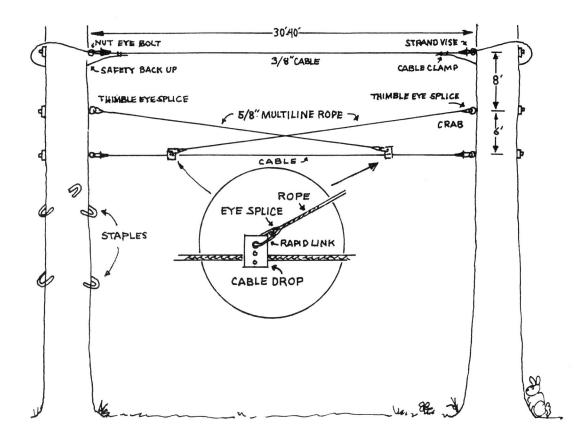

vertical or horizontal orientation — makes no difference. The placement of this stape must be secure, so if the tree is a hardwood that is resisting your massive sledge blows, yield and pre-drill the tree, (3/8" bit to a depth of 1 1/4") to protect the tree from errant blows— also ensuring bomb-proof staple placement.

Using an extension ladder leaned against the lower cable to gain access, loosely attach two 3/8" cable clamps onto the cable. Each of these two clamps will separately secure an eye spliced end of the 5/8" rope section. Locate each clamp one third the length of the cable away from the nearest support tree. Orient each clamp on the cable so that the threaded ends face down and the closed part of the **U** is up. Turn this page upside down and the closed

part of the **U** will be up. (I tried to electronically do it for you, but the computer won't let me.)

If the bottom cable is higher than your ladder will extend, you get to take a ride out on the cable using a harness/pulley arrangement — not comfortable, but not difficult either. An alternative to harness-hanging is accurate measuring and pre-fabing of the rope/cable clamp juncture before installing the cable. I've never had much luck with pre-measuring; I'm one of those cursed measure-a-hundred-times-and-cut-once people.

Measure the diagonal distance from where one of the clamps will be attached to the 5' staple that is on the furthest support tree. The measurement from the second clamp location to the other far staple should be identical to the one you just made. Cut two lengths of 5/8" multiline rope that equal this measurement plus 7'. (The extra 7' allows tying a prusik knot.)

Eye splice separate ends of these two ropes and (now you can slide out on the cable) U-bolt [clamp] the spliced eyes onto the cable, then reeve the unattached working rope ends through the 5' staples so that the two ropes end up crossing one another approximately in the center of the traverse. Tie a prusik knot arrangement in each rope (as the working end comes back onto the standing part), both to secure the rope and to allow future tension/slack adjustments.

The illustration (round insert) shows the ropes attached to the cable via a combination of rapid link and cable drop. Either way works fine.

Do not secure the ropes together where they cross, as this free play of rope provides part of the *Heebie Jeebie* challenge. Surprise! — you're done.

I have, since writing the above instructions for the *Heebie-Jeebie*, talked with Tom Quimby (one of **PA**'s National Certified Trainers), and he passed on this variation to me.

Build the event no higher than 6' (no belay) and make all the lines from 3/4" rope. (Splice where the diagonal rope intersects the bottom horizontal rope.) In this way, more people can try more often, since the completion percentage isn't very high. Make sure the ground is well turned under this event, and spot well, as falls to the turf are common.

The Heebie or The Jeebie

If you "string" the foot cable (as above) and then install just *one* of the angled ropes, you have constructed a difficult crossing event called either *The Heebie* or

The Jeebie:—your choice. This event requires a belay, unless it is built as a low element.

The Hour Glass

This low event is much like the *Heebie Jeebie* except that it's easier to build and much harder to accomplish.

Choose two support trees that are about 15' apart. The ground between these two trees needs to be clear of all rocks and stumps. Clear all dead and living limbs to a height of 10'.

Drive in a 1/2" staple (V) at about 7' so that the **U** portion of the staple points at the other support tree. Drive in a similarly oriented staple one foot off the ground. Place two more staples in the adjacent support tree that duplicate what you have just done. Sledge these four staples in as if they were going to serve as climbing belay anchors.

Measure the tree to tree distance diagonally from high staple to low staple, and cut two lengths of 3/4" multiline to equal that measurement plus 6'. Eye splice (use a thimble) one end of each separate rope.

Using 11/16" rapid links, connect the eye spliced ends to the high staples, and reeve (that's a fancy word for threading the rope through something) the other ends through the low staples so that the ropes cross just about midway between the trees.

Bring the rope end back on itself and tie a prusik knot. If you don't want to mess with a prusik, just finish off the end with a couple half hitches around the low staple.

There you go, it's ready to use. Just start at one tree and try to make it to the other tree without touching-hitting-smacking the ground. This low ropes event is deceptively difficult and requires attentive spotting.

Centipede

Here's an exciting high event that is easy to build, install, and of course, fun to mess around on. The scenario suggests climbing; your vertiginous psyche suggests discretion.

Picture 4-6 vertically connected 4 x 4's (end to end), swaying gently from a high eyebolted branch. Each 4 x 4 displays varied sequences of hammered-in 1/2" staples.

The Centipede is a simple climbing event that offers unique access to higher things. Take a look at the photographs and the following text for instructions on how to make your own. Don't hesitate on this one — it's easy to fabricate and simple to suspend.

- Measure the height from whatever tree branch or cable that you want to hang this event.

- Considering that you will be using 6-8' sections of 4 x 4 boards to fill the vertical space, determine how many boards you will need.

- Using a 1/2" drill bit, drill through each board on-center about 3" in from each end. Insert and nut-down a drop forged bolt into each of these holes. Don't forget a washer at each end of the bolt.

- Hammer in 1/2" staples along the length of each board, using 14-16" as a vertical spacing guide and your imagination for spatial orientation (side-by-side, alternating, spiral, free form). You must pre-drill twice with a 7/16" drill bit for each staple, to prevent splitting the board. Tap the staple with a hammer to mark the board at the desired location, and drill to a depth of 1" at those two marks. Each 1/2" staple should be hammered horizontally into the holes to a depth of approximately 2". Don't

over-drive the staples or splitting will occur.

- Connect the boards (eye bolt to eye bolt) with 1/2" rapid links.

- The branch (cable) that you wish to connect with should have an additional 5/8" eye bolt (or juxtaposed cable clamps) for belay rope use.

- Haul this segmented contraption up using a single rope/pulley arrangement and clip the top eye bolt into the 5/8" nut eye bolt in the overhead branch, using a wide-opening locking steel carabiner, or a 5/8" rapid link. Done!

Ideally, the end of an 8' bottom board should be about 8' off the ground so that a short (4-5') stapled bottom segment of 4 x 4 can be removed, to preclude unauthorized use.

If this event is not being utilized for access to other high ropes course elements, to facilitate the lowering process, ask a student to pull the bottom 4 x 4 away from

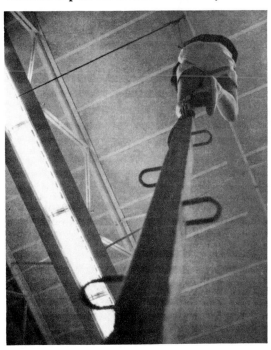

plumb (as you would on the *Dangle Duo*), so that you can lower the participant briskly without having to worry about body contact with the staples or boards.

Staples

If you build ropes courses, or plan to string a few cables for your own program, this next time and $$$ saver will more than pay for the cost of this book.

Use 1/2" galvanized staples to establish a climb up your high ropes course support trees. That's it. I could just stop there, because everything else I write is simply supportive, but . . .

The staples are placed in a pole or tree with the use of a hand sledge. It takes me about 10 good hits to place a staple in hardwood, and 5-7 whacks for softwood.

Leave enough staple sticking out to provide a sufficient hand or foot hold. Here's a photograph of a marked 1/2" staple to give you an idea of about how far I slam it in.

Notice that the part sticking out of the tree provides an ideal foot hold, and also allows a firm hand grip without having to worry about losing your finger (like sticking your finger through the eyehole of a 1/2" or 5/8" SLES), as the result of a fall. Makes me cringe just to think about it. 3/8" galvanized staples also have numerous uses on a ropes course. The following list will give you an idea where I use the two sizes.

1/2" staple

1. To establish a climb up a support tree. (H)
2. Clip-in points for a *Fidget Ladder*. (V)
3. Connector point for *Tension Traverse* hand ropes. (V)
4. Supports for *Rebirth* (Hole in One) Tire. (V)
5. Self-belay points on a tree climb. (V)

3/8" staple

1. Attachment points for the *Spider's Web*.
2. Attachment points for the *Maze*.
3. Lock-up point for a swing cable or haul system.
4. Tent pegs in hard soil.

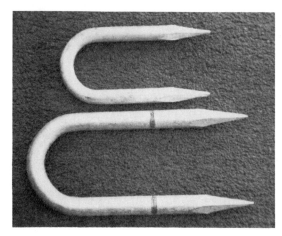

5. Used to stake out the *Unholy Alliance* ground rope.

I can remember ropes course building without using staples . . . but I'd rather not.

Here's how to staple a tree or pole to gain access to higher things.

You are going to need at least a 2 lb. hand sledge, and if you can manage it, I think you are better off with a 2 1/2 lb. head. You cannot place staples with a frameing or claw hammer, don't even bother trying.

The handle should be long enough to develop efficient head arc speed, and to allow occasional use of a two handed swing. The handle is usually made of hickory, ash, or fiberglass. Personally, I like a synthetic handle; it lasts longer (stays in one piece after numerous off center blows) and seems to cause less fatigue after the 50th ± staple placement.

Swinging a hand sledge with leverage and accuracy takes practice—so practice! It

sounds a bit compulsive, but if you know that you will be placing many staples over a period of time, it pays work related dividends to practice swinging that hand sledge. Search for a still-vertical dead tree, then, with your feet on the ground, and tree belt slung around the dead trunk, slam away at an imaginary staple on the tree. Try to direct your blows accurately and consistently, occasionally switching hands to gain some practice with your non-dominant arm.

There is also something primally satisfying about smashing a hand sledge repeatedly against a chosen target. I can't remember a day coming home frustrated with work, life, etc. after having stapled-up a couple trees. Sound simple? Life should be so simple.

You will also need a tree or pole belt. This is a workman's belt that encircles the tree or pole, and allows you to use both hands for whatever task needs to be accomplished. Stapling up a high tree without a belt is either a ludicrous display of stubbornness or reveals a distressing level of poverty. Use of this type of belt takes some getting used to; i.e., trusting the hardware to support you at height. Get used to it, or you're not going to get much done after you transfer off the ladder onto the staples.

Affix a hammer holster to the belt for obvious reasons, and also purchase a canvas bag for carrying staples. Generously sized wide- mouth bags are available that attach conveniently to your belt. Stapling up a high tree requires carrying two bags. I also use a 16 gauge shot gun shell bandolier made of stretch nylon to carry staples, (see photo at left.)

Fill your bag with 1/2" staples, and tie a small diameter rope onto your belt in order to haul up all the things that you will eventually need or have already forgotten. Don't forget your sledge.

Climb a short ladder to about a 12' mark

Photo by Brahm Schatia

on the trunk, and place the first staple at that height; i.e., high enough to preclude casual unauthorized climbing, and low enough to be reached by a short/light ladder.

Climbing staples should be pounded in perpendicular to the trunk and parallel to the ground so that they provide an easy grab and a comfortable stance. Choking up on the sledge handle, smack the hand-held staple a few light blows to get it started. Then with controlled vigor, slam that sucker as accurately and as hard as you can. It takes me about six good one-handed shots to drive a staple into a white pine trunk, (2 1/2" in the tree, 3 1/2" available for grabbing and standing.) Slamming staples into a red oak trunk, I'm more apt to use a double handed blow, and it usually takes between 8-9 solid hits.

Some trees (Live Oak, Causaurina, Hop Hornbeam, and others) need to be predrilled, simply because they are just too hard. I know someday you'll try to drive a staple into one of these hyper-hard trees just because Karl said you can't, but the result is predetermined, either no penetration at all (accompanied by flying bark and staples) or a flattened staple head without sufficient depth achieved; either way results in funny looking staples, and lots of whacked-off bark from frustrated errant blows.

If the temperature has been well below freezing for a few days and then warms up enough to tempt you to do some building, you might find that the tree's surface has frozen enough to preclude staple placement. After half a dozen good hits trying to place a staple into a frozen white pine, it'll spit the well-whacked **U** right back at your head.

In either case, if too hard or frozen, predrill with a 3/8" drill bit to a depth of about 1 1/4".

After you get the first staple in, measure

about 14" up the trunk (a handle and a half of the hammer I use) and 12" to the side of that staple. Smack another staple in there. Depending upon your ladder height and placement you can usually get a third staple in before transferring your weight onto the first two. The third staple measures up another 14" and 12" over; i.e., about in line vertically with the first staple. Now throw the belt rope around the trunk, clip in, and transfer your weight to the bottom two staples, one foot on each staple.

Continue this alternating left and right stapling system all the way up the trunk until you have reached whatever height is necessary for installation of the planned ropes element. The staples will form a zigzagged path up the trunk, with all the right hand and left hand staples lining up just about vertically. If you want the climb to be more challenging, increase the distance between staples or vary their placement around the trunk. Don't spiral around the tree as it will cause problems with the belay rope.

On the way up you will probably and

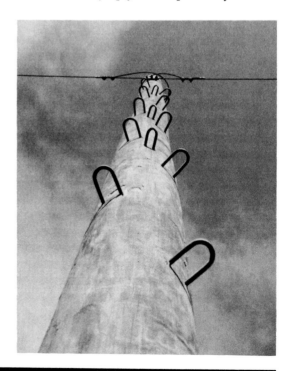

eventually have to clear (cut) off a few limbs; dead and alive. Do a neat job of trimming the live limbs (undercut the limb first to one quarter its diameter before making the top cut), otherwise the falling limb will strip bark from the trunk. After a few of these ugly cut & strip disasters you might as well kiss the tree goodbye, because those large gouge marks are irresistible becons for boring insects.

If you come to a large limb that does not need pruning, situate yourself solidly on the staples, undo your rope sling, move it efficiently above the limb and reclip smartly. During the unclip/clip time span you will be off belay — I just wanted you to know that.

As you are establishing the climb, you might as well take care of placing the needed belay staples. These somewhat off-vertical oriented staples are placed every 6-7 feet on the trunk, starting about 6 feet above the top of the ladder, and centrally paralleling the climb. Place these belay staples directly up the center of the ladder-like side staples (see photo on page 184). Staple belay anchors are for use by that otherwise unprotected individual who is climbing the tree using "bear claw" (lobster-claw) self-belay ropes.

The off-vertical orientation (somewhat oblique) of the belay staples is necessary to keep from splitting the trunk. If the two shanks of the staple are situated in line vertically, their combined diameters can cause the trunk to split, with a resultant harmful open-wound scenario.

If you notice that even your horizontally driven staples are causing the bark of the tree to split, it would be wise for the future health of the tree to predrill before placement.

Drive the first off-vertical belay staple into the trunk (pole) about six feet above the top of the ladder and directly in the middle of the zig-zag line of climbing

staples. The belay staple must be able to hold a potential fall, so sledge it in to the extent that the inside curve of the staple is approximately 1 1/2 inches out from the trunk. It has been proven through UIAA-type drop-test falls that a vertically placed staple will hold a much greater shock-load fall than a horizontally oriented staple, even if both the staples are driven to the same depth. Do not clip into a horizontally driven staple.

Staple Tricks

- Extra staples can be carried in an old shot-gun-shell bandolier. Don't use the leather type; look for a synthetic, stretchy material loop that will hold the individual staples in place. Wearing a full bandolier of staples with sledge in hand, makes quite a work ethic statement, also providing a photo-op of rare proportion.

- When you are so situated on the trunk that you cannot use a free hand to position the staple for tapping in place, hold the **U** portion of the staple in the palm of your dominant hand and slam the points into the trunk. It will tenuously stay there while you aim carefully and get in a couple medium effort blows to set the points. (Any errent strike at this juncture will result in a flying staple). Then give it the ole two handed smack-er-oo for as many hits as it takes for secure placement.

- When you end up at the height necessary to work on a cable or install a platform, sometimes it's necessary to knock in a couple staples at foot level so that you can stand comfortably and move by degrees around the trunk. Do not over-drive these standing staples because you will probably want to remove them later. Two good hits in a pine is all that's necessary.

As you attempt to remove a staple, remember to hit it from side to side, not up and down. Control your removal blows so that you can eventually hand-wiggle the staple out of the tree, and not watch it plummet toward the scattering workers below. Three or four solid side-to-side hits should be all that's necessary.

When the staple is removed, two obviously open wounds are left in the trunk. Fill these with a squirt of 50-year-silicone from your caulking gun. This type of clear caulking is useable for other ropes course building applications ("Paint and putty cover the devil."), so don't hesitate to buy a couple cylinders.

- For some after hours adventure-type recreation, try using a 1/2" staple like a throwing knife. Staples are well balanced and thunk solidly in wood as the result of a good throw. Do I have to tell you not to throw at live trees? Good!

Single Line Potpourri

Read this and pay attention if your budget is limited and your sense of frugality likes multi-use ropes course elements.

Since you're still reading, I have obviously snared the interest (curiosity) of a skeptic or a ropes course aficionado . . . or maybe you're bored sitting on a New York to Boston commuter flight, and the flight attendant just told you that there aren't any magazines, and reading the airbag sickness instructions just doesn't grab you like it used to — so, you down two or three cups of rank airline coffee, look out the double (scratched) plastic windows at nothing ('cause you're over the wing and at 17,000 feet with a low cloud cover, what's to see?), and out of desperation, reach between your legs into the bulging carry-on pack that never fits under the seat in front of you, and attempt to find some "work," but by acci-

dent you grab December's BOT's. You figure, "What the heck," and begin to read — before the coffee nails your nephrons and initiates not-to-be-ignored synaptic bladder signals, necessitating asking the two obese people snoring next to you to move so you can . . .

This is the stuff of imagination, because all the following events are based on a simple swing rope.

1. *Swing for Distance* — There is some skill associated with attempting to swing for distance on a rope; i.e., swinging forward and letting go of the rope. If the starting point is elevated (off a stump, pommel horse, Swedish box), more distance is gained by grasping the rope and jumping up and backward than can be accomplished by simply thrusting forward, as per the length-of-pendulum principle.

   Adjust the landing area so that a jump mat or loose sand/dirt will meet the flying swinger. Judge the distance on this impromptu event as you would the running long jump. You will find that most participants will want to try this event over and over, notwithstanding their distance as compared to other swingers' efforts. Emphasize PB's, (Personal Bests).

2. *Stump-to-Stump Swing* — Offer an elevated take-off and a similar landing area, and you have an event that is given to many attempts, even if the first try is successful: point-to-point swinging just feels good.

   Try to arrange the take-off and landing points (adjustable stumps or boxes) so that swinging to and from can be accomplished with varying degrees of difficulty. Do not make these areas so high that spotting becomes either impossible or of the *puleeez*-don't-fall type.

3. *Sea Gull Swing* — This swing and pivot combination is a continuation and embellishment of the stump-to-stump swing and landing described above. The swing itself is so constructed that the landing platform appears to be misplaced or more accurately, badly placed. If the swing is attempted directly toward the landing area, most people would whack their shins or completely miss the landing, so an alternate, wide-arc approach must be taken. This is a swing that may have to be eventually demonstrated by an instructor if the participants are having trouble "making it."

Emphasize to the swingers that their safety is ensured by their grip on the rope, and that they should not be tempted to let go *until their feet are solidly on the platform and their body is in balance.*

If the swing arc is either too great or too little, the participant will miss the landing area. This event is a let-me-have-one-more-try winner. The illustration shows the proper swing path and angled orientation of the landing board.

The following events can also be accomplished with a single line swing rope. These events are included and explained in the book *Silver Bullets*, or elsewhere in this book.

1. Prouty's Landing
2. Nitro Crossing
3. Prusik Climbs
4. Scooter Swing
5. Disc Jockeys

Ride the Wild Log

This bouncing, jerking, log-ride activity injects some role-playing fantasy and surfer-like balance movements into a staid old ropes course element (which name is as predictable as its action — the *Swinging Log*).

Pretending briefly that you are Buck Hornbeam, acclaimed saddle-hardened bronco buster, or Duke Reefhound, the hot curl idol of the surf set, try swinging onto the swinging log (an arcing swing around one of the support trees), then, precariously balanced and *holding onto the rope with only one hand*, attempt to "ride the wild log" for 6 seconds. If you have a hat, it should be held in the free hand during your "ride": a hat is a necessary accoutrement in order to score more "rider style-points."

The swing onto the log need not be long, just enough to arrive there and impart some action to the log itself. Attach the swing rope to one of the support trees about 30' up the trunk, (1/2" vertical staple). The start of the swing can be initiated from a placed section of vertical log that provides an elevated (12") takeoff point. Try the swing a few times off the steps of a supported step-ladder to determine where to best place the take off stump.

Clear the area around the swinging log of all sharp or hard objects (rocks, limb sections) because spotting this event is difficult and potentially dangerous to the spotter, resulting from the erratic action of the swinging log. Critical spotting areas are near the cable and next to the support tree.

Through Bolting Trees and Poles

A "better" method for attaching a cable to a support (tree, pole) is to drill through the support and place an eye bolt. Tree surgeons regularly do this to reinforce weak limbs or to protect valuable trunk sections

from wind and ice. Here are a few sweat-hog drilling tips gleaned from many hours of "making holes."

Au Naturel (by hand) — If you can afford to rent an alternator (alternating current); terrific! Refer to *Power Tools* below. If your budget won't allow the rental fee, hold a bake sale, plead with the parents, or ask your Mom, but try like the dickens to avoid hand drilling the **many** holes necessary to construct a ropes course. However, since I also went through a Thoreauvian period (simplicity, simplicity, simplicity), here's a pat on the back (with liniment), and some ideas for you hard folks.

Buy or obtain a decent bit brace. It's hard enough to manually drill through a 14 inch hardwood trunk without having to combat excess friction. A bit brace with ball-bearings pays for itself soon enough in time saved.

Keep the tip of the auger bit sharp by not throwing or storing it unsheathed in a tool box. Cover at least the tip of the bit

with something (cork, foam, metal tube, etc.) to maintain its feeding and cutting edges.

Try to position yourself (on the ground, in a tree, or on a ladder) so that you can apply moderate pressure on the bit brace. It's impressive to the slack-jawed gawkers to drill through a hickory trunk 12 inches over your head, but so, so wasteful of your time, energy, and patience.

As you drill, remove the bit every two inches or so in order to clean the hole of shavings. Take 2-3 turns counterclockwise to free the drill tip, then pull back hard to achieve this cleaning. (This clean hole suggestion is not an anal compulsive thing. If you let shavings build up in the deepening hole, friction will soon slow and eventually stop your rotation efforts.) Make sure the chuck is tight on the drill bit, or check your belay, before pulling back too hard.

Switch arms occassionally for turning the brace, if you anticipate drilling many holes. Although this may seem initially awkward, switch hitting with the bit brace postpones the 2 p.m. limp arm syndrome.

After drilling at height, don't just drop the bit brace or drill to the ground as an expedient means of "lowering" the tools. Trying to drill with even a slightly bent bit or brace will convince you to respect the tools.

A quick and efficient way to get almost any tool down is to improvise an im-

promptu zip arrangement. Hold onto one end of your haul rope and have your "down" partner walk the other end of the rope away from the base of the tree. Attach the zipable tools to the rope with a carabiner and release, courteously indicating to your partner that you are sending a few pounds of tools zinging in his/her direction. A couple yards before the tools reach the end, your partner gives major slack to the rope and the tools come satisfyingly to a stop. This technique not only saves time and the tools, but is obviously more fun than simply lowering the heavy things, and what's wrong with a diversion or two? . . . since you have been working so hard and all.

Power Tools — What a treat! These torquing demons eat right through the supports with little effort, leaving more time for planning, curriculum design, and getting to the restaurant before it closes.

    Checklist for a good drill: (1) Industrially rated with a minimum 1/2 inch chuck. (2) With a reverse — not absolutely necessary, but a time-saver. (3) The permanent ON button should be in a position that precludes accidental pushing. As an aside and a warning, if while drilling you lose control of the drill (it spins out of your hands), and the ON button has been depressed, negative things usually happen in a hurry. Unless the spinning drill cuts its own power source, your partner must quickly pull the plug.

    High or low speed RPM is OK. It's easier to control a low RPM drill, but it's obviously slower. A low RPM drill is best for metal drilling. Variable speed is a plus.

Drilling Tips:

If you let the drill bit pull itself all the way into the trunk, past the spirals, it will probably jam; i.e., continue spinning but

not come out. If you have a reverse switch, use it. Otherwise, remove the drill by loosening the chuck, then turn the bit out counterclockwise with a vise grip, or more dramatically, knock the bit through with a smaller diameter length of steel rod.

    Use an 11/16" diameter drill bit. The slightly larger bit size (1/16" larger than the bolt shaft) allows easy bolt insertion into the just drilled hole. If you use a 5/8" drill bit, you will have to hand sledge the 5/8" bolts into place.

    When you plug the end of the drill wire into the extension cord(s), tie a knot (square knot or figure eight) using both ends of the cords before plugging them together. This prevents unplugging at inconvenient times.

    Pre-drilling for a SLES (shoulder lag eye screw) is best done with a spade or speed bore drill bit. Drill about one inch in at a time, pulling back frequently to clean the hole. Use a 5/8" drill bit for a 3/4" SLES.

    I have seen at least three SLES bolts snap during ropes course use, once when I was demonstrating an element! Don't use these lag eye screws for any cable attachment that results in flexion of the cable; i.e., shock loading the cable.

Through Bolts — NEBs & TEBs

There is an on-going and general concern about the load placed on bolted-through-the-tree eye bolts by the force resulting from a missed trapeze jump attempt. (There are other belay situations on a high ropes course that occasionally result in a "catch," but none as frequently and predictably as a result of the trapeze attempt.)

    I can understand the concern, and it's this "what if?" type of thinking that often results in safer rigging being developed. The concern is heightened after watching a ropes course participant plummet past the safety of that slim PVC trapeze (silver dollar eyes, churning legs, flailing arms — awesome!).

But the belay works: the belayer is well trained and confident, the "jus-rite descender" adds controlled friction, the "shear reduction block" maintains the rope's tensile strength, and the anchor bolts remain secure. Yeah, but what if the bolt breaks? I have never experienced or heard of a through-the-tree belay bolt that *Project Adventure* installed as ever having failed, but even if it did, there is a back-up system on all belay cables of equal or greater strength than the original set-up. This is an example of responding to the "what if?". . . thinking that I referred to above.

A ropes course cable belay is dynamic in the following ways: (1) The nylon mountaineering rope, because of its elasticity, absorbs much of the fall's impact. (2) The two trees through which the anchor bolts are placed are flexible enough to be pulled inward as the result of a fall. (3) The belayer (if the Jus-Rite descender is *not* used) provides another dynamic (moving) factor.

Thimble Eye Bolt Placement

Thimble eye bolts are obtained from electrical supply companies (Graybar Co. in Boston), or from local power companies. *Project Adventure* also sells them. Their advantage is that they have a thimble arrangement forged into the head of the bolt to help reduce cable shear.

After an 11/16" diameter hole is drilled through a tree or pole, the 5/8" diameter thimble eye bolt (TEB) is inserted into position. The thimble eye configuration should be aligned in a vertical position. If the thimble grooves are aligned obliquely or horizontally, the cable will slip off the grooves, cancelling the effectiveness of the built-in shear reduction groove.

Use a galvanized fish plate washer (2" X 2") at both ends of the bolt. The head end washer slows the tree's tendency to grow around the bolt head.

Notice that the TEB nut has square and beveled edges. After you put a washer on the inserted bolt end, turn the nut on the threaded bolt so that the beveled side of the nut is toward the trunk. This bevel will allow the nut to turn against the washer even if it is not perfectly flush with the washer, which it rarely is, considering that the trunk has irregular contours.

The protruding threaded end of the bolt should be cut off if it's part of a low element because: (1) A threaded bolt end can cause injury (2) A cut and peened-over (buggered-up) end of a bolt makes the fixture permanent and not the target for prankish theft.

On a high element, the protruding bolt can often be used as a hand or foot hold or as a back-up cable support. A vandal's interest seems to decline in proportion to increased height.

Use a hacksaw with a quality ($) toothed blade, and cut flush with the end of the nut. It will take approximately 75 firm strokes to cut through a 5/8" bolt (that's a thinly veiled challenge . . .), but don't bother cutting all the way through. When you're a bit past halfway (40 strokes), use a hammer to smack the end of the bolt at right angles and the shaft will snap off. Take a 360° clockwise turn on the nut with an adjustable wrench, then peen-over the remaining threaded end with a hammer.

Ropes Course Longevity — Soil Compaction

It should concern you as to how long the trees on your ropes course are going to last, because without them, utility poles become the answer for element supports. From an aesthetic standpoint, I'll take trees any day.

It's amazing how fast a wooded area can be trampled down by participants' feet over the course of only a few months. The undergrowth will completely disappear (a temporary benefit), and shortly thereafter, the soil will begin to compact. A manifestation of soil compaction is the appearance of roots that you didn't know were there. These exposed roots are damaged inadvertently by participant foot traffic, as students walk from event to event. Additionally, as the soil becomes more compacted, less water can penetrate to the tree roots. The trees suffer in both instances.

To alleviate this heavy use problem, something organic must be put on the forest floor, particularly in the area of the highest foot traffic. Wood chips provide a good natural covering; stuff called *duff* by woodland folks-in-the-know. Chips are easily attainable, blend in well with the forest scene, are biodegradable and, most importantly, alleviate the environmental problems mentioned above. Check with your town's road department, they are usually looking for a place to dump chips.

In the flush of building a new ropes course, don't forget the consequences of upsetting the delicate balances that occur in a forest ecosystem.

The down side of using wood chips is that the chipped trees might have been diseased. Bark mulch can also be used, (smells good) but it's considerably more expensive.

Wood Preservatives

If you are using creosote, Penta, or Cuprinol for preserving wood on your ropes course — check out these paragraphs from *Harrowsmith* magazine.

"The three most common oil-based preservatives are creosote, pentachloropenol, and copper naphthenate. Creosote, the gooey, dark brown stuff used to preserve railroad ties and telephone poles, has some 200 major chemical constituents and several thousand minor ones. Many of these chemicals are toxic; some are carcinogenic; others, while not necessarily harmful to people, are damaging to plants."

"Pentachlorophenol, or "penta," was once readily available and is still occasionally sold, though its sale was restricted by the Environmental Protection Agency in 1984 because it contains dioxin, one of the worst toxic substances known to man."

"Copper naphthenate (best known by the brand name Cuprinol) — a sticky, dark green liquid — is less effective as a wood preservative than creosote or pentachlorophenol. It is also thought to be less harmful to plants and people."

"Water-based preservatives, such as those used in pressure-treated wood, are generally safer than the oil-based varieties. The green-tinted wood sold in lumberyards has been impregnated under pressure, or pressure-treated, with one of two water-based preservatives: chromated copper arsenate (CCA), or ammoniated copper arsenate (ACA). In their liquid states, CCA and ACA are toxic chemicals. But in the pressure-treating process, the arsenical compounds are chemically bonded with wood molecules so that they can neither leach into the soil nor be absorbed into the skin of people or animals coming into contact with the wood."

"Apparently, the only way to absorb the arsenical compounds into one's system is to ingest the wood itself. Short of taking a bite out of a green-tinted 2 x 4, the only way one might inadvertently take in small doses is by inhaling sawdust from pressure-treated lumber, or by breathing the fumes when burning it. Wearing a protective mask when sawing the wood seems like a wise precautionary measure."

Wood Rot

To those ropes course builders who plan to be around for a few years, it is of some concern as to how long their masterpieces of ingenuity and perspiration are going to last; i.e., when will I have to replace the *Beam, Swinging Log, Stump Jumps*, etc. The following information is the result of some research, but mostly experience in the New England area.

First and last rule: If you anticipate your program lasting for at least three years, choose your cut trees wisely and buy pressure-treated lumber; variously called **wolmanized** or **outdoor wood**.

Some types of cut wood (felled trees) are more susceptible to rot (action of bacteria and fungus) than others. A brief comparison follows:

Wood susceptible to rot — ash, aspen, beech, birch, cottonwood, elm, oaks in the red oak group, poplar, fir, willow, spruce, maple.

Wood resistant to rot — cedar, black locust, oaks in the white oak group, sassafras, osage orange.

Cut log sapwood (phloem) rots faster than heartwood (xylem), so just because the surface of your Beam looks a bit time-worn doesn't mean that a break is imminent, but it's an indication that replacement should be on your mind. I had to replace a sugar maple *Beam* that measured 12" in diameter because it literally broke in half (with some help). This impressive section of wood came from a tree, cut five years earlier. A piece of white oak might have given me 8-10 years, and a section of black locust would probably still be there when you and I are

pulling down a pension. So, the choice of wood does make a difference in element longevity.

A handy test for wood fiber soundness is to stick the log with the blade of a pocket knife (or with the Rockwell hardened C65-68, seven inch hand-crafted, carbon steel blade of your staghorn, and nickel silver-handled, folding magnum deer slayer.) If the blade enters the log over an inch with just a moderate push, it's replacement time. As a further test, you can jump up and down on the log and listen for cracks, but this is obviously a poor image move, and not recommended without a belay.

It helps to remove the bark before placing the log. The bark, as the cambium quickly decays, provides an ideal protected habitat for various boring insects, bacteria, and fungi. The bark will slough off in less than two years anyway, so you might as well strip it initially.

Wood or lumber that is going to be placed in the ground must be chemically treated, or it will rot within 3-4 years, and in some cases, less than 2 years. Lumber that has been pressure-injected with Cuprinol (*Wolmanized* and *Outdoor Wood* are trademarks for this pressure-treated lumber), will last a minimum of 20 years in the ground (so the guarantee says). Treated lumber often costs no more than normal kiln-dried material.

If you have the forethought to cut and cure a log, you can soak the end in preservative to achieve a longer "in ground" life. The most practical idea and application is to use a section of utility pole that has already been pressure-treated with a preservative.

I learned recently that the chemical pressure treating process for logs is not effective in getting the chemical into the heartwood (xylem). Therefore, the center of a utility pole will rot much sooner than the exterior fibers—just thought you'd like to know.

Tree platforms are best made from 2" x 6" sections of treated lumber. The section of a platform made from untreated lumber that rots most swiftly is that part juxtaposed to the tree; the wood interface which remains moist. The vulnerable inside of that bolted section next to the tree is practically impossible to re-paint and, because of trapped moisture, is an ideal spot for decay-producing organisms to proliferate. Slop on some Cuprinol a couple times a year.

As a last $$$ saving suggestion: When buying lumber for a Wall, the four 4"x 4" sections should be pressure treated lumber because of their bolted position on the support trees (potential rot area), but the 2" x 10" sections can be kiln-dried fir, spruce, etc. Look how long an unpainted New England barn can last.

Telephone Pole Esoteria

Want to be conversant about utility pole imprints at your next gathering? Are you embarrassed when someone asks, "How deep should I set a 35' pole?", and you don't know a posthole from a pole hole? Here are some exotic facts that may or may not be pertinent to your knowledge bank

Length of Pole in Feet	Setting Depth in Feet
25	5
30-35	5'6"
40	6
45	6'6"

"Continues in 5' lengths as to 6" depth increments up to an 80' pole, which is set at 10'."

Backfilling

"Thoroughly tamp the fill material *by layers* until hole is completely filled around pole. Tamp any stones available against pole surface and finally form a dirt mound to give drainage away from the pole."

Pole Breaking Strength

"The average transverse load applied 2 feet from the top, which will break the pole."

Class I (min. top circumference 27") - 4,500 lbs.

Class II (min. top circumference 25") - 3,700 lbs.

Estimated Weight of Creosoted Poles		
30' Class I	—	1,122 lbs.
50' Class I	—	2,563 lbs.
35' Class II	—	1,254 lbs.
75' Class I	—	5,375 lbs.

Reading a Pole

The burned-on imprint at the base (about eye level) of a utility pole tells you (top to bottom) where the pole is from geographically, what type of preservative treatment was applied, date of treatment, what the height is in feet, and what class pole it is. (*Class* pertains to diameter and/or circum-

ference. A Class I pole is "thicker" than a Class II pole.)

The bottom set of numbers (sometimes hyphenated) is of most interest to you. It will appear, for example, as 3-35, or 2-40, etc. The first number is the pole class and the double digit number refers to the pole height in feet.

Just for fun, go out to the street by the front of your house and "read" a pole or two.

In order to collect utility poles for your ropes course, why not have a pot-luck pole party, where each guest must bring their own Class I, 40-footer? Maybe just an imprint rubbing would be sufficient to qualify for dessert.

All of the preceding quoted information is from a training article by the New England Electric Company.

How To Cut Cable

Let me get right to the crux of the cutting. Cable (wire rope) is either easily cut with the proper tool, or the cutting (?) becomes a time-consuming, exhausting exercise in frustration.

A triangular jaw cable cutter (not a bolt cutter; its parallel jaws will only squash the cable strands), when kept sharp, will efficiently slice through cable up to 1/2". The tool is advertised to be capable of cutting 5/8" cable and that's true, but it requires considerable strength of limb and

a good leverage position. As an aside: A cable slicer of this type does a bang-up job of cutting rope, actually better than any knife I've ever used.

If you have access to a portable circular saw, buy a metal cutting blade and you have a combination that will zip through 3/8" cable in seconds; not bad at all for the price. Its only drawback, aside from an irritating screeching noise and an abundance of sparks, is that cutting at heights is a bit awkward (and ludicrous). Just be careful with your ground cable measurements and no trimming in the trees or beams will be necessary. Well . . . it sounds good, anyway.

A guillotine-like cable slicer is available that allows you to cut cable with a few well-placed hand sledge blows. Buy the expensive model (comparatively) made by Morse-Starette; others I have tried or heard of do a lousy job, dull quickly, or malfunc-

tion. This whacker/slicer is efficient and cuts the cable cleanly, but must be supported on a hard, unyielding surface — not a tree limb.

Let me make brief mention of using a hacksaw — DON'T!

Tightening Cables

Please recognize that a taut cable can withstand less strain than a loose cable — actually, the looser the cable, the more weight (strain) it can withstand; measured within parameters of the cable's anchor point tensile strength. But, it's often necessary to tighten the cables in order to make a ropes course event possible. For example, the cables of the *Mohawk Walk*. But, if it's a *Pamper Pole*/trapeze jump belay cable (and it's not also part of a *Two Line Bridge*), the cable can be left quite slack.

According to the title of this brief essay, I am supposed to be telling you about tightening cables, so let's *come-along* and start with a pair of Haven's grips, because I want to indicate how two of these handy grips are utilized for pulling a section of cable taut: the double Haven's grip technique.

Your efforts, so far, have resulted in one end of a 3/8" cable being strand vised to an eye bolt (or cable clamped or swaged). The other end (working end) is reeved through another distant anchoring eye bolt and is received (cammed) by the first Haven's grip, which is itself attached to a hook on one end of the come-along. Let out or release 3-4 ft. of line (small diameter cable or chain) on the come-along and attach the second grip as far out on the standing part of the 3/8" cable as possible. This second grip is attached to the other hook on the come-along. (If you are working at height, it's a real convenience to be able to lean out

against a lineman's belt to secure this second Haven's grip.)

With both Haven's grips camming the cable in opposition, start cranking in with the come-along. The two grips should now be working against one another, causing a tightening of the cable.

After re-reading this somewhat murky bit of Haven's-grip-this and come-along-that, I'll understand if things don't just snap together the first time. Give it (me) another try, expository writing isn't easy, you know.

Extraneous Tidbit — When you are tightening the cables on a *Two Line Bridge* (actually three cables), watch the first cable that you tightened as you tension the second cable. As soon as the first cable shows any slack developing, stop tightening the second cable — they are now as close to being equally taut as you can get them. Ditto for the third cable.

Measuring Cable — "Measure 100 times and cut once."

To keep cable waste to a minimum, think a bit ahead before cutting your desired lengths. With a measuring tape (50-100' fiberglass), measure from tree to tree (bolt to bolt). Utilizing this measurement, pay heed to the following *if's*.

- If you are using a strand vise at one or both ends, subtract about 6" for each vise used.

- If you are using cable clamps, add 18" for each clamped end.

- If you are swaging, add 12" for each swaged end.

- If you are running the cable around the tree, use the tape to duplicate the cable needed and read the measurement right off the tape.

- If you are still in doubt, add a foot or two to your desired cable length — splicing short sections of wire rope is an esoteric art and beyond the scope of your needs or bandaid supply.
- At the end of a looong work day, I once cut through my fiberglass measuring tape rather than the cable; did it twice actually . . . don't tell anybody.

Trapeze Construction

Here's how to make a safe, long-lasting trapeze. Fashion your trapeze from some unbreakable material. I recommend using 1-1/2" PVC (poly vinyl chloride), U/V resistant rod, which can be drilled and shaped like wood, but which is stronger, as flexible, and is impervious to decay. Do not use wood dowels; they will eventually decay and break if left outdoors.

Make a mark 1-1/4" in from each end of the 30" long PVC rod and drill through the rod at these marks with a 7/16" spade bit. Do your best to drill these holes in the center of the rod and parallel to one another.

It's much easier to get a hole started with a pointed spade bit than attempting to start drilling with a drifting high-speed spiral bit. If you have access to a drill press, use it. The holes you make will be predictably straighter than the ones attempted by hand.

Place a drop-forged 3/8" x 1-1/2" nut eye bolt into each of the two holes and secure them using an SAE 3/8" washer and single nut. The top portion of the eye should run parallel to the trapeze. Cut off the protruding threaded end of the bolt (just beyond the nut) with a hacksaw and peen over the ragged cut ends to secure a tamper-proof fixture.

To achieve a peened-over bolt end, further tighten the nut 3/4 turn or so, to expose about 1/16" of the cut end of the bolt. Grasping the trapeze, place the eye portion of the eye bolt on top of an anvil, vise, or substantial mass of metal. Strike the vertically placed cut end of the bolt with controlled, slightly angled blows of a hammer, until the edges of the bolt are beveled over and contoured to the nut.

Use a medium rasp or hacksaw blade to roughen up the smooth surface of the PVC rod, offering a secure grip for the sweaty palms to come.

The strongest, most permanent way to hang the trapeze is to use swaged cable and strand vises, but first plan where you are going to suspend this aerial target.

Trapeze Suspension

Fortunately, most gymnasium ceilings have exposed beams. Use these beams to hang the trapeze so that the swinging bar is about 7 1/2 feet from the end of the platform (for a high school student) and at about chest height for a 5'6" person. You should get about a 70% completion rate using the above measurements; i.e., actually grabbing the bar. It may be that the beams are serendipitously arranged, allowing you to place 5/8" X 4" eye bolts between the beams (usually juxtaposed L-beams) offering adjustable (comparatively easy or difficult) dives for the bar.

You can also drill through the beam and place Dickin's bolts (1/2" x 1 1/2" nut eye bolt) to hang the trapeze. Or, if you have big bucks (or no drill, or no permission to drill), you can install beam clamps. They cost about $60 bucks apiece: PA sells them.

Do not adjust the height of the trapeze so that it hangs below the waist level of a student standing on the platform. A downhill dive will result, and most people cannot handle the G forces generated by catching the bar in this low position; possible shoulder injuries may result.

If there are no exposed beams in your gym, you may have to forego rigging this event. Drop ceilings often hide useable beams, but utilizing the area above a drop ceiling usually involves a cosmetic hassle with the building super or custodians.

Another potential ceiling structure, suitable for anchoring belays, trapezes, etc., is a poured concrete beam; tremendously strong, but laced with lengths of reinforcing steel rod. When you start drilling a hole, you "takes your chances," because even a carbide-tipped drill isn't going to make it through steel. Another negative tidbit about concrete; it is super-duper hard drilling stuff. I don't want to discourage you, but considering the hidden re-bar and the solidity of the concrete, it's like playing Russian Roulette with a jackhammer.

As a result of whatever drilling or bolting arrangement you succeed with, attach the two 5/16" trapeze strand vises into each one of the two beam bolts—measured slightly wider apart than the 2-½' trapeze length.

With someone standing on the platform, it becomes an easy task to adjust the height of the trapeze by having that person tell the worker on the ladder (or among the beams) to push more cable through the paired strand vises until the trapeze is centered, parallel to the floor, and at a functional height. Push cable through the strand vises with care and in *small* measure, remembering that the cable only moves through the strand vise in one direction.

It is somewhat more difficult to hang the trapeze using rope. Measure what you think is the right length of rope (1/2" multiline) needed by dropping a tape measure from the support eye bolts and having someone standing on the platform "eyeball" what appears to be the right length. (Between chest and chin height on the jumper is about right.) Add 14" to each length to compensate for the eye splice at each end of the rope. The splices will take up more than 14", but don't forget the added length resulting from the use of a rapid link on one end of the rope. If you splice it too long, a knot takes up about 6" of the rope. If you splice it too short, add a couple rapid links or splice it again. And, if you splice it juuust right, you win the Goldilock's JUST RIGHT Award!

Put a 1/2" thimble into each trapeze bolt and perform an eye splice around these thimbles with the ends of separate and equal lengths of rope. At the other ends of these ropes, perform another eye splice around a 1/2" thimble. Using a 1/2" rapid link, clip these latter eye splices into the ceiling support eye bolts. If you measured the ropes accurately and performed the splices well, the trapeze should hang evenly and just where you want it. To be honest, most of the time my rope-supported trapezes are slightly askew and a couple centimeters away from an ideal height, but uniqueness is what you get with a hand crafted product—so they tell me at craft fairs when I ask why a product is flawed.

The Vertical Trapeze

If you don't orient carabiners and rapid links in the gate-down position, a rare few will unscrew themselves over time due to gravity and jostling around. To prevent this, tighten the gates with a wrench — now wait a minute — not THAT much; you might want to take this connector off someday. In fact, if you plan to leave the rapid link out there for the entire season or maybe even a year or so, you better put a dolop of grease on the threads; otherwise a hack saw replaces the wrench.

I hadn't planned for this to be a lesson

in ropes course maintenance, but it's good stuff to know. The reason I mentioned the unscrewed rapid link in the first place, was because of something that happen recently on a *Project Adventure Pamper Pole* trapeze. Because of a spontaneously loosened rapid link, one half of the trapeze fell off the suspension cable. This happened while a participant was standing on top of the pole. (The belay cable and trapeze had just been jostled by another person jumping from the adjacent *Pamper Plank* for a trapeze that is connected to the same cable.) If you didn't understand that last parenthetical reference, don't bother re-reading it, just picture someone standing on top of the *Pamper Pole*, struggling desperately for balance and sputtering that half his target had disengaged. The vertically dangling trapeze apparently did not present an attractive challenge to that not-so-stable person, so he decided to climb down.

But it looked challenging to me, so I tied in (good ole bowline around the waist — keeps you honest) and had a dive at this weirdly vertical section of PVC rod. I caught it fairly, did a couple pull-ups, was lowered down, and decided to replace what was there (definitely untidy) with a "store-bought" vertical trapeze. We already had another typical horizontal trapeze for the *Pamper Plank* dive, so this new vertical challenge was well received.

From my observations over a two year period, about 70% grab the bar firmly, and of those, perhaps one in six will hold on. I'm not sure if it's because they grab, then relax, or maybe just a relationship of body weight to arm strength, but the results are predictable — rapid descent and a strong desire to try it again.

To build this uniquely vertical target, take a 3-foot section of inch and a quarter diameter PVC rod or any kind of similar

diameter hardwood dowel, and drill a 3/8" hole, one inch in from the end. Then either swage a section of 1/4" cable or splice a length of 1/2" multiline rope through that hole. The length of the cable or rope should be such to allow hanging the trapeze at about chest level of the jumper. Rough up the bar with a rasp to provide the best grip. A smooth section of PVC rod is a bad joke. You might even want to provide a rosin bag for the jumpers, as sweaty palms are a common by-product of this event. This is a dandy variation to the normal trapeze jump, (you gotta be kidding; none of this stuff is normal).

A tip from an experienced jumper and observer — when you go for it, grab high on the bar, squeeze like the devil, and keep your arms bent. If you grab at the bottom of the bar with straight arms, the immediate drop is impressive.

Ding-a-Ling

If you already have a ropes course, this high commitment activity is a natural, and can be added at minimal expense and effort.

Erect a 20-25' ladder in a vertical position directly underneath a high (30-40') belay cable. Ask 6-8 people to steady the ladder. The student of choice (his/her own choice, of course) ties into a belay rope, which is attached (via carabiners, rapid links, S/S pulley, etc.) to the belay cable above. A separate rope is also tied to the top of the ladder and anchored to a solid object (e.g., a tree) to prevent the ladder from falling to the ground. This rope is not used for supporting the ladder, simply to keep it from falling to the ground and possibly injuring one of the ladder holders.

The belayed student begins climbing and continues to the top of the ladder, diligently eyeballing the overhead goal; a bell hanging from the cable and positioned about six feet above the top ladder rung. The object is for the climbing student to ring that bell. The chief ingredients of this ladder-to-nowhere event: fun and fear.

If you haven't thought it through, the climber is required to precariously stand on the top ladder rung and thrust upwards to ring the bell. The subsequent fall is programmed and occurs frequently.

Try making your own ladder, using 2" x 3" lumber sections for the rails, and 1" hardwood dowels for the rungs: commercial extension ladders are expensive.

Most of the time, I encourage people to name their own event, or change the name to suit the situation. I encourage you to keep this one — it's near perfect.

Flying Squirrel

I assume you know, but the name above and all the other fanciful and whimsical names that have been applied and adopted by the *Project Adventure* staff are chosen and used primarily so that everyone knows which activity or ropes course event is being referred to in a conversation, discussion, etc. "Did you notice the poor spotting on event #17?" "Hey, let's play #6!" See what I mean?

The Flying Squirrel event (explanation to follow) has little to do with a flying squirrel, but one day . . . I was installing a high limb belay anchor and noticed a lower dead limb that needed trimming. After making a few reciprocal passes with a bow saw at the base of the limb, I noticed what seemed to be a large dead leaf detach from mid-limb and begin floating to the ground. The "leaf" radically changed direction two or three times on the trip down! Only as the blurred UFO approached the ground (from about 50'), and flared its airbrakes did I realize that I had just witnessed a rare diurnal event, the flight of a nocturnal flying squirrel. This squirrely scenario was worth remembering, and so it is, via the name designation of this high ropes course experience.

The purpose of this passive element is to allow a physically and/or emotionally disadvantaged student to: (a) experience the sensation of height on a ropes course without having to climb and (b) to experience the trust of being on-belay.

Sounds intriguingly complex. Nope — very simple, actually — here's the M.O.

Install a cable at height (40+ feet), or choose a stout hardwood limb at about the same height. On this cable or organic support, affix (NEB and rapid link) an S/S pulley arranged in the non-belay pulley mode; i.e., the sheave wheel turns. (Or use a

ROSA-RED aluminum sheave pulley.) Reeve a length of KM III static rescue rope through the pulley set-up so that the rope is long enough to measure from the ground to the pulley and back down, plus 15 feet.

Tie a bowline-on-a-bight in one end of the rope and clip (locking steel carabiner) the two formed loops into the front of a student's harness or Swiss seat/Studebaker Wrap pelvic tie-in. The pulling group (minimum 8, alternating sides of the rope) grabs the other end of the rope and *walks* away from their position under the pulley, at which juncture the clipped-in student begins to "fly."

To back up the system, simply swage or cable-clamp a length of 3/8" cable around the support limb so that the formed circular loop includes the static haul rope.

From a student decision-making standpoint, it is important to establish communication between the person being lifted and the others . . . otherwise, this event is simply hauling a "sack of potatoes" up in the air. Encourage the student to control his/her ascent/descent by verbal control of the lifters. This command status should be as the result of some pre-flight conversation by both parties. You should remain nearby to make sure this "mid-flight" communication remains an intelligible two-way conversation.

Considerations:

- Tie a few overhand knots in the lifting end of the KM-3 rope to aid gripping the rope.
- Do not use the S/S pulley in the static mode. It makes the lifting process too difficult because of increased friction.
- If you are concerned about your group's lifting ability or commitment level, clip two pelvic wrapped students to the end of the rope via a split bowline-on-a-bight (Ref. Australian back-up belay).
- Control the speed of ascent (and descent, obviously), because 8-12 people pulling on a rope can raise a 150 lb. person with surprising ease.
- Be aware that whatever pendulum action is occurring to the "flyer" near the ground will be exaggerated as the rope shortens near the top.
- Make sure the footing is good where the lifters will be consistently walking.
- Do not use climbing rope in place of

static KM-3. Dynamic climbing rope stretches too much, and has 2,000 lbs. less tensile strength.

The Hickory Jump — Construction and Use

The stimulus for developing the *Hickory Jump* as a low ropes course event resulted from a nostalgic recollection of time I had spent during pre-adolescence, pretending I was Batman and wishing that I could heroically dive to a temptingly close tree limb which extended near to the top of my family's suburban roof garage. I did not attempt the jump (my survival instincts prevailed), but that long-ago challenge was powerful enough to stimulate the creation of today's *Hickory Jump*. Now, I jump with impunity, and encourage others to do the same, knowing that the consequence of missing the "limb" is a welcome landing in the arms of willing spotters.

This dive-to-your-limit ropes course element allows any latter-day Batman or Wonder Woman to jump for their imagined tree limb, comforted by knowing that if their goal isn't reached, a chain-link fence or cartop will not have to provide the landing area. Willing hands and arms "catch" the ersatz avenger if the trapeze bar is missed. The sequentially-placed take-off stumps of the *Hickory Jump* event are so arranged that almost everyone eventually finds their distance limit. The event is not so much a nostalgic "super friends" indulgence, but a combination self-challenge/trust exercise, that requires a significant personal commitment, and confidence in the spotters.

The Hickory Jump involves a minimum of purchased material for construction, but requires moderate-to-hard labor, depending upon the ease of digging at your chosen site. The dive to the trapeze is given to repetition by participants — "Let me have another try; I'm sure I can make it this time." — and is well worth whatever time and labor is involved.

Planning and Construction

Spend some time looking for two appropriately-sized and spaced-apart trees. A support tree for this element should measure a minimum of five inches in diameter at a height from the ground of eight feet, and be six to ten feet from the other support tree.

Take into consideration what the digging will be like at the potential site; otherwise, you may spend an inordinate amount of time placing the jump stumps. There is often no choice, and in such a case, just literally dig in, consoling yourself with a mental image of how dramatically useful this event will be for the students' developing sense of group trust and her/his self-image.

If two utility pole sections (about 12') are available, and you don't mind digging a couple more holes, use them as trapeze supports. The benefits of utilizing utility poles are that wood decay is practically eliminated, and you have the luxury of locating the poles wherever you like. Or, combine one tree and a pole or a pole and a bleacher support, or a pole and a goal post, or . . .

This low ropes course element was named the *Hickory Jump* because the first few jump bars were fashioned from hickory saplings. (As an historical aside: The first *Hickory Jump* was built at Hamilton-Wenham Regional High School in Massachusetts in 1975.) Tough stuff, that hickory — tensile strength akin to iron I've heard, but alas, being a "natural" product, the wood does eventually rot, leading to replacement hassles every few years. However, if you take the trapeze indoors after each use, there's no reason not to use wood, particularly if you have a source of straight-grain hardwood.

For years, a permanently bolted bar (wood or metal) was used for the *Hickory Jump*. The disadvantages were:

1. Liability (not being able to secure the event).
2. Replacement problems (constant exposure to the elements).
3. Vandalism (availability at all times).
4. Breakage or bending (poor construction geometry).

The advantages, besides aesthetic, were nil, and so the logical change was made to using a synthetic trapeze jump bar.

Here's the synthetic alternative (BOOoo-HISSss). Inch and a half PVC (poly vinyl chloride) rod is now generally used as a trapeze bar. PVC's battleship gray color fits into most woodsy scenes; it has as much or more resilience (spring) than hickory; its plastic make-up can be drilled and shaped like wood; heat and cold have relatively no effect on its strength, and it will *hang* around longer than you will. Apparently, its only drawbacks are:

1. Comparatively high priced.
2. PVC is a proven carcinogen (don't eat it).
3. There is evidence that PVC is affected by U/V exposure.
4. It's just not *hickory*! (You should know how to pronounce hickory, since you will be utilizing and talking about this event as part of your adventure curriculum. It is said, *Hick*-ry [accent on the HICK], not Hick-or-ry. Now you know.)

Remember to rough up the smooth surface of whatever trapeze material you choose—to help sweaty palms adhere. Having a rosin bag available isn't as strange as it seems.

PVC can be purchased in five or ten foot sections from a local plastic distributor (ask for U/V resistent PVC), or from *Project Adventure, Inc.* PA will either sell you the stock rod or a finished product.

Cut the length you want (2'-2-1/2') using just about any type of saw you have around; even a hacksaw. Drill a 7/16" diameter hole at each end of the trapeze rod, and 1-1/2" from the ends. Try to make the two holes as parallel to one another as your eyeball drilling technique allows. If you have a drill press — use it.

Use a spade bit (Speed Bor is the commercial name) if you are going to hand-hold the drill. The pointed tip of a spade bit won't dance around the surface to be drilled.

Insert a 3/8" x 1-1/2" shoulder nut eye bolt (drop forged) in each hole so that the eyes of the bolts are both on the same side of the trapeze (Did I need to say that?) and parallel to the trapeze bar. Put on a 3/8" SAE washer and an anti-vibration nut, tighten down and cut off the remainder of the bolt with a hacksaw. Done. If you can't find an anti-vibration nut, don't sweat it, just turn on a regular hex nut. After you have cut off the excess bolt end, peen over the remainder with a hammer to prevent the nut from working itself free; and to preclude vandalism attempts.

Now, hang the trapeze. Drive a 1/2" staple (V) into each support tree at a height of about 10 feet, so that the staples face one another. Using either cable or rope, fashion two lengths that will support the trapeze from these two staples and so the trapeze hangs level at a height of eight feet. Use carabiners to connect the trapeze to the support rope/cable, so that disconnecting the bar can be accomplished easily. If you do nothing else from this point, at least you now have a boffo swinging pull-up bar.

OK, the technical stuff is over. It's time

for the type of work that slams the door on romantic notions about ropes course construction; digging a ditch.

Five or six sequentially placed take-off stumps need to be set in place. Considering that you will want the jump from the first stump to be challenging for shorter people, but not impossible, place the first stump five feet back from a line perpendicular with the trapeze's plumb. This first stump should protrude about two feet, nine inches above the ground.

After having established where to place the first stump, use that mark to begin a ditch that will be approximately one and a half feet wide by three feet deep by five feet long, and dug along a continuation of the perpendicular line mentioned above.

If possible, use sections of utility pole for the stumps. Utility poles are pressure-injected with a chemical preservative, which precludes rot and the need for stump replacement. Otherwise, use any type of logs available, except those which are particularly susceptible to decay; e.g., birch, hickory, poplar, which rot faster than oak,

maple, locust and cedar. Cut and cured logs absorb liquid preservative and last longer than treated freshly cut, wet logs.

Measure and saw each following section of log or pole in relation to the first, shortest stump. Each stump subsequent to the first one should be two to three inches higher than the next, and juxtaposed immediately behind one another; i.e., actually making contact. The fifth or sixth stump should be far enough away from the bar so that not many people will be able to make the jump, and that's intentional. Each individual should be allowed to find their physical limit and eventually be required to *really* trust their spotters — programmed trust.

After the log sections are cut and placed in the ditch — vertically, and in sequence — alternately shovel in dirt and *tamp vigorously* until the ditch is filled. Use a cut limb or pick handle as a tamper. The best procedure is to fill/tamp, fill/tamp, remembering to tamp that loose dirt with vigor. Without firmly set take-off stumps, this event becomes a dangerous joke. An instructor should give each stump a lateral kick before each day's use, to ensure a solid take-off.

After the stumps are in and set, their height relative to one another can be easily adjusted with a chainsaw, so don't be dismayed if your initial measurements are incorrect; mine usually aren't either.

WARNING — Read this . . . or Else
This spotting recommendation *must* be followed, or someone will eventually be injured.

The intention of the jumper is to grasp the bar, and if that is accomplished, it becomes the spotters' job *not* **to let the jumper swing through** (complete the arc of the swing). The swing-through causes an increased pull on the jumper's grip and can result in a spontaneous release, resulting in a quick trip to the turf, usually on the participant's back or neck. Frightened? Good — don't let it happen.

Suggestions

1. At a preliminary get-together, offer each student the chance to try a trust dive; i.e., simply diving off a stump into the spotters' arms.
2. Use a minimum of eight spotters. Use a couple more spotters if the jumper is XL, but do not place spotters so close to the first stump that their arms impede the jumper's dive.
3. Have spotters remove their wrist-watches, otherwise the forward momentum of the diver may break the strap, band, etc.
4. Ask jumpers to remove large buckles, belt knives, or any sharp objects from their pockets.
5. Occasionally remind the jumpers, as they approach their distance limit, that it is much easier to catch a laid-out body than a I'm-not-going-to-make-it, folded pike position.
6. Suggest to the jumpers that they aim above the bar with their eyes, in order to get more distance from their dive; the old 45° up-and-out trick.
7. After everyone has made an attempt or two, suggest an additional challenge. Ask a volunteer if s/he would commit to dive for the trapeze blindfolded. Suggest that they make their blind jump

from the stump in front of the one from which they made their final sighted dive. This challenge is offered as a "step beyond the expected," so don't expect 100% participation (or 50%, for that matter). Allow more than one blindfolded attempt per person, because the first dive is usually short.

These blindfolded jumps should not be viewed as simply a daredevil stunt. Don't hesitate to ask more from your students than they are initially prepared to give; after all, the name of the game is Project *Adventure*. The commitment is real, the trust level is high; group support and enthusiasm is generally 100%, and the satisfaction from an attempt is apparent.

Do not let the blindfolded participant jump until s/he is facing directly toward the center of the trapeze. Ask the potential jumper to extend their his/her hands, held together, toward the trapeze, and then, if necessary, rearrange their direction as per **your** instructions (this is a time for everyone else to stop talking). Watch each jumper carefully so that they maintain a correct orientation to the bar.

If a student plans to dive blindfolded from the *Pamper Pole*; i.e., if you plan to offer this high challenge, a low-level attempt provides a tremendous confidence boost.

Go get 'em, Batman! POW! WHAM! ZAP!

The Mohawk Walk

This very popular low ropes course group initiative problem is simply a zig-zag extension of the *Tension Traverse*, with no rope to add support.

The object is to move the entire group from the initial support tree to the last support tree, using only the taut cables in between, and one another, for balance. There are usually some adept (well-balanced?) students who can walk on the cables without support, like a tightrope performer, but since the emphasis is on problem-solving and group completion, it's

MOHAWK WALK

everyone on the cables (one at a time from the start), and go for it.

Hopefully the person with the best balance will lead, but this is a student decision, not yours. It is the first person (and the last person) who most frequently find themselves in the least-balanced position. Falls (steps to the ground) will vary from occasional to frequent.

If you ask the group to begin from the start of the event after each fall, you better bring bivouac gear, because you're in for a long stay. The falls are going to happen, so have some fun, encourage laughter, and suggest a realistic goal (the improbable "failure is fun" concept).

Set a goal of trying to make the entire traverse without incurring more than 10, maybe 20 falls (after a few tries, a workable number will present itself). If the number is bettered or equaled, offer much fuss over world records; etc., and if the goal is

doubled, respond with good-humored jibes and encouragement to try again.

Ask the group to record their own falls (honor system), then record a total number after all have completed the traverse. The beauty of this activity is the total group involvement toward achieving a common goal and the unrestrained physical fun in attempting to reach it.

Another approach requires that if anyone touches the ground, that person must retreat to the end of the line—wherever that happens to be. This type of redistribution consequence appeals, because it allows more than one person to lead.

Hey, if it's that great, let's get one built. OK, here's how.

Choose a location that has a level, uncluttered ground area and enough well-spaced six inch to sixteen inch diameter trees, at the base, to provide anchor points for the taut cables.

If where you're standing is good enough, pick the support trees so that five to ten cable spans provide the best challenge for the students and the easiest drilling for you.

The cable lengths (distance between trees) should vary, with only the last cable being more than fifteen feet long. The final cable can be up to thirty feet in length, only because there will be a tension rope attached to the second-to-last support tree. This rope is attached and used exactly like a regular tension traverse rope (spliced and clipped to an eye bolt or tied to a limb at about fifteen feet), except that in this case, the rope is measured about six feet short of the final support tree. You ask why? I deign to answer as the challenge fairly announces itself.

Let's begin with the first tree and by-the-numbers, so that I can better record (remember) the sequence.

1. Drill through the trunk diameter on center so that the drill bit is pointing through the tree toward the next support tree.

   Brief clarification: the *drill bit* is that piece of fluted steel that rotates through the wood, while the *drill* itself represents that helpful mechanical device that holds and rotates the *drill bit*.

   The *Mohawk Walk* is not a high event; not even average height — it's a short event. The cable heights shouldn't exceed 18-20 inches (about knee high) to ensure an intact crotch if a participant's legs accidentally, and almost always suddenly, straddle the cable.

Use an 11/16" x 16" auger bit for the hole making. If you plan to use a bit brace instead of an electric drill, more power to you. That was a small joke, folks, and if you aren't smiling, from this point on, I'll be technically serious, directly-to-the-point, and *boring*. You're smiling? — Good, me too! BORING, did you get it?

2. Place a 5/8" diameter thimbled eye bolt of appropriate length in this newly bored hole (thimbled end toward the next support tree), and turn a nut down on the threaded end over a fish plate washer. The thimbled groove in the head of the bolt should be perpendicular to the ground.

   Tighten the nut with an adjustable wrench and cut off any protruding threads with a hacksaw. Peen over the cut end with a hammer. This cut and peening procedure reduces vandalism and removes a shin-battering obstruction.

3. Drill a hole in the second support tree similar to the hole in tree #1, and pointed directly toward hole #1. Try looking through the completed hole, thinking of it as a sighting mechanism, and see how accurate your estimating abilities proved to be. If the hole doesn't sight directly at the other hole, that's OK — What the heck, we're not building furniture here!

4. Measure a length of 3/8" diameter cable (I use 7x19 galvanized aircraft cable) that is one and a half feet longer than the measurement from tree #1 to tree #2; i.e., bolt-to-bolt.

   Using cable clamps, attach one end of the cable (either end: this is one of those unlikely times when you can't make the wrong choice) to the thimble eye bolt in tree #1. Attach the three 3/8" cable clamps (also called wire rope clips and, sometimes erroneously, U-bolts), so that the **U** portion of the clamps go over the working end of the cable — refer to the photo.

To hold down the last short section of the working end, you can either (1) copiously wrap electrician's tape around and around the cables, or (2) squeeze on a serving sleeve. If you don't know what a serving sleeve is, use tape or call (508) 468-7981 (PA's #), and ask to speak to a builder. Notice, that's (508), not (800).

5. Reeve (that's kind of an *in* word meaning to insert a rope or cable through something, like reeving a rope through the cheeks of a pulley—and I can't get into a further discussion of cheeks here, because this is a family publication),

the other end of the cable through the thimble eye bolt (TEB) in tree #2. Thread the cable end up through the TEB opening so that the working end lies on top of the standing part of the cable. That sounds confusing, but it's simply done and allows you to put the **U** portion of the clamps on the cable so that the threaded ends point down. This orientation reduces the chance of getting scraped or gouged by the threads if they were sticking up.

Use the double Haven's grip technique to pull the cable taut. Then, attach the cable clamps and tighten them down. Using a socket wrench, torque the nuts on the clamps as tight as you can physically manage, alternating the rotation from nut to nut. This is one instance where you can't overdo the muscle.

6. Drive a 1/2" staple (V or H) into the last tree so that the staple points toward the final support tree and is approximately fifteen feet above the ground. This staple is the anchor point for a tension rope. Cut the rope (5/8" multiline is a good choice) to a length that is about 6'-7' short of the final tree. Eye splice one end of the rope in order to facilitate attachment to the staple by use of a carabiner or rapid link. If you can't splice, tie a bowline knot in the rope end. You can learn to splice next week . . .

There are more exotic techniques for attaching cables that I have not mentioned (thank goodness, eh?) that are fine to use, but necessitate the use of more expensive and hard to find gear (strand vises, swaging, and nut eye bolts).

If you want to include more than just zig zagging cables, good, I like some variety in a *Mohawk Walk* myself. Think about

adding a *Wild Woosey* section or simply parallel cables, a la the *Tired Two Line* event. If the trees allow, include an arcing swing from cable to cable. Add anything you want, it's your ropes course.

The popularity of this event stems from the infectious nature of a non-intimidating challenge, and the group cooperation needed to finish the "walk" successfully.

Remember, it helps to get things started if the first person out on the cable has better than average balance: You, for example. No? Come on, embarrass yourself — it's fun.

Multi-Vine Traverse

From the tropic and torpid depths of the Ohio jungles comes this delightfully challenging ropes course element, via Gary Moore of Ohio State University, and more recently D.I.S.S. Inc.

The object is to cross a low or high taut cable (about 30-40' long) with balance help only intermittently available from dangling short spliced ropes. These interestingly sequenced ropes hang from an overhead cable that parallels the bottom one (the one

you walk on). The dangling vertical ropes (5/8" multiline) should be spliced short enough or be spaced far enough apart so that a participant cannot hold onto one rope to reach another.

As a participant launches her/himself (the fine art of wire-walking is abandoned for the immediacy of survival leaps) toward a rope, be aware that you can offer substantial and largely unnoticed belay help by simply tightening up on the belay rope. Most successful traverses are in the hands of the belayer — success is where you find it.

As a safety consideration when this event is used as a low element (maybe on the *Mohawk Walk*?), construct the bottom cable low enough to compassionately consider all crotch levels. Completing this Tarzan-like crossing as a group is a cooperative and confidence-building gem. A fabricated challenge? Too true, but so were Tarzan's impossible tree top stunts.

Materials Needed for Construction

170'	3/8" cable (approx.)
6	18" nut eye bolts (or whatever the tree diameter dictates)
6	fish plates
4	3/8" strand vice
8	3/8" cable clamps
4	7/16" serving sleeves
4-5	cable drops (This is a 1/4"X2"X4" rectangular piece of steel that attaches to a cable with a cable clamp. A stamped out hole in the steel is used for connecting a carabiner or rapid link. Cable drops are manufactured for and sold by *Project Adventure*.)
4-5	5/16" cable clamps
5	1/2" thimbles
35'	5/8" multiline rope
5	1/2" rapid links

Construction Procedure

When choosing two trees as anchors for this multi-commitment event, exercise your sense of proportion for challenge and go for the long traverse. Even if the support trees have to be guyed, a 50' span between trees isn't too demanding. As always, when picking a ropes course element site, pick an area that requires the least amount of clearing unless your ideal support trees lie amidst a green hell of prickers and briars - now where's that perfect sense of proportion and personal commitment to build the best?

Install a belay cable at the maximum height you feel comfortable with in the chosen trees. No, cancel that. Build it higher . . . safe, but higher.

Drill the bolt holes for the belay cable to the right or left of trunk center. Be consistent (right or left) for both trees; this off center orientation will soon make sense.

Install the bottom cable at least 15' below the belay cable. Bolt holes for the bottom cable are drilled on center.

The third and final parallel cable will support the vertically hanging ropes. Support bolts for this cable should be placed off center also, but this time to the side opposite the belay cable, and at about the same level. I recommend attaching the "vine" ropes to this third cable before installation to save yourself some tedious hang time in a harness, not to mention precluding numb legs and groin from "hanging around."

Standing comfortably on the ground, attach a 3/8" strand vice to one end of this third cable. Measure 12' out from the strand vice on the cable and attach a cable drop. If, after attaching this cable at height, you determine that the first convulsive step-lunge toward the rope (vine) is too demanding, simply staple (V or H) a short section of eye spliced 5/8" rope to the tree trunk about 3' above eye level, providing initial extended support to a very precarious starting position. This short (3-6') rope section is also useful for coaxing hesitant people away from the relative security of the trunk.

Considering that the distance between support trees is 50', attach cable drops beyond the first drop at 9'-10' intervals for a total of four cable drops. If you want the last hanging rope to be used as a tension traverse finale, then the fourth cable drop will be the last "vine" connector, leaving about 18'-20' for the final traverse. Hang a 15' rope from this last cable drop.

The other cable drop "vine" ropes should measure between 6'-7'. To make up these ropes, eye splice a 5/8" multiline rope end around a 1/2" thimble. Put a 1/2" rapid link into the thimble before splicing and save yourself the task of trying to force the link into the finished spliced eye. Forcing the link into the eye splice can be done, but it's a hassle at height. Remember, the longer the "vine" rope, the more distance between vines is necessary, otherwise a comparatively easy series of rope-to-rope grabs will be made; i.e., no challenge.

Back splice the other end of the hanging rope. Attach the other rapid links and "vine" ropes to the cable drops and prepare to string the cable. You do have someone helping you do all this, I hope!

Install the "vine" cable, making sure that you attach the proper cable ends on the correct support trees or no amount of challenge rationalizing will make this event possible. Remember the anchor bolt holes for this vine cable are positioned to the opposite side of center as compared to the belay cable positioning. This offsetting of cables will allow an easier belay run of the ROSA pulley resulting in less belay rope hang ups on the cable drops. If this doesn't

make sense, read it again and think through how the belay will function. If it still doesn't read right, just trust me and do it.

It's up? It's done!

Considerations:

- If the hanging ropes seem too long (too easy), tie an overhand knot or two to shorten them: each knot uses up about 6" of rope.
- When belaying, be prepared for some spectacular falls as the result of go-for-it lunges. If you're skilled with handling a belay rope, (you better be!) you can provide unsolicited and unrecognized support during those less-than-coordinated lurching grabs for the "vines."
- If you want to use this event as a low element, simply exclude the belay cable and install the walking cable at about 18" off the ground. Don't forget, there is no belay on this low variation, so provide good spotting for the inevitable go-for-it short falls.

Tired Two Line

Performance Objective:

To walk, slide, shuffle, etc. from one support tree to another, standing erect on top of two tautly strung sections of cable that run parallel, and measure approximately 9" apart Use of the belay rope for balance and security can be allowed if minimum performance is anticipated by the facilitator. This medium height element (15' - 25") functions as a short connector for a contiguous ropes course set up, or it can be used as a stand alone element.

Use a steel sheave ROSA pulley on the top belay cable to alleviate tugging the belay rope, allowing application of some tension to the belay rope without the participant's being aware of the help. The belay rope should be affixed behind the participant (Peter Pan position), unless you plan to allow holding the rope for support; it all has to do with whatever challenge/success level you are trying to develop.

As on cable/balance events, jogging shoes with knobs on the soles do not work well — the knobs catch on the cable. Flat soled tennis shoes work best. Bare feet are contraindicated: too painful!

Materials Needed For Construction:

6 - 5/8" nut eye bolts of required length
12 - fish plate washers (soft wood trees)
12 - slug washers (hard wood trees)
70' - 3/8" cable
6 - 3/8" strand vices
2 - 5/8" X 12" take-up, hook & hook turnbuckle
4 - 3/8" cable clamp
2 - 7/16" serving sleeves

Construction Details:

Choose two trees that are on reasonably flat ground and located about 20' apart. If the choice is available, pick supports that require the least clearing; i.e., both limbing the trunks and cutting surrounding brush. The support trees must be of substantial diameter at the cable level to provide and maintain stability for balance walking on taut cables. Since a large diameter trunk at cable height is necessary, this event is usually not installed over 25" (on the East coast anyway), and therefore most of the tree work can be done off a ladder.

Start by connecting a belay cable between the support trees at least 12' above where you plan to install the walking cables — the term walking in this case is a euphemism for hesitant shuffling.

About 10'-12' below the belay cable, install two side-by-side, parallel, 3/8" cables approximately 9" apart. Use 5/8" nut eye bolts of appropriate length as anchors for the cables.

Measure the distance from bolt to bolt (tree to tree) and cut each cable 33" short of this measurement. The extended hook & hook turnbuckle used on each cable will take up about 30" of that . The 3/8" strand vice at each end of the cable also adds a total of about 10" to the 30" take-up total.

Attach, via a strand vice, the two cables separately to the two nut eye bolts in one support tree. Slip two more strand vices on the far two ends of the cable. Use two separate turnbuckles to tighten the cables. By either tightening or loosening the turnbuckles you can decrease or dramatically increase the challenge of walking on the two cables. A claw hammer provides a convenient "cheater bar" for leverage while tightening the turnbuckles.

Remember that you are using a hook and hook turnbuckle, so don't make the cables too loose or there is the chance that one end of the hook arrangement might slip off the strand vise bail.

Strand vices are the easiest way to connect a cable to an anchor, but also the most expensive. The ends of the cable can also be eye-swaged (with a nico-press crimping tool), or the ends can simply be cable clamped into eyes.

Clip in the belay rope to the rear of the *Studebaker Wrap*; i.e., at the person's back. This posterior positioning of the rope allows unfettered walking along the cables, and also reduces the temptation of grabbing the belay rope to aid balance. This type of retro rope support is quaintly referred to as a *Peter Pan belay*.

Rope Ladders

A wooden-runged rope ladder provides access and egress with style from any ropes course element. In addition, a hand-crafted ladder is aesthetically pleasing, and its construction is surprisingly easy. Include

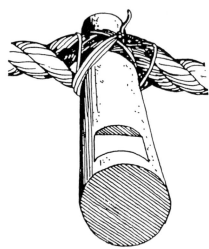

your students in the construction of the ladder. It's genuinely fun (in contrast to digging post holes), and the good-looking result of a handmade rope ladder generates many satisfied smiles and predictable nods of approval.

Rope Ladder Construction

To build a 20' rope ladder, you will need the following materials:

1. 43' of 5/8" multiline rope. The extra three feet of rope is necessary in order to include an optional short splice in the bottom of the ladder. Manila rope of the same diameter can also be used, but it's harder to work with and will not last as long outdoors because of its comparative susceptibility to rot.
2. Four 3' sections of 1" hardwood dowel (birch is serviceable, but ash is better) to be cut into sixteen 9" sections.
3. One 1/2" galvanized thimble.
4. Approximately 100' of waxed nylon cord.

Tape the ends of the hawser-lay multiline with plastic electrician's tape before you cut the rope so that the ends

don't unravel (cowstail) while you are working on the ladder.

Find the center of the 43' section of rope and seize in the thimble at that juncture. Seizing is the wrapping/whipping process of securing a thimble in the bight of the rope that designates, in this case, the measured center of the rope.

Using a dado blade on a table saw or a circular saw, cut two grooves 1" in from the ends of the 9" dowel sections (rungs) so that the grooves oppose one another; i.e., so they occur on opposite sides of the dowel. Cut the grooves to measure 3/16" in depth by 1/2" and 5/8" wide respectively. Be consistent with each dowel so that the narrow grooves are on one side and the wide grooves are on the other. These grooves are made to receive the three strands of rope; one strand in the narrow groove, and two strands in the wider groove. Refer to the illustration above.

If you don't have access to a power saw, use a round rasp to make the grooves; more time-consuming certainly, but in some ways more satisfying.

Using a power sander (or hand sanding), slightly bevel the edges of the rungs to remove the sharp circumference edge.

Dip each birch rung into a container of Cuprinol to stain (mahogany, redwood, teak) the blond wood and appropriately match the decor of your gymnasium and, of course, to preserve the wood.

After performing a secure seizing, reeve a rope (cord) through the thimble and tie the unrunged side-ropes onto a temporary tree or pole support. Grab the two loose rope ends at the bottom and pull equally hard to help remove any kinks or turns in the ropes. Pull on the ropes frequently while inserting the rungs to make sure that the rungs remain parallel to one another.

Measure 18" down the ropes from the base of the thimble and insert a rung in both ropes so that the rung forms the base of an isosceles triangle, with the thimble as the apex. Twist the three strands of the rope in such a way as to provide an opening for the insertion of the rung, or use a fid to separate the strands. Make sure the single rope strand goes in the narrow groove of the rung and the double strand fits in the wider groove.

Measure 14" down the two side ropes and insert another dowel. Eyeball this rung with the first one to make sure that they are parallel to one another. Pull on the rope ends each time a rung is inserted to facilitate this visual placement, and to help set the rung. Continue to insert rungs at 14" intervals until there is approximately 2 feet of rope left on each side.

Cut the waxed nylon cord into 4' and 3' sections. Using a 4' length, make an **X** lashing at each juncture of rope and rung. This very basic lashing doesn't involve fancy knots or intricate tying procedures, just tightly wrap the cord back and forth across the rope/rung juncture until you have used up about half the cord, then change direction and criss-cross the remaining cord on the unwrapped part of the

juncture. Finish off with a square knot or two. Leave enough cord, while tying this knot, to get sufficient leverage in order to make the knot tight. This lashing will work loose if each wrap isn't taken tightly and if the final knot isn't secured well.

Use the 3' length to tie a seizing around the rope beneath the rung. This is necessary to prevent the rung from being displaced downward by a climber's body weight.

Perform a short splice in the two loose bottom ends of the rope in order to finish off the ladder. This splice also provides a bottom rung to the ladder. If you haven't learned to splice and don't want to bother, leave the two ends taped and dangling: splicing is an ego trip, anyway.

Vertical Playpen

A *new* ropes course element! These don't come along every day, so you better check it out. I've found over the years, as a ropes course builder, that we (builders) get into a routine of what we build. Although ropes course construction is viewed as an innovative undertaking, it's actually like any other construction job, satisfying upon completion, but otherwise just physically demand-

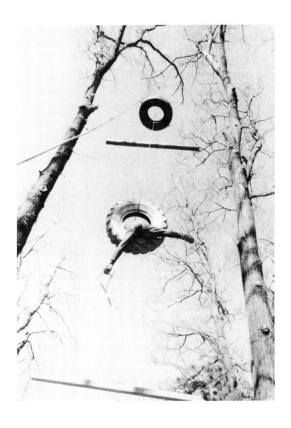

ing and fairly repetitive. "You want a *Two Line Bridge*?" Bang, bang, bang . . . there's your Two Line Bridge — hey, it's a business.

But occasionally, a new element forces itself onto your consciousness; sometimes as a serendipitous mistake, often as the result of on-the-job conversations with other builders; rarely as a pure gem of inspiration. The *Vertical Playpen* is the result of some "light bulb" innovation and a generous dollop of sharing, particularly with PA employee Bob Ryan.

The *Vertical Playpen* (VP) resembles the *Dangle Duo* event, in that a series of obstacles must be overcome to reach the top of the event, however, the VPP offers a series of varied challenges rather than the predictable ladder-like ascent on the *Dangle Duo*. As each level (5-7 challenges) is reached, the climber must evaluate her/

his position, look ahead, and decide on the next plan of ascent, the cognitive and physical approach that so well defines the adventure education ideal.

The Vertical Playpen high ropes course element can be daunting to both participant and installer. As a result, many practitioners are now presenting this element as a pairs challenge; i.e., asking two people to climb and assist one another during the ascent. If you decide to utilize tandem climbing on this event, safety dictates that you should install two separate and parallel belay cables.

Installation angst is mostly imagined because of the unique nature of the event itself. My reference to the word daunting above has to do with how an installer perceives their own experience and confidence to work beyond standards. Most ropes course element installation is straight forward; a Two Line Bridge is a Two Line Bridge . . . whereas the VP allows planning and implementation beyond a blue print scenario.

Planning and installing a VP allows the builder to use his/her imagination in order to create a challenge commensurate with; the potential audience, the materials available to build with, and the geographical layout of the site. Every "Playpen" that I have installed has looked, and been in some way functionally different from the previous one.

As you approach the exciting task of installing a VP, make up a layered list of cable supported items that might offer a reasonable challenge for a climber, remembering that the criteria for success is not necessarily reaching the top, but experiencing the attempt along the way. Some "vertical" challenge items might include:

- A horizontally hung and edge-routed 4"X4"X10' board. This wobbly 4" platform makes a good first obstacle for the vertical challenge, because it can be easily removed to limit after-hours access. Install this board so that it hangs horizontally about 5'-6' off the ground. Rout the edges of all boards used on this element.

- A vertically oriented truck tire. Hang the tire from two 1/2" diameter forged eye bolts (Dickin's bolts) that are drilled and placed 24" apart on the circumference tread part of the tire. Don't forget to drill a drain hole in the bottom of the tire with a 1" (or thereabouts) multispur bit. Photo below.

If you are trying to cover quite a bit of vertical space with this tire, hang a short section of rope ladder from the bottom of the tire; say 4-5 rungs. Sus-

pend the rapid link attached ladder from another forged eye bolt, placed about 2" away from the drain hole. If you decide to use this type of tire attached auxillary ladder, leave a generous 3 1/2' between the horizontal 4"X4" bottom board and the bottom of the rope ladder.

- Two horizontally strung sections of 1" multiline provides a strength and balance challenge not to be denied. Suspend these thick diameter *smile* ropes (so called because of their cheerful camber) about 3' above one another, with the top rope about 4' below the next dangling object, but no more, otherwise you will have created an impressive challenge that no one can accomplish. The distance from the top of the suspended tire and the bottom rope should measure about 4 1/2 ft.

- A suspended rope, as above, allows you to "fix" an exaggerated space between two vertical challenges. To be more specific, you made a mistake and the move from one suspended item to another is too difficult or impossible. Installing a well arced rope (the working vernacular is, "install a smile") allows some planned serendipity — and there's not much of that around.

- Suspend an 8' length of 6" X 6" board from four suspension points (four 1/2" SLES bolts, two at each end of the board). This "spring" board will give the participant a fairly secure base from which to try and reach the next and perhaps final vertical obstacle. Moving from the rope to this beam requires a high level of commitment and balance, so the distance between the two will vary considerably as to the challenge considered. I usually leave 4' twixt rope and beam for a high school group.

- Hang a PVC trapeze so that it is suspended 5 1/2 feet directly above the 6" X 6" board. This "too high" trapeze provides a go-for-it finale to an exciting and demanding series of unique challenges. The final upward thrust to the trapeze is probably the event's most difficult move, from a personal decision making standpoint. The vertical distance between beam and trapeze is not unreasonable if the participant is motivated and willing to go for it.

• Suspending a truck tire horizontally as a final move is also appealing in that the climber must move through the tire and emerge on top. Suspend this tire from four lengths of 5/16" cable. Four equally spaced dickin's bolts secured around the tire's circumfrence (through the tread), provide the means of cable attachment.

Before you start hanging the stacked challenges that make up the whole, conceptualize what the event will look like by doing a rough paper and pencil draft. This will give you an idea of what props and equipment you will need, and also allow you to pre-fab each challenge level on the ground.

After these preliminaries have been taken care of, staple your way up the trees and install two parallel belay cables at a height that will allow the vertical stacking of your chosen challenges. The reason for installing two cables is to provide a safe belay for two people.

If limbs have to be pruned or removed, do that. If you are cutting a live limb, under cut the limb first in order to prevent ripping of the bark. The future health of the tree depends upon your trimming techniques.

While you're up there, hang a haul line from one of the belay cables using a pulley/ carabiner combination. Use this rope to haul the heavy challenge items (tire, logs) into position. For the lighter items (rope,

4X4s), have the two climbers (you need one person in each tree) individually take a haul rope with them.

Here's the part that will save you a lot of measuring time and post-installation recriminations. Hang all the prop sections (tires, ropes, boards) from generous lengths of 5/16" cable that include a strand vice on one end (for attachment to the tree trunk anchor staple) and an eye swaged into the other end for rapid link attachment to the suspended challenge item. (If you don't have access to a swaging tool, cable clamp an eye into the end of the cable.) Using the cable and strand vice combination allows easy adjustment of whatever prop you have decided to suspend.

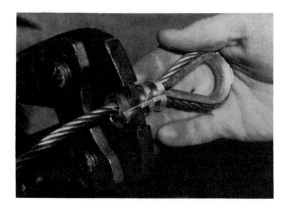

For example, if you suspend a length of 1" multiline rope or even separate parallel lengths, perform a thimbled eye splice into each end of the rope(s) and suspend the rope using extra long lengths of cable as above (you can trim off excess cable later); precluding hassles of knot tying or measuring rope length accurately enough to allow a functional fit between the support trees.

Just so that I'm sure that you're sure — clip (use an 11/16" rapid link or a dog-leg carabiner) the swaged end of the 5/16" suspension cable into the spliced eye of the rope. The other end of the cable is strand viced to the tree trunk staple.

Another time saver is to use 1/2" diameter staples as support anchors in the trees (not for the belay cable) rather than through bolts. Whack the staple in with an almost *vertical* orientation to the trunk so that about 1 1/2" remains from the end of the staple to the surface of the tree. If you are having trouble hitting the staple in that far without flattening the curved end, or you haven't been doing your daily magnum-arm-blaster bicep curls, pre-drill the tree to about a 2" depth with a 3/8" drill bit before force-feeding with the sledge.

If you do decide to use staples as challenge supports (rather than drilled through NEBs), make sure that there is sufficient cable drape built into the challenge; i.e., suspend the hung challenge item well below the level of the supporting staples. Remember, drape = strength.

Also, don't forget when all is done, including installation of the shear reduction devices and hanging of the lazy lines, slap that belay rope on and giv'er a try, mate—to make sure that you haven't indulged yourself in a challenge fantasy that's fun to look at, but impossible to accomplish.

All of the above vertical measurements have been used successfully with adult groups. Don't hesitate to adapt these distances for whatever population you will be working with. If in doubt, make it harder than easier. *"Moderation is for monks."*

The included illustration is more for your enjoyment than to be regarded as a building model.

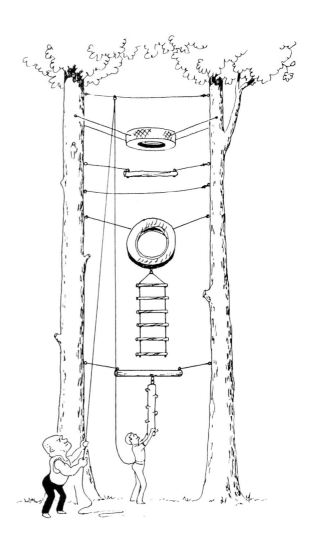

The TP Shuffle

Can't drive a nail without whacking a digit or two? Get the hives when you look at a blueprint? Develop a headache when you read, ". . . and then put Tab A into Slot B, when B has been folded under Slot C"? Here's balm for your shattered ego, a genuinely easy to build initiative event called, "The TP Shuffle."

Materials List
One 25' - 30' utility pole

Tools Needed
None, Zero, Not any

Building Instructions
With a class or a few friends, place the chosen telephone pole (TP) horizontally on a flat grassy or ungrassy area. Done! Hoo Ha — was that great? I could build ropes courses all day!

If you are also interested in what to do with that pole lying out there, here's the low-down, and it's even more fun than building it.

Ask a group of about twenty students to halve themselves and with their newly formed group to stand (balance) on opposite ends of the TP so that the two groups are facing one another in single file. Establishing this face-to-face queue does not represent the initiative problem. The challenge lies in having the two groups exchange ends of the pole without touching the ground. Time the entire procedure and assign a 15 second time penalty for *every* touch with the turf (man and woman eating alfalfa sprouts). After an attempt, ask the group to talk things over and give it another try; the sprouts are still hungry.

As the individuals exchange ends, they do not have to assume any particular sequence at the beginning or at the end of the task, just so that the groups have switched ends from N to S, or E to W, or NE to SW, or SSE to NNW . . .

If you have just purchased a new set of tools and feel chagrinned that you are not going to get a chance to ". . . let Stanley help you do things right," here are two variations that require some building.

1. Dig two holes with a posthole digger (PHD) about 18 feet apart and 2½ feet deep. Cut two 3 foot sections of pole, place them in the holes and tamp in dirt firmly around them. **Do not** cut these 3 foot sections from your 25 footer.

   Lift the long pole and rest it horizontally on top of the two short poles; the longer pole then being parallel to and six inches off the ground. Drill the top pole at each end with a 5/8" extension auger bit so that the holes extend well into the two vertical short poles. With a sledge hammer, drive 5/8" machine bolts through these holes and into the lower support poles so that the bolt heads are smacked flush with the pole. These bolts might be obtained, with a bit of luck and cajoling, from an electric or telephone company.

2. An even easier method of elevating and situating the pole (if you have access to a chain saw) is the following:

   Cut two 3 foot sections of telephone pole (again, not off the end of your TP pole!). Now, cut a **V** notch in the middle of each 3' piece. Try to shape the **V** more like a **U** so that the TP pole will rest solidly in place. Locate each notched 3' pole section perpendicularly at each end of the TP pole (about 2' in from the ends), and lift the pole (lots of people) into the notches: so simple.

The people problem is the same, but the approximately twelve inch elevation of the log allows a bit more maneuverability for the participants and facilitates penalty spotting by the instructor. The elevated pole also proves easier to move on because there is no roll to the pole, but take your pick of techniques and have some fun.

Trolley Construction & Use

Trolley 4" x 4"'s can be as short or long as your group needs dictate. A trolley two feet long with only room for two people is useful for a special needs population or for younger students that have trouble cooperating beyond a one-on-one situation. Trolleys up to 16' long have been built for large groups to offer an additional communication challenge; "What did you say at that end?"

Buy the least expensive 4" x 4" stock available. Even rough cut green wood is OK for this event. Don't try fabricating the trolleys from 2" x 4" stock, because the 2" wood depth isn't enough to countersink the knots. If you leave the knots on the surface of the boards, it makes the "walking" attempts frustratingly difficult and not as much fun.

Using a beveling bit, rout all the edges of the 4X4s. This will save you much sandpapering time later, and it makes the finished product not only look better, but safer.

Using a try-square, draw a line across the board every 12", and on this line, find the center of the board. Using a 1-1/2" drill bit, drill each one of these center marks to a depth of 2". A spade bit (speed-bor) does a good job of making these holes (set up a drill powerful enough to handle such a large-headed bit).

These holes can also be drilled using a bit brace and an Irwin adjustable bit. I mention this only because I have done a few this way (years ago) and know that it can be accomplished. If your boards measure 12', that means you have 20 holes to drill; a substantial physical commitment for one person. If you have students helping, maybe a bit brace is more functional from an I-helped-build-it standpoint.

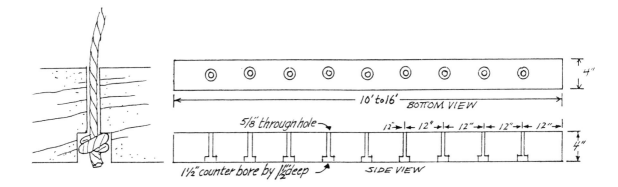

Using a 5/8" bit, drill through each large hole on center. (To keep the drill bit from splintering through the far side, watch for the tip of the spade bit to just break the surface and then turn the 4" x 4" over and, using this pin-hole as a guide, turn the 4X4 over and drill in the reverse direction.)

Cut 20 five foot long pieces of 1/2" polypropylene or 1/2" multiline rope. Reeve a cut section of rope through each hole. (It will be necessary to tape an end of the rope to make it fit through the 5/8" hole without cowstailing.) Tie an overhand knot in the rope end exiting from the large countersunk hole. Tighten the knot as close to the end of the rope as possible without dissolving the knot. Pull the knot into the countersunk hole with a jerk on the other end of the rope. Any part of the knot which sticks above the plane of the board can be tapped into the hole with a hammer.

Either tie another overhand knot in the opposite end of the rope, or if you have the time and patience, perform a back splice in each rope end. This end knot or splice provides the students with a handle.

Implementation

If you want to make the event a bit more difficult, drill the first and last hole only an inch in from the ends of the 4" x 4".

This provides rope for two additional people, but 2 less board feet to stand on.

When you ask the group to use these props to move from point A to point B, don't set the 4" x 4"'s on the ground parallel to the destination. Throw them down or cross them so that their position doesn't indicate possible usage.

Tie another overhand knot about 1/3 of the way down each rope. After the group has mastered the 1-2-3 right; 1-2-3 left technique, suggest that they try making forward progress by all holding onto the lower knots. This bent-over "spoon" position makes the group more vulnerable to the *domino phenomena.*

If you have a hot-shot, I-can-do-anything leader type that needs a bit of humbling, suggest that he/she take the first position on the boards and call signals from there.

A video tape of the whole problem-solving process, particularly with this problem, is a valuable and entertaining teaching tool.

Trolley Variations

If you need a trolley for 16 people and don't have room in your Chevette to transport two 16' lengths of 4" x 4" boards, and . . .

If you want the group to move the trolley over an obstacle, but you're afraid that the boards will crack, and . . .

To add a distinctly bizarre touch to the regular Trolley approach, do this: cut the 4" x 4" boards into 6 or 8 foot lengths, then add the holding ropes in regular one foot increments. Place 1/2" SLES's (shoulder lag eye screw) into one end of each board, and clip the two eyes together with a 1/2" rapid link. If you want to make the trolley problem even more of a problem, use boards only 4' long and attach four of the boards together. This approach may cause a disjointed group to become even more so.

As you and your group try to make it from point A to B on top of the rope festooned trolleys, and someone happens to step off the trolley into the poisoned peanut butter, et al.; rather than assigning a time penalty, simply ask the faller to get back on the trolley backward from his/her starting orientation; i.e., a 180° switch. The faller is then vis-à-vis the person who was formerly viewing their backside. This penalty adds to the confusion and makes forward progress even more difficult and giggle-prone.

Zig Zag

Object: To transport a group across a designated area without touching the ground with either the available boards or any part of a participant's body.

Rules:

1. For the boards to be used, they must fit into the slotted posts; i.e., they may not be turned flat and placed on top of a post.
2. If a participant's body or a board touches the ground, a time penalty may be assigned or the group may be required to start over.
3. 2" X 6" lumber should be used as traversing boards.

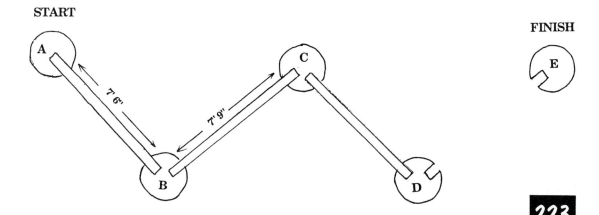

4. Board BC should be equal to the space DE.
5. Board AB and CD should be less than the distance between DE so that only board BC will fit space DE.
6. Posts are placed so that approximately 14 inches of the post is above ground and 3 feet is in the ground. The top of the posts are notched appropriately for the boards with a chain saw initially, and squared off with a sharp chisel.
7. Distances AB and CD measure 7 feet 6 inches, and distance BC measures 7 feet nine inches.

8. Refer to the illustration on page 223.

Chicken Wire Crossing

I have not participated in or introduced the following initiative problem for over twenty years, but it keeps coming back to mind ... so, you're about to share one of my reoccurring reveries.

It was a stark and dormy night at the North Carolina Outward Bound School in the fall of 1968, as amidst darkness and bluster, I contemplated the downed and precariously balanced log that provided the only way across the precipitous canyon that yawned abysmally before my trembling size 12's. (Ref. Bulwer-Lytton Contest book, *It Was a Dark and Stormy Night ...*)

The OB program was introduced at the North Carolina site, I think, in 1966, so that by the time I began instructing there in '68, a ropes course had already been built and some initiative problems (called initiative *tests* at that time) had also been installed at the various woodsy sites. One of the "tests" was the *Chicken Wire Crossing*, located in a deeply cut stream bed near the old zip wire site. After twenty years, I'll bet the

event (and even the memory of the event) is long gone locally, so maybe this expository revisitation will rejuvenate what I remember as an engrossing physical and mental group problem.

Take a look at the illustration on pg. 224. The object is to move your entire group across the log (for whatever fanciful reason you want to make up), without touching either the ground or the chicken wire (which is, of course, galvanically sensitive to human touch). Contact with the ground under the log results in a trip back to the start for the offender, but the merest touch of the chicken wire causes a polarity reversal of the creosoted log's hydrochlorine gas which quickly diffuses throughout the entire area, necessitating that the entire group begin again — yes, including everyone who has already safely and laboriously made it across the log.

Note that the construction of the chicken wire barrier is such that a person cannot crawl across on top of the log *and* under the barrier. The only prop allowed is a 15 ft. section of 9mm sling rope.

Considerations:

- Do not suspend the horizontal log more than 6 feet above the ground for safety reasons; any higher and spotting becomes unreasonable.

- Conceptually, the chicken wire and adjacent support poles extend indefinitely upward; i.e., no one may climb the poles. Wrap chicken wire around the poles as part of the installation process, and no on will even think about climbing the poles, considering the potential for chlorine gas being produced.

- More than one person is allowed on the log at a time, but no more than four. Assign at least one spotter per person on the log.

- After a participant has made it under the chicken wire without touching, they must regain to the top of the pole (log) before getting credit for making a successful passage. It may be useful to paint a white stripe on the underside of the log about five feet from where it is suspended from the vertical support. This stripe would act as a NO TRESPASS sign to the upside-down log rider.

- You don't actually have to use chicken wire as a barrier; criss-crossed bungee cord works just as well.

Swing Aboard, or Prouty's Landing

This activity is a simple and enjoyable combination of the *All Aboard* and the *Nitro Crossing* initiative problems.

Set up a portable 3' x 3' *All Aboard*-type portable platform a few feet away from your *Nitroglycerine Crossing* initiative problem rope. Exactly how far to set the platform can be easily determined with a bit of trial and error swinging. Think: challenging, but not frustrating. Perform your T&E swings before the students show up. Don't forget to set up the "trip wire" length of bamboo at the START end of the swing. I set my bamboo pole on top of two caffine free, diet Coke cans, but . . . it's obviously your choice.

The object is to swing an entire group (12-16 players) onto the platform and maintain a balanced group position for 5 seconds. Since you have already set the

platform into toxic PCB (peanut colored butter), any transgressions into this highly corrosive material results in a trip back to the starting point for detoxification (. . . you want to end up sterile? . . . you do?) and another try. You may want to outline the toxic area with a rope, or just scratch a circle in the dirt.

Disc Jockeys

The object is to choose one of the two available swing ropes and move the entire group from a designated safe area out and into the situated hoops, discs or bicycle tires (refer to the illustration on pg. 227). The first attempt is not timed; succeeding attempts are performed under the clock. The same rope used for the *Nitro Crossing* can also be used for this event.

- Make available wooden discs, hula hoops, or bicycle tires equal to the number of participants.
- These discs, hoops, or tires are arranged in a pyramidal fashion with the pyramid base located about 8 feet from the two swing ropes. Discs are somewhat symmetrically set about 14" apart.
- Any two feet on a disc is the limit. If

three feet end up on a disc, both participants must return to the start.

- A participant can step to only one more
  disc or hoop beyond the one they
  initially land on, IF only one foot makes
  contact with the first disc or hoop. As
  soon as both feet are located on a disc,
  that is where you stay.

- It you can't swing or step to a disc, a
  participant must be physically passed
  to a disc further on in the pyramid. A
  passed player must accept the first disc
  they touch; i.e., no steps after being put
  down.

This initiative problem has all the right
elements for classic status, except for the
comparatively large number of props

necessary, but in a ropes course setting,
that should pose no problem.

Go out of your way to try this one — it's
better than most. And don't forget to try
twice so that the students get a chance to
appreciate how efficient they have become.

Do-I-Go

Set four 2X2 platforms symetrically around
the single hanging rope so that the platforms represent the outlined four dots on
the number 5 die (you know, like a pair of
dice), with the rope being the center dot.
The platforms should be so positioned that
it is impossible to jump from one to another. To start, ask the 16 or so students to
stand on one of the four platforms.

The object is for each student to end up on another platform. No one is allowed to swing diagonally across, unless you need to make the problem easier.

A variation is to see how long it takes to move each student clockwise (or counter-clockwise) from platform to platform so that they end up on the platform from which they started.

Do they have to get the rope themselves at the beginning of the problem? S'up to you, mate.

Hang an additional rope for more swinging action. (Photo below) Then it really becomes a question of, "When *do I go?*

How to Install a Climbing Block

I wrote a book about ten years ago entitled *High Profile*, that outlined and detailed wall building and indoor ropes course installation; the book is no longer in print. The following instructions for climbing block installation are from that book and will provide what you need to know about securing wooden or synthetic blocks (as offered in *Project Adventure's* equipment catalog) to a brick, cinder block, or concrete wall.

All of the holes drilled in the climbing blocks are sized to fit various lengths of 3/8" lag screws. They are also counter bored to fit 3/8 SAE washers. If you bought the blocks from *Project Adventure*, all needed connecting hardware would have been provided.

Various companies are now manufacturing synthetic, one hole climbing blocks made from a combination of resin and grit (to simulate the feel of real rock). They come in beau coup varieties, and I have to admit, feel good to the touch.

You will need the following pieces of hardware for drilling into the wall and securing the blocks.

* **A hammer drill**. This type of drill provides a simultaneous rotary and hammer operation. Try not to use a homeowner's hammer drill, as this type of wimpy tool will add considerably to your building time. Buy or rent an industrial 5/8" X 4" drill bit and drill. You will need a longer drill bit if you plan to place belay anchors, but for the blocks only, a 4" bit will do the job.

* **A socket wrench** with a 9/16" socket.

* **A hammer**

Procedure

Where you put the blocks on the wall as you establish your climb is up to your sense of aesthetics, compassion, and climbing experience. You should consider that starting a climb at floor level opens the climb to anyone who discovers what the blocks are for. Most schools require that *Project Adventure* builders begin the climb; i.e., install the first block, at a minimum height of 10'. If your wall is only 20' high, that doesn't give you much operating room, but the reality of the situation is that you either start at height or secure the climbing area.

Choose a block and place the two supplied washers in the two holes. Insert both lag screws into the holes, and hold the block on the wall where you want it to be. Use a hammer to strike the ends of the bolts in order to make two marks on the wall. If the marks are distinct, fine, if not use a magic marker to define their location. This may seem superfluous, but marking the small dented area will save you considerable time and frustration at the top of a ladder in poor light, troublesome winds, and cool temperatures.

If you are installing the one hole synthetic blocks, just drill away where ever you want to place the block. One hole, one bolt—get it?

If installing the blocks on brick, I usually choose to drill into the concrete between bricks, because the drilling is predictably easier. The only contraindication is that some brick layers don't put a full layer of concrete between bricks with the result that your drill bit may break through prematurely. A good drill and bit will make short work of either concrete or brick, so just slap the block up there and go.

It pays time dividends to obtain an individual cinder block before beginning the job and look at the inside of the block in order to determine the best place for making a hole. Cinder block construction varies, so choosing a solid placement takes some experience. The good news is that, most of the time, anyplace on a cinder block will provide enough cinder material for holding a lag screw/lead shield combination.

Drill at each hammer mark to a depth slightly deeper than the length of a short lead shield. (If you are going to be making a lot of these holes, use some type of hearing protector. WHAT?) If the drill bit breaks through the interior of a cinder block, it's usually no problem. However, if the lag screw won't "take", fill that hole with some quick dry patch of appropriate color and try again closer to the edge of the cinder block.

Place a lead shield in each finished hole so that the wide opening on the end of the shield is facing you. You may have to tap the shield in with your hammer. The end of the shield should be flush with the wall.

Hold the block up to the wall so that the two lag screws are aligned with the shield openings. Holding the block against the wall, begin turning the lags by hand until it becomes too difficult. Use the 9/16" socket to continue turning the lags clockwise until you begin to feel a tightening; i.e., the lead shield expanding against the sides of the hole. It will require more turns of the socket to reach this tightening point than you might anticipate; be patient.

Do not over tighten the lag. Anyone with normal strength could strip the lead shield. Tighten only to that point where the block is drawn securely against the wall. Done !

If the installation was accomplished indoors, come back after a few days and gently retighten all wooden blocks. The wood will shrink because of the dry indoor gym environment.

There are obviously other types of anchoring systems that can be used, but lead shields are easy to install and hold well. Their only limitation is that if you are going to be removing a block frequently and reinstalling it, the shield will eventually wear away the sides of the drilled hole. If that's the case, try the Hilte epoxy anchor. You will know it when you see it at the store, the insertion piece looks like a condom made from chicken wire.

DANGLE DO (DUO-TRIO)

Performance Objective

For one, two, or three people on belay to ascend this "giant ladder", using only the horizontal wooden 4X4 cross pieces for support or aid; i.e., the two vertical support cables cannot be used for maintaining balance or assistance in getting to the next higher rung.

Photo by Nicki Hall

Materials Needed For Construction

4 to 12 - 4" X 4" X 10' boards (pressure treated)
80' - 5/16" cable
40' - 3/8" cable
12 - 5/16" cable stops or 12 - 1/4" cable clamps
12 - 1/2" slug washers
2 - 5/16" strand vices
2 - 5/16" nico-press sleeves
4 - 5/16" thimbles
2 - non-locking carabiners
2 - 3/8" strand vices
4 - 3/8" cable clamps
2 - 7/16" serving sleeves
4 - 15" (approx.) nut eye bolt
8 - fish plates
2 - 1/2" X 4" nut eye bolt & 4 washers
20-30 - 1/2" staples

Construction Details (For a six rung Dangle ladder)

Locate two tall, straight, large diameter trees to serve as supports. (I know you aren't going to choose two short, crooked, skinny trees, but I have a writer's expository obligation to fulfill.) Each tree will need to be cleared of most branches to a height of about 40', especially those branches that extend inward between the two trees; i.e., the space to be occupied by the dangling 4X4's. Straight trunked trees that require the least amount of limbing are obviously the best choice.

BEST - tulip poplar, ponderosa pine, jeffery pine, southern yellow pine

NOT BAD - white pine, hickory, some oak, some maple, walnut, hemlock (involves much limb cutting), beech

NOT GOOD - poplar, cedar, white birch, cottonwood, cherry

Use a tree climbing belt to allow the maneuverability necessary for hand sledging half inch diameter staples into the trunk, as you establish a stapled climb up to the event height. Clear all (dead and alive) interior facing limbs from the support trees. If you have a small (10" bar) chain saw for this job, use it. If you don't know how to use a chain saw on the ground, don't use it up a tree.

At a height of 30-60+ feet, install a 3/8" belay cable, with back up loops. (This presupposes that you know how to drill through the trunk and place proper length nut eye bolts.) A minimum 12" diameter of the support tree trunk dictates the maximum chosen height for Dangle Do ladder installation. Remember that participants do not have to make it to the top rung in order to "succeed" or feel a sense of accomplishment (that's up to your insightful presentation and compassionate comments), so do not hesitate to build an event that some students will have trouble completing; built it with *functional challenge* in mind.

Measure down about 12 inches from each belay cable anchor bolt and install another nut eye bolt in each support tree. These bolts provide the two opposing anchors for suspension of the Dangle Do itself.

Begin making up the Dangle Do ladder on the ground in the cleared area directly beneath the belay cable.

Using a router, chamfer all four sharp edges from each 4X4 board. Beveling these edges is necessary for safety, aesthetics, and climbing comfort. Don't leave out this step because you can't find your router.

Measure 3" in from the ends of each board and, on-center, drill a 1-1/4" counter bore hole to a depth of 3/4". (Use a speed-bor drill-bit, held in a 1/2" chuck electric drill.) After finishing the counter-bore holes, change the drill bit to a 3/8 inch diameter spade or auger bit, and, starting at the center of each counter bore hole, drill all the way through the board.

Building this particular Dangle Do is based on a 40' belay height, but by looking at the photos you can estimate how the measurements can be adjusted proportionally. In this case, you will need two sections of 5/16" cable that measure at least 35' long each. Don't hesitate to add a few fudge feet to each length, considering that it's easier, and ultimately less expensive, to trim off extra cable than to start over.

Arrange the boards on the ground like ladder rungs, so they are all parallel to one another, and resting on a side so all counter bored holes face in the same direction. Reeve an end of a 37' cable length through the respective 1/2" holes of five board ends, so that the cable enters a board on the side opposite the counter bore. Leave a sixth 4X4 set aside for later use.

If you are using nicopress stop-swages to separate and support each board on the cable, reeve a 1/2" washer and stop-swage (in that order) onto the cable between each set of 4X4 boards. If you can't afford a nicopress swageing tool or don't know what I'm referring to, use cable clamps for this support purpose. If you do plan to use cable clamps to support the 4X4s, just continue reeving the cable through the boards, because the cable clamps will be attached later. Reeve the second 35' cable length through the holes at the other end of the boards, (as above).

Use a cable cutter to neatly trim the two frayed cable ends that you have been force feeding through the boards. Pushing cable through a series of 3/8" holes is bound to fray the end of the cable, so don't waste time being ultra-careful with your reeving. You only need to cut off an inch or two of cable to provide a clean end for swaging an eye. Even if you plan to use a 5/16" cable clamp to form the eye, a trimmed cable end is safer and looks better.

Walk to the other end of the cables, and place a 5/16" strand vice on the two respective cable ends.

Now determine how much of a physical challenge you want to establish by how far the 4X4s are positioned apart from one another. If you start off with 5 feet between the first and second rung, and add 2-3 inches for each additional spacing between 4X4s, you will have created a truly exceptional challenge, but perhaps one that only the most adept can hope to accomplish. Try starting with 4 feet between the first and second boards and add two inches for each additional spacing.

Starting with either cable (at the swaged eye end) move the bottom 4X4 down and against the swaged eye. Using a tape, measure 4 feet up the cable from the top of the board and squeeze on a stop swage; or

use your socket wrench to attach a 1/4" cable clamp at that 4 foot level. Pull the swage/clamp solidly up into the countersunk hole of the 4X4, then measure 4' 2" up the cable from the top of that 4X4. Hold the already reeved cable stop at this 4' 2" mark and swage it in place there, (or place a 1/4" cable clamp at this same juncture). Pull the stop (or clamp) up into the countersunk hole of that second board, and measure up the cable 4'4" from the top of the board. Mark this spot and swage on the next stop or place the next clamp, etc., etc.

Continue this measuring and swaging (clamping) sequence, insidiously increasing each between-board measurement by 2 inches. Because of the climber's down-looking-up perspective, the increasing distance between boards cannot be determined from below—perfect. *"Hey, these rungs are getting farther apart!"*

When completed with one side, switch to the other cable and repeat the above procedure, checking as you proceed that the boards are secured on the two cables parallel to one another.

Make your measurements on the cable accurately, otherwise the rungs will hang askew; functional certainly, but not aesthetically acceptable. If the rungs are misaligned, there is no recourse except to confidently declare (don't mumble or your lost), "That's the kind of challenge you don't see every day!"

If for some serendipitous reason you end up with too much space between the dangling 4X4s, or you don't have enough boards to complete your vertical scheme, try *adding a smile*. For example, say you end up with six feet between rungs, an improbable challenge for normal people. *Add a smile* by draping a cut section of 5/8" diameter multiline rope beneath the top 4X4. The climber can grab the rope's belly (smile), stand on the lower 4X4, and step onto the smile (belly of the rope) as access to the top 4X4. Adding a draped rope or two also adds to the variety and visual challenge of the event.

To actually *add the smile*, measure about three inches in from the nut eye bolt and countersink an inch and a half hole about 1 1/4" deep. Then using a 7/8" bit, continue the counter-sink all the way through the 4X4. Do this on both ends of the board.

Reeve a length of multiline rope through one of the holes and tie a simple overhand knot and pull (jam) it into the countersunk hole. Establish the drape of the rope (smile) so that it is just above half way between the two boards — the rope will stretch with use — and establish an identical knot arrangement in the other counter-sunk end of the board: there's your smile.

Before you start hauling this bizarre ladder into place, make sure that there is sufficient length of cable between the top board and the strand vice. Considering that the boards are 10' long, and that you want at least three feet between the ends of the board and the support trees, the length of the cable from the top board to the strand vice needs to be at least 6' to allow enough of an angled drape to preclude excess strain on the anchors, cable, and board itself.

Attaching the two support cables directly to the anchor trees will cause the angled cable to bite deeply into the wood of the top rung. To prevent the cable from eventually making a deep groove in the board end, screw a three hole galvanized plate directly juxtaposed and perpendicular to the angled support cable so that the cable rests on the plate rather than digging into the board. These three or four hole galvanized plates are readily available at hardware stores.

Climb both support trees in turn, and hang a strong pulley (ROSA type or industrial grade) in each tree, using a steel carabiner attached to the belay eye bolt or a round-the-trunk sling arrangement. Reeve a haul rope (KM 3 or a similiar static rope) through each pulley, a rope long enough to double the height distance (pulley to ground) plus 15 extra feet for a bowline on a round turn knot, and some hands-on hauling space.

Using this pulley/rope arrangement, tie one end of each haul rope (bowline-on-a-round-turn) to the top board near where the cable enters the board. Tie on the rope to the inside of the cable to keep the rope from possibly slipping off the end of the board.

Before hauling away, use a socket wrench to tighten a 1/4" cable clamp onto the 5/16" cable just above the board. These temporary clamps can be removed after hauling the Dangle Do into position. Their function is to keep the top board in place and the top cable section loose so that clipping-in under tension will not be a problem. If the slack cable idea doesn't make sense, do it anyway and thank me later.

If you have a couple Haven's Grips in your tool kit, simply use their camming action on the cable (placed just above the board) to accomplish the same result as the wordy cable-clamp plan above. Don't try to buy a Haven's Grip from your local hardware store, they won't have one.

Prepare to haul, using all interested onlookers, conscripted students, and reluctant (". . . this isn't in my contract) teachers that you can cajole into helping. Actually, the lifting can be accomplished by four strong people, but a few more willing hands ameliorates the do or die haul scenario that may develop. Additionally, if you can position your truck in such a way that horsepower can get the job done, do it. If you have *Jumars* or the like, and know how to use them, use them.

Before hauling begins, you and someone else need to climb the two support trees to be ready for the nut eye bolt/strand vice attachment. Use a tree climber's belt so that both of your hands will be free to attach the strand vice to the anchor eye bolt. Attempting to attach a strand vice with one hand can be equated to eating spaghetti with a single chop stick.

Okay, *haul away, evenly now, keep the boards horizontal,* **STOP!** - *clip-clip: All slack!* Does the bottom board hang between 9-10 feet off the ground? Are the boards pretty much parallel? Are the ends of the boards about equidistant from the support trees? Yes? Done!

Now step back and enjoy the visual aspect of your well crafted woodland anomaly.

The ulttra-high Dangle Quad depicted in the photo to the right was installed at Georgia College in Milledgeville, GA. It has 15 rungs (eat your heart out Adrian) and measures 85' to the top rung. The person standing near top is 6' 3" tall.

Photo by Lee Gillis

Some Finishing Touches

- Go back to that lonely sixth board on the ground, and install a 1/2" X 4" nut eye bolt, three inches in from each board end. Cut and peen the end of the bolt. This portable bottom board can be attached to the cable eyes (just below the bottom dangling board) with carabiners or rapid links (carabiners are faster) to provide first-step access to the event, also allowing easy removal of the board, precluding unauthorized, after-hour attempts.

- If you are going to use this event with three participants (Dangle Trio), install two *separate* belay cables. Preparatory to the climb, arrange for the two lightest climbers to be belayed on one cable. The third, *well covered* climber, gets their own cable.

- One of the belay cables will have two S/S Pulleys attached. To prevent the pulleys from banging against one another and to preclude tangled belay lines, before securing the belay cable, slide on a 2 foot section of 1/2" diameter PVC pipe. The PVC pipe conveniently keeps the belay pulleys apart. Installing this section of pipe isn't necessary, just convenient, and it makes you look like you know what you're doing.

- If high winds are common at the installation site, you must provide some means of teathering the bottom rung to one of the support trees, otherwise that rung, and the one or two above, will act as battering rams during high winds. Bark will be knocked loose, cambium will be exposed to insects and decay organisms, and the tree's health will dramatically suffer, (that's a euphemism for dying).

- Are there lots of limbs growing into what could be useable photographic space? The Dangle Do can be dramatically photogenic, so try to selectively remove surrounding vegetation to allow striking silhouette photographs.

- Dan Post and I recently built a Dangle Do that had alternating 8' and 12' 4X4 lengths. What a visual treat; we called it the *Dippsy Doodle Do*.

PAMPER POLE & PLANK

Performance Objective

Using sledge placed staples (H), to climb a tree or pole to a platform, then dive, on belay, to catch a trapeze suspended a challenging but reasonable distance away.

Materials Needed For Construction

75' -	3/8" cable (approx. length)
30' -	1/4" cable (approx.)
2 -	3/8" strand vice
2 -	1/4" strand vice
4 -	3/8" cable clamps
2 -	7/16" serving sleeves
2 -	1/4" nico-press swaging sleeves
2 -	1/4" thimbles
8 -	fish plates
1 -	Shear Reduction block
35 -	1/2" staples
30" -	1 1/2" PVC rod
2 -	3/8" X 2" nut eye bolt
2 -	3/8" SAE washers
2 -	1/2" rapid link
85' -	#4 nylon cord (approx.)

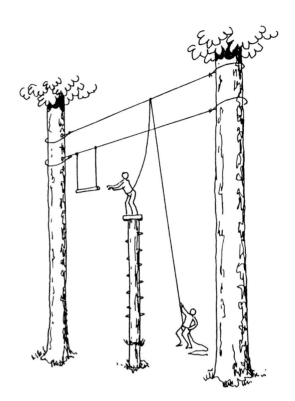

4 -	5/8" forged nut eye bolts (approx. length)

Wood for the Pamper Pole

4 -	2" X 6" X 1' pressure treated boards
12 -	16d galvanized common nails
8 -	1/2" X 6" galvanized lag screws
8 -	1/2" galvanized slug washers

Wood for the Pamper Plank

2 -	2" X 6" X 10' pressure treated wood (approx. length)
2 -	2" X 6" X 12' PT wood (approx. length)
3 -	2" X 10" X 8' PT wood

Diving for a trapeze from the top of a wobbly Pamper Pole, a tree supported platform/plank, a field house balcony, or from a block supported wall platform is the recognized *sine qua non* of ropes course commitment activities. I have heard combat veterans, pilots, sky divers, bungee jumpers, and rock climbers all express the same general gut feelings about the trust, fear, support, commitment, letting go . . . etc. that are so intimately involved with the climbing and diving attempt — and the dry mouth, sewing machine legs, accelerated speech, yielding sphincters . . .)

Construction Procedure for the Pamper Pole

If you have already constructed a high (25'+ minimum) Two-Line Bridge, building time for the Pamper Pole and perhaps the Pamper Plank belay set up will be reduced considerably by using the bottom cable of the Two-Line Bridge from which to hang the trapeze, and utilizing the top, backed-up belay cable of the Two Line Bridge, as the belay cable for the trapeze jump.

If a high Two-Line Bridge isn't part of your ropes course set up, spend some time looking for two strong, straight-trunked trees that will serve as belay cable anchor supports. There should be a minimum of 20' between the two trees, and be located in an area where post hole digging is possible. Minimal clearing of trees, shrubs, and rocks is always a consideration.

The choice of poles for the Pamper Pole itself are limited to either a utility pole or a felled tree. Consider them individually.

- A utility pole is the best choice, because the wood has been chemically pressure injected with a preservative to prevent fiber decay and insect damage. However, most donated utility poles are low quality because of their in-ground age; usually over 25 years. Even though a new pole will cost $400.00+ delivered, it will look better, last much longer, and not be coated with skin irritating creosote. (Creosote has been designated as an illegal substance to use for wood preservation because of the toxins used in its chemical make up.) A benefit of placing a pole rather than using a topped tree is the programmatic choice of jumping distance to the trapeze — additionally, a topped tree will soon rot.

- If you are going to use a felled tree, strip off all bark before installation. Removing bark speeds up the wood drying process and removes an organic layer that protects grubs and other saprophitic wood gobblers. A freshly peeled log will absorb practically no liquid wood preservative, so let the log cure for a couple weeks before attempting to soak the trunk.

I do not recommend topping a tree *in situ* to use as a climbing pole, because of: accelerated decay, hassle, and danger. A topped tree will decay faster (in ground), and eventually having to replace the tree with a pole is a half-day hassle that's avoidable. Also, and most significantly, topping a tree safely is beyond the skill level of most weekend Mini-Mac loggers; don't try it.

Whatever type of tree or pole you choose, drive in all the 1/2" climbing staples (H) and bolt on the platform while the pole is still horizontal; there's no use doing unnecessary vertical work. Also, staples enter a fresh cut log easier than in wood that has dried out. If you must staple a dried out log, pre-drill for the staples with a 3/8" bit.

What measurements represent the distance and height that exudes challenge ("I'll go for it!"), precludes boredom ("No problem"), and minimizes frustration ("No Way, Ray!")? A jumping distance (end of platform to trapeze plumb line) of seven feet, with the trapeze hanging at about chest level (six foot tall jumper), will offer a first rate challenge, and be just difficult enough to appear initially impossible — particularly from a ground-looking-up perspective.

After approximating where the pole

should be placed, have-at the site with your Phd (post hole digger). Try to choose an area that isn't all rock ledge, construction fill, or a leeching field. The joy of post hole digging decreases, as dredging out rocks, construction fill, or sponge-like cess pool soil increases.

The hole must be at least 5' deep (deeper if the pole is more than 30' out of the ground—see *Utility Pole Esoteria* pg.194 in this Chapter) and at least 6" larger in diameter than the pole itself. This concern about differentiation in pole/hole diameter relates to needing enough space around the pole to allow forceful tamping of dirt fill. If the pole is lowered into a tight-fit hole, there won't be enough space between pole and ground to allow effective tamping of returned soil, resulting in a loose pole. A well set Pamper Pole vibrates and wiggles enough without having to overcome high angle shifting. The quaint descriptive phrase, "sewing machine knees" used by dispassionate climbers to describe the fatigue/fear trembling in a novice's knees becomes "sewing machine body" at the top of a loose wobbly pole.

While the hole is being dug by an associate (keep reading, I'm getting you out of the sweat-hog work), climb one of the belay cable support trees and carabiner-clip a strong pulley (a ROSA or industrially rated snatch block pulley) into the belay anchor nut eye bolt. Reeve a suitable length of haul rope (KM-3 or any strong static synthetic rope of at least 1/2" diameter) through the pulley cheeks. Both ends of the rope should reach the ground plus 15 feet. Make sure that after one end of the haul rope is tied onto the log, that the rope runs fairly through the pulley; i.e., no sharp angles that increase friction and weaken the rope.

Repeat your climb up the other support tree and arrange another similar pulley/haul rope system.

Raising a log of Pamper Pole size places a considerable strain on the pulley and rope system, so don't use a $2.78 laundry-line pulley or clothes-line rope; I'm exaggerating, but you know what I mean. If there is substantial shock-loading of the rope during the pole raising, an inferior natural fiber rope may snap, and that massive angled log becomes a hammer looking for a nail. Do not use sisal, jute, or inferior manila rope for any construction purposes; most natural fiber rope is just too weak for hauling and lifting purposes.

Back to the deepening post hole — briefly. After a 5' depth is reached, shovel in about 6" of gravel (any ole rocks will do) to allow water drainage away from the bottom of the log. If your hole extends below the water table, forget the rocks, but make sure the bottom of the log is well soaked with preservative.

Measuring from the bottom (butt end) of the log, make a mark at the 5' level (in-the-ground section) and also at the 12' level. Begin sledging 1/2" staples into the log at approximately 8' above ground level. Try not to make the staple climb too difficult, considering that the commitment value of eventually standing on the platform is half the challenge; 7/16 anyway.

If a platform on top of the pole needs to be built, do it now. Place a short fulcrum log under the upper end of the pole to elevate the top end of the log enough to make the platform work easier. A platform may not be necessary if you have decided to use a naturally bifurcated Y end of the tree for a two-footed stance. Each of the two cut ends (tops of the Y) should have a minimum diameter of 5" to provide a realistic, albeit temporary foot stance. Or you may want the jumper to simply stand on top of the horizontal trunk cut, in which case a minimum diameter of 8" should be used.

There is something about a platform, however, that strengthens resolve by providing a visual, if not substantial goal. A small simple platform can be fashioned as follows:

- Cut two 12" section of 2" X 6" pressure treated lumber.

- Orient these two boards at the top of the pole so that they are aligned parallel to one another on either side of the pole and so that their 2" sides are flush with the top of the pole. Trimming the sides of the pole (top eight inches) with a chainsaw provides a flatter surface for a bolted-on board.

- Bolt these two 12" boards into their respective positions using 2 - 1/2" X 4" galvanized lag screws per board. Don't forget to use washers with each lag screw. You might find it easier to nail the boards on first (16d galvanized), then drill the necessary bolt holes (1/2" first through the board, then 3/8" into the pole) with the boards in place.

- Cut two more 2" X 6" X 12" boards and nail them both (use 10d common galvanized nails) to the top of the bolted boards, leaving a small gap between boards to ensure a square platform. (2" X 6" boards actually measure only 1 -3/4" X 5 -5/8"; don't ask, that's just the way it is.)

- Done, except for rasping off the sharp edges of the boards. Consider stencilling or writing a sympathetic and inspiring note on top of the platform; perhaps, "Relax, it's all down hill from here."

With a group of 20+ people to help, lift the log and jockey the butt end next to the hole so that the long axis of the log is perpendicular to the belay cable mentioned above. After you have lifted this massive

peeled pole and moved it as suggested, you will understand why the "Iwo Jima" method of raising a long log to vertical doesn't work. The Easter Island folks came up with an unbelievably tedious technique for raising heavy objects to vertical (Read Kon-Teki by Thor Hyderdahl), but they had unlimited time, and you don't, so . . .

Tie (bowline on a round turn) both of the haul ropes to the platform end of the log. Also tie on two additional lengths of rope at about the same height, to act as lateral stabilizers during the lifting process.

If you have about 24 helpers, distribute them this way (If you don't have 24 lifters, lift with more gusto, set up a block and tackle system, or use your brother-in-law's 4X4 truck):

- Nine on the end of each pulley haul rope.

- Two mesomorphic males to lift vertically on the platform end of the log (straight backs, bend your legs) in order to "break the inertia." These two can join the eighteen rope haulers as soon as their initial efforts have served their purpose.

- Put two committed hefties on the ends of the stabilizing ropes.

- Locate yourself at the butt end of the log with a pry bar or stout sapling length to guide the pole butt into the hole. Angle a 2" X 10" X 5' pressure treated board section into the far side of the hole to act as a git-into-the-hole guide for the sliding butt end of the log. If you can't get the board out of the hole after the pole is adjusted to vertical, leave it there; the treated board is rot-resistant and makes a dandy shim. Beware the inertial power of the moving log and its effect on the lever you are holding.

After the log drops into the hole (amidst

numerous directional calls, goads to greater effort, and finally cheers) ask your helpers to adjust and maintain the pole vertically as you fill in dirt and tamp vigorously; actually it's a fill-tamp, fill-tamp sequence that best firms up the log. *Go for the 4X4 truck, it's mucho easier.*

Concrete footing or fill is not necessary if the hole is deep enough, and the dirt is well tamped. Using concrete fill is seldom indicated, but if used, the top area of the cured concrete must taper away from the pole surface, otherwise water will collect at the concrete/pole interface accelerating eventual decay of even a treated pole.

If the just-placed pole needs to be turned in order to align the platform with the trapeze, place a peavey or log lifter on the pole at about waist height and, using the tool spike as a fulcrum and the tool shaft as a lever, turn the pole in the hole (with help) as many degrees as necessary; not as difficult a task as you might imagine. I think it's obvious, but . . . finish your platform angling adjustments before filling and tamping the hole.

Climb the pole and remove the haul

ropes, unless you need the ropes to adjust the pole's lean. If, after you have tried a jump to the trapeze, you find the dive too difficult; i.e., you miss, adjust the distance by either: (1) lowering the trapeze a few inches or, (2) angling the pole closer to the trapeze.

To cause the pole to lean toward or away from the trapeze, grab one of the lateral adjusting ropes and utilizing some group muscle, pull until the platform is where you think it needs to be, then vigorously re-tamp that area behind the pole where a gap between dirt and pole has appeared. As the result of trying #2, you will notice a slight tilt to the platform, but that's okay because it's tilted in the direction you're going anyway.

After the pole is set and tamped in place, pour a copious amount of acceptable wood preservative around the dirt/wood interface at the bottom of the pole. Repeat this chemical application once a year. Without treatment, the pole will need replacement within five years or less because of wood decay.

If a *Two-Line Bridge* was utilized as a pulley attachment point for lifting the log, hanging the trapeze will be comparatively easy. Let's take a look at the easy way first, and maybe save you a couple hours work.

Tie into a belay rope that runs through an S/S pulley on the top cable of the Two Line Bridge, (I'm making sure that you do this following work with some protection). Take these items up with you.

- trapeze set up (see below)
- socket wrench and socket (11/16")
- 2 - cable drops with 5/16" cable clamps attached
- shear reduction block and 2 - 1/2" rapid links

Considering that you have already

climbed one of the support trees, walk (slide-step) out onto the Two Line Bridge foot cable until you are located directly across from the Pamper Pole platform. Ask your belayer for a bit of slack and sit down on the bottom cable. I know this apparent balancing act is "above and beyond . . . ," but with a tight belay it's easier than it seems. Don't straddle the cable as you sit down or an ultimate weggie will result: sit side straddle.

Let go of the belay rope so that you have the use of both hands. Use a leg for balance and stability by wrapping it around the tensioned belay rope. Be confident!

Place the two cable-drops on the 3/8" bottom cable — the one you are sitting on — attaching one to the left of your comfortably seated bod, and one to your right. Don't tighten them down yet. Adjust each

clamp so that the platform is located at the imaginary apex of a triangle, with the attached clamps and cable forming the base. Now tighten the clamps. Open the two 1/4" strand vices individually and hang the trapeze from the two cable drops.

Move back to the support tree and ask someone to tie into a belay rope, then have them climb the Pamper Pole, and stand erect on top of the platform. Ask that intrepid person to eye-ball the trapeze for levelness and proper height. Move back out to the cable-drops and make the needed adjustments by cautiously pushing cable through the 1/4" strand vices. Do not stay out on the cable while your helper is eyeballing the results of your adjustments, as your mid-cable weight will lower the trapeze considerably, offering an incorrect visual estimation of where the trapeze should hang.

It may be necessary to make a couple trips back to the tree in order to get the "hang" just right. Make small adjustments with the 1/4" cable, because once they are made, the one-way characteristic of the strand vice does not allow easy readjustment of the cable in the other direction. Actually, reversing cable direction in a strand vice is possible by using a narrow headed screw driver or scratch awl to lever against an internal spring through an access slot in the vice body. Delicately balanced "en derriere" on the cable, such esoteric manipulation is a bit of journeyman work that I don't think you will want to pursue.

Rarely, one of the 1/4" cable lengths that make up the trapeze suspension, may feed spontaneously through the body of the strand vice; not slipping out, mind you, but feeding through. This feeding-through happens because of the bouncing action that regularly occurs when someone lets go of the trapeze. To prevent this "self adjustment" apply black electrician's tape tightly to the cable then continuing the wrapping onto the narrow end of the strand vice body. Tape's cheap, don't hesitate to make a few turns.

After the trapeze is hung to your satisfaction (and since you're already there), attach the SR belay block about 14" laterally to the left or right of the trapeze by attaching two 5/16" cable clamps directly to the 3/8" belay cable above your head. (Make sure this placement jives with where you are going to place the *Jus-Rite descender*, or where the belayer is going to stand.) Situate these two clamps about an inch and a half apart, with the threaded bolt ends pointing skyward. Hang the SR block in between these clamps by using the two 1/2" rapid links attached linearly to one another. The two links are arranged in this way (linked to one another lengthwise) to allow a partial swiveling action of the SR block with resultant optimum alignment of the belay rope.

Since these links will probably remain exposed to the elements for some time, grease the threads before installing and save yourself a future take-down hassle. Also remember to orient each rapid link so that their gates screw closed toward the ground. Such down-hill, gravity-friendly gate orientation helps prevent accidental gate opening.

And, since you are still there, why not thread some #4 nylon cord (lazy line) through the SR block; it'll save you a climb later on. You didn't bring the cord up with you? Sorry, I can't think of everything.

If there is only a single cable for the trapeze attachment (no Two Line Bridge), getting out there to suspend your trapezial target requires a poignantly different work set up. If you have a long extension ladder, long enough to reach the cable, lean the extended ladder on the bottom cable at a comfortable climbing angle (recognizing

beforehand that for most humanoids there is no such thing as a comfortable climbing angle) with at least 8" of ladder extended above the cable. Ask your partner to laterally support the ladder and up you go — on belay.

If the ladder idea comes up short (and it usually does). you must climb one of the support trees, and using a combination of locking carabiners, ROSA pulley, and harness, slide/roll out on the cable to a position that allows centering and securing the trapeze. I usually suggest using a Studebaker Wrap for most situations where you need some torso support while suspended, but in this case I'd go for a commercial climbing harness and take advantage of the increased comfort factor.

If you don't know what I am talking about in the paragraph above, stop reading here and find someone who does. Don't play trial and error games with your body. I have been purposefully unspecific about how to set up this rolling suspension system, because it's easy to roll into trouble.

As you roll out to the work area, you will find the going easy because you are travelling on a declined caternary (downhill), so it should be no surprise that the trip back to the support tree will be correspondingly difficult (uphill). To make the return easier (possible, in some cases) attach a length of rope to the tree and take one end with you, using it eventually as a self-haul line on the return trip. Use a separate ground belay also, in case Murphy's Law acts as a corollary to Newton's.

Situate the trapeze on center as above, and place the belay block 14" to the right or left of the trapeze suspension cable drops. Hang the block and trapeze efficiently, as dangling in any kind of harness is not comfortable; all kinds of body parts go numb. Use the retrieval rope to pull yourself back to the support tree.

Now ask your partner, standing/sitting patiently on top of the teeny-weeny platform, to try a leap for the trapeze, ". . . just to see if any further adjustments are necessary." You are looking for about an 80% completion rate; i.e., actually grabbing the trapeze. Holding onto the trapeze is entirely another percentage category.

Install a *Jus-Rite Descender* log in a position that would duplicate a natural belay stance; somewhat off to the side, with the afternoon sun at the belayer's back. A Jus-Rite log is not a necessary belay device, and in some cases becomes a crutch, but it works wonderfully well, so if you like it, use it.

The photographic possibilities for this event are considerable, IF you are able to clear some of the surrounding high limbs that get in the way of those dramatic go-for-it silhouette shots. Taking high angle photos with a leafy back drop are predictably blah.

If a person misses the trapeze or spins off it, and the belay set up is such that the pendulum action of the fall and lowering sequence cause the jumper (faller in this

case) to swing toward and make contact with the Pamper Pole or Jus-Rite Descender, require that the participants wear helmets. If the pole/climber contact is consistent, something's wrong with the belay system or pole orientation.

Remember — Current ropes course standards do not recommend clipping or tying into the rear of a tied Swiss Seat or commercial harness. The Swiss Seat does not provide enough support, and the harness manufacturers will not gurantee the use of their harness for rear attachment falls, particularly self-generated falls. Use either a front clip/tie in with the above two methods, or clip/tie into the back of a Studebaker Wrap.

Again, if you don't know what I'm talking about, don't tie/clip into anything and don't make the jump until an experienced person okays your safety set up.

Historical note: If you didn't already know, the name *Pamper Pole* was first applied during the early days of *Project Adventure* when an unfortunate participant , because of a combination of fear,

anxiety, and too much coffee, momentarily lost control of his/her bladder sphincter, and . . .

The first Pamper Pole was installed at *The Hamilton-Wenham Regional High School*, Hamilton MA, c. 1974.

Construction Procedure for the Pamper Plank

In some construction scenarios it makes practical and ecological sense to build a platform off a living tree to serve as the launching area for a trapeze jump, rather than attempting to vertically place a utility pole or tree trunk in an impossible spot. Don't even think about topping a tree to serve as a Pamper Pole: the tree will rot from the roots up, and topping a tree safely is a job for highly experienced workers.

The Pamper Plank offers: a solution to a no-pole situation, a more stable area for the trapeze dive, a lead up to an adjacent Pamper Pole, and negligible harm to the support tree.

Building the Pamper Plank is identical to the procedure for installing a tree plat-

form, with the exception that the platform dimensions are considerably larger. A Pamper Plank may be anywhere from three feet to over ten feet long. In order to get such long sections of 2X6 lumber into position, something other than balance and strength are necessary.

Two haul systems are utilized. The first rope/pulley combination, suspended from the support tree, lifts the body end of the platform; i.e., those two board ends which are to be bolted to the tree. The second haul rope is suspended, via a ROSA pulley/carabiner combination, from the cable that supports the trapeze. The end of this haul rope is tied to the jumping end of the 2X6 platform boards (where they are held together with 1/2" carriage bolts). If these two haul ropes are used in tandem and unison (by two workers on the ground) with two workers in/on the tree pushing, adjusting, drilling, hammering and tightening, an unlikely collection of boards can be fashioned into a spectacular platform/plank arrangement.

I particularly like fashioning the plat-

form so that the top walking area narrows from the tree to the end of the platform. Perhaps starting off with a three foot length board at the tree and gradually tapering to a 9" board at the end.

If, despite all your careful measuring, the jump from the end of the platform proves to be too challenging (read impossible), install a couple Beaver Boards, 2"X6" PT boards bolted (or nailed and clinched) to the top of the platform so that an appropriate amount of board extends over the end of the platform. This extra 6"-14" might makes the difference between impressively difficult and programmatically doable.

Beaver boards are installed parallel to one another and about 2" apart. Make sure that at least three feet of Beaver Board is bolted or nailed to the platform.

Install or write something on the platform to lessen the perceived seriousness of the event. Perhaps a large stenciled arrow on the platform pointing toward the trapeze. Maybe a crypic note printed in bold letters, SMILE, YOUR BELAYER LOVES YOU ! How about an installed toilet seat near the tree end of the platform, that can't be seen from the ground? Come on, don't be so serious — this is fun!

Chapter 10

Ropes Course Implementation

Zip Wire Endings — How to Stop a Zipper

Enthusiastic Instructor — "Just look at the initial drop on that cable. What a ride!"

Concerned Administrator — "How do they (*they* means anybody but her/him) slow down?" "How do they stop?"

And that's as it should be — concerned enthusiasm. As there is a beginning, there will be an ending and hopefully a gradual one, in this case.

Here's another zip wire innovation to ease the concerns of riders and worriers, called the Bungee Brake.

There are basically two types of zip braking systems, the gravity and trust brakes. The gravity brake uses the force of gravity to slow and stop the rider — the zipper accelerates down and decelerates up.

The 2-3 auto tires located at the end of the ride act as buffers in case you engineered the ride too swiftly: a safety fudge factor. These tires are reeved onto the cable before the cable is attached. Use a 1/2" diameter drill bit to drill the tires — through the tread, with holes drilled 180° from each other.

The trust brake necessitates some kind of apparatus to slow the rider down; something that the rider must "trust" to keep her/him from hitting the lower support tree or pole. The trust brake is usually longer and incrementally swifter than the gravity brake ride, with the bottom attachment point of the cable located considerably lower than the starting point.

A somewhat primitive and eventually

expensive braking device was initially tried by clipping a carabiner onto the cable with a 75' section of slash (retired) climbing rope attached to the carabiner. The descending pulley (rider attached) would hit the carabiner and a belayer holding the rope would try to provide a dynamic belay and gradually slow the rider to a stop.

Problems

1. The carabiner had to be changed frequently because of excessive and rapid wear on the carabiner.
2. Unless the belayer was experienced s/he could be pulled off their feet as the result of providing too static a belay.
3. The pulley became a cosmetic mess due

to the metal-on-metal contact with the carabiner.

We needed a detachable "soft" device to take the place of the carabiners and a solid belay mechanism to take the place of the "soft" belayer. *Project Adventure* now uses (and sells) a rubber-ended block of mahogany that bolts onto a zip cable to take the place of a carabiner. This block, which measures 4" x 4" x 10", has an integral through eyebolt for shock cord (bungee cord) attachment.

The human belay factor has been replaced with a length of bungee cord. The zip-stop scenario goes like this. The rider takes off from a platform and after gradually picking up speed (the trust brake ride is not as initially fast as the gravity brake zip), the pulley strikes the zip wood block approximately 3/4 of the way down the cable length. The block is pushed by the pulley (negligible resistance) until the attached length of 1/2" bungee cord (length varies as to the speed of the ride; i.e., maximum speed), gradually brings the rider to a comfortable stop. Some trial and error is

necessary for each new zip construction to determine the best place for the bungee holder(s) to stand, and how long a length of bungee cord is necessary.

If you have read this section just to be polite, thank you and continue on to the next engrossing tidbit. If you are interested in installing a bungee brake system, and my explanation hasn't been explicit enough, give the folks at PA a call at (508) 468-7981, and I'm sure one of the friendly builders will fill in the gaps. The information is free, but the call is your nickel.

Sizzle Seat

Getting tired of fried buns as the result of extended belay stints? Here are a couple ways to combat the heat without using mechanical shearing belay devices.

Put on a pair of oversized *cotton* cut-offs (levis, etc.) over your regular attire. This double padding takes the sting out of belaying, but can be uncomfortably warm on a hot day. A visit to a Good Will store should supply the XL cut offs required.

Do not wear nylon shorts or pants for belaying. A long, dynamic standing hip belay can literally melt your pants, and put permanent stripes on your buns.

Sylvia Shirley of William and Mary College in Virginia sent me the plans for a belay apron some time ago. The canvas aprons work quite well and fit loosely enough to provide good air circulation. You can embellish an apron in many ways, but basically the canvas simply puts another layer between your sensitive seat and the rapidly running rope.

Larry Rorick, PA trainer from New York state, uses a leather apron to cover his buns, and reports that a considerable amount of friction is achieved and disippated by the heavy leather. This is true, I've tried it.

Be advised that just because you are using a belay apron you still need leather-palmed gloves to prevent rope-burned hands.

High Belay Set-Up Solution - Lazy Lines

This "solution" has been used for years as a workable and sometimes frustrating way to set up belay ropes at the beginning of a school day, without having to lead climb (lobster claw or carabiner clip-in techniques) or climb without a belay.

The technique involves stringing a length of nylon cord from the ground up and through paired rapid links that have been previously placed on the cable and back to the ground; kind of like a vertical out-haul clothesline, if you tilt your head and imagination. The object is to attach your belay rope to this cord and pull it up and through the two rapid links or spin/static pulley, and then back down. The frustration mentioned above results from the rope getting stuck as an attempt is made to pull the cord/string through the belay device, causing a no-go situation or breaking the cord (depending on the frustration level), or dissolving of the knot (usually a clove hitch) tied onto the end of the rope.

Here's an embellishment that reduces the above problems and even lets you pull the rope through an SR block *or* an SS pulley with a 98.5% success ratio.

Purchase a few 3/4" eye screws. Hold an eye screw with a pair of pliers so that the eye portion is held firm by the jaws. Heat the screw length with a propane torch until it glows and then push the entire threaded shaft (right up to and including the bottom of the eye) directly on center into the end of a belay rope. The hot screw will literally melt its way into the nylon end of the rope (amidst much acrid smelling smoke), resulting in a solid heat-sealed bond when cooled.

The eye size of the screw head is less than the diameter of the rope so that tying a cord to the eye will allow a direct pull through a comparatively small orifice (SS pulley cheeks). Such a direct pull cannot be achieved by tying

the cord around the end of the rope using a clove hitch, timber hitch, etc.

Don't bother tying a bowline — simply reeve the end of the #4 nylon cord through the eye and tie an overhand knot in the end of the cord. Too simple? Sorry, go ahead and tie the bowline if you want to.

Considerations

If you are going to leave a rapid link on the cable for a period of time, you must liberally grease the threads of the link, or they will rust in a permanently sealed position.

If you leave an SR block out in the elements, the steel portions will rust unless painted. The rust will not reduce the strength of the block, but it's unsightly and might result in a diminished trust situation.

Shear reduction devices are expensive to replace if stolen.

Use unattractive cord (to mitigate rip-off temptations) and tie it to a placed cleat or staple at least 12' up on the trunk of the support tree to reduce the chance of theft or curious tampering.

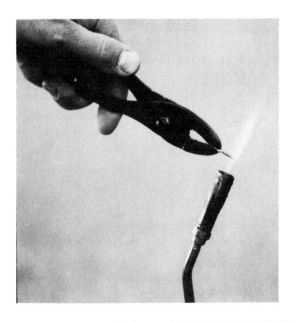

Belays

There are lots of reasons to tie on a belay of some sort while building high elements in trees. A couple of reasons deal with responsibility to self and family, and it's obviously going to slow down the day's work if you slam into the turf from 30-40'. But the real reason for a belay is to preclude PAIN. Never a truer phrase was offered than by the battered sage who uttered (gasped, moaned, etc.), "The fall wasn't bad, but the ending . . . !"

Avoid the inevitable, and use some type of belay set-up to protect yourself at height. And for you folks interested in the quality and length of life — a belay produces dramatically better results than massive doses of vitamin C.

It's fairly obvious that a bottom belay set-up provides constant protection, but it necessitates involving a belayer who could be doing other work. So, consider the following static and dynamic self-belay techniques. The static tie-in is deceptively simple, and effective. The moving (prusik) belay is a time-honored tree workers' belay system.

Static Tie-In

I just realized that this technique has no name and there's not much to recommend *Static Tie-In* as being worthy of remembering. How about *Rollo's Wrap*? Rollo was (probably still is) an inept climber I knew a few years back. It seems an appropriate name, considering Rollo's propensity for *falling* — an exclamation I heard with some frequency whenever he got more than few feet off the ground.

There you are, 30 feet up amidst the branches of a _____ (fill in your favorite) tree, and ready to do some work, but you don't want to take up any more of your belayer's time, so you situate yourself solidly amidst the limbs and ask for some slack.

Take a large bight-loop in your belay rope and pass the formed loop over and around the *base* of a convenient and substantial limb. The base of this branch should be slightly above you. After the loop comes around the limb, clip a *locking* carabiner through the loop and then also include the standing part (rope leading to belayer) and working end (rope leading to you) in the same carabiner (photo below). Lock the gate and pull the loop snugly to the limb. Yell "Off Belay" to your belayer and

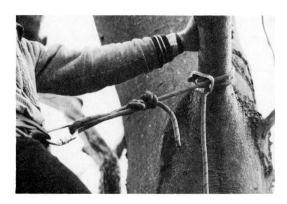

relax, because you have established a self-belay. Rollo's Wrap is secure and can be easily adjusted if you need more rope for working. Don't give yourself more rope than absolutely necessary; even a short fall on a static rope can be _____ (fill in your favorite pejorative phrase from "Accidents in North American Mountaineering").

Dynamic Prusik Self-Belay

Tie a length of 5/8" diameter multiline around your waist or clip a formed loop (figure 8, bowline-on-a-bight) in the multiline to a harness or Swiss seat. As the result of the bowline tie-in or loop clip-in, there should be a tail (working end) left over of about 6'. The standing part of the rope that stretches away from you should measure at least two times the height that you plan to climb. If you are going to clear a tree trunk of limbs to 50', you will need 100+ feet of rope.

Ascend the tree to the height that's needed and climb over or through a *substantial* living limb or crotch that will serve as a belay point, and descend a few feet. Make sure your rope is suspended next to the tree trunk and not hanging out on the limb. Take the 6' tail mentioned earlier and tie a prusik knot with the tail's free end around the descending standing length of rope. There should be no more distance between you and the prusik knot than 1/2 the length of your arm.

This self-belay prusik system allows you to work with both hands free at whatever height you choose by simply moving the prusik knot up or down the vertical standing length.

You can use rope other than the multiline mentioned above, but be certain of its safe working load and its ability to hold a prusik knot tied onto itself.

Practice this technique near the ground and with a bottom belay until you have confidence in the system and yourself.

The Munter Hitch

Over the years, Project Adventure workshop leaders have been emphasizing and teaching the body belay (standing hip belay) as the best way to develop a one-on-one trust situation between belayer and climber. I still personally believe this to be true, but there are so many useful and effective ways to belay that we are now demonstrating a number of proven belay methods and letting the workshop participants choose which technique will work best for them in *their* work situation. Here's one that functions well, but is not well known in this country.

I feel justified in suggesting that you give this method a try, as outlined in the following description written by Andreas Kubin. I was surprised to hear that a special threaded carabiner was necessary for maximum safety, so be aware, but use any ole "crab" just to see how it works. It's interesting to see the hitch reverse itself when the pull is alternated from working end to standing part. Go get a rope right now and try it. You *know* you'll forget it if you put this down.

"There is a belay method that has gained almost universal acceptance in the last ten years among the climbers of Europe. It is called the half-mast release (Munter hitch) and was introduced by Werner Munter of Switzerland. The technique gained prominence through publications of the German Alpine Club's Safety committee after an impressive demonstration by Italian Climbers during a U.I.A.A. teaching convention.

Of sole importance to the half-mast system is a particularly complicated locking carabiner with a wide opening and a screw gate, because in performing the Munter, the rope can be laid over the spring-loaded catch and conceivably be pushed open under stress! Since most screw carabiners close against the catch, it repeatedly occurs that through the letting out or taking in of the rope, the screw gate opens. The new Chouinard reverse locking carabiner whose screw closes on the joint of the catch, removes this source of danger.

The enthusiasm Americans have for the bare-handed hip belay lies in the fact that most have never caught a sudden leader fall of any length. Like a mediocre insurance policy, it's great until you need it. More than 90% of all European climbers protect themselves with the half-mast release, a belay method which because of its simple application and small source for error, has gained wide acceptance over all other methods — why not by the Americans?"

Because we like gear — that's how come.

Superfluously Redundant Award

The winner of this bi-decade award will remain anonymous due to the predictable deluge of laudatory cards and letters that result from this much-awaited announcement.

The nice-going, slap-on-the-back and camaraderie-filled hug this time goes to the originator of the *Sticht Plate Gang Belay.* Believe it or not, folks, here's how it works.

Person one handles the rope coming from the climber; largely a two-handed "Old Man of the Sea" hauling technique.

Person two provides the well-known "speedshift" (2nd-gear-to-3rd) motion that exemplifies the braking action of the Sticht plate.
Person three ties a simple overhand loop for every 3' of rope that comes through the

Sticht plate. The knot closest to the plate provides the failsafe element of this gang belay, because it is said in *the book of rocks and ropes* that a "camel can't pass through the eye of a needle, nor an overhand loop through the slot of a Sticht plate."

Person four unties the knots as they come from person three, making sure to always leave one knot in the rope.

Person five neatly coils the unknotted rope.

This technique, although presented tongue-in-cheek, is workable and has been used successfully by instructors interested in maximum student participation and a failsafe belay system.

Nice going, anonymous belayer, wherever you aren't.

A Peter Pan Belay

As the student clips a locking carabiner into his/her Studebaker Wrap as preliminary to a climb, the question is, should the rope remain in front of the body or be switched around to the back?

Some feel that if the rope remains in front that the novice climber has more of a tendency to reach for the rope in a tight spot than relying on his/her climbing

ability. Also, while climbing a tree on a ropes course, there is more chance for the rope to get tangled or hooked onto a peg or limb if the rope remains in front. However, if a fall occurs, the faller's position (flight attitude) becomes almost horizontal to the ground (Peter Pan style), lining up the individual's head as a potential battering ram. Fortunately, there are few obstacles underneath high ropes course elements to ram into; except the ground.

If the climber is attempting to climb up a wooden blocked wall, the presence of the wall itself indicates that the rope should be left in front. A wall is a fairly large target to miss as the result of a fall, particularly if your belay rope is attached to an eyebolt in that wall. The climber's proximity to such a large mass of uniformly hard material is also a good reason for having the students wear helmets.

But, standing on a high wire with the rope behind the individual lends itself to increased commitment. (You know the rope is there, but you can't see it or touch it.

Surely you have seen students reaching behind for the rope for no other reason than to check and see if it's still there.) And, the occasional belayed face-first trip to the ground is an unavoidable visual experience, unless it's an eyes-closed descent.

It's not strictly a case of one way is bad and the other good, but rather where and how the belay is being used, that makes the difference.

A Belay Problem

The Balance Beam, more commonly called the "Cat Walk" in ropes course parlance, is a high log walk element and is the subject of the following belay poser.

If a student falls off the left side of the log and the rope to the belayer is on the right side, is it necessary to climb up the tree and pass the climber's end of the rope back to the right side of the log before the next climber ties in? No fair reading on until you at least try to think of an answer.

If you are using a bowline-on-a-bight/ carabiner in the rope end and clipping into a Swiss seat, tie a bowline-on-a-bight in both ends of the belay rope and use which-ever end facilitates the belay.

I apologize if this explanation seems superfluous to you experts, but the problem is real and often an embarrassing one. I also apologize to you folks who have no idea what I'm writing about.

Down Under

I had the opportunity recently to lead a workshop in Australia. The weather was fabulous (any place is better than New England in March), the participants were enthusiastic and friendly, and the hospitality superb.

I never used to take the expressed affliction "jet lag" seriously, having only travelled to the west coast and back a few times. After having experienced, en route to Brisbane, a "coach" seat (euphemism for cattle car) for 23 hours, losing an entire day from my life (international dateline) and having been fed an interminable number of plastic meals, I became acutely aware of something that kept tugging at my eyelids and causing my head to seek the horizontal. The "lag" was worth it — Australia isn't a place, it's an experience. Ripper Mate!

During the workshop, I learned a new (new to me) method of belaying on a ropes course that is worth passing along.

Australian Back-Up Belay

A problem situation concerned with belaying that has plagued adventure teachers struggling with 30 or 40-to-one student-to-teacher ratios, is how to handle the need for more trained and responsible belayers on high elements. One solution is to use more static belays. Another means is to utilize student belayers, a somewhat risky but often workable solution.

The following belay technique provides another answer that is surprisingly reliable and disarmingly simple, in fact so much so that if I hadn't tried it myself (as faller and belayer), I would have summarily dismissed the idea as laughable, and potentially dangerous.

Acting as the belayer, tie on a Swiss Seat arrangement, Studebaker Wrap, or put on a commercial harness. Using a figure 8 loop or bowline-on-a-bight in the end of the belayer's end of a rope (imagine a bottom belay situation on a *Burma Bridge*), clip the formed loop(s) into the harness (ventrally) with a locking carabiner. Here comes the simple part. As the climber climbs, the belayer backs up and continues

backing up until the climber reaches his/her goal, in this case, the cables of the Bridge. If the climber falls, the belayer literally does nothing, except eventually walk forward to let the climber smoothly down. There is nothing to let go of and no rope movement to burn exposed skin.

So, where's the mystique? Sorry, it's all gone — in this case, replaced by bare bone functionality.

Problems? Contraindications? A couple.

1. If the climber is much heavier (over 30 lbs.) than the belayer, clip the two loops of the bowline-on-a-bight, at the end of the belay line, into two side-by-side "back-up" belayers.
2. The belayer must have an obstacle-free

So, if your problem is how to safely train enough belayers for use with additional students on high ropes course elements, try the back-up belay. It works "down under."

Prusik Knot Ascent

This vertical, monkey-on-a-string activity is a rainy day must.

Climbing ropes, those traditional vertical fixtures which all too frequently dangle unused in a gymnasium, can be utilized for this technical and satisfying technique of ascending a rope.

The actual climbing procedure (seek experienced help to actually learn the knots and procedures) is a mountaineer's rope ascending technique used primarily in rescue situations.

back-up path to follow for the length of the belay. This technique does not work if the climber plans to move laterally on an element; e.g., across a Two Line Bridge; well . . . maybe on a telephone pole course in the middle of a field, but not amidst a stand of trees. Beware the clear-cut mentality. "Woodsman, spare those 432 trees."

3. After the belay "catch" is made and lowering begins, there is a natural tendency to be pulled forward at faster than a walk. Simply be aware of this and control your forward speed by leaning back.

4. If the belay is a long one (over 200'), supply the belayer with an ice axe on frosty days. That's a joke — I say, *that's a joke, son!*

From a practical standpoint in a school setting, the use of the ropes and technique allow almost any student to reach the top of the rope (usually 20') under their own power; a considerable accomplishment for a student that has trouble with one pull-up.

Ordinarily, three 8' sections of 9mm kernmantle rope are tied individually end-to-end forming three 3' or 4' diameter rope circles (slings). The knot of choice for joining the rope ends is the double fisherman's knot, also called a barrel knot.

Each of these three slings is tied onto the vertical climbing rope by means of a prusik knot, a knot closely resembling a taut line hitch. This knot, properly tied, maintains a grip on the climbing rope when the sling arrangement is pulled downward, but can be slid up or down the rope after the pressure is released.

One sling goes under the arms, leaving the two remaining slings, one for each foot. As each sling is moved (no pressure exerted), the other two slings hold the weight of the climber. Develop a repeated 1-2-3 sequence for a smooth, relaxed ascent.

For a bit more comfort and efficiency while jockeying up the rope, tie on a Swiss Seat/Studebaker Wrap arrangement, and tie a short sling onto the vertical rope using a prusik knot and clip the other end of the sling into the harness via a bowline/carabiner combination. Only one foot sling is necessary, also tied to the vertical rope with a prusik knot, so that a 1-2, 1-2 movement system develops. Reverse your sequence of moves for the climb down.

Considering that the ascent, particularly the first time it's tried, will be physically taxing, indicate to the students that some energy should be reserved for the climb down. Coming down requires as many physical moves as ascending. The descent is not a gravity-fed slide to the floor.

Caution: If you have any questions as to whether a student, because of ineptness, corpulence, hives, etc., will poop out, require that they use a belay so that there is a means of getting them down without having to call the fire department.

There are mechanical rope ascenders (two or three popular types) available at rock climbing specialty stores that allow much greater ease in moving up and down the ropes (1/2' KM 3 kernmantle rescue rope, in this case). These ascenders come in sets of two and are rather expensive, but offer the advantages of being easy to use, attach and detach to and from the rope quickly and allow more students to participate per rope in use. A belay is still a prudent choice with the use of these mechanical ascenders.

Set up a number of these vertical sections of KM 3 rope in the gym to involve as many students as possible, but consider how many belayers will be necessary or available, before you festoon your rafters with rope.

To add variety, fix a bulb horn or bicycle bell at the top of each rope to provide an audio reward for having reached the top. HONK! DING DING! Relax, coach. A little stress, a little fun — it's all part of the experiential game.

Rope Vault or Tarzan's Triumph

Continuing the precept that "the simplest are the funnest," a single swing rope is the essential prop in this physical/fun stunt. You will also need portable high jump standards, in addition to some landing pads. (*Landing pad* sounds better than *crash mat*, but you know what I mean.)

"The object is for 'Tarzan' to stand back as far as possible (from the bar) and let the rope swing toward the high jump standard. When the rope returns, the young swinger runs alongside, reaches up and grasps a tight hand hold, jumping as s/he nears the bar. His/her momentum, if timed properly, will carry the jumper/vaulter over the bar. Coupled with a quick hand release, the vaulter will end up clearing the bar and

landing on the mats — where s/he can beat on her/his breast/chest to signify their triumph.

Safety Hints
1. Caution the students that if they do not have enough momentum to clear the bar — just hang on and enjoy the return ride.
2. Make sure the landing area is smooth enough to preclude ankle injuries.
3. Caution the students to make a feet-first landing — headstands smart from 6 ft. up.
4. Set the high jump standards in opposite directions so a cross bar hit does not upset the standards.
5. To give the rope its initial momentum, do not swing the rope, simply let it go from a pulled-back position.

The secret to this event is timing. Start low and let the gang develop their skill in small height increments. It is possible to clear 10 feet or more if you have some real swingers in the crowd.

This is a good one! Instructors will have to beat the kids with sticks (ed. note: use foam swords) in order to close down the activity."

I'll attest to the popularity of this kind of swinging event, having set up a similar situation in a workshop that involved vaulting over stacked paper cores (photo). I don't know if it's the swinging movement, the inherent challenge in clearing an obstacle, the self-competition, or what — but it does stimulate and hold the interest of an active group.

Swing to Safety

This simple swinging element is included in *Cows' Tails & Cobras* (pg. 84), but I would like to emphasize and expand on the event

because of its usefulness in: (1) Teaching a student how to achieve a long pendulum swing on a rope. (2) Building upper body strength or the determination to achieve more strength. (3) Capturing the intrinsic joy of movement that a rope swing engenders.

Hang the swing rope from a limb at least 20' high, remembering that the higher the anchor point, the longer and softer the pendulum of the swing. Grasp the dangling rope in your hands at about eye level (mark where you grasp it with tape), and walk away from the plumb line to a point that allows you to still grasp the rope at that tape mark, while standing on the 2nd rung of a step ladder. Dig a 2' deep hole directly below where you are standing and firmly place a section of utility pole or a section of hardwood log (locust, if you can find it), so that the pole measures to the

2nd rung of the step ladder. The diameter of the pole should measure at least 8" and a bit more, if attainable.

Swing from this pole (over a cleared area that includes no rocks, punji sticks, or poison ivy), a number of times to determine where a logical maximum swing arc would end; i.e., where you would land after letting go of the rope at the end of the pendulum. Ask two or three other people to perform the same swing and release to determine where an average landing point should be located. Using this "scientifically" determined landing point, measure about 6" back toward the take-off stump and erect a hurdle 12" high and perpendicular to the line of the swing. The hurdle itself is simply a small cut and trimmed sapling balanced on top of two 12" vertical sections of cord wood placed 6-8 feet apart. The pieces of cord wood are not placed permanently in the ground, so that they can be moved forward or backward to vary the swing's difficulty. The object, then, is to develop enough momentum on the swing to clear the hurdle after releasing the rope.

The novice Tarzan will attempt to throw himself/herself forward toward the hurdle to gain the necessary speed and momentum. This convulsive attempt at propulsion usually results in a quick trip to the turf or a foreshortened swing.

The thinking-man's Tarzan will jump backward away from the stump (while holding onto the rope, right?), thus increasing the length of the pendulum and therefore the arc of the swing, resulting in more distance and the desired result of easily clearing the hurdle.

This event is infectious — an initial short-fall often leads to repeated failing-forward attempts to clear the hurdle, either ending in a successful landing or self-promises to build additional arm strength.

Rosin Bag

Ever watch a big league pitcher reach down off the mound, grab a small whitish bag, perform a quick hand-rubbing ritual, and toss the sack unceremoniously aside? Do you know what's in that dusty bag? Rosin is what. This powdery substance serves the dual purpose of drying sweaty palms and acting as an object of inspiration.

A rosin bag doesn't cost much, but the amount of use and inspiration available on a ropes course is worth the couple bucks.

Offer a rosin bag to a participant who is about to dive for the Hickory bar. It's amazing how much confidence a simple pat-pat-pat to the palms can offer a hesitating student. There is, of course, the advantage of having dry palms when diving for a trapeze (or swinging on a rope), but the real advantage results from offering an "edge" to a doubtful or hesitating performer. The edge is mental, as most marginally helpful substances or talismans offer, but mental is the name of the game on a ropes course.

Try a bag, but don't get hooked; high grade rosin is surprisingly addictive.

The Green Box

Storage of ropes course material on-site has always been a temptation because of what-to-bring-with-you worries and transportation hassles — (Here, you carry it!). Various schemes have been used; some more successful than others. For example, if you have a pre-existing storage shed nearby, use it if security of the structure is lightweight, vandalproof — lightweight in contrast to heavy-duty vandals; i.e., serious, tool-toting lock smashers.

If a shed is not available and hundreds of dollars worth of gear are the snatchables at risk, try storing the valuables (and not-so valuables) in a "green box."

Project Adventure began using a Greenlee 2' x 2' x 4' sheet metal box (green, of course) two years ago, with continuing satisfaction and success. The interior volume of the box is large enough to hold **everything** you need to run the ropes course, including *you*. Contents of the box normally include: belay ropes, swing ropes, fidget ladder, foldable stretcher, blanket, helmets, carabiners, and assorted slings and webbing — all stored without having to fold, tuck, or compartmentalize each item.

The lock (ordinary master lock type) is recessed into the box, protecting it from moisture and attempts at cutting or sawing the hasp. There are two large folding handles on the ends of the box through which a cable or chain can be reeved, to allow locking to a tree. Making off with this hefty, gear-filled box would be no small task for wimpy vandals on foot.

If your "ropes" area is subjected to only minor vandalism, try the #665 Greenlee storage box as a welcomed convenience factor for heavily-used ropes courses (and similarly used instructors).

A Reagle Net

Project Adventure usually has one or more interns in attendance at our Wenham site during the year. Charles Reagle, from Radford University in Virginia, was with us during this last summer and as the result of a what-should-I-do-now? day, he painstakingly and laboriously handcrafted a small (4' x 8') cargo net. I forget how long he said it took to make, but you don't want to know from a $/time standpoint. But, Charles did a bang-up job, so we *had* to find a function for this mini-net; I mean a real program function. Surprisingly (and typically serendipitous), the two classic ropes course activities we used for incorporating the net were arguably changed for the better; the net actually worked and worked well. Here's how and a brief report.

Trust Fall Net

If you don't know what a trust fall is, look in *Silver Bullets*, pages 80-82; I can't bring myself to explain it again. Anyhow, one of the potential dangers of falling backward into a spotting line has been the tendency for some fallers to fling their arms akimbo and smack their erstwhile protectors in the chops — largely painful; usually no serious damage. But, the trust that is slowly building is significantly reduced: enter the Reagle Net. If the net is held by the spotters (about 16 people, 8 on each side), in a position that takes the place of their arms, the problem of getting whacked by flailing appendages is almost eliminated.

After having set up the trust fall for years by having people catching people (flesh on flesh, so to speak), I was a bit reluctant to give the net high grades on trust building (there was no question of functionality), because the net was doing the catching (. . . producing a comfortable landing, by the by). As I questioned the group, however, I found that trust was in the eyes (and emotions) of the beholder and that these beholders cared not a wit what did the catching, as long as they were sufficiently caught. The net won a few points that day and grudging acceptance from a middle-ager who thought he had seen it all.

Fidget Ladder Net

Unless you have considerable padding or an airbag under the Fidget Ladder, you know that someone is going to hit the ground fairly hard. And, it's also well known that this dervish of a ladder is difficult to spot without risking injury to the spotters from the whirling ladder rungs. Re-enter the Reagle Net!

This time, hold the net on the ends only, as it is placed under that part of the Fidget Ladder which receives the most falls; i.e., the first move the participant makes. With about 6 people (3 on a side) holding the net and moving with the participant, the chances of hitting the ground or getting hit by the rungs is greatly reduced. AND (big and), there are more people involved in a meaningful way.

For you folks who don't want to spend your hours splicing and reeving, I don't have many solid recommendations for substitute nets, but try these ideas:

- Use sections of old tennis nets.
- Deep sea fishing nets (heavier rope).
- Nylon semi-trailer net covers are strong and about the right net opening size.
- Contact me and I'll give you Charles' address.

So, Charles, as you read this in December, comfortably situated in the semi-south, know that you have made the big time — a feature section in *The Bottomless Bag*. It's worth a smile and a Coke, eh?

Knot Terminology

When teaching knots to a group, learning is facilitated if the students know a few simple vocabulary words and terminology phrases associated with ropes and knots. The following is a *very* basic primer.

Knot — a tie made in the rope itself. Example: Overhand.

Hitch — a "knot" used for attaching a rope to an object. Example: Clove Hitch.

Bend — the "knot" used for tying two ropes together. Example: Sheet Bend.

All three of the above terms seem to be related by the knot designation, and indeed they are. Differentiation of terms facilitates explaining the different uses of knotting.

Working End — that end of the rope used to tie with.

Standing End (Part) — that end of the rope opposite the working end and often attached to an object.

Hawser Layed — refers to rope construction that is twisted to provide strength and flexibility.

Kernmantle — parallel synthetic rope fibers surrounded by a woven sheath of similar synthetic material.

Bight — that curved, uncrossed portion of the rope that forms between the working end and standing part.

Loop — when the working end crosses over the standing part, or vice-versa.

Studebaker Wrap

Folks in workshops over the years have asked for a tie-in method that would combine the relative comfort and support of a regular Swiss Seat and the security of a waist wrap. While fooling around with a length of rope, I came up with this attempt at a combination compromise called the *Studebaker Wrap*. The name, for those of you not familiar with the 1950's Studebaker automobile, refers to that model made famous by its designers for its Push-Me/Pull-You appearance; i.e., looking the same fore and aft.

The wrap is tied so that the classic Swiss Seat is doubled and combined from a functional and visual ventral/dorsal standpoint.

I'm writing the following description for those of you who know how to tie a Swiss Seat. Using a 26' long section of 9mm kernmantle rope or l" tubular webbing, tie on the well-known front Swiss Seat and, as you finish, rather than tying off, continue the sequence by duplicating your initial maneuvers to include your posterior. This finished torso wrap is simply a double Swiss

Seat and allows clipping in to the front or back with improved support.

Give it a try and let me know what you think. If you don't know the Swiss seat tie-in, don't attempt two of them.

Finish off the rope or webbing wraps with a square knot and adjacent safety knots (half a double fisherman's knot).

Say What?

Everything that goes up, must come down, but when?

What do you say to a nervous student who has been in the "position of potential" long enough and sometimes too long? Are there effective words of wisdom that can be confidently offered to cause the knee-shaking, gulping, misty-eyed student to boldly "go for it"? Sometimes yes, sometimes no — how's that for concise ambivalence?

The first right words or word offered at the right time often makes a difference, and will on occasion cause a hesitating participant (trapeze jump, rappelling, etc.) to make the move that completes an activity. Such well-intentioned words of encouragement are often unequivocally rejected by a student ("Keep quiet!"; "Leave me alone!"; "I don't need that!"), and that's a pretty good indication that further attempts at ground-level, profound rationale should be zippered up by *all* good-intentioned spotters, spectators, and instructors, at least until another plateau of commitment has been reached.

Situation — Student has been crouching on a wall platform for about five minutes, anticipating the jump (dive) to a trapeze. Close contact has been kept with the wall (tree), as the obviously nervous participant attempts to convince his/her body to make a move that the mind wants nothing to do

with. It should be apparent, at this juncture, whether the student really wants to complete the activity.

As an aside — I believe that a student who has come this far has more than completed his/her class requirement: a conscientious try at the offered obstacle. Remember, instructors — constant cajoling borders on coercion and if a student attempt is eventually made because of your impelling personality, the choice to perform becomes more your decision than the student's.

If it seems obvious that no attempt will be forthcoming within a reasonable length of time, offer a compassionate escape; to descend and try again at another time. There's nothing wrong with mañana, and success manifests itself in diverse ways.

If the student "wants it," but is having trouble making the right move, try the following lines that have and have not proven effective for the author in the past. "Wanting it" is demonstrated by repeated movements to and from the point of no return. Each of these, often spasmodic attempts are punctuated by exclamations of self-deprecation, usually associated with several deep rapid breaths. Other manifestations of the syndrome (for the clinically interested reader) are: rolling of the eyes skyward, re-establishing contact with the closest solid object, repeating approximately the line, "I can't do it; I really want to, but I can't," looking out toward the horizon, or in the case of a first rappel, looking directly and agonizingly into the eyes of the belayer (or a trusted person), almost committing to the task, and then drawing back at the last possible instant.

Don't say, "I know you can do it." You *don't* know that. I have never experienced a positive response from this often used cliché. I think instructors say it to make themselves feel better when the situation becomes tense.

1. After a student has made a few unsuccessful attempts, suggest that the next try be *the* one, and make it coincide with a counting sequence. Let the student decide which number is the GO signal. Try this technique only twice. If the counting doesn't work, repeating the 1-2-3 GO sequence simply reinforces the negative aspect of not trying.
2. Ask the student to turn around and face away from the intimidation aspect of the event. When a level of composure is re-gained and the participant seems calmer and re-committed, a turn and try often results in a successful attempt.
3. "I've been standing here belaying and attempting to help you for over 15 minutes. This is no longer just your thing, it's mine, too — you owe me a good attempt."
4. "Trust me — I am not going to let you fall."
5. "Do you want to do this?" (Answer is a tremulous "yes.") "Then let me help you." "Follow my directions exactly." Then proceed to talk them through the event. Don't verbally stumble — know what you are going to say and voice it confidently. If the answer to your first question is "no," then initiate a sequence for letting the student retreat. Sometimes the knowledge that there is an escape will compel them to completion.

    Occasionally, words don't work and are obviously inappropriate. Be confident and understanding enough to be quiet at times.
6. I'm giving away a professional secret on this one, because I've had more success with the following few words than with

any others, but timing is important.

The action must occur toward the end of a class or session. The student should have made more than one abortive attempt. Other students should be in attendance and obviously (not verbally) waiting for a try.

"Janice, you know the choice to do this or not do it is up to you, but I'm going to have to ask you to make a decision now; we just don't have any more time today. Now step up there and GO, or let me help you come down." This is at least a 50% ploy.

How Long Is Too Long?

Situation — Student standing anxiously on a Flea Jump platform, Pamper Pole, Cat Walk, etc.

"I really want to do it, but my feet won't move." "Oh, wow — I can't believe I'm so scared." "Can I come back and try this later?" "Do I *have* to do this?"

Dissolve to tears, self-recrimination, embarrassment, and perhaps a convulsive, inept attempt that occurs more as a result of emotion than determination.

The above scenario is not an uncommon predicament on high ropes course events. Unfortunately, because of misunderstanding or instructive oversight, the hesitating student begins to perceive the event as a win/lose situation, rather than recognizing the intended challenge; a sentient, conscientious attempt.

The answer seems to be in effectively outlining what the curriculum expectations are, and what you (the instructor) physically and mentally expect from the students.

There seems little value in leaving a student on a platform or cable to agonize for 15 minutes about whether to "take that step," etc. Being in a position of potential is enough to qualify for the TRY, that stepping stone to the next level of commitment or completion. The longer a student dwells on the attempt, the more it can become the instructor's personality or peer pressure or fear of failure that provokes the completion move. Any resulting decision is most likely not the individual's, but the result of various good-intentioned anxiety ploys. There is no doubt that an individual can be prodded (coerced) into extraordinary efforts by the pressures mentioned above. The military uses such stress techniques effectively ("No one eats tonight, Mr., until you make that jump . . .") and with justifiable cause: discipline above all. But to emulate the DI's methods and means within a school setting is negative, unproductive, and unacceptable.

The KB Syndrome

"I can't do anything at heights, except hug the beams." An expedient way to combat the *Koala Bear Syndrome* and become functionally at ease with height is to spend time at height (comfortably) in a belayed position.

When you look down from 20-30', things take on a different perspective in comparison to ground level viewing; smaller, often upside-down — frightening.

It takes a while to become accustomed to that disconcerting difference in perspective and the time spent acclimatizing should not require precarious positions or exaggerated expectations ("Come on Esther, I know you can do it!").

Try sitting for a couple hours on a platform at about 30' (don't forget to use a belay and keep your eyes open) on more than one occasion. This time spent at height, coupled with a developing trust in the belay system and your own inner cool (0oomm) should reduce the what-am-I-doing-here? horrors. I'm not putting you on about this, as I have seen it work numerous times with individuals who professed chronic (but sometimes convenient) vertigo.

Chapter 11

Disclaimers/Opinions

function. Make up a few of your own; it's kind of fun, displays a compassionate concern for your clientle, and may impress someone.

Disclaimer — of Sorts

Bag of Tricks is not meant to be an instructional tome, rather a lighthearted presentation and sharing of current ideas and procedures in the field of adventure education. If an included area requires technical knowledge and you feel unsure of your skill level, put that idea aside until your training is commensurate to the activity. There's enough silly stuff here to take its place until your technical *bag of tricks* is plumb with confidence.

Do I sound like your mother? Sorry, just doin' my job.

Every now and then (much more *then* than *now*), an insistent sense of responsibility urges me to make sure that you all are using BOT's material in the safest possible way. This compulsive caring has resulted in the following collection of "posterior protectors," more decorously referred to as disclaimers. These you-better-be-careful platitudes satisfy an author's need to feel responsible, but serve practically no legal

Ye Olde Blanket Disclaimer

I would like to formally exonerate myself and everyone I have either talked to or looked at, from everything that has anything to do with whatever you're upset about — also to include weekends.

Other Disclaimers

Bag of Tricks is written and edited by Karl Rohnke. He enjoys writing and editing this periodical and thanks you for perusing its contents, but beware the Jabberwocke and other unseen hazards of adventure programming. Proceed carefully with abandon and try out your schemes personally before allowing your students to taste the "thrill of victory" — you aren't allowed many official "agonies . . ."

* * * * *

Please use good sense in attempting to utilize the games, climbing techniques, initiative problems, etc., that are included in *BOT's*. Some of the activities require specialized training or esoteric know-how. Be overt about being baffled by the covert — seek experienced help when necessary.

* * * * *

If you've got it, flaunt it. If you haven't got it, don't fake it — somebody will get hurt. So much for this quarter's disclaimer — a study in sledgehammer subtlety.

* * * * *

Bag of Tricks is an educational quarterly written and edited by Karl Rohnke. Since I have not tried all the ideas and schemes sent in by readers, I trust you will approach any trial and error situation with caution. Everyone needs some adventure — no one needs injury.

* * * * *

Bag of Tricks is written and edited by Karl Rohnke, but he isn't taking the blame for misuse of any of this disparate material — so be careful; use common sense and all those other pay-no-heed platitudes that make up your basic disclaimer.

* * * * *

This author has almost achieved maladroit immortality on a couple badly chosen occasions by not following his own survival instincts. In other words, I can't take responsibility for the misuse of any information offered in *Bag of Tricks* . Use the ideas as you best interpret them and

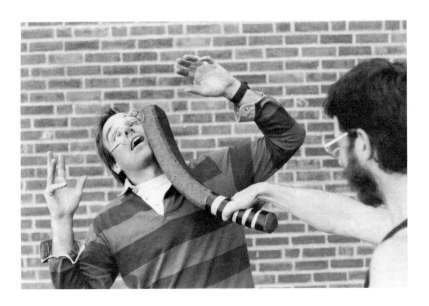

seek experienced (not well-intentioned, but experienced) help with technical problems when necessary.

Self-Serving Justification

"Men resemble one another in that they do best those things which please them most." — Juan Manuel

If you keep reading and looking long enough, you can find someone who agrees with you about anything. To wit, the following quotation from *Success Magazine*:

FOR, AS THE EDITORS OF *DECORATING YOUR OFFICE FOR SUCCESS* OBSERVE, "THE SUITABILITY OF YOUR OFFICE DOES NOT DEPEND ON IT BEING NEAT, MODERN, ELEGANT, OR STYLISH. IT DEPENDS UPON HOW IT SUPPORTS YOUR MORALE AND SELF-DETERMINATION. THE IDEAL OFFICE IS ESSENTIALLY ONE THAT WILL ELEVATE YOUR SPIRITS WHENEVER YOU ENTER AND STICK IN YOUR MEMORY AS A PLACE YOU WANT TO GO BACK TO. *IT SHOULD SUGGEST INTERESTING AND EXCITING THINGS ABOUT TO HAPPEN.*"

This wide angled photo shows a 117° section of my office as of January 1993.

It didn't get like this overnight, you know. There's a lot of time, tradition, *joie du vivre* and benign neglect depicted here.

A Rational Rationale

. . . climbing then, is not simply a matter of several thrill-seekers thrashing about on an impossibly difficult rock face. It is rather a sport of fine challenges, demonstrating a satisfying spectrum of accomplishment levels; a something for everyone sport.

The availability of a challenging and climbable set of rocks or rock faces is a matter of geographical location: no rocks, no climb. However, a practice climbing wall build of sized hardwood blocks or synthetic ersatz "rocks," bolted at various angles and positions onto the bricks or concrete of a gymnasium wall, provides an exciting and innovative approach to a variety of needs.

1 The further and aesthetic utilization of school facilities.
2. Provides an indoor (all weather) physical education station.
3. Allows beginning climbers to develop strength, expertise, and confidence toward improving their performance at an actual rock climbing site.

4. Allows students (whether or not they want to continue their efforts in actual rock climbing) to participate in something new without a pre-sensitivity to failure. Remember to emphasize that student success is simply a genuine **try**.

5. Because of the various stresses involved (fear: of failure, of physical harm, or human fallibility, etc.), there is the unparalleled opportunity for the establishment of gut level trust.

6. Provides a physical and mental challenge with pizzaz. Participation is genuinely fun.

Tegwar

Tegwar is an acronym for, That-Exciting-Game-Without-Any-Rules, and as a game it presents a classic mental/physical exercise in logical confusion. Any obvious lack of rules within or surrounding a game requires a fairly complex set of non-rules or acceptable confusers to make play possible.

For example, if you are going to plan a Tegwar variation of soccer (and you can't really, because Tegwar is Tegwar, only alluding to soccer in order to explain Tegwar), you must ignore all the rules — better yet, recognize that there are no rules, and then establish touchstones of play; i.e., those gems of illogical participation that suggest sequence, scoring, win, lose, etc., but which are only pivotal focal points of concentration. To score or make a good play is an illusion that lasts only long enough to feel good, then melds into the next acceptable sequence of physical action. Recognizing that there are no established guidelines, operating meaningfully within a game context without consistent regulations is the key to understanding how a decently unorganized, semi-serious potpourri of play can be exciting and fun *without any rules*.

I've burdened you with all this twaddle

to simply indicate that Tegwar is child's play, which is probably the best kind. Think of the above rhetoric as a roundabout introduction to an initiative problem, then try this—take any game and reduce or change the rules to that point where the structure of the game remains barely intact, **all** participants feel good about being part of the action, and the joy remains or has increased. A formidable task, but it's worth a try or two, and who knows what might emerge? It's better than running laps.

How Safe Is Too Safe?

Can an individual or a program be too safe? . . . What did he say? I must have read that first sentence incorrectly. Safety is the cornerstone of adventure programs, on a par with concepts like, "home," "trust," and "belay": a bastion of unassailable acceptance and truth in concept.

But, the answer is yes, you can not only be too safe, you can suffocate a program with it. Blasphemy! Heretic! Anti-American! But you can go too far toward each end of the *Safe-Hazardous* spectrum, and it's not difficult to spot the extremists.

Solo climbing (unbelayed), for most, is an example of genuine hazard; going overboard in the pursuit of a greater adrenaline boost. Or more programmatically, canoe tripping through white water without flotation devices: an obvious breech of common safety practices. But these examples are easily found, pinpointed and eliminated by folks who want their programs to continue. A consistently unsafe approach will eventually lead to a physical disaster and a weakening or dissolution of procedures and program.

The commitment thief is a much more difficult curriculum offender to recognize, because everything s/he does is safe . . . stultifyingly safe. Recognizing that there

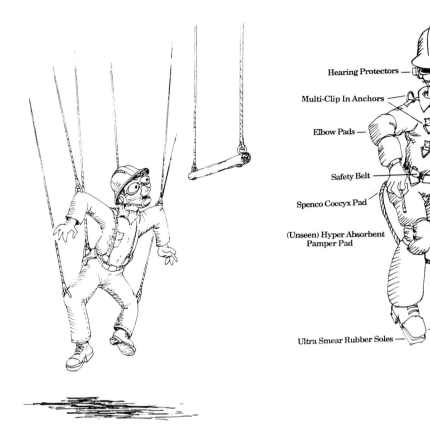

Approved ANSI Helmet

Hearing Protectors —

— Tinted Goggles

Multi-Clip In Anchors —

— Micro Particle Spore Mask

Elbow Pads —

Kevlar Gloves

Safety Belt —

Spenco Coccyx Pad —

— Kevlar Genital Cup Protector

(Unseen) Hyper Absorbent
Pamper Pad

— Knee Pads

— Ensolite Lined Coveralls

Ultra Smear Rubber Soles —

— Steel Toed Boots

GO FOR IT! I *KNOW* YOU CAN MAKE IT.

must be a hint of hazard to make the **GO** commitment meaningful, a zip line that begins at a height of 10 feet is not only ho-hum, it's impractical. A double-belayed student on a Two Line Bridge (2 belay ropes, 2 sets of crabs, 2 belayers) involves so much rope, the perceived danger becomes less of falling and more of getting tangled in the excess belay line. A trapeze that is practically at arm's length doesn't make the event safer, it just eliminates the challenge. Etc., etc., etc.

A program, to remain viable, must be safe (low accident record). To quote a program truism I've used many times at conference presentations and workshops,

"We (Project Adventure) wouldn't remain in business very long if we were dropping kids out of the trees." The parameters of safety become more recognized as a concerned approach continues and matures.

The danger of weakening the student's potential commitment is the lack of perceived danger (hazard, risk), and it's difficult to generate that perception when it's obviously not there. The students know . . .

After a period of time, many of the students will recognize that the events are not really as hazardous or difficult as they first appeared: experience, insight, perception — growth. Score one for the teacher's team!

Adventure Angst

I was responsible recently for a one day curriculum workshop that was intended and designed for experienced, tenured elementary and middle school teachers who had been administratively directed to implement a PA component into their physical education time slots. The first questions asked by this tense group of teachers (their body language indicated tight minds and possibly sphincters) were survival oriented. "How do we start?' and "What do we say to the students during the first class?" As the day progressed, I recognized that they really didn't want to know how to start, what to say, or anything that had anything to do with techniques that differed from their previous 20+ years of experience; i.e., one year repeated 20+ times.

They were nice people, smiled a lot, paid attention most of the time, and gobbled up any new game or initiative problem that I suggested might fit into their curriculum or help fill their class time on a day to day basis. They were absolute gluttons for new information, but simply polite listeners when it came to suggesting a change in their personal teaching tactics. I hinted that Project Adventure does not lend itself to a clip board style of teaching ("Take a lap, then come back here so I can take the roll."), and then suggested a couple ploys that would help involve the students, but would also require that they step out of their recognized pedagogic patterns, take a histrionic chance or two, and perhaps begin to establish themselves as occasionally zany, predictably unpredictable and consistently fun. You would think I had asked them to take a pay cut, work in a ghetto, or start a personal exercise program. As I indicated, polite, but adamantly secure in their established roles and polished teaching styles. Have you ever seen jewelry made from fossilized dinosaur dung? It (coprolite) polishes up beautifully.

It's not necessary to wear a red nose, be silly, or flamboyantly display any kind of prop, but it is necessary to involve yourself occasionally in an activity where there is a chance of being recognized as a regular person, outside the pedagogic aura that, as time goes by, unfortunately establishes unequivocally how we see ourselves and how we want to be seen.

Get yourself a copy of the book *Silver Bullets* and read over page 14, particularly Play Pointer #1. I know that's not fair (smacks of commercialism and laziness on my part), but what I tried to say there and more specifically here is that to get any student of any age to take a chance (cognitive, affective, or psychomotor) you have to be seen as willing to take the same chance; not all the time, but it has to be general knowledge and regularly reinforced that you have tried what you are asking the students to try. Also memorize this adage, *"An ounce of image equals a pound of performance."* And remember, you get to pick the time and place for your inspired attempt. The older you get the more sense it makes: at 50+ I'm irretrievably into image.

Please notice the emphasis on the word *try* above. If you know anything about adventure programming, or have heard the frequently used shibboleth *Challenge By Choice*, you should recognize that performance is not key, it's the conscientious attempt (trying) that makes the difference. So, if you aren't adept at what you are asking the students to try, you have an excellent opportunity to reinforce the concept of eventual success being made up of many failures.

Try the Fidget Ladder and do your predictable spin-a-roo ; laugh, try again. Ask someone else if they would like to become part of the humor, so that the laughter becomes part of what's shared rather than who it's directed toward. The only caveat is, *don't become too good at everything you try*. No problem? Good; Go for it - share a few failures.

"Yeah, but do you have any sure-fire activities to guarantee a good beginning with a group?" . Sure fire? No, because there are so many variables, people particularly, but also location, the weather, time of year, the school's political climate . . . Guarantees? There are no guarantees, just fortuitous precedent. The activity oriented book you're currently reading weighs over 2 1/2 pounds. There's a few ideas within that I'm sure would be well received."

The game *Moon Ball* is a good "starter" because it's easy to present, easy to play and the level of individual involvement can be adjusted by each player. I think you will find that any non-onerous activity (any middle school activity that requires holding hands, promotes meaningful sharing, or partnering-up for over 30 seconds is usually onerous), is initially well received if its easy-to-understand, activity oriented, kind-of competitive, and does not require a partner.

A first time audience needs an active, simplistic game to serve as a subtle introduction to their own sociologic and physical needs before you begin presenting off-the-wall contests and initiative problems that require some compassionate awareness of one another, and a comparatively sophisticated, discussion oriented (conversationsal) approach to problem solving. Simply, the participants (age notwithstanding) have to be re-introduced to their roots and learn how to cooperatively play like children again.

The game Moon Ball provides a slam-bang, I've-got-it! You've-got-it! activity that builds trust and a sense of wanting to

participate, wanting to be part of a team, if only for that fleeting ball-strike moment. And if you think that the "first time audience" mentioned in the paragraph above refers to children only, remember that, "an adult is simply a broken down child."

For the sake of simplicity and brevity, I'll list the pros of Moon Ball and its genre. Try to use or adapt activities that parallel or duplicate these keys to joyful play.

1. Easy to explain and correspondingly simple to understand.
2. Play begins without a lot of posturing, choosing sides, worrying about boundaries, etc.
3. Participants can choose their own level of participation without fear of censure.
4. The group operates as one team, competing against its own best effort; win/lose scenarios are avoided.
5. Good or bad hits are only meaningful to the individual, as the ball continues in play without pause or hesitation.
6. The Moon Ball itself is, in commercial terms, a beach ball, providing an implement of play that is inexpensive and generic enough to preclude those competitive urges surrounding more familiar catch and throw drills. There is little or no pre-sensitivity to failure when playing with a beach ball.
7. Everyone's eyes remain fixed on the rebounding ball so that attention is not drawn to skills, playing style, who's hitting or not hitting the ball, dress code, skin color, etc.
8. A beach ball is lightweight and harmless so that any hard strike is usually successful and a rebound off a head or crotch is not painful.
9. Game variations are usually well received because there are no traditional rules associated with a beach ball.
10. As the student anticipates playing with a

Beach Ball, an attitudinal leveling occurs that would not have happened if a basketball or volleyball were introduced as the object of play.

Creativity

"If you know exactly what you are doing, you are not being creative."

Some people seem to be inherently more creative than others, but maybe it's just a matter of on-going interest rather than productive proclivity. I have a feeling that most folks are, or can become, creative, but unconsciously choose not to, in favor of the "bible" approach; i.e., referring to a compilation of facts and techniques that apply to their area of interest or need. And that's OK; it's certainly not copping out, just saving time and energy for other scholastic or recreational pursuits.

The capability to be creative is there if given half a chance. Here's what I do to encourage the flow and if it works for you — great! If it flops, look to other suggestions or continue to use prepared texts and lesson plans as guides for your ongoing curriculum. Some create — some implement — some administrate.

By the numbers:

1. Refer to other texts on your preferred subject to gain leverage on the inertial status of where-do-I-start? Use other peoples' ideas to act as a stepping stone for embellishments that make an idea work within other environments or contexts. Changing the rules, vocabulary or setting of a game or puzzler can produce a strikingly fresh and new situation. Examples: The Clock (formerly "Ring Around the Rosie"); Aerobic Tag (a variation known in the vernacular as "Boy With the Ball Gets

Smeared"), 2 x 4 (gleaned from a book on coin and match stick problems).

2. If you are a coffee drinker, drink two cups while making a long, solo interstate drive somewhere and then orient your thinking toward creating in some specific area of program need (a new initiative problem, ropes course event, belay device, working tool, etc.). Let your thoughts drift, but keep them on the subject area, even if the same lousy idea keeps cropping up. If an idea seems like a good one, write down a word or two only (remember, you're driving) to remind yourself of where this fragile and fleeting inspiration came from and where it's going. This brief notation is important. If you mistakenly think the idea is so good and significant that forgetting it is impossible, by the time you attempt to think it

again (what?) it may well be gone and not retrievable. (Comparisons of the mind to a computer are interesting and apt, but the automorphic button for idea retrieval hasn't been located yet— it must be near the thymus.)

If you are not a coffee drinker, drink only one cup or try a no-doze type of pill. I know it seems facetious, some-how unhealthy, and smacks of cheating, but the brief caffeine boost works for me. It must be an increase of blood flow to the brain due to the vasodialator characteristics of caffeine. It's only temporary, but all you need is a start.

3. When you wake up early some morning and aren't still tired, hung over, emo-tionally distant, cold, full bladder, etc. (it's hard to be creative when other signals are getting in the way), direct your thoughts as in #2 above. This relaxed, mentally floating position is one of my favorites and has resulted in a few curriculum elements of note — *The Pamper Pole, Hickory Jump, Warp Speed, Frantic . . .*

4. Go alone to the geographical area that needs your cerebral time, lie on your back and let the area and artifacts flood your thinking (ideally, but sometimes not possible because you're not sup-posed to lie down on the job — I know, it's a corny aphorism, but in application it's too true). I saw a cartoon recently that showed a fellow sitting at a desk staring dreamily out the window. Two co-workers were watching and one remarked, "The boss lets him do that because his last idea saved the com-pany $1,000,000." Creative thinking is a tremendous asset to any business, but its perpetration does appear sometimes too relaxed; i.e., too relaxed for a "no pain, no gain" corporate mentality.

5. This next suggestion is an adjunct and aid toward creating the setting for uninterrupted thought. Buy a pair of shooter's "ears," those earphone-like appendages that shut out sound, rather than enhancing it. They are sold to reduce the risk of injury to your inner ear because of loud sounds (gunfire, machinery, engines, etc.), but their efficiency also cuts out almost all other distracting sounds. If you can get used to people mouthing their words (every office comedian thinks this is an origi-nal and hilarious joke), and the reputa-tion of being a recluse, the "ears" often make a hectic, noisy day more toler-able. You *can* hear the phone ring.

Being creative is fun when it works, but the stage must be set; otherwise, a good idea is pure chance or more often, the result of necessity (good ole serendipity).

"The truth is that each one of us is creative. It was more evident when we were children and playing, because creativ-ity is play-oriented and depends on a faith in ourselves and what we are doing. It is associated, therefore, with those adjectives we use to describe children's play — spontaneous, effortless, innocent and easy."

"Creativity is a different way of looking at things, a different way of looking at ourselves. When we are creative, when we are at play, we open ourselves to our own experiences. We discard preconceptions. We become aware. We begin to live."
— Dr. George Sheehan

I have undoubtedly popularized and embellished more peoples' ideas than I've had original ones of my own, but that's part of the creative game. Every now and then, a sparkling new idea will surface and you will feel justified for all the daydreaming and creative plagiarizing.

Cooperative plagiarism is a productive mind game that I constantly pursue during creative down time. When there's just nothing there (in the windmills of your mind), that's the time to grab a book on the subject you have loggerheaded with and begin designating new thought directions by assaulting what you have (muddled mass of non-functioning ideas) with other folks' notions and inclinations. It's amazing how a simple written comment by another person can stimulate an idea or cause the branching out from a weak idea toward a web of fascinating alternatives. Change size, direction, kinesthetic orientation, rules — make it different, really different, and you make it yours.

An Insight

So often in adventure clinics and classes student responses are immediate, boisterously positive and largely superficial — there's not much time for introspection in a fast-paced workshop. Occasionally, someone will write a letter, after a few days (usually weeks), and pass along a time-mellowed insight concerning people, a moment, or an emotion. Sometimes a response is beautifully sensitive, even artistic. I hesitate to lay that on you, Monique, but anyone who can so clearly see through the smokescreen of *Fire in the Hole*, and so accurately (subtly) pinpoint the real rationale of "just popping balloons" deserves to be quoted.

"'Fire in the hole,' he yelled
with smiling enthusiasm.
We reached out to our partners,
laughing and squirming, and hanging on
tightly.
A delicate balance
between struggle and embrace
weaved through the pairs,
as the discomforts of hugging a stranger,
vanished with each bursting balloon.
It was the gentle transition into familiarity,
(filled with nervous laughter),
as the stubborn balloon resisted the force
of two clutching friends (resulting in a
shattering 'pop'),
that made falling into each other,
more than just a game."

— Monique Gil-Rogers

Debriefing, Processing, Values Clarification — whatever cognitive jargon seems currently appropriate

Ropes course activities and initiative problems are great fun and variously stimulating, but a large part of their educational value can be diminished if an instructor rushes from one physical/emotional high to the next without pausing and offering the group an opportunity to reflect upon and talk about the experience. Watching an otherwise bored class turn on to an adventurous curriculum element can be a tempting stimulus for a teacher to move quickly to another activity before the "magic" is lost.

I think a time for talking about "what went on" during an activity can often be captured by an alert/experienced teacher, without having to formally sit the group down and program the debriefing. "Hey, chicken, whatsamatta with your knees? They get the shakes?" Such demeaning comments provide the opportunity for a discussion of program rationale and how come we're here. Pick your spots at emotional high and low points, when morale is at ebb or flood, not just when the clock says it's time.

To completely eliminate discussion wastes a valuable teaching tool and probably indicates an instructor's (1) lack of caring or confidence (2) ignorance of the value of such an experience (3) boredom level.

Debriefing can also be overdone with many groups. Stopping after each activity for an in-depth "meaningful" discussion is probably too much for a normal group. Interest will wane if the group knows a "heavy" time awaits them after each action experience. However, some groups (adjudicated youths, emotionally disturbed students, etc.) need more scheduled discussion time.

To help you develop your own patter and line of questions, here are a few debriefing topics that you can bring up to stimulate discussion, or change the direction of a deadend dialogue.

Leadership & Followership	Spotting
Group Support	Sexism
Peer Pressure	Carryover
Negativism - Hostility	Fear (Physical -Psychological)
Efficiency	Joy - Pleasure
Competition	

Read *Islands of Healing*, Project Adventure's Adventure Based Counseling book, for a detailed presentation of how to facilitate a functional debrief session.

General Reading for Extra Credit

Everyone knows that insurance coverage, liability concerns, and premium payments provide prime topics of discussion and debate whenever adventure educators get together. Amidst this seemingly endless round of issues is an uninformed attitude that really bugs me; i.e., the cavalier acceptance (mostly inadvertent) of accident-prone activities because they are traditional, followed by the mass non sequitur that insinuates any activity is dangerous (risky) if it appears to be. (This is a letter-to-the-editor written by the editor: noblesse oblige.)

I'm not going to quote a bunch of supportive statistics or try to write around the issues, so here's the tell-it-like-it-seems story!

We'll visit the traditional school gymnasium first and consider the ubiquitous 20' climbing rope (4 on the male side and 4 on the female side of the gym; c. 1949). What are these ropes for, swinging? I wish that were true, as more fun and upper body development would result than from their intended purpose — to climb. That's right, straight up 20', **no belay**. A 3/4" pad on the floor is situated beneath the rope to prevent scuffing the basketball court surface.

How many pull-ups can the typical American student do? I think the answer is 0.75! Climb a 20' rope? Maybe that's why the activity has a fairly good safety record — no one can get off the floor. But, is the climb potentially dangerous? Of course. So, why is it continued? As the *Fiddler on the Roof* would exclaim — **Tradition!**

A newspaper report recently quoted the following unbelievable statistic. (I'm paraphrasing this because I don't have the article in hand.) "Over the past five years, 44,000 (that's 3 zeros) individuals in the United States suffered a paralyzing type of injury as the result of participating in football." How many "paralyzing type of injuries" would result in cessation of all adventure programming? 5,000? 1,000? 200? How many fingers do you need to answer this one. Why the ridiculous discrepancy? **Tradition!**

I recently observed a school-sponsored activity that has been performed yearly for decades — the building and burning of a substantial pile of wood as part of a team sports pep rally. "Yeah, team — burn them Tigers!"

As I watched the students building and climbing the potential pyre (eventually 40-45' high), I kept my camera ready to record what I suspected would be the A.P. tragedy shot of the year. The building, torching and dancing (all quite impressive and entertaining) went off without a hitch — no falls, burns, or beer spills (they drank it all). But, the potential for disaster was undeniably near the surface (any closer than passing an oncoming car at 55 m.p.h.?). The fact that

nothing happened provides an undisputed reason for a bigger and better fire next year — **Tradition!**

Here we are on the playground. **Whack!** There go a few teeth, or add a line of facial stitches from getting bopped by a hard seat swing.

Scrunch! Billy just jumped off the teeter-totter and let his sister drop, posterior first from six feet — broken ankle, compressed vertebrae, concussion.

Hey, let's centrifuge the new kid off the merry-go-round and see how far he goes. How about playing tag on that geodesic monkey bar dome? Or, let's run backward up the slide and . . . OK, I'm obviously (I think) making fun of traditional activities that have entertained children for years, including you and me, but you have to admit that the general feeling (cuz-that's-the-way-it-is) has a lot do do with what's accepted without question and what is suspiciously and tentatively attempted, or disregarded as a fad; i.e., *Project Adventure* and its genre.

It just bugs me, that's all. Thanks for listening. Editor's note: Letters to the editor that disagree with the editor are generally disregarded.

Conservative Reveries

When and where should I consider using helmets on my climbing wall? How long should I continue using the same rope? What kind of rope is best? Should students be allowed to belay?

I could add considerably to the above question list, because people are concerned about safety and safety systems — and rightly so, as accidents tend to produce a reluctance toward continued programming. Considering all this, I thought you would be interested in some pertinent quotes from an overseas publication on climbing walls.

"A suitable indoor climbing wall site is one that allows virtually unrestricted access."

"Put simply, there is no need for any rules or regulations to protect individual climbers on climbing walls."

"Nobody is more aware than the climber of the risks involved and to interfere by insisting on the use of ropes or helmets is to distort the normal process of training and inhibits the climber from developing the judgement on which his safety depends."

"How climbers climb is a matter of personal choice and nobody should interfere. Put simply, climbers can be left to conduct their own affairs without interference."

These quotes were under a chapter entitled, "Professional Management for Climbing Walls." These comments are not tongue-in-cheek, but were written by knowledgeable individuals well-schooled in climbing techniques and ethics.

The obvious discrepancy in safety concepts points out how different ideas concerning safety can develop among groups that have little contact and less communication. It might also indicate how the U.S. suit-conscious mentality has affected our conservative decision-making about risk activities.

In this case, I'm just reporting, not judging.

Where Did "Guns" Go? or Pop Gun Paradise Lost

On my tenth birthday party, I received (from the six party-goers) six cap pistols and a couple holsters. No fake lasers, flashing lights, recorded ricochets or popping corks — just plain **click-click** (occasional **bang**) cap guns that detonated their onomato-poeia projectiles with a full-mouthed explosion that was punctuated by a combination of facial, throat and salivary gymnastics that far surpassed any miniscule **snap** produced by the black-dotted red rolls of caps.

The smell of used caps was great ("rockets' red glare, and bombs bursting in air . . ."), and it almost made the tedious loading procedure worthwhile. But who wanted to mess with caps when your life was on the line? I needed at least 200 rapid-fire shots for my imaginary combat exploits and being limited to 50 unreliable caps was an unthinkable handicap. Caps were fine for setting off with a rock on the sidewalk (3 & 4 deep — not much louder, but more smoke) or for some laid-back target practice, but when the action started, there was no better incendiary than that produced vocally by the oral imagination of the warriors. I had some of my best exploits with a homemade plywood machine gun. How can I possibly write what the staccato oral bursts from that treasured bit of wood sounded like? I can still do it — I just tried out my air-cooled .30 caliber Browning Automatic Rifle imitation (BAR for you aficionados), and it sounded pretty good — but at over 50 years old, you just don't go around orally imitating a machine gun without checking out the immediate area: I'm in the bathroom, so it's OK!

Why don't kids play "guns" anymore? Vietnam horrors? Handgun tragedies? Vicarious fascination with electronic games? Whatever — it's too bad in some ways, because games involving imagination (currently like D&D) are the most vivid and require the best role-playing situations. As violent as our society has become, it's lamentable that "guns" (I'm referring to any game of the genre, like Cops & Robbers or Cowboys), can be a vehemently resisted substitute for Little League and other organized small folks' sports, or TV, or transistor radios, etc. I liked "guns," I don't like guns.

If I have inadvertently tripped anyone's letter-to-the-editor switch by my flippant referral to your favorite cause — I apologize. Relax . . . put the pen down . . . it's OK.

Sound Familiar? . . .

This discourse on risk, etc., is part of a letter I wrote in 1980. It's mildly interesting to see how much things don't change.

". . . as a result, everyone thinks they know how to tie a bowline the right way, and, of course, their method of rappelling is the only safe technique. I think this, I'm-right-because-I've-been-doing-it-for-10-years, mentality is beginning to permeate the ropes course field.

When not many people were 'ropes courseing' it, the techniques of building and use were pretty much ignored by everyone except the people who were using the facility. Now the programmed adventure niche has been educationally established and the prophets of doom (protectors of the kiddies) are suggesting that this is high risk stuff. So, predictably you have the oldtimers who resent having limitations put on their efforts and innovations and a newly concerned set of individuals (concerned about environment, safety, liability, their own regularity, etc.), that are in conflict, so you don't know what to think.

To be more specific . . . A ropes course is as risky as the people who build it, the material they use, and the techniques they employ. Driving a car with bald tires is a genuinely high risk activity. Walking across a high (30-50') Two Line Bridge that is made of aircraft cable with a back-up system, and with a capable person belaying with approved rope is a low risk activity, but it's perceived as high risk: therein lies the value, and the dilemma.

PERCEPTION - difficult, dangerous, risky, exciting

ACTUAL - fairly demanding, not dangerous, risky from a personal failure standpoint. Contains the common factor *excitement*, without which there is little to sustain the activity.

Perceived risk is a valuable teaching tool — actual high risk (drunken driving, drugs, solo climbing, rush-hour traffic) has nothing to do with programmatic adventure.

A Developed Philosophy Toward Adventure Through Quotes - or the Mellowing of an Ex-Outward Bound Instructor

"Anything that doesn't kill you makes you stronger."
  – Paraphrase of a Nietzsche quote

"If the only choice is between pain and nothing, I would choose pain."
— Unknown

"Pain levels come and go, but a recorded effort is here to stay."

"Be fit or be embarrassed."

"If you take care of your ass, your ass will take care of you."
— Old Muledriver's saying

"I don't mind being challenged, as long as I'm comfortable."

"A little adventure is better than no adventure at all."

All non-credited quotes are the author's fault.

Serious Play

Please answer:

- Can you maintain a sense of play if your companions consider fun and games as childish?

- Is play a childish pastime that has no place in a responsible adult's life?

- Can you handle being occasionally child-like? Do you know the difference between childish and child-like?

- Can you personally use the words play and fun as they relate to your own daily experiences without feeling guilty?

- Can you, at your age: Play without competing? Play without having someone tell you exactly how to play (golf, tennis, etc.)? Play without a goal in mind?

- Can you purposefully change the rules?

The questions above are obviously rhetorical, and are asked simply to help rearrange your mind-set about fun and play.

I've made a successful career of professional funmanship. Organizations pay me a substantial consulting fee to teach them how to play *meaningful* games, but it's not the teaching per se that is covered by the fee, it's for a personal appearance by someone that can validate the play experience. "Karl's here, now we can play, have some fun, and become a team." I am not being entirely facetious.

I stuck the word *meaningful* between play and games above to emphasize a ludicrous juxtaposition. Administrators and teachers often feel obliged to make their play purposeful by verbalizing their way around funn. That's why I stuck an extra n on fun(n) to produce the following acronym—functional understanding's not necessary. Don't get me wrong tho', I am not advocating pure play for all situations, just making sure that the opposite doesn't take place simply to appease an office type who schedules and compartmentalizes fun, and determines that play must be validated - like a parking ticket.

I go out of my way to let fun find me;

you don't find fun, just be open to it. And since I don't have a "secret" to share about fun and games, consider the following tips about playfulness.

• Personal fitness is a big part of the enjoyment picture for me. I've tried to maintain a high level of fitness since high school - a looong time ago - finding that, if something exciting makes itself available, I can take part without hesitation and respond to the max, not worrying about pulling muscles, pooping out, getting stiff, and all the other excuses that keep you from experiencing the fun.

• Get out and do some potentially fun things by yourself. I'm not trying to turn you into a loner, but when you're just getting started as an adult fun hog, it's tough to know what you are going to enjoy. There's no use dragging someone else into this trial and error period of serious fun experimentation, it's just you and fun: sorry.

• Don't try to lump your fun. Full time fun is very hard to accomplish and even more difficult to maintain, besides, excess leads to addiction, compulsion, and eventual boredom. Try to establish a lifetime game plan that feeds fun doses at intervals. Fun should not be overwhelming, rather an unplanned but expected series of rejuvenating interludes sandwiched between PTO meetings and car pooling.

• Avoid anything where you have to take lessons or wear specialized clothes and shoes, especially shoes. Did you ever notice how much money and advertising space is devoted to activity footwear? Air soles, gel soles, pumps . . . it's no wonder kids are literally killing for the status that surrounds shoes. And if trophies are part of the participation package (particularly if they are all displayed on a table) get out quick. Find activities that you can learn via trial and error, where the errors are laughable/shareable, and where the necessary clothing is whatever you happen to have on.

All of the above has to do ultimately with your mental attitude and adventure aptitude. If you have spent years and years doing your job and fulfilling family responsibilities, and now want to grab some of the fun you hear about, (I'm not talking about the heavily advertised aspects of smoking, drinking, and sexual involvement that are pitched as fun, but seem more like escape mechanisms and psychological crutches) you can skip all the preliminary stuff and go for the big A (Adrenaline) event of your dreams by signing up for sky diving classes, SCUBA lessons, The Bob Bonderant School of High Speed Driving, etc., but . . . you might be better off initially committing to a weekend experience of hiking, canoeing, or square dancing. You don't have to risk life

and appendages to experience adventure, play, and fun.

Age should have little to do with an individual's potential for play, afterall. Growing up and aging are equated in our culture to being serious, responsible, mature adults. That's fine, but where's the fun?

It's difficult to remain "young" when people are always telling you to grow up and when a fun-loving attitude is relegated to immaturity and a lack of seriousness. We read, quote and extol the writings of great philosophers, because this defines us as mature, intelligent adults, then we ignore their maximums and teachings. Plato is quoted as saying, "I can learn more about a person in an hour of play than in a year of conversation." but for some, experiencing an hour of play is an unrealistic expectation, they don't know how. Play is unfortunately often defined as what children do, or on a higher, more competitive plane, as something adults pursue as sport.

Huge tip coming up - *Pursue those activities and situations that have the highest potential for fun.*

• If the people you live with don't want to play, play by yourself or with like-minded friends and let the fun roll.

• Don't plan activities where you have to consistently compete against yourself or someone else. It's hard to have fun when you're losing, and winning all the time isn't that great either.

• Get involved in something where joking and laughter is the primary means of communication.

• Don't go just to fulfil a responsibility, or if that is necessary (and there are times when you have to do your duty) reward yourself later with an experience that makes you smile and that YOU look forward to.

• Do things with people that you like. Playing golf with a business contact might result in a sale, but you are not playing; you are playing at golf, but you are not playing.

• Find things that you like to do by yourself occasionally. I like to fly big kites with other people around, but I also enjoying doing it alone. Give yourself a chance to get to know yourself.

• Don't wallow in discomfort, either emotional or physical. If the fun factor declines below your pre-set level, split. That's not being irresponsible. God knows, the rest of your life oozes with responsibility. This is your funn we're talking about; be choosy.

. . . and *here's a few pedagogic tips related to fun.*

• Differentiate between an effective, spontaneous, outrageous approach and a stupid, prepared, fabricated attempt at being spontaneous. This has to do with charisma, an innate sense of timing, experience, and a willingness to occasionally appear the fool. There isn't much difference between a safe approach and using calculated abandon effectively, but the subtle variation makes all the difference in how the students perceive their instructor, and eventually how effective they will become as instructors.

• Differentiate the fine line between being the center of attention and the ability to empower a group. This requires considerable self confidence and "having your act together". Someone who is still questioning the effectiveness of their own approach, will have trouble empowering a student group.

• Know the rules to the games and activities well, well enough so that your presentation is easy to understand, puts your students at ease (they know that you know what you are talking about), and is entertaining.

Be careful most of the time, stay healthy, have some fun.

Chapter 12

Safety

Flying Squirrel Rescue

No, you won't need a rescue scenario for the Flying Squirrel event, but since I detailed previously in Chapter #9 how the rope-haul system works, I'd like to pass along how this pulley system can be used in a ropes course rescue situation.

Imagine someone stuck on a zip wire cable about 25' away from the take-off platform and maybe 35' off the ground. One current student retrieval method involves sending a suspended rescuer down the cable from the platform to the stuck student (hanging less-than-merrily from his/her Swiss seat). The rescuer is suspended from a sling-shot section of static rope. Using a pair of locking carabiners, the rescuer clips harness to harness, then cuts the stuck person's static suspension rope with a knife (scissors are safer). Both

individuals are lowered to the ground, helped by an overhead figure eight descender.

In order to preclude the rescuer having to descend the cable, try this hauling up and down technique, and notice the *Flying Squirrel* similarities.

The following rescue gear package should be always available on site. ROSA gold pulley (steel sheave) attached with a locking carabiner to a ROSA red pulley (aluminum sheave).

The staff person on the zip platform attaches (snatch block capability) the ROSA gold pulley to the zip cable and reeves a length of KM III rope through the ROSA red pulley, so that both ends of the rope reach the ground, plus 15 feet.

Allow the pulley/rope arrangement to "zip" slowly down to the stuck student, then pull on the doubled ropes in the direction of the cable slope to see if this simple action will cause the lodged double wheel zip pulley to become unstuck. If the zip pulley remains stuck, tie a bowline-on-a-bight in one end of the KM III rope and clip both loops into a rescuer's harness using a locking carabiner.

The following rescue action practically duplicates the *Flying Squirrel* haul system. Using 8-10 people, haul the rescuer up to the person to be rescued. The rescuer clips into the rescuee, face-to-face (use 2-3 interlocked carabiners to facilitate this attachment), completes the cut-away as above, and both individuals are lowered to the ground.

If you have been to a *Project Adventure* Advanced Skills & Standards Workshop, this Flying Squirrel explanation should make sense, and provide you with an alternate rescue technique.

If you are trained in ropes course use, but have never tried a high rescue, proceed with caution and with a back-up belay, in case . . .

If you are a reader who just wants to try something new — don't.

Tested for Safety

"The U.I.A.A. (International Union of Alpine Associations) has established several standards regarding the strength of rope when subjected to a fall (fall test), its ability to reduce the shock to a falling climber (impact force), and its elongation (static and at impact).

"The U.I.A.A. Fall Test duplicates, in the laboratory, the effects of a severe fall. 'Severe' designates large forces on rope as well as a climber. The free-fall test is performed as follows:

"An 80-kg weight is dropped from a height of five meters. It is held by a 2.8 meter length of rope passed over a 10 mm

carabiner edge. Two measurements are taken: the number of falls held (five is the minimum for U.I.A.A. approval), and the impact force on the weight (1200 kg maximum). These figures provide a useful starting point in the comparison of different climbing ropes."

Staples Testing

There was some initial doubt as to a staple's potential to withstand a leader fall, if used as a belay anchor point. So, a test was arranged that would duplicate a lead climbing fall on the ropes course. Two anchor points were tested: a 5/8" shoulder lag eye screw (SLES) and a 1/2" galvanized staple.

A 16" diameter red oak was chosen for the first test series. A 5/8" SLES was placed by pre-drilling the tree with a 1/2" spade bit to the entire depth of the screw portion of the lag and then turned in the remainder of the way with a cheater rod. The 1/2" staple was hammered in with a hand sledge (a claw hammer won't work), so that there was approximately one inch remaining within the interior space between end of staple and the trunk.

Both anchor points were located in the tree about 12' above the ground, and about 10" apart.

The object, as per this U.I.A.A.-type drop test, was to apply a consistent falling force to the anchors individually. The falling object chosen was a 150 lb. spool of cable. The attachment between spool and anchor was a 7' length of 1/2" diameter static kernmantle rescue rope.

Using an overhead pulley, the spool was hauled seven feet above each tree anchor and dropped, insuring a free-fall of approximately 14 ft. Each anchor was tested three separate times.

Results — The 5/8" SLES exhibited the slightest downward bend (which may well have been separation of wood fibers) and the 1/2" staple showed no movement at all.

The second phase of this test was performed identically, except a large diameter white pine tree was used.

The 5/8" SLES was started with a few blows from a hand sledge and then turned in the remainder of the way using a cheater rod. Two 1/2" staples were also placed with the hand sledge; one oriented vertically to the trunk and the other horizontally.

Resu lts — The 5/8" SLES broke on the first fall. Apparently, the softer wood of the pine allowed a bending of the outer portion of the SLES shank, while the deeper fluted portion remained stationary. The break occurred at the first turn of the screw.

The vertically driven 1/2" staple showed

no movement after three falls. The horizontally placed 1/2" staple bent noticeably on the first fall and even more so on the second. The third fall caused it to pull out. (see photo)

It had been our initial thinking that a horizontal placement of a staple was stronger than a vertical orientation (due to an earlier pull-test using a come-along), but the results of this more realistic shock load fall test were undeniable.

A couple years later we performed identical drop tests on the same trees, but used a 7' section of eye swaged 5/16" cable as the connector between spool and anchor. All SLES bolts and staples (vertical and horizontal orientation) pulled out on the first drop. The difference between using a static section of cable and an identical length of static kernmantle rope was dramatic and kinetic.

As an aside to all these wham-bam tests, the bowline knots used on each end of the attachment lines were easily undone after the testing; another indication why not to use a figure 8 loop in a situation where you know the knot will be severely stressed.

Many thanks to the unselfish efforts of PATT (*Project Adventure's Testing Team*) who gave up valuable (?) office time to brave the rigors of a spring afternoon (sun, bugs, sore muscles).

Helmets — Who Needs 'Em?

You want to know what I think about helmets? . . . I'm going to tell you anyway!

Helmets cause my head to sweat and my ears to get cold. They are troublesome to adjust and often still don't fit right. Shared by lots of heads, helmets are at the least a hassle, and at the worst, a health and safety concern. However, helmets are necessary safety apparel for selected ropes course elements.

Helmets are necessary to: lessen potential liability concerns; reduce the severity or chance of head injury from things being dropped or knocked loose (wrenches, rocks, bolts, canned fruit), and more pertinently, to prevent a bare moving head from making contact with hard stationary objects.

Project Adventure (as of this printing) requires wearing helmets on the following high ropes course elements.

Cat Walk — Dangle Duo — Pamper Pole and Pamper Plank — Fabricated Climbing Wall (indoor and outdoor).

Purchase quality rock climbing helmets that adjust easily, fit well, and are certified to protect heads. Wear head protection when the situation demands prudence (your judgment). Try not to let your judgment be guided (manipulated) by fear or intimidation.

If an individual feels more comfortable wearing a helmet on all the elements, and if that sometimes symbolic head protection allows the student to feel more comfortable trying a difficult ropes course event, let 'em wear it.

End of helmet diatribe.

Demon Rings

Ever been hit by the flailing arms of a trusting faller? Ever seen the "hit" happen during the Trust Fall sequence? Unfortunately, the whacked nose or bruised cheek is bound to happen eventually, no matter how tightly the trouser material is gripped or fingers are interlocked. I've contemplated using long velcro bands around the chest area, and experimented with bungee cord wrapped around the wrists, but such voluntary bondage smacks of partial participation, or evokes emotionally devestating scenarios involving physical and/or emotional abuse. So, during a June workshop that I was co-leading with Ken Demas, when Ken came up with the following simple solution to the occasional lateral karate-like chops that changed the Trust Fall to the Fend-Off Fall, I was delighted; so much so that I immediately named the rubber bracelet — Demon Rings: Demon = Demas.

Take one of the rubber deck tennis rings that you use for the game *Italian Golf*, and slip it over the faller's hands, which are held in a palms-together, prayer-like position. Then, with the ring encircling the wrists, ask the faller to interlock his/her fingers. Even a person so unnerved by a backward fall from 5+ feet will not be able to extricate their hands during the short time span of the actual fall.

This ring/wrist arrangement will

"You have been chosen to implement the Project Adventure curriculum." Fade to poignant images and pictures of people flying through the air while disengaging from cables and trapezes . . . Aargh!

Having used a variety of these save-your-life devices over the years, here's a personal recommendation and a couple caveats.

If you are going to be working in trees or positioning yourself on a pole for an extended time (over 15 minutes), I think the Klein tree climber's belt is a best buy. You will have to add a section of 1/2" diameter multiline rope as a tree wrap-around, but that's no big deal, and if you can't figure out the rope/harness arrangement, ask the guy at the store where you bought the harness.

function well for comparatively large hands and wrists. For smaller hands, two rings may be necessary. Squeeze one ring slightly so that it fits inside the second ring. So arranged, the rings will be perpendicular to one another — not concentric. The hands are inserted into the obvious openings. (Photo)

Hello, Demon Rings. Goodbye, whacked faces.

OPB's (Occupational Protective Belts)

People who are newly involved with adventure programming and particularly with ropes courses predictably develop a tactile and functional fascination with harnesses and protective belts. This may be a survival reaction to the superintendent's edict that

If he can't tell you, he shouldn't be selling the harnesses. Come to a PA Advanced Skills workshop and learn how to splice your own.

There are many OPB's on the market, but don't buy one for ropes course work. These narrow belts are not made for leaning against (freeing your hands for work) and, more significantly, they are not manufactured to sustain a substantial static fall. A static ending to a 4' fall might rupture the buckle arrangement and if it didn't, the single no-stretch belt around your midsection might cause internal problems, resulting in more than a tummy ache.

If you're climbing on a ropes course, either wear a commercial rock climbing harness or tie on a Studebaker Wrap using 1" tubular webbing or 9 mm kernmantle rope. Wearing one of these pelvic protectors is still not going to make a static fall feel good, but at least you'll be around for another one.

Write to the following company for the address of a local distributor of their products. Klein sells utility pole hardware including high quality safety gear. Ask for a catalog and the location of a local distributor.

Klein Company
7200 McCormick Boulevard
Chicago, IL 60645

To purchase or look at a rock climbing harness, check your yellow pages for a climbing retail store near you, or write to the following company for their catalog.

R.E.I. (Recreational Equipment, Inc.)
Seattle, WA 98188

Project Adventure, Inc., also sells rock climbing and mountaineering harnesses. Write for a free Ropes Course Source Catalog. Box 100; Hamilton, MA 01936.

Climbing Rope Replacement, Etc.

Of all the technical questions that I'm asked, "When should I replace my climbing ropes?" is the one for which I have become most reluctant to offer a definitive answer. There are so many variables and unknowns in the "life" of a climbing rope that a definitive answer is at best presumptuous and at the least, dangerous. Here are some cordage facts to ponder.

- New England Ropes, Inc. (the rope company in New Bedford, Massachusetts, that provides *Project Adventure, Inc.*, with most of their cordage) has the following to say about checking rope for wear. "*No type of visual inspection* can be guaranteed to accurately and precisely determine actual residual rope strength. When the fibers show wear in any given area, the rope should be respliced, downgraded, or replaced."

- Estimating rope usage or wear by measuring rope elongation is not a valid technique. A well used rope length will actually measure shorter than the same rope length when new.
- Use of shear reduction devices dramatically increases the load-bearing capacity and useable "life" of a rope.
- Climbing ropes display an impressively large ultimate tensile strength, but this same rope can be easily cut by sharp edges and as easily burned by cigarettes.

Threaded Rod

Do not use threaded rod for critical connectors on a ropes course. If there is any flex movement of the rod under pressure, the rod has a greater chance of breaking because of its threaded nature.

Another inherent danger is that a threaded eye may rotate off the rod unless a cotter pin is installed.

The only advantage to using threaded rod is its length (usually up to 72"), and the

capability of using an eye on either end of the rod.

If the rod head is loose or placed under alternating pressures (walking on a cable?), the chance of eventually snapping the rod is greater than your program can afford.

Cable Strength

People who are thinking about building a ropes course often ask, "How long does a section of cable last?", or "Just how strong is that stuff?" As the result of a winter storm, I now have a firsthand answer, rather than having to quote destructive testing tensile strength figures.

The folks at the Hamilton-Wenham Regional High School (the site of *Project Adventure's* original ropes course) called our office recently, and said that we should come and take a look at the storm damage on the course, and suggested that we bring our chainsaws.

That was no joke, because two large beech trees had come down as the result of high winds (and old age). One of the trees had fallen directly onto the 280 ft. zip wire cable. They had mentioned this, so when I arrived, I expected to see broken cable and snapped bolts. What I did observe was a surprise. The falling tree had pushed the zip cable all the way to the ground, but the cable had not broken and although the connector bolts had bent, they were also still intact. The near support tree (18" diameter trunk with the platform attached) had been pulled over to about a 45° angle. There was still a considerable amount of tension on the cable. The significant fact remains that the entire length of a 12-year old non-galvanized fiber core cable and the connectors were intact.

It's pertinent to also report that the falling tree (diameter at the base was 27") was not simply uprooted, but snapped off about two feet above the ground, so that the force of the falling tree was considerable. The zip wire was actually hit about 30 feet up the trunk of that snapped-off tree.

The dénouement of this action-packed adventure vignette is: there's a lot of beech in 2 ft. stove sections curing for next winter's use, and a mess of cable has been retired to that ole junk yard in the sky. Now, on to a bigger and better zip.

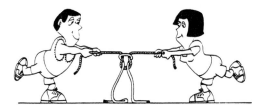

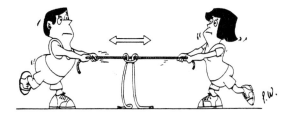

Not a Knot

This is what happens when a square (reef) knot collapses as the result of not being protected by overhand safety knots tied on either side of the square knot.

This simple but dramatic demonstration is quite effective toward convincing students that safety knots are more than just "window dressing."

Hickory Jump Trapeze Bar

A young girl broke both of her wrists as the result of an unfortunate accident on a ropes course, because she was swinging on the *Hickory Jump* bar without spotters' support and she lost her grip. Such unsupervised use can be alleviated by substituting a trapeze arrangement for the bar. In this way, the trapeze can be removed after the supervised activity is over by simply unclipping the carabiners or rapid links that connect the trapeze bar to the support cables.

This case was mentioned elsewhere in *Bottomless Bag* — I just want to make sure you read it.

Warning — Unsafe

Wow! Heavy rubric. But, worthwhile knowing.

One of the original Project Adventure publications that preceded *Cows' Tails & Cobras* recommended an initiative problem called, *The Four Poster*. The problem involved supporting a number of students off the ground using only 4 sub-

stantial posts (cut limbs) and a sling rope. The solution involves piling people on top of a hastily fabricated tee-pee arrangement utilizing the poles and rope.

The solution (the only solution that makes sense) is unsafe. There is almost no way of insuring an individual's safety because of the variables of body position on the tee-pee, knot unreliability and ground condition (mud is a sure-fire ankle breaker). Cut up those well-cured poles into 2 ft. lengths for the ole wood stove and pile your students with confidence onto the *All Aboard Platform*.

Destructive Testing, or "You Make It — I'll Break It"

Here's good news for those of you trying to prove a safety point. The following load figures represent the breaking or disfiguring points for a number of commonly used ropes course fixtures.

The tests were performed by the Arnold Greene Testing Laboratories in Natick, Massachusetts, as a contract fulfillment for Project Adventure, Inc.

5/16" strand vise - cable broken inside the strand vise at 8,520 lbs.

3/8" strand vice - 11,300 lbs. (cable broke)

3/8" pear-shaped link - connecting 5/16" cable broke at 9,660 lbs. Link did not disfigure.

SARA Rescue Pulley - *One* eye broke at 6,220 lbs.

5/16" swage - slipped at 8,400 lbs. No breakage.

"Spring Thing" - 600 lbs. for complete compression. 3,660 lbs. for disfigurement.

Open 1/2" rapid link - 1,650 lbs.

Closed 1/2" rapid link - 22,000 lbs.

ROSA Gold Pulley - 11,400 lbs.

Spin/Static Pulley - 11,650 lbs.

The tests also indicated that cable clamps hold best when they are tightened down to 45 foot pounds (as measured by a torque wrench). So that you don't have to carry a torque wrench in your tool kit, just remember to torque the clamps with your socket wrench as tight as you can manually get them. Don't worry about over-crimping the cable; put some muscle to it.

Running Self-Belay

Based on personal experience, other teachers' war stories, and an article I recently read in the *Climbing Magazine*, "Off Belay" #46, I want to re-emphasize some negative feelings about static self-belays on ropes courses.

If you are not familiar with this type of belay — good; you're better off. But for the sake of being knowledgeable in the field, here's a quick run-down.

Picture a high *Two Line Bridge* set-up. The climber ties or arranges something around his/her body (Swiss Seat, sit harness, Studebaker Wrap), and from this tie-in, a short length of rope extends to the belay cable, and via a carabiner/bowline, is clipped to this cable. If a fall takes place, the static rope obviously prevents the

climber from falling to the ground, but the hapless hanger usually ends up somewhere below the bottom cable, suspended.

It is this suspended position that presents a serious health problem. It is an unusually adept student that is physically capable of climbing her/his own static belay rope to get back up onto the *Two Line Bridge*, or *Burma Bridge*, or whatever. The suspended student is temporarily "safe," but stuck and becoming rapidly and increasingly uncomfortable. If the tie-in is a single strand bowline around the waist, unconsciousness can result *in less than a minute*, and depending upon the position of the suspended body (horizontal or vertical), brain damage can result unless there is a *quick* (less than two to three minutes) means of getting the student safely down.

If the student is in a harness arrangement, there is more "hang" time available, but according to results that have been gleaned from carefully controlled tests, even the most expensive harnesses can cause "loss of blood pressure, respiratory distress, intense pain, and a loss of consciousness" within 15 minutes.

Think it through, could you get a suspended student safely down in less than 15 minutes? In one minute? Do you have an extra coil of rope at the ropes course site? Extra carabiners? A knife? Do you or your working partners have the knowledge or expertise necessary? (Refer to *Flying Squirrel* rescue at the beginning of this chapter.)

What I'm suggesting is, "You might want to rethink your use of a running self-belay." A sling-shot bottom belay (belayer-to-upper cable-to student) is the safest method, and is applicable under almost all circumstances where a belay is necessary.

Static belays are probably as safe *if* the static belay rope is short enough to pre-

clude a fall, but in shortening the static rope you have removed the most significant part of the challenge, the real chance of disengaging from the cable.

Where the Accidents Occur

There is a generally held misconception that adventure programming leads to a higher rate of accidents (per time of participation) than in more traditional physical education classes. Not true, as questionaires have pointedly and repeatedly indicated that more accidents take place during regular physical education classes than during high ropes participation. (Write to **PA** for a copy of this documentation; there is a nominal charge.)

On most of the high events, there is a built-in "perceived danger" that is further cultivated by the programmer to make the event more challenging; hopefully resulting in a greater sense of accomplishment when the "impossible" has been attempted.

There are some ropes course elements that, because of their nature (safety depends on spotting), result in a higher chance of an injury occurring. I'm not in any way trying to blacklist these following events, only trying to make you aware of things that have happened in the past, so that being forewarned, you can take steps to make the events safer in the future.

Unfortunately, I don't have the space to explain the rules for each event. Refer to the books *Silver Bullets* and *Challenge By Choice* for a write-up on most of these stunts, initiative problems, and events.

1. *Electric Fence* — injury areas: ankles, wrists, and neck.

   Do not allow . . .

   (a) . . . indiscriminate (but well-intentioned) tossing of people over the rope.

(b) . . . diving over the rope and attempting a shoulder roll.

Encourage . . .

(a) . . . constant spotting — instructors should spot the first couple of students over the rope.
(b) . . . a compassionate attitude.

(c) . . . a concern for efficiency rather than time.
(d) . . . lowering the "electric cord".

2. ***Stump Jump*** — injury areas: sternum, ribs, ankle.

Do not allow . . .

(a) . . . rapid sequence jumps; the spotters can't keep up.
(b) . . . attempts that are the result of peer pressure and emotion, rather than a personal desire to "make the jump." This is a hard one to judge; be conservative.

Encourage . . .

(a) . . . surrounding the landing platform with at least 4 spotters.
(b) . . . making a trial jump from the landing platform to an outlined area on the ground.
(c) . . . read #2
(b) above.
(d) . . . spotters, watch the jumper's feet—the body has to follow.

3. ***Hickory Jump*** — injury areas: back, neck, sternum, ribs.

Do not allow . . .

(a) . . . swinging through after a jump.

The spotters must stop this action to prevent a dorsal trip to the turf.

Encourage . . .

(a) . . . a minimum of 8 spotters.
(b) . . . removing spotters' wrist watches.
(c) . . . checking the stumps for soundness before allowing a jump (give the stump a good, lateral kick).
(d) . . . pre-jump stretching exercises of the shoulder muscles

4. ***Reach for the Sky*** — injury areas: wrist and arm.

Do not allow . . .

(a) . . . stacking people 4 high, unless a belay is used.
(b) . . . the top person to jump in order to make a higher mark.

Encourage . . .

(a) . . . lateral spotting (right next to the wall on both sides of the people pile).
(b) . . . removing pencils, pens, combs from pockets.

5. ***Wall*** — injury areas: wrist, arm joints, ankle.

Do not allow . . .

(a) . . . more than 4 participants on top of the wall at one time.
(b) . . . anyone to hang over the wall, unless they are supported by two people.
(c) . . . jumping off the back of the wall to save time.

Encourage . . .

(a) . . . lateral spotting as in #4.
(b) . . . spotting for those people descending the Wall.

6. ***Balance Broom*** — (Witches' Broom) — injury areas: fingers, shoulder.

Encourage . . .

(a) . . . spotting (N.E.S.W.) by 4 people (let the participant achieve a disoriented state, but prevent a "crash").
(b) . . . a dispensation for those who characteristically suffer from motion sickness.

7. ***Cargo Nets*** — injury areas: wrist, arm, neck.

Do not allow . . .

(a) . . . rolling head-first over the top of the net.
(b) . . . climbing up and over a net that is 10-15' high, without an overhead belay.

Encourage . . .

(a) . . . spotting by 2 people at the bottom of the net if someone is swinging into the net.

8. ***Swing to a Stump*** - injury areas: non-specific

do not allow:

(a) . . . swinging attempts by people who cannot support their own suspended weight.

encourage:

(a) . . . not releasing the rope until the swinger is <u>solidly</u> balanced on the target stump.

I have observed or heard of documented injuries having occurred on all of the elements mentioned; these are not empty concerns. Take note of how many of these elements involve a belay.

Those of you who have taken a chance or two in life (getting out of bed or driving to work), realize that living is chronic chance-taking. A number of people were killed a few years ago while eating ice cream at a soda fountain by a badly aimed airplane — how would that look on your epitaph? Kinda' makes you want to go out and do something crazy . . . like taking cholesterol pills.

If we can share an awareness of the hazards that are combined with our work, we're better able to anticipate and reduce the consequences.

Chapter 13

Miscellaneous

Tic Tac Tedium

I've never liked the game Tic Tac Toe because when I was a kid, someone always seemed to be using up or messing up my clean sheets of paper by scribbling

# # # #

on an empty sheet and *then* saying, "You wanna play?" or "Come on, you first." People artlessly criss-crossing my un-touched 3 hole lined notebook paper with a messy #1 pencil (crayon was the worst), and the fact that I usually lost did not increase my tic-tac-toe training time. But some

people like the game, so here's a variation to extend your playing time — uck!

Create the minimum grid cypher on someone else's clean white sheet of paper. Give one player 4 pennies and the other player 4 nickels. Play the game in a regular fashion. If the metronome-like moves end up in a "cats" game (about every time, if the players are paying any attention at all), continue playing by alternating turns and sliding a coin until someone eventually ends up with THREE IN A ROW. Great fun, eh? No? Forget it.

Word Association Adventure Potential Test — More universally recognized as the WAAPT

Here's a test that measures practically nothing (sound familiar?), but it's fun to take and administer. The list can obviously be added to or subtracted from, depending on your audience. The real beauty of this non-evaluative gem (as compared to those super-serious tests steeped in validity), is that you can feel justified in completely ignoring the results — because Karl made up the questions and format, and what does he know?

Offer the following words printed on a photocopied sheet with a space left next to each word. Record the sport, activity, or item associated with the word. If you don't want to go to the trouble of recording answers, give the words verbally and ask for a response — self-grading for fragile egos.

Try the test yourself! How can you refuse? I'm not offering any answers because you are the resident expert, and anyway . . . we might disagree.

There are some words included in this list that are practically generic and can be associated with more than one activity. Grade liberally; remember, everyone gets a ribbon.

Ensolite	Beal	Ambient Pressure
Bent Shaft	Hang Ten	5.10
Counter Force	Self-Arrest	Schraeder
Pintle & Gudgeon	UIAA	EB's or RD's
Fish Scale	Herringbone	J Stroke
Wedeln	Bong	Kabar
Shimano	Klister	Side Pull
Embolism	Kevlar	Draw
Loft	Sticht	Jam
Telemark	REI	Jibe-O-Duck
Zipper the Pins	Friends	Ferry
Eddy Turn	Optimus III	Arch-Thousand
33 PSI	Glissading	Cordura
Belay	Svea	Wanigan
Brace	Gaiters	Etrier
Sheets	BCD	Presta
Cadence	Nikonos V	ANSI
Gaff Rig	Munter Hitch	60/40
Mantle	Loran	End Shifter
Chock	Piolet	Jumar
Blue Wax	Bergschrund	Victorinox
Vibram	Catching a Crab	J Valve
Rolling Resistance	May Day	Hot Curl
Skirt	Sun Cups	PFD
Standing Waves	Feathering	Skeg
MSR	Slalom	Prusik
PLF	Dia-Compe	Declination
Blue Hole	Silva	Randall
XXX Beaver	Lignostone	RURP
Spenco	Twist Lock	Bat Hook
Tumblehome	Bonk	Shark Skin
Para-Pente	Pipe Line	Hot Pogies
Third Hand	Grundwalla	DIN or ASA
Smearability	**Long Horn**	**Keeper Hole**

Fabricated Fun

OK, enough specifics; here's a really specious attempt at rationalizing fun quotient (FQ) enhancement—no . . . really!

To have a lasting effect on FQ enhancement, you must first remove a fun sponge from his/her own environment—this includes yourself, if you happen to be part of the problem. Just like the difficulty experienced in reducing recidivism among urban adjudicated youth, you can't extol the satisfaction of a 9-5 minimum wage job to a 16 year old that's pulling down a couple hundred a day hustling on the streets. We're talkin' change of venue here. Get your problem individual(s) out of their geographical comfort zones by seducing them with some out-of-town fun.

You're still a bit fuzzy on this, right? I said specifics (look above, it's just after the word enough), so no more theory, here's the nitty gritty. Do something vaguely enjoyable in an unfamiliar environment. Sounds easy, eh? Well, it's not. I never said having fun was easy.

Typical scenario — You and your wife/husband/friend don't want to go camping because of the envisioned discomfort (bugs, rain, bears, dirt, constipation, freeze-dried food, motor cycle gangs, wet sleeping bags, body odor, teeth scum, blisters, etc., etc.) It's true, all of those experienced and imagined disasters are part of the avoidable aspects of camping, but anticipating the worst invariably initiates reality fulfillment because of unrealistic expectations about the fun you are supposed to be having.

When comedienne Carol Burnett immortalized the lines, "Are we having fun yet?" she defined the essence of the FQ (fun quotient) problem—most people don't know when they are having fun (if it's not happening now, it's not happening), when it's supposed to happen (good fun is spontaneous), or what it's supposed to feel like, (. . . like you can't think of anything else you would rather be doing).

Disengage yourselves from the quintessential role of the Great American Catalog Trailblazer (part of the L.L. Bean Gortex rotten-weather testing team) and find out what's really fun for your partner—your own good buddy—then try as a team-of-two to let the fun happen in a comfortable extended-forecast outdoor environment that's unique to you both. You can look forward to being miserable at a later date, after you have established a buffer comfort zone.

The fun-enhancement guarantee that goes along with this approach is not validated (free parking at Bloomingdales) unless both partners commit to TRY. Remember try and fun are both three letter words—truly, a non sequitur of profound proportions.

Oxymorons

Oxymoron - A pairing of contradictory or incongrous words.

Oxymorons don't have much to do with anything, I just like them as paradoxical twins . . . and a good one makes me smile. Here's a few favorites, starting with my all time favorite:

pretty ugly	clearly confused	Soviet Union
instant classic	genuine imitation	exact estimate
working vacation	larger half	conservative liberal
unsung hero	almost perfect	freezer burn
war games	silent scream	Dry Beer
friendly fire	jumbo shrimp	randomly organized

The last oxymoron almost *perfectly provides* an *instant classic* of my office, that location of *extensive briefings* and *randomly organized* gear. A rhetorical . . . have you ever? Have you ever . . . read a sentence that had five oxymorons contained within?

Annotated Ropes Course & Adventure Curriculum Black-Listed Word & Phrase List

There are a few words and terms that, although frequently used in the abstract and often out of context, denote such pejorative bodily and emotional consequences, vis à vis adventure, that their use must be assiduously avoided . . . and occasionally abetted if things get too serious.

1. Almost all those gems of graffiti which have been clandestinely inked, cut, burned, and otherwise emblazoned on THE WALL. A 12' wall, that fabricated bastion to the attainment of the impossible, is the quintessential "blank page" for unknown authors to anonymously vent anger, joy, frustration, and, of course, to vividly describe in the vernacular, the vice-principal's sexual preferences, generic quirks, and other idiosyncratic exotica.

2. "Oops!" Not well received as a belay or spotting exclamation.

3. As a means of explaining the braking system (not breaking) on a zip wire, describing the terminus as coming to a *dead stop*, seems a bit final.

4. Carabiners are called many things, and some of the abbreviated terms are both descriptive and useful. However, with a group of interested onlookers in attendance (parents), calling to your belayer, "Do you have any *crabs*?" might result in some understandable confusion.

5. A shoulder lag eye screw, a useful ropes course hardware item, produces a colorful acronym: SLES, pronounced, of course, sleaze. It makes obvious sense then, that the leather pouch which attaches to a worker's safety harness is called a SLES-bag. Again, be sure of your audience before calling for carabiners and shoulder lag eye screws in the workmen's vernacular.

6. The buried anchor point that secures a guy line is called a *dead man*. It would be occupationally unthinkable to call it anything else. Notwithstanding the other worldly aspect of the term, could *dead woman* be substituted 50% of the time?

7. If a ropes course builder uses 5/8" diameter cable to build a *Burma Bridge*, s/he has used cable that is obviously overly strong for its intended use. In this context, the phrase "over-kill" has been inappropriately and frequently used. Try "over-engineered" — much more acceptable and technically accurate.

Sand Sliding

During my teenage years, growing up in Hawaii (c. 1954), I learned how to sand slide. I continued beach skimming while living in California and have even pursued some summer gliding here in Massachusetts at Crane's Beach. If you live near the shore or vacation there, this little-known, fast-moving activity is worth trying to learn.

Of the 500 or so people that BOT's goes out to each quarter, I'll bet there are less than 5 that will actually try sand sliding, but writing about skimming is nostalgic therapy (it's December — HELP!) if only for me, and if just one person becomes proficient, it will be worth the space and time. Even if

you are a sand board cognoscente, I'll bet my board design dimensions will provide you with a longer and more stable ride. Is the hook set? Better read this, or you may miss out on the next national fad, and certainly the potential for some personal adventure.

The object of sand sliding is to stand-up ride a shaped plywood board on the beach for as long a distance as possible over the thin layer of water that results from a breaking and receding wave.

Rides of 100 feet on a gentle beach slope are not uncommon on a good day (smooth flat sand at near low tide), and even longer rides (100-200+ yards) can be accomplished when working as a team. But first you need a board.

If you have ever watched someone sand skimming, they were probably using a round or lemon shaped boardboard. After having tried many shapes and sizes over the years, I think the following board dimensions will give you the best ride.

Buy a 4' x 8' section of 1/2" marine plywood (it's the smallest section that most lumber yards will sell). Cut the 4' x 8' in half so that you have two 2' x 4' pieces. Measure down 9" and across 9" from one of the corners, and draw a line connecting these

two marks. Scribe the same measurement lines on the opposite short corner. Using a circular saw, or whatever kind you have, cut along these two dotted lines, producing a board shape as illustrated.

At the opposite end of the board, measure 2" up and 2" across on both sides. Cut along the connecting dotted line as above.

Using a medium rasp and then sandpaper, smooth off these cut corners to produce a contoured rounded shape that is less apt to do harm to your body if the board hits you or if you hit the board.

Using a power sander (or by hand if you're on an island with nothing else to do), contour the front end (9" cuts) so that at the board tip at least 1/4" has been removed from the depth (thickness). Begin sanding 18" back from the front of the board. Also, contour the two rear corners, but not nearly as much.

After you have sanded and fine-sanded (120 grit sandpaper is good enough) the entire board, put on at least three coats of polyurethane varnish or whatever color(s) of paint you choose (use marine paint). We used to decoupagé Playboy centerfolds onto our boards, but this requires considerably more work, time and inclination. Being 16 years old helps.

Round skim boards are ok, but you can't get the distance obtainable with the "bitchin'" board that you are now holding.

Sand sliding can be practiced at any time of year in New England if you don't mind (I do) wearing wet socks and suit in winter. Check the tide tables so that you arrive at around low tide. Also, check the calendar so that you arrive around July.

Stand holding your board (we're at the beach) with both hands at waist level so that the big bevel is forward and the flat of the board is parallel to the beach. As a wave comes in and begins to recede, step and throw the board as above; forward in a sliding movement. Watch the board skim over the 1/8" of water film. Do this a few times until the board skims predictably — avoid throwing the nose down first.

First ride (attempt) coming up. Again, watch for a good wave, begin running forward and throw the board. If you are right-handed (and throw the board well), you should now be running slightly behind and on the left side of the solo skimming board. As you move to step on the board, put your left foot on first and then almost immediately afterwards, the right, so that your feet are set approximately as depicted in the photo below. This step-hop onto the center of the board is the key to a good start — now, ride! You won't have any trouble recognizing when the ride is over because (1) The board will hit a dry patch of sand and stop immediately (you won't), (2) The board will glide down toward the ocean and stop (gradually) in deeper water, (3) Your feet inadvertently change position; an edge digs into the sand, and . . .

I'll mention a couple of other things and then stop because I find that I'm really enjoying myself and the words are piling up rapidly.

After you become a proficient rider, ask a sand-riding partner to run along next to you and offer the end of a knotted rope (5'), or more indigenously, a knotted towel. Grab the rope and let your partner haul you down the beach for as long as you can guide the board to thin water, or until your hauler begins to experience serious oxygen debt. Be empathetic and change positions after a couple rides. You can even change pullers in mid-ride (tag team technique) for a long, long ride — my P.B. is close to 1/4 mile.

If you throw the board down consistently well, try a belly-flop ride. With your head closer to the beach, the sensation of speed is dramatically increased. Remember to take your fingers out from under the board before flopping on top.

There's more, but . . . I appreciate your forbearance; back to 30° and slush. Merry Christmas and if you're going surfing over the holidays, I hate you.

Don't Just Stand There

Watching a group stumble, giggle, and bludgeon their way through the "Nitro Crossing" initiative problem for the umpteenth time is bound to have a stultifying effect on your enthusiasm and humor and flexibility and what all. Remember the key

to enthusiasm for your students? Variety! Treat yourself to some variations on life when you have the opportunity, or try to make that opportunity happen. Go white water rafting, hot air ballooning, parachuting, something, so that you can renew that dry mouth, what-am-I-doing-here sensation that so poignantly slams the door on vicariousness.

Experience for a change that unique position of being a student and trusting what someone else is telling you. "You'll be OK, just keep your . . ." "I'll be right here if you need . . ." "Keep your hand on that line and try to . . ."

Compassion. Fear. Empathy. Joy. Exhilaration. Pumped -Up. Glow. Commitment. Dry Mouth. Worthwhile. Satisfied. Self. Together. Anticipation.

Go on a weekend scavenger hunt and see how many of the above words you can check off as the result of participation in some activity.

Australian Survival Information

As the result of a recent sojourn to the land "down under," I have recorded a number of facts and situations that might be of interest to travelers, or just fun to read for the typical *YANK*.

Writer's note — The following comparisons are the result of cultural and distance differences between countries and are not meant as demographic situations to be intellectually dissected or held up to the light of pure nationalistic truth. Read for fun, mate!

1. Hot and cold faucets are often reversed from what you would expect; i.e., hot is on the right and cold to the left. With soap in your eyes, this information may save your skin.

2. When writing the day and month, reverse them; i.e., 5/28/86 becomes 28/5/86. Why? Because that's the way it is.

3. All driving is on the left side of the road; not the wrong side, mate, the left side. Interestingly enough, the steering wheel *and* shift column are also reversed.

4. The toilet is *not* in the bathroom, therefore if in extremis, don't ask to go to the bathroom. The WC (water closet) is the toilet, which flushes (by pushing a button) in a most explosive way. Toilets down under do not swirl clockwise or

counterclockwise — they implode.

5. Most orange juice is only one star quality. Drink beer — *Aussie* brew is best!

6. Vegemite is an Australian breakfast institution and has a taste and consistency that is distinctly acquired. Use sparingly and smile. I like it, but in excess it's deadly.

7. Barramundi fish is excellent (****) eating. It's the fresh water fish that Crocodile Dundee spears in the movie.

8. The coins used as currency pretty much duplicate ours in the U.S., but since the switch from British currency was only about a decade ago, vernacular names have not developed for the individual coins. Nickel, dime, penny, etc., are non-existent. It's one cent, ten cents, etc.

9. When dishes are hand washed, the dishes are put directly from the soapy water onto the draining rack; i.e., no rinse. I never noticed any stomach problems as the result of this.

10. Men — Individual urinals in public toilets are rare. An entire section of wall, with a convenient trough beneath, is set aside for your aiming pleasure (or lack of). I particularly liked the painted tile motif.

The following word comparisons are interesting. Aussies reading this — pity a poor Yank who took incomplete notes.

Australian	American
crooked (not crook-ed)	sick
take away	take out (food)
give away	yield (road sign)
wind cheater	sweater
doona	quilt
bloke	fellow
overtake	passing (driving)
tick	to check (list)
spanner	wrench
torch	flashlight
prawn	shrimp
tinnie-stubby	beer can - bottle
Rice Bubbles	Rice Krispies
aeroplane	airplane
the Monday, the Tuesday	Monday, Tuesday
caravan	trailer
holiday	vacation
pig hour traffic	peak (rush) hour traffic
tall poppy	anyone who thinks they are hot stuff, usually obnoxious

There are many more comparative similarities than differences between our cultures. The differences make up the spice that makes the travel and interaction stimulating. Bonzer mates — it was a fine journey. S'truth.

Brief Report on Adventure Brewing

It works! Zymurgy is not just a good scrabble word. Combining the simple elements contained in a brew kit, plus sugar, water, and yeast, makes beer — and not a bad brew, at that. John Rittermeister and I whipped up the first batch with some trepidation, but the immutable laws of science and a robust gang of yeasties worked their cosmic magic to produce a highly palatable beverage with, as they say, "a lovely head"; and at about $.16 a pint, the price is right. Definitely a low-risk adventure with considerable potential for libatious rewards. (Photo pg. 309).

Check out the creative label that the PA folks in Vermont came up with. Tom Beddel consistently turns out innovative and tempting brews . . . the fruity after taste lingers on the middle palate. Truly a memorable brew; bold, but not presumptuous.

The Big Bang Theory in Zymurgy

If you will remember awhile back, I made mention of home brewing some beer . . . well, I've continued doing it on a small scale because I kind of like beer, and brewing your own reduces the cost and increases the taste.

I found out something about following directions that I would like to pass along — *follow them*, particularly those pertinent to the formation of dissolved gasses in a sealed container.

If you want a "head" on your beer, it's necessary to add a tad more sugar to the bottled brew to act as supplemental food for the various yeasts. In so doing, some gas is produced as a by-product of this additional fermentation. Most of the gas is held in solution, because the brew is now bottled and *sealed.*

I have said all this leading up to a zymurgical caveat — don't add more than 1/2 teaspoon of sugar (not cane sugar, CORN sugar) to each bottle before capping, or the bottle may burst. If it doesn't blow while sitting there "curing," chances are it may when you start jostling the bottle around before opening — and, if it's still unblown at the point of removing the cap, all that potential will shoot itself straight up and out the bottle neck, manifesting Bernnouli's principle right up your olfactory orifice.

Weather Balloon

This suggestion may well be inappropriate or unusable for most programs or situations, nonetheless you should know of the potential for glee (I can't think of a more descriptive word in this case), that an inflated 12' (that's foot) diameter balloon produces within a group.

I'm sure there are a number of games that can be (or have been) developed for use with large balloons; i.e., Earth Ball types, but just the Gargantuan presence of this bubble-like plaything is enough to produce smiles, and exclamations of disbelief.

As this Godzilla of balloons descends toward your group, hands and feet press into the undulating rubber surface expecting a substantial resistance, but encounter only a fleeting, bubble-like wobble as IT blobs slowly . . . so slowly away from your push toward the next ambivalent receiver. Things this big should be inertial, but this big thing isn't — overwhelming in some ways, but kindly persuasive in its enveloping rubberness.

When it breaks, you may experience that poignant sorrow, so long set aside and

lately unappreciated, of a child that pops or releases a favorite or only balloon.

Such a humongo balloon is not sold at local five and dimes, but searching around surplus stores may turn one up. Remember, each state has a government surplus properties center that has goods available to non-profit organizations, including schools. See *Government Surplus Wants You!*

You will need a power inflator to blow up a balloon of this size...there just aren't enough alveoli around to do the job by mouth. Sounds like some great oral adventure, eh? Don't bother; this is supposed to be fun, not a residential experience. A commercial vacuum cleaner will do the job; that's blow, not suck!

Don't use helium. It's expensive (compared to vacuum cleaner exhaust) and some of your smaller students may disappear.

Rubber Band Man

Portable fitness, that's what I'm telling you about.

As the result of undefinable mid-back pain a couple years ago (resulting from things I probably shouldn't have been attempting — but it was fun, etc.), I found myself casting about looking for symptomatic relief and hopefully a "cure." After visiting a number of chiropractors (a story in itself), one particularly knowledgeable fellow, who was sympathetic to an ex-jock's laments and age-eroded self-expectations, made a suggestion that not only helped my personal joint/muscle/nerve situation, but has since provided me with a lightweight, functional and inexpensive means of maintaining upper body (arms and torso) conditioning. This is a male/female thing, so don't stop reading 'cause of gender.

Surgical tubing it is! Buy a 5/16" (O.D.) x 6' length (about $2.50) and tie an overhand knot in one end and a bowline loop in the other end (or any-kind-of-do-it loop, if your bowline resides in the circle file of your mind). The loop should be big enough to slip in three or four fingers. Various tubing diameters and whatever length you want can be purchased at a surgical supply store — one of those I-don't-want-to-go-in-there places that sells wheelchairs, bed pans, emesis basins, and such.

Find a door that closes inward; i.e., toward you (best to go home and do this, or the tubing salesperson will steal the idea or think you're nuts). Close the knot into the door jam at a height that seems convenient to each exercise sequence. Pass your hand (fingers) into the loop and step back until some tension is put on the tubing and your muscles. The difficulty of each exercise is varied by the distance you stand from the door and the number of repetitions that you choose to attempt.

I had specific arm movements and number of repetitions that I was assigned to do as physical therapy. I found that the exercises were so easy to accomplish (notice I did not say "easy to do"), that after the affliction pain was relieved, I continued and expanded on the various movements as part of my personal fitness plan.

The type of exercises are pretty much up to you. With your hand in the loop, there are many movements and planes to use and operate within — swimming motion, lateral and back draws, cross-chest pulls, etc. Experiment and set up your own program — that's what I did and I'm always changing it as per boredom level and wherever I happen to be.

The tubing travels well in a suitcase, so there's no reason to leave it home.

If you can't find a convenient door to use (or can't figure out my spatial door closing instructions), tie a bowline loop and slip it over a door knob.

If one strand doesn't provide enough of a workout for your finely-tuned upper bod, double the rubber strand — but I'll bet 50-70 reps will tax most muscles.

*   *   *   *   *

Adventure Camp Song

When workshop people get together in the evenings, it's not uncommon for a few "pops" to be shared and such socializing often produces a sense of euphoria and camaraderie that results in an on-the-spot song. Most of these ditties have a life span that is commensurate with their content and melodic quality. This song is an exception and I think you will agree if you take the time to juxtapose verse and tune.

That PA State of Mind

To the tune of The Gambler,
by Kenny Rogers
Words by Edward E. Gamble
June 10-14, 1987

On a cool summer's evening, in a mansion
  south of Ipswich,
I met up with a bunch of folks — outdoor
  freaks by trade;
And the thing that makes them different
Is the way they make their living,
swinging through the treetops making sure
  they're all belayed.
  (Refrain)
You've got to know when to hold 'em.
Know how to mold 'em.
Know when to take up slack and when to let
  out line.
You never give them the answers while
  they're working on the problems,
'Cause they've come here to develop — that
  PA State of Mind.
When the day starts a-dawning, there ain't
  no time for yawning.
We just grab a bite and hit the field to dry
  the morning dew.
Soon my clothes are just a sopping, as I
  learn the Cobra flopping,
playing Toe Tag, smelling dirt, and learning
  games these folks call "*NEW!*"
  (Refrain)
Now the Dangle Duo's beckoning, as I cross
  the Burma's reckoning,

just how much nerve it's gonna take to
  climb the Pamper Pole.
But I find the task exciting, once I flush the
  fear I'm fighting,
and they vanish in a flash, right down that
  high up toilet bowl.
  (Refrain)
As I finish up my training, I don't notice
  that it's raining,
I can't feel the soreness, bug or rope 'neath
  my behind.
'Cause they challenged me by choice, so
  that now I can rejoice,
knowing as I do that I've attained that **PA
  STATE OF MIND!**
  (Refrain)

Aerobies

From California, of course. The only
innovative thing that I know for a fact
started in the northeast and moved west is
Project Adventure. Nonetheless, this
streamlined, long-distance toy is a gem,
particularly if you are disappointed with
how far you can't throw a frisbee. This
rubberized anorexic donut goes farther
than any thrown object should go, producing rapturous feelings of Olympic capability. I have always liked throwing things for
distance: the javelin, discus, flat rocks, 45
r.p.m. records, so the Aerobie device was
made to order for fantasy fulfillment. The
world's record for throwing an Aerobie is
over 1,000'; try to imagine throwing something that far. I love world records!

There are games to play with an
Aerobie, but the pure joy is in the throwing.
Beware! Aerobies like to get stuck in trees
— that big center hole is made for limb
insertion. They also get lost faster than you
can say eight dollars, so limit long distance
throws to wide open areas.

An idea — which I'm sure has already

been tried in California — is to form a
foursome and play a regular round of golf
using the Aerobie as object of play. A
good golf drive goes 200+ yards, which is
also true of the distance to be expected
from a well-thrown disc. What a treat to be
able to walk the links carrying only three or
four Aerobies. Sand traps? No problem.

(Ed. Note: Written about six weeks after
the above.)

I was recently in Washington, D.C.,
doing the tourist bit with my family. While
visiting the Air/Space Museum, I saw a
prototype of the Aerobie made of paper and
dated 1967. So, if you have a good idea and
are dismayed that no one is paying attention, just think of how long it took the
Aerobie to become commercially acceptable.

The Minimums for Health

I like these charts that threaten you via
statistics; subtly indicating that you are
going to die if you don't . . .

So, insert your non-biased participation
level of activity (choice of 8 — how can you
go wrong?), and personally estimate
whether you have 40 or 50 years left of
"shuffling about this mortal coil."

*Minimums for cardiovascular fitness
per week**

Walking	12 mi.
Swimming	900 yd.
Skiing (downhill)	6 hr.
Running	9 mi.
Rope skipping	75 min.
Racketball	4 hr.
Cycling	24 mi.
Aerobic dance	3 hr.

*Spread over 4 days per week.
Insurance against heart attack
Calories expended per week:*

Miles Walked**	Risk Drops By:	Death
Less than 500	4%	6 or less
500 to 999	22%	6 to 12.5
1,000 to 1,499	27%	12.5 to 19
1,500 to 1,999	36%	19 to 25
2,000 to 2,499	38%	25 to 31
2,500 to 2,999	48%	31 to 37.5
3,000 to 3,500	54%	37.5 to 44
Over 3,500	38%	44 or more

*The average person burns 80 calories per mile. A 175-lb. man burns 100 calories.
**Includes background exercise such as walking to the bus stop and climbing stairs.

Haiku

The following Haiku was offered as an answer to a question on an exam. The question was, "What is adventure?" The author is Lawrence (Muncie) McLeod.

Brink wish,
Not death wish.
Security at the end of its tether.
Stretched thin,
Taut,
Tense,
Straining,
But not quite,
Letting go.
To fall,
Caught,
By back-up lifted
Or lowered
Securely
To a stable area,
Thankful,
Wondering,
Next time?

Rockwell Enigma

I've carried a folding knife for years, ever since my first professional involvement in the outdoors. I wore a few holes in my pockets from the constant presence of the knife until I discovered a small belt holster at L.L. Bean and copied it — except I left off the snap-top for easy access, but that's another story.

A knife has become my vademecum (for your lexicon buffs, there's even a toothpaste carrying that odd name), and I find it indispensable as a tool. As a weapon, my 2-1/2" manually-operated switchblade isn't very useful, and in these days of the ubiquitous handgun — what's the use?

I'm running off a bit here — back to the reason I started to write this section: to unlock the secrets of the Rockwell scale of hardness.

For years, I have seen the numerical symbol (C55-60 or C58-60 or C "something" referring to the hardness of a particular knife blade, but I had no idea what the numbers meant and no one I asked seemed to know (or care).

Maybe it had something to do with the number of quenchings, firings, or incantations necessary to produce, as they say, a fine blade. I really wanted a blade with a C57-60 rating measured on the Rockwell scale of hardness, just because it sounded like you needed a C57-60 blade: I'm an easy sell. Well, blade fans, I recently read an article that destroyed the mystique Rockwell had established over the years, but replaced it with some great trivial knowledge that I'll pass on to you.

This hardness scale, established by the Rockwell Tool Company, measures the hardness of steel in a scale measuring from C3 to C68. The letter C refers to the test of a hard metal and the higher the number, the harder the steel. "Hardness is tested by measuring the penetration of a diamond cone into the steel under a force of 150 kilograms — C3 to C68. The lower the number, the faster the steel will lose its edge, the easier it will be to resharpen: the higher the number, the harder and more brittle the steel."

So now you know, and being awash in metallurgic knowledge, the choice of your next nickel silver bolstered Rosewood-handled magnum trophy-hunter will be simplified. If it's not between C3 and C68, don't buy it!

Climbing Grades

I have, in past BOT's, blithely referred to or inappropriately compared some physical action to a decimal configuration that began with the digit 5, such as 5.3 or 5.9, etc. For example, "getting out of his poorly parked car involved a 5.6 move."

These numerals refer to a difficulty grading system in rock climbing called the YDS (Yosemite Decimal System), or internationally called the American system.

This system (and many others that use numbers and letters) allows rock climbers to grade or rate various climbs to either inflate their egos (sour grapes on my part), or advise other climbers of that particular route's difficulty.

Using the YDS, a 5.0 is a **very** easy climb. Currently (with some disagreement among climbers — controversy is part of the sport — the highest grade is an unbelievable 5.14a (imagine climbing an overhanging sand dune).

If this grading folderol interests you at all, the following comparison chart is worth perusing.

Under the American (YDS) column, note that the numbers start at 9 — that's actually 5.9. So, this chart is a bit elitist in that it begins at about the highest level I've ever climbed. Do I mind this type of journalistic humbling? Nah . . . , but I do want to quote something Chouinard (if you don't know who *he is*, stop reading now and begin the next item) said recently in an interview. "In the greater scope of things, how important is it that Americans climb 5.14? The grading system has to be flawed anyway when an out-of-shape 48 year-old (himself) can now do a 5.11 when in 1960 at his prime, he could barely do a 5.10."

So, since Chouinard and I are both over 45, logic has it that it's the system that's skewed, rather than an eroding of the spring steel and dynamite body I used twenty years ago.

Removing yourself from a blocked auto at a 5.5 level of difficulty adds to the color and variety of your speech and doesn't hurt the image much, either.

P.S. The Brits, in a masterpiece of rhetorical succinctness, rate climbs as either "Bloody Hard or Bloody Easy."

Rolling Out the Ropes

While leading an adventure curriculum workshop in Georgia a while back, one of the participants facetiously (I hope) said that he was an advocate of the 3 R's in his "fizz ed" program; i.e., "Readin' the Role, Rollin' out the balls, and Relaxin'."

Ignoring or forgetting that an adventure curriculum has more components than just a high ropes course can result in a lot of "rope rollin'," resulting in unsafe attitudes and practices — specifically, letting students participate on elements of the ropes course without supervision, and rationalizing that since the class is so big, it's the only way the kids will get anything done.

If it's necessary to revert to "rollin'" anything, let it be balls — at least it's safer.

Social Concern Forum

Considering the large subscribership of BOT's, I believe it to be the moral responsibility of those involved in production of such a socially-aware periodical to attempt on occasion to address various concerns of the world's population. This quarter, the editor has chosen a broad spectrum concern to fit a demographic cross-section of the readers.

September's topic (to rival June's fascinating presentation of how to build and use a Mohawk Walk) is World Contentedness, and is aptly titled, "Happiness Through Responsible Hedonism."

The following checklist represents an excerpt from that timeless tome, "60 Minutes or 60 Years to Possible Happiness." Simply seek and achieve each item on the list (the time line is up to you), and a certain sense of fulfillment will infuse your heretofore jaded psyche.

HAPPINESS (contentedness)
WISDOM (a mature understanding of life)
MATURE LOVE (sexual & spiritual intimacy)
TRUE FRIENDSHIP (close companionship)
SENSE OF ACCOMPLISHMENT (lasting contribution)
SELF RESPECT (self-esteem)
AN EXCITING LIFE (stimulating existence)
FAMILY SECURITY (taking care of family)
PLEASURE (an enjoyable life)
A WORLD OF BEAUTY (beauty of nature and the arts)
SALVATION (eternal life)
A WORLD AT PEACE (free of war and conflict)
EQUALITY (equal opportunity for all)
A COMFORTABLE LIFE (a prosperous life)
SOCIAL RECOGNITION (respect, admiration)
FREEDOM (independence, free choice)

Not a bad checklist, all in all. Keep it around; it's worth referring to every now and again when your priorities get screwed up. The rhetoric is tongue-in-cheek; the list is pure gold.

Values Clarification via Murky Discussion

Need something intense and meaningful to talk about? Here's a useful list of randomly arranged topics that are crying for prioritization. Give a copy of these topics to each student and ask him/her to list each item as to its importance, as they define their own values.

There are, of course, no right or wrong answers. Fine tune your noncommittal responses and be prepared for some insightful discussion.

CLEAN
(neat, tidy)

BROADMINDED
(open-minded)

INDEPENDENT
(self-reliant, self-sufficient)

FORGIVING
(willing to pardon others)

INTELLECTUAL
(intelligent, reflective)

CHEERFUL
(lighthearted, joyful)

LOGICAL
(consistent, rational)

RESPONSIBLE
(dependable, reliable)

CAPABLE
(competent, effective)

HONEST
(sincere, truthful)

AMBITIOUS
(hard-working, aspiring)

LOVING
(affectionate)

COURAGEOUS
(standing up for your beliefs)

OBEDIENT
(dutiful, respectful)

SELF-CONTROLLED
(restrained, self-disciplined)

POLITE
(courteous, well-mannered)

HELPFUL (working
for the welfare of others)

Stereograms — Stare-e-os Ω

98% of you are really going to like this; the remaining 2% will surely think I'm putting you on.

I was thumbing through a recent edition of GAMES magazine (April 92) and came on an article that was illustrated with five pictoral blocks of black and white rectangular mish mash, just like the illustration at the base of page 317. The article said that each computer generated picture was a 3-D representation of whatever the title indicated (balls, various symbols, words, anything . . .). I said, "Yeah, right! Where's the April Fools disclaimer?" But there *is* a 3-D picture within the snowy nothing that seems to fill the square.

To quote from the article: "Now available as posters and calendars, and passed hand to hand on ever dimmer photocopies of photocopies (the one included here is only second generation), are single-image random-dot stereograms (SIRDS). At a glance they look like nothing at all, but there's plenty going on within the computer-generated random array of black and white dots. With practice and patience, you should be able to achieve 'deep sight' and enter these captivating images."

Here's how to achieve "deep sight" and experience the stimulus of "watching your brain work." Look at the two dots at the top of the picture. Throw your eyes out of focus so that the two dots become three. (If you can't defocus your eyes, try looking "beyond" the dots.) When this occurs you are ready to see the six balls. Let your fuzzy gaze drop down to the center of the picture and be open to whatever happens. Don't try to see anything, just let your brain process the black and white dots and "see" whatever has been programmed in. When the six balls manifest themselves they will be in rough textured perfect focus, but everything outside the square will be fuzzy.

The 98% I mentioned above is the magazine's estimate of how many people

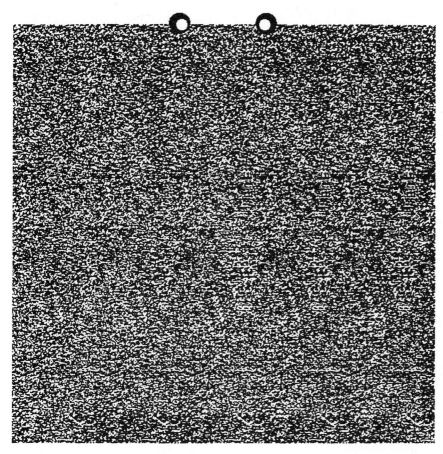

can see the balls if they commit to trying. It took me about 5-7 minutes, but my son Drew saw them within a minute. Some people I have given this picture to, still haven't seen anything. One staff member got so involved that he complained of headaches and disorientation for over 12 hours, so moderate your attempts. Once you know how to see the balls, it will still take a few seconds each time to make the synaptic transfer from surface to deep vision.

The first half dozen times that I mentally entered the 3-D picture I saw the six balls as indicated in the article. Then the next time I tried I saw 12 balls with a few indistinct symbols floating above the balls.

The only reason I'm mentioning this is in case you happen to see 12 instead of, or in conjunction with, the more obvious 6.

I know all this sounds weird, but it's for real, and as soon as you see the balls, even if it's only 6, we'll be simpatico again. If this type of mental flagellation appeals, drop me a line (SASE) and I'll send you the name of the company who developed the concept, but for now:

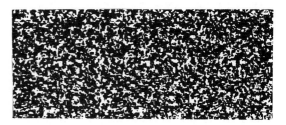

Chapter 14

Quarterly Quotes

While reading, driving, listening, playing, working, I always keep an eye and ear out for quotes that appeal to me, for no other reason than I like to re-read them at a later time. *Bag of Tricks* is advertised as idea-sharing, reporting of what's new in adventure education, and all that good pedagogic stuff to help you implement and/or build your own program, but *Quarterly Quotes* is something that I include for myself. I hope you have enjoyed these occasional quotes over the years: here's a bunch of my favorites.

"Always listen to experts. They'll tell you what can't be done and why. Then, do it."

"$100 placed at 7% interest compounded quarterly for 200 years will increase to more than $100,000,000 — by which time it will be worth nothing."

"Climate is what we expect; weather is what we get."

"A committee is a life form with six or more legs and no brain."

"To enjoy the flavor of life, take big bites. Moderation is for Monks."

"Courage is the complement of fear. A person who is fearless cannot be courageous."

"Do not handicap your children by making their lives easy."

"Don't try to have the last word. You might get it."

Robert Heinlein —*The Notebooks of Lazarus Long:*

"A child is a person who can't understand why someone would give away a perfectly good kitten."

— *Doug Larson*

"When I was younger, I could remember anything, whether it happened or not."
— *Mark Twain*

". . . you have to understand that in dealing with these kids, the **Challenge By Choice** philosophy doesn't start until they are at least ten feet off the ground.
— *summer camp ropes course leader*

". . . a regular beer stays on the tongue like ice cream; a light beer slides off like a sherbet." — *William Least Heat Moon*

"If growing up means it would be beneath my dignity to climb a tree . . . I'll never grow up . . . not me!" — *Peter Pan*

". . . we play for the sake of the game, for play itself. In this manner, we participate in the essence of existence."
— *George Leonard*

"Conscience is the inner voice that warns us that someone may be looking."
— *H.L. Mencken*

"Everything is a subject on which there is not much to be said." — *C.S. Lewis*

"Possum settin' up on a branch of a tree,
Can't jump down cause he got a trick knee!
Got a trick knee by walkin' after dark,
Stepped in a hole dug by an Aardvark!"
— *newspaper cartoon*

"I refuse to arrange a world war in every generation to rescue the young from a depressing peace." — *Kurt Hahn*

"I thought the window was down, but I found out it was up when I put my hand through it."
— *from an insurance form*

"Imagination is more important than knowledge." — *Einstein*

"Nothing succeeds like excess."
— *Oscar Wilde*

". . . there is no literature which proves that competition is inevitable. It seems instead that competition is learned."
— *AAHPERD book reviews*

"One thorn of experience is worth a wilderness of warning."
— *James R. Lovell*

"Balloonists have an unsurpassed view of the scenery, but there is always the possibility that it may collide with them."
— *H.L. Mencken*

"It may be that wet wool is warm, but dry cotton is warmer."
— *Rufus Little*

"Better to wear out than rust out."
— *Anonymous*

"Lack of vigor is often mistaken for patience." — *Kim Hubbard*

"Egotism is the anesthetic which nature gives us to deaden the pain of being a fool." — *Herbert Shofield*

The essence of education: "Realizing that you didn't know that you didn't know."
— *Anonymous*

"As a city bicyclist, you're part of a team sport. The only problem is that the other players often don't realize you're on the court." — *Josh Lehman*

"Experience is like a light on a caboose, illuminating only where we aren't going." — *George F. Will*

"To find order in anything, it is most important to know the limits imposed from outside the game, to know what the game is **not**." — *George Leonard*

"If youth be a defect, it is one that we outgrow only too soon."
— *H. Prochnow*

"Truth is obvious, after its discovery."
— *Anonymous*

". . . I want you to face each other, back to back."

"... we also included cross country skiing, rock climbing, and other vicarious activities."

"... you don't understand, because you're taking what I say in context."
— *S. Webster*

"I was only joking when I told you I didn't mean what I said about reconsidering my decision not to change my mind."
— *Anonymous*

"Ulcers are hereditary ... we get them from our kids." — *bumper sticker*

"If you don't know where you are going, you will probably end up someplace else."
— *Anonymous*

"Winter is Nature with Her pockets turned inside out." — *Anonymous*

"If practice makes perfect, then failures — even lots of them — might just be part of success?" — *Anonymous*

"Most great discoveries are made by mistake and the bigger the funding, the longer it takes to make the mistake."
— *Ann Landers*

"What we don't know is much more interesting than what we know."
— *NOVA — WGBH TV*

"It now costs more to amuse a child than it once did to educate his father."
— *Herbert Prochnow*

"The only people who mind getting wet are the ones that are dry." — *KER*

"I have found that the best way to give advice to your children is to find out what they want and then advise them to do it."
— *Harry Truman*

"We lived for days on nothing but food and water." — *W.C. Fields*

"Happiness makes up in height for what it lacks in length." — *Robert Frost*

"The vitality of thought is in adventure. Ideas won't keep. Something must be done with them."
— *Alfred North Whitehead*

"When large numbers of men are unable to find work, unemployment results."
— *Calvin Coolidge*

"Originality is undetected plagiarism."
— *Dean Inge*

"My memory is the thing I forget with."
— *a child's definition*

"The white man's real burden is a lot of other white men." — *Anonymous*

"Watch out w'en yu er gittin all you want. Fattenin' hogs ain't in luck."
— *Joel Chandler Harris*

"She has a nice sense of rumor."
— *John H. Cutler*

"Those who live in stone houses should not throw glass." — *Anonymous*

"You can't fool all of the people all of the time — but it isn't necessary."
— *Anonymous*

"Many would say, 'I'm afraid,' if they had enough courage." — *Anonymous*

"Bore: A person who talks when you wish him to listen." — *Ambrose Pierce*

"No matter where you go — there you are!"
— *A.E. Newman*

"Sure, you're as tough as when you were thirty, you're just falling apart faster."
— *Gloree Rohnke*

"Logic is the art of going the wrong way with confidence." — *Peter's Quotations*

"If you don't say anything, you won't be called on to repeat it."
— *Calvin Coolidge*

"One final paragraph of advice: Do not burn yourselves out. Be as I am — a reluctant enthusiast ... a part-time crusader, a half-hearted fanatic. Save the other half of yourselves and your lives for pleasure and adventure. It is not enough to fight for the land; it is even more important to enjoy it. While you can. While it's still here. So get out there and hunt and fish and mess around with your friends, ramble out yonder and explore the forests, encounter the grizz, climb the mountains, bag the peaks, run the rivers, breathe deep of that yet sweet and lucid air, sit quietly for a while and contemplate the precious stillness, that lovely, mysterious and awesome space. Enjoy yourselves, keep your brain in your head and your head firmly attached to the body, the body active and alive, and I promise you this much: I promise you this one sweet victory over our enemies, over those desk-bound people with their hearts in a safe deposit box and their eyes hypnotized by desk calculators. I promise you this: you will outlive the bastards."

— *Edward Abbey*

"Play so that you may be serious."
— *Anacharsis (C. 600 B.C.)*

"Play is the exultation of the possible."
— *Martin Buber*

"In every real man a child is hidden that wants to play." — *Nietzsche*

"Play is vital to all humanity. It is the finest system of education known to man."
— *Neville Scarge*

"The right to play is the child's first claim on the community. Play is nature's training for life." — *Frederick Froebel*

". . . we take chances, risk great odds, love, laugh, dance . . . in short, we play. The people who play are the creators."
— *Holbrook Jackson*

"In the early formative years, play is almost synonymous with life. It is second only to being nourished, protected and loved. It is a basic ingredient of physical, intellectual, social, and emotional growth."
— *Ashley Montague*

"A rut is a grave with the ends knocked out."
— *Frank Hubbard*

"Teamwork is essential — it allows you to blame someone else." — *Anonymous*

". . . yeah, but!"
— *often heard in a ropes course context*

"No member of a crew is praised for the rugged individuality of his rowing."
— *R.W. Emerson*

"A good idea doesn't care who has it."
— *passed on by Plynn Williams*

"The secret of effective leadership is sincerity; once you can fake that, you have it made." — *Anonymous*

"A lot of parents pack up their troubles and send them to summer camp."
— *Raymond Duncan*

"Fools rush in — and get the best seats."

"All probabilities are 50%, either a thing will happen, or it won't."
— *Murphy's Law — Book 2*

". . . personal and substantive growth is both predictable and measurable when one's reach slightly exceeds one's grasp."
— *Nancy McLaughlin,*
Adventure workshop participant

"The quickest way to a man's heart is through his stomach."
— *Harry Sphincter (the first proctologist to attempt heart surgery)*

"I've always longed for adventure, to do the things I've never dared — now here I'm facing adventure — then why am I so scared?" — *Rogers & Hammerstein*

"The experience is over for now
            but I have learned . . .
            I know it can happen...
I reach out for tomorrow,
        ready,
            excited,
                open . . .
Today has changed my life.
    I have grown . . ." — *George Betts*

"I looked up and saw a squirrel jump from one high tree to another. He appeared to be aiming for a limb so far out of reach that the leap looked like suicide. He missed — but landed, safe and unconcerned, on the branch several feet lower. Then he climbed to his goal, and all was well.

    Since then, whenever I have to choose between risking a new venture or hanging back, I remember those crazy, air-borne squirrels and think, 'They've got to risk it if they don't want to spend their lives in one tree.'

    So, I've jumped again and again. And in jumping, I've learned why the squirrels so often do it: it's fun."
— *Oscar Schisgall*

"If you're waitin' on me, you're backin' up."
— *forgettable country & western song*

"I'd like to go by climbing a birch tree,
And climb black branches
up a snow-white trunk
Toward heaven, till the tree
could bear no more,
But dipped its top and set me down again.
That would be good both going
and coming back.
One could do worse than be a swinger of birches."
— *Robert Frost*

"You get what you get, when you go for it."
— *Barry Manilow*

"Writing was meant to be a hobby. An act of willful play . . ." — *J. Updike*

"If it's clean, it isn't laundry."
— *Murphy's Law — Book 2*

"A blue light danced before her eyes, painting phosphorescent figure-eights on the velvet dark. She turned her head aside, blinking away the retinal afterimage, which lingered like a fading stain of color." — *Edward Abbey*

"A good scare is worth more than good advice." — *Ed Howe*

"But wait a bit, the Oyster cried,
Before we have our chat;
For some of us are out of breath,
And all of us are fat!" — *Lewis Carroll*

"In 30 years, a man can remember a good many things that ought to have happened." — *Farley Mowat*

"Do not fall into the error of the artisan (teacher) who boasts of 20 years' experience, while in fact he has had only 1 year's experience — 20 times."
— *Trevanian*

"It never occurs to an adolescent that he will someday be as dumb as his father."
— *Mark Twain*

"I would have to say our best buy was the IBM 4331, which gives the whole company a means of communicating electronically and neatly. But it also gives everyone the ability to screw up at the speed of light."
— *Purchasing Manager, Lexidata Corporation*

"Some things have to be believed to be seen."
— *Ralph Hodgson*

"This is either a forgery or a damn clever original."
— *Frank Sullivan*

"When choosing between two evils, I always like to try the one I've never tried before."
— *Mae West*

"The object is not to completely avoid butterflies in the stomach, but to attempt to get them to fly temporarily in formation."
— *Tom Del Prete*

"It takes a big zipper to make an elephant fly."
— *Disney World Jungle Cruise Guide*

"In two words: im possible."
— *Samuel Goldwyn*

"Most of the time I don't have much fun. The rest of the time I don't have any fun at all."
— *Woody Allen*

"A hyperactive child is a kid who can't sit still for long periods of time and listen to Colonial History."
— *Richard Baudler*

". . . we may be in the brink of an actual seller's market for wild and free-wheeling creativity for the clever, the goofy, the whimsical and playful. If ever there were a time to cultivate one's own audacity, foolishness, and wit, this is it."
— *Success Magazine*

Tombstone inscription: "Died at 30. Buried at 60."

"Many epitaphs signify a grave error."
— *Anonymous*

"It is useless for the sheep to pass resolutions in favor of vegetarianism, while the wolf remains of a different opinion."
— *Dean Inge*

"I have never been hurt by anything I didn't say." — *Calvin Coolidge*

"It may be that the race is not always to the swift, nor the battle to the strong — but that's the way to bet."
— *Damon Runyon*

"Woman was God's second mistake."
— *Nietzsche*

"If basketball had never been invented, where would they hold high school dances?" — *Anonymous*

"Scream when you want to scream. Roll on the floor. Surprise everybody!"
— *Leo Buscaglia*

"What do you mean, she fell into an open personhole?" — *Ladies Home Journal*

"If you cross a fly with an elephant, you'll get a zipper that doesn't forget."
— *Who Cares*

"In humor, there is truth. We need to take humor more seriously."
— *Ralph Nader*

"Eschew obfuscation"
— *Bumper sticker on VW diesel Rabbit observed recently on the Massachusetts Turnpike. Back window decals read MIT and Harvard. Driver (so lively and quick): smoking a pipe; moustache, turtleneck, sports coat — perfect!*

"Craftsmanship affords the antithesis of instant results." — *NCOBS*

I was recently offering a student the opportunity of trying a lower rappel than the more intimidating one that was initially presented. Her reply is a study of resigned confidence: "If I'm going to drown, I'd just as soon it be in the deep end of the pool."
— *Name withheld due to my Swiss cheese memory*

Edward Abbey, a lover of landscapes, about littering roadsides with beer cans —

"Beer cans are beautiful — it's the highway that's ugly."

"Sometimes I've believed as many as six impossible things before breakfast."
— *Lewis Carroll*

"...genuine, pure play is one of the main bases of civilization."
— *Homo Ludens: A study of the play element in culture.*

"To be first and be correct is the most important. To be first and wrong is not so good." — *Samuel Ting*

"Beware of our lawyer."
— *warning sign on a residence*

"A rolling stone gathers momentum."
— *Anonymous*

"Young men are fitter to invent than to judge, fitter for execution than for counsel — men of age object too much, consult too long, adventure too little."
— *Francis Bacon*

"Tell me, Oldtimer, where did you get your good judgment?"
"Experience."
"And how did you get your experience?"
"Bad judgment!"
— *Anonymous*

"We find ourselves striving for the all-American dream; good job, house, family, color TV and new car. When we

obtain these goals, we will be happy. We go to school or work each day and then come home to read, watch TV, have dinner and go to bed. On weekends, we clean house and the yard and maybe go out for dinner or a movie or a ball game. We look forward to retirement. Our life is routine. We are comfortable. We know what to expect from each day. We are bored."
— *Penny Bolio*

"All an education does is open an empty mind; it doesn't fill an empty one."
— *Malcolm Forbes*

"Bad weather always looks worse through a window or sounds worse on a tent fly."
— *KER*

"Self-centered people are the ones who spend so much time talking about themselves that we never get a chance to talk about ourselves." — *Bits & Pieces*

"We are so ruled by what people tell us we must be that we have forgotten who we are." — *Leo Buscaglia*

"For he knew, as all students did, that the basic purpose of instruction was not so much to teach young people good things as to fill up all their time unpleasantly. Adults had the notion that juveniles needed to suffer. Only when they had suffered enough to wipe out most of their naturally joyous spirits and innocence were they staid enough to be considered mature. An adult was essentially a broken-down child."
— *Piers Anthony, Centaur Aisle*

"I took the other road, but only because it was the lazy road for me, the way I wanted to go. If I've encountered some resistance, that's because most of the traffic is going the other way."
— *Edward Abbey*

"Forget your opponents; always play against par." — *Sam Snead*

"A nose conjures more than it reveals — it is a luxury in the economy of the senses."
— *KER*

"Life is what is happening to you while you are making other plans."

"Some people will believe anything if it is whispered to them."

"Fate is blamed for many accidents, but we feel personally responsible when we make a hole in one."

A workable and refreshingly brief philosophy of life . . .". . . love, trust, dare — and keep on doing it."

"Not one person in a thousand can keep his/her hands in their pockets while giving directions." — *Bits & Pieces*

"Your first line of defense should be the thoughtful use of your head, not the covering of it."
— *Magazine article, Learning to Rock Climb*

"The meek shall inherit the earth, but not the mineral rights."
— *Success Magazine*

"Humor bridges the gap between the perfection we seek and the imperfections we're stuck with." — *Robert Wieder*

"The weather is here, wish you were beautiful." — *bumper sticker*

"John Cogi's 4:3 is a piano composition that calls for four minutes and thirty-three seconds of total silence as the player sits frozen on the piano stool. I have not heard 4:3 performed, but friends tell me it's Cogi's finest composition."

"Don't just do something, stand there."
— *Robert Hutchins*

"Give me gradual improvement rather than postponed perfection."
— *John Murray*

"I don't want to achieve immortality through my work. I want to achieve immortality through not dying."
— *Woody Allen*

"Definition of a genius: a person who aims at something no one else can see . . . and hits it."

"One of the great mysteries of life is how the idiot that your daughter married can be the father of the smartest grandchildren in the whole wide world."
— *Bits & Pieces*

"There are three kinds of lies: lies, damned lies, and statistics."   — *Mark Twain*

"The only thing keeping us from our fondest dreams is our fondest fears."
— *Patricia Sun via Animal Town Game Company*

"A keychain is a gadget that allows us to lose several keys at the same time."
— *Bits & Pieces*

"**LIFE** — the one race you lose by finishing first."   — *Lung Cancer poster*

". . . a ropes course is the Swiss Army Knife of experiential education."
— *Mike Stratton*

"Campers roughing it in a county park in Iowa plugged in so many coffeemakers, TV sets, electric blankets, and refrigerators that the park transformer exploded from the overload."   — *news item*

"If a person is standing with one foot in a bucket of ice and another foot in a fire, you could say — statistically — that on the average, the person is very comfortable."   — *Unknown*

"Take some more coffee! I've had nothing yet, so I can't take more. You mean you can't take less. It's very easy to take more than nothing."
— *a liberal paraphrase from Lewis Carrol*

"To laugh is to risk appearing the fool.

To weep is to risk appearing sentimental.

To reach out for another is to risk involvement.

To expose feeling is to risk exposing your true self.

To place your ideas, your dreams, before the crowd is to risk their loss.

To love is to risk not being loved in return.

To live is to risk dying.

To hope is to risk despair.

To try is to risk failure.

But the risk must be taken, because the greatest hazard in life is to risk nothing.

The person who risks nothing, does nothing, has nothing, and is nothing.

S/he may avoid suffering and sorrow, but they simply cannot learn, feel, change, grow, love, live.

Chained by certitudes, they are slaves, they have forfeited freedom.

Only a person who risks — is free."
— *Anonymous*

"It's fun to do things you're not made to do. I was playing when I invented the aqualung. I'm still playing. I think play is the most important thing in the world."
— *Jacques Costeau*

"All other species play to play. We're the only species that plays to win. Maybe that's why there are so many losers."
— *Lily Tomlin*

"Every child has inside him an aching void for excitement and if we don't fill it with something which is exciting and interesting and good for him, he will fill it with something which is exciting and interesting and which isn't good for him."
— *T. Roosevelt*

"Don't be so humble, you're not that great."
— *Golda Meir*

Response to a famous quote and recent discoveries about how various chemicals are naturally released in situ.

"... It's apparent that 'because it's there' has at least become a valid explanation for the climbing urge — but only when the 'it' is understood to be chemicals within, not mountains without."
— *Glen Randall*

Chemicals considered (norepinephrine, phenylethylamine, endorphins).

"A desire to have all the fun is 9/10 of the law of chivalry."
— *Dale Sayers*

"Three o'clock is always too late or too early for anything you want to do."
— *Sartre*

"Show me a nation whose national beverage is beer, and I'll show you an advanced toilet technology."
— *Mark Hawkins*

"You can discover more about a person in an hour of play than in a year of conversation."
— *Plato*

"In spite of the cost of living, it's still popular."
— *Kathleen Norris*

Overheard in a summer camp situation: "Who cares who wins; it's only a game."
— *Anonymous*

"It's better to have loved and lost than to do 40 lbs. of laundry a week."
— *Lawrence Peter*

"... the facts are wrong!"   — *Einstein*

"An ounce of image is worth a pound of performance."
— *Anonymous*

This book represents a compilation of rewritten and heavily edited back issues of the adventure curriculum quarterly *Bag of Tricks.*

I began writing *Bag of Tricks* in December of 1979, and after 64 issues (16 years) decided, in December of 1994, to change the timing and format of the subscription.

I plan to continue collecting, creating, and writing about adventure curriculum material, but will make this information available on a biannual (twice a year) basis as a published journal. Kendall/Hunt has agreed to work with me on this, so starting in the Fall of 1995, Number One of a yet unnamed journal will be available including all the newest adventure stuff, embellished with photographs and illustrations, and written in the same conversational, irreverent, humorous style that characterized the first 5,840 days of *Bag of Tricks.*

For information about this journal contact Kendall/Hunt Publishing Co. at: 1-800-228-0810.

This book's about finished (if you noticed how many pages are in your left hand), but don't leave yet—check out the index, it makes a great activity list and you have my permission to copy it.

Also, don't forget to look up *xyst.* Here's another bonus word, *zax.* If you play Scrabble—you're welcome. Bye for now...

Index

Other Books by Karl Rohnke

Slightly Skewed Vignettes

Confessions of an Incorrigible Kid

Since publication of the original Cowstails and Cobras in 1974, Karl Rohnke has provided Adventure Education practitioners with a steady supply of games, Initiatives, challenge ropes course events, and other Adventure activities. *Silver Bullets, Challenge By Choice, Cowstails and Cobras II, The Bottomless Bag* — where does he come up with this stuff? Well, if you've been fortunate enough to have Karl as a workshop facilitator, or if you've ever attended one of his Silver Bullets days, you know that Karl's writing is a reflection of his life.

As Dick Prouty (Executive Director of Project Adventure) has observed, "One of Karl's unique gifts is his ability to have fun and truly enjoy everything he does." In these 18 vignettes, Karl shows us just how he accomplishes this. He takes us from his boyhood home in Hawaii, *Kitchen Capers*, where he attempts to corner the local lead market, with nearly disastrous results, to his brief tenure as a professional pigeon exterminator, *The Pigeon Contract*, and finally to a desert island in the Caribbean to capture a troop of egg thieving monkeys, *Monkey Business*.

Humorous, insightful, poignant — but always classic Rohnkesque, *Slightly Skewed Vignettes* provides us with a rare glimpse into the life of one of the true characters and founding fathers of Adventure Education.

1992/144 pages/paper/ISBN 0-8403-7852-1

Forget Me Knots is a book specifically written for use with rope course-related activities. The artistic skills of Plynn Williams were employed to freeze the various knots in a most revealing manner. Clearly defined line drawings in combination with photos and the descriptive text make the book easy to follow. So, here's a specific reader-friendly reference that will show-and-tell you how to tighten a fidget ladder or fashion a studebaker wrap in addition to clearly reviewing the more classic knot sequences.

1992/75 pages/paper/ISBN 0-8403-7138-1

Cowstails and Cobras II is a re-write of Karl Rohnke's classic guide to games, initiative problems and adventure activities. It contains much-and-more-of what made the original a standard in the field of Adventure Education. This revised edition has been thoroughly updated and now includes a sample curriculum and a chapter on leadership and debriefing. The text offers a thorough treatment of Project Adventure's unique education philosophy and approach to team building.
1989/224 pages/ paper/ISBN 0-8403-5434-7

Silver Bullets is a fun and valuable collection from Karl Rohnke featuring 165 adventure activities that require few, if any, props. All activities have been field-tested, are rated as indoor/outdoor, props/people only, and high/low activity level. Many helpful hints toward program implementation are also offered. **Silver Bullets** is used by a variety of teachers, counselors, therapists, camp personnel, church leaders, and others who want to build trust.
1984/192 pages/paper/ISBN 0-8403-5682-X

Quicksilver has been in the creative stages for the past ten years. This book includes a plethora of programmatic play that will delight even the most avid games collector. Karl Rohnke and Steve Butler have combined their 43 years of adventure experience to provide you with new; Icebreakers, Warm-ups, Games, Stunts, Initiatives, Trust Activities, Closures and even some insights into leadership.
1995/320 pages/paper/ISBN 0-7872-0032-8

To order call: 1-800-228-0810
KENDALL/HUNT PUBLISHING COMPANY
4050 Westmark Drive P.O. Box 1840 Dubuque, Iowa 52004-1840